The Beetles of America

The Beetles of America

of

America

RICHARD HEADSTROM

EXCLUSIVE LIBRARY DISTRIBUTORS:

classic publications

P.O. Box 1228
Covina, Calif. 91722
PHONE: AREA CODE 213
332-1194

South Brunswick and New York: A. S. Barnes and Company
London: Thomas Yoseloff Ltd

A. S. Barnes and Co., Inc.
Cranbury, New Jersey 08512

Thomas Yoseloff Ltd
Magdalen House
136–148 Tooley Street
London SE1 2TT, England

Library of Congress Cataloging in Publication Data

Headstrom, Birger Richard, 1902–
    The beetles of America.

    Bibliography: p.
    Includes index.
    1. Beetles—United States. 2. Insects—United States. I. Title
QL583.H4 1975   595.7′6′0973   74-14
ISBN 0-498-01469-X

PRINTED IN THE UNITED STATES OF AMERICA

To My Wife

Contents

7

Preface

If numbers were the criterion for popularity, beetles should be the most popular of all insects—if, indeed, insects can be said to be popular at all. A few can be most annoying as well as posing a health problem.

It is said that there are a million species of insects, though actually we do not know how many; beetles comprise perhaps two-thirds of that number. Now, few of us will ever come in contact with all the species of beetles, but many of us do encounter some throughout the year as we walk along a country road, follow a woodland path, or pause for a few moments by the edge of a pond or stream. As a matter of fact, we do not even have to leave our home, for within the environs of our house and in the garden, we are sure to see a number of species; insect visitors are even in the house itself, despite our precautions to keep them out.

The beetles are a colorful group, many of them having brilliant colors that rival those of the butterflies, and having many interesting habits. Most people merely give a cursory glance at the beetles they see and immediately forget about them. But some of us give them a closer look and perhaps wonder what kind they are and by what name they are known. The present book has been written for those people and for others who might want to know a little more about these fascinating insects. There is no need to refer to some book of technical terminology sufficient to discourage anyone from pursuing the matter further. Some technical terms have been used quite unavoidably, but they have been kept to the minimum and those terms that have been used are clearly explained in the glossary. Needless to say, I have not attempted to include all the beetles found in the United States, but only those that most of us are apt to see in the course of a year, as well as a few others to make the book more complete.

Introduction

The Abundance and Distribution of Beetles

It is said that there are about six times as many species of insects as there are of all other kinds of animals combined. Stated differently, about eighty percent of all known animals are insects. It is generally believed that somewhere between 625,000 and 1,250,000 different kinds of insects have been named and described. And these appear to be only a fraction of the total number that are presumed to exist. There are some entomologists who believe that there may be as many as 2,000,000; others put the figure at 10,000,000. The number of species alone is staggering and, if we should multiply the minimum number of species by the total number of individuals of each species, we would arrive at a fantastic figure.

Of the many different kinds of insects, the beetles form the largest group; it is believed that over 600,000 have already been described. One family alone, the *Curculionidae,* includes some 50,000 species (which is more than the total number of species of birds, mammals, reptiles, and amphibia found throughout the world) , and there possibly exist some 150,000 to 200,000 species that yet remain to be described.

Since there are so many different kinds of beetles, it is to be expected that they are widely distributed throughout the world and so they are being found almost everywhere, except in the oceans and at the poles.

The Place of Beetles in the Animal Kingdom

All matter, organic and inorganic, is divided into the three great kingdoms: mineral, plant, and animal. Some scientists have added a fourth, the synthetic kingdom, which includes substances or products developed from the other three. The animal kingdom includes all living forms that are free moving, ingest food, grow, and reproduce, and is divided into a number of large divisions called *phyla* (singular, *phylum*), which in turn are divided into smaller divisions called *classes*. The classes are further divided into *orders,* the orders into *families,* and the families into *genera,* which are made up of the *species*. All animals are classified by structure and so the animals belonging to a phylum, class, order, and so on have certain structural characteristics in common.

The insects belong to the phylum called the *Arthropoda,* a word derived from the Greek words *arthron,* joint, and *pous,* foot. Hence, any animal having a jointed or segmented foot is an arthropod, but the word has generally come to mean any invertebrate animal with jointed or segmented appendages.

The phylum *Arthropoda* includes such animals as lobsters, crabs, crayfish, shrimps, barnacles, millipedes, centipedes, scorpions, spiders, mites, sow bugs, water fleas, and insects. The insects belong to the class *Insecta* and the beetles to the Order *Coleoptera,* which is derived from the Greek, *koleos,* sheath. In the case of the beetles, the word *sheath* applies to the forewings, which are hard and sheathlike and protect the hind wings, which are membranous and folded beneath them. The beetles also have biting or chewing mouthparts and complete metamorphosis; that is, they have four stages in their life history: egg, larva, pupa, and adult.

Should we want to classify a beetle, such as the common Two-Spotted Ladybird Beetle, we would proceed as follows:

PHYLUM *Arthropoda*
  CLASS *Insecta*
   ORDER *Coleoptera*
    FAMILY *Coccinellidae*
     TRIBE *Coccinellini*
      GENUS *Adalia*
       SPECIES *bipunctata*

The scientific name of the Two-Spotted Ladybird Beetle is *Adalia bipunctata* (Linné), Linné (better known as Linnaeus) being the name of the person who first described it.

The Fossil Record

From fossil remains of insects or parts of insects that have been preserved in such substances as amber, resin, copal, lignite, and limestone, we know that insects first appeared during the period of the geological timetable known as the Carboniferous, some 300 million years ago. One of these ancient insects, which resembles our present-day mayfly, appears to have been the ancestor of all our modern species.

The Characteristics of Beetles

What Is a Beetle?

A beetle is an insect, which leads to the question: What is an insect? An insect has been defined as an air-breathing arthropod with a distinct head, thorax, and abdomen, one pair of antennae, three pairs of legs, and usually one or two pairs of wings in the adult stage, although there are some insects that do not have any wings.

The External Anatomy of a Beetle

Beetles, like all insects, have a hard, tough, outer framework that supports and protects the softer parts of the body and that is known as the *exoskeleton*. It has been likened to a coat of mail, tough enough to protect the vital organs but jointed and hinged in order to permit freedom of movement.

The exoskeleton consists of three distinct layers: the *cuticula*, which contains chitin, pigments, and various substances that give it color, toughness, and hardness; the *hypodermis*, a layer of living cells that produce the cuticula; and the *basement membrane*, which holds together the lower ends of the hypodermal cells.

Associated with the exoskeleton or derived from it are various structures such as hairs, spines, scales, and a number of different kinds of glands. The exoskeleton also contains receptors of sound, sight, taste, and touch, as well as nerve cells and complicated structures, such as the *chordotonal organs*, which transmit the impressions received by the receptors in the form of impulses to the nervous system.

Head

The head is the first of the three body regions and bears the eyes, antennae, and mouthparts (Fig. 1). In addition to these structures, the head has several distinct characters that serve in identification; these are the head regions, the position and shape of the eyes, and the *locus* or place of the attachment of each antenna. The head regions are: the *front* or *frontal region*, which is simply the insect's face; the *vertex*, which is the tip of the head between the eyes; the *occiput*, which is the extreme back of the head (Fig. 2); the *gena* or cheek, which is below and behind the eye; the *gula* or throat, which is the extreme lower part (Fig. 3); and the *submentum*, which bears the lower lip or *labium* (Fig. 4).

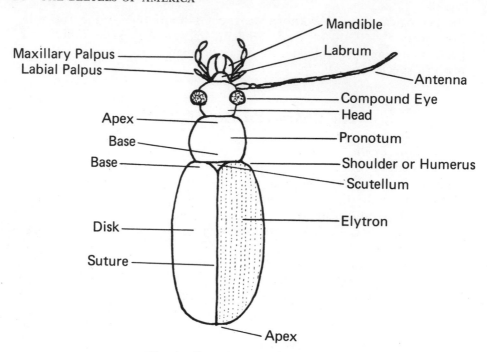

Fig. 1. Dorsal View of a Beetle

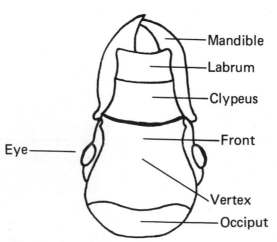

Fig. 2. Dorsal View of the Head of a Beetle

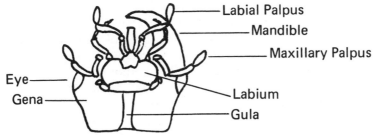

Fig. 3.   Ventral View of the Head of a Beetle

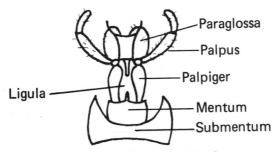

Fig. 4.   Labium of a Beetle

Eyes

Adult insects have two kinds of eyes (though both may not occur on every species): simple eyes called *ocelli* and *compound* or *faceted* eyes (Fig. 1).

The simple eye is constructed on a plan similar to that of the human eye, but its capacity for producing images is extremely limited. The form of the lens is fixed and so is the distance between the lens and the retina, hence there is no power of accommodation. Most external objects are therefore out of focus. Probably all a simple eye is capable of doing is to distinguish between light and darkness, though it may possibly form a crude image at close range. Simple eyes do not occur in beetles except rarely in a few families and thus are not shown in Figure 1.

The compound eye is quite different. The convex surface of the eye is covered externally by a modified transparent section of the cuticula called the *cornea*, which is divided into hexagonal areas or *facets*. Each facet is but the external part of a long, slender rod known as an *ommatidium*. Thus a compound eye is made up of a number of similar ommatidia lying side by side but separated from one another by a layer of dark pigment cells. It forms a mosaic image, it can detect movement, and it is sensitive to the various wave lengths that compose the light spectrum.

Normally the eye is always on the side of the head, but its exact position may vary in the different groups. Thus the eye may extend well up onto the top of the head and sometimes even touch the one on the opposite side. The words *round, oval,* and the like refer to the outline of the eye against the head. Often the eye is partly scooped out where it partly or completely surrounds the antennae, in which case it is said to be *emarginate* or *notched.* When the surface is more or less rounded, the eye is said to be *convex,* but when the convexity is great, it is said to be *prominent.* When the individual facets that compose the compound eye are so small that they are rather difficult to distinguish, the eye is said to be *finely granulate;* when they are large enough to be seen easily, it is *coarsely granulate.*

Antennae

Insects have one pair of *antennae,* or feelers as they are popularly called, which are usually conspicuous and long, though in some species they are minute (Fig. 1). They are composed of joints or segments: the first called the *scape,* the proximal end of which is often subglobose and called the *bulb,* appearing like a distinct segment; the second, the *pedicel;* and the remaining collectively known as the *clavola* (Fig. 5). In some species the first one or two segments of the clavola are much smaller than the others and are called the *ring joints;* in others, the distal segments are more or less enlarged and are termed the *club.* The part of the clavola between the club and the ring joints, or when there are no ring joints between the club and the pedicel, is known as the *funicle.*

The antennae may have a number of different forms: *filiform* (the segments are all of the same size and shape so that the antennae appear to be threadlike) (Fig. 6); *moniliform* (the segments are all rounded with constrictions between them so that the antennae appear to be beadlike) (Fig. 7); *clavate* (the succeeding segments gradually become broader toward the tip so that each antenna resembles a club) (Fig. 8); *capitate* (the segments toward the tip or apex become suddenly enlarged to form a knob or head (Fig. 9); *lamellate* (the segments at the tip are expanded laterally to form leaflike or platelike structures) (Fig. 10); *serrate* (the segments are more or less triangular or have notched edges like the teeth of a saw) (Fig. 11); *pectinate* (the segments are equally elongated so that each antenna looks like a comb (Fig. 12); *flabellate* (the segments are unusually elongated so that each antenna becomes fan shaped) (Fig. 13); and *geniculate* (an antenna that is elbowed or bent at an angle (Fig. 14).

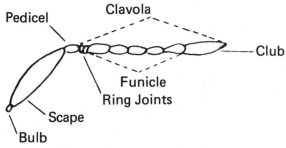

Fig. 5.   Parts of an Antenna

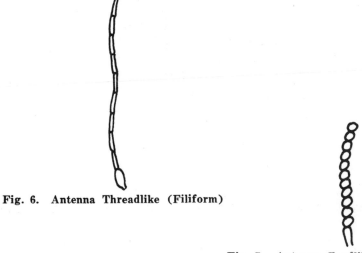

Fig. 6.   Antenna Threadlike (Filiform)

Fig. 7.   Antenna Beadlike (Moniliform)

Fig. 8.   Antenna Club Shaped (Clavate)

Fig. 9.   Antenna with a Head or Knob (Capitate)

Fig. 10.   Antenna with Platelike or Leaflike Structures (Lamellate)

Fig. 11.   Antenna Sawlike (Serrate)

Fig. 12.   Antenna Comblike (Pectinate)

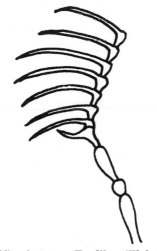

Fig. 13.   Antenna Fanlike (Flabellate)

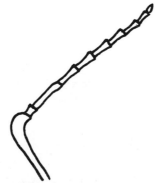

Fig. 14.   Antenna Elbowed or Bent at an Angle (Geniculate)

The antennae may serve as organs of touch, smell, and hearing, or they may be adapted for other than sensory purposes, as in an aquatic beetle where they are used in connection with respiration or in the male of a certain beetle where they are employed to hold the female when mating.

Mouthparts

The structures that enable insects to obtain food are called *mouthparts*. These vary considerably in form according to whether they are used for seizing and tearing prey, for chewing leaves, for sucking the fluids contained within the tissues of leaves, or for obtaining the sweet liquid found in the nectaries of flowers.

Beetles have chewing mouthparts that typically consist of an upper lip, the *labrum* (Fig. 2); an under lip, the *labium* (Fig. 3); and two pairs of jaws that act horizontally. The labrum, which is attached to a part of the head called the *clypeus,* is used to help in grasping food (Fig. 2). The *mandibles* or upper jaws which are usually horny and are often provided with teeth and grinding surfaces, are the principal organs of mastication and in some instances serve as a means of defense as well (Fig. 2). Beneath the mandibles are located the lower jaws or *maxillae,* which aid in manipulating the food and directing it into the mouth (Fig. 15). Each maxilla bears a segmented appendage, the *palpus,* which is believed to be tactile in function (Fig. 15). The lower lip or *labium* is more

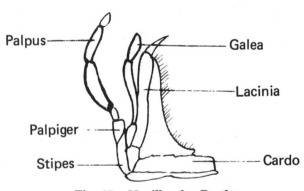

Fig. 15. Maxilla of a Beetle

complex in structure than the labrum and is composed of a number of parts: the *mentum* and *submentum* (Fig. 4), the latter connecting the structure to the *gula* or throat (Fig. 3); the *ligula,* the central portion of the outer part, on each side of which is a *palpiger* (Fig. 4), which bears the *labial palpus;* and the *paraglossa,* which lies between the ligula and palpiger (Fig. 4). The labial palpus functions much the same as the maxillary palpus (Fig. 3).

Thorax

The thorax is the second of the three body regions and is itself divided into three regions called the *prothorax, mesothorax,* and *metathorax.* Each of these regions bears a pair of legs, while each of the last two has a pair of wings. The upper surface of the prothorax is known as the *pronotum* (Fig. 1). As a whole, the pronotum is probably more diversely modified in shape and in sculpture than any other part of the insect's body, and for this reason is of considerable taxonomic value (Fig. 16).

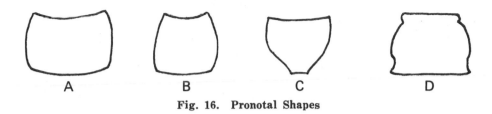

Fig. 16. Pronotal Shapes

Wings

With few exceptions, wings are present in all adult insects and are more or less triangular in shape. A wing is a saclike fold of the body wall or exoskeleton; its saclike structure is not apparent, since the two walls extend outward over the same area and are so thin and so close together that they appear as a single membrane. The dual nature of the wing may be seen, however, where the walls remain separated. Here they are thickened and form the firmer framework of the wing. These thickened and hollow lines are called the *veins* of the wing and the manner in which they are arranged are peculiar to a species. Hence, they and the spaces between them are often used in classification.

Wings may vary in texture. Thus they may be membranous, hairy, scaly, horny, leathery, or partly leathery. In the beetles the upper pair of wings are hardened and are known as the *elytra* (singular, *elytron*) (Fig. 1); the lower or hind wings are membranous like those of a fly. The base of the wing is that part which is adjacent to the pronotum when the wing is at rest. The tip of the wing is the *apex,* the central part is the *disk,* and the shoulder or *humerus* is the point where the lateral edge and the base meet (Fig. 1). This point is also usually rounded or angulate. The line formed by the two internal straight edges of the elytra is the *suture* and the more or less triangular area between the bases of the elytra is the *scutellum,* which is sometimes absent (Fig. 1).

Legs

Adult insects have three pairs of legs, a pair being attached to each of the three segments or regions of the thorax. A leg consists of a number of segments: the *coxa,* the segment by which the leg is attached to the thorax, *trochanter, femur, tibia,* and the *tarsus* or foot (Fig. 17). The coxae, particularly those of the front legs, may

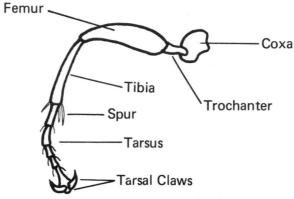

Fig. 17. **Leg of a Beetle**

be of several types. They may project from the body when they are said to be *prominent,* they may be more or less in the same plane as the undersurface when they are not prominent, or they may be rounded or conical. The trochanter is usually small, unmodified, and of little importance. The femur or thigh is usually cylindrical but sometimes it is enlarged or clubbed at the apical end or even spindle shaped. Generally speaking, the tibia is usually cylindrical, thin, and slightly enlarged at the tip, though in some families it is quite complex.

The tarsus or last segment of the leg is, however, extremely variable and may be absent altogether. When present it usually has five segments, but may have only three or four. It may be short or long, cylindrical or broadened toward the tip, smooth or fringed beneath, or with dense patches of setae. On the last tarsal segment are attached one or two claws, which may be *simple* or *divergent.* They are divergent when the two claws form a distinct angle (Figs. 18, 19). At times the two claws may be so divergent as to be *opposite* each other (Fig. 20). Some claws are provided with a tooth (Fig.

21); others are split (cleft) for almost their whole length (bifurcate),
and in still others the base may be rather long before the claw itself begins. This last example is said to be *appendiculate* or *with
an appendage* (Fig. 22).

Fig. 18.   Simple Claws

Fig. 19.   Divergent Claws

Fig. 20.   Opposite Claws

Fig. 21.   Toothed Claw

Fig. 22.   Appendiculate Claw

Abdomen

The abdomen is the third of the three body regions and is divided
into a series of somewhat similar rings or segments (Fig. 23); each
segment is composed of two parts, the *tergum* above and the *sternum* below.

Genitalia

Adult insects are normally without abdominal appendages, except
for those of reproduction, the *genitalia*. Some species have a pair of appendages at the end of the body known as the *cerci*. The appendages
of the genitalia are called the *genital claspers* in males, and the

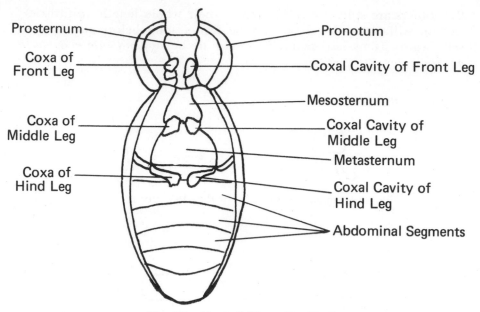

Fig. 23.   Ventral View of a Beetle

ovipositor or egg-laying apparatus in females. In beetles the genital claspers are absent and the ovipositor is usually hidden within the abdomen.

Sculpture

The surface of a beetle is often variously modified into *impressions* and *elevations* and these are generally considered under the name of *sculpture*. Impressions include *punctures, pits, grooves, striae, wrinkles,* and the like; elevations include *ridges, keels, tubercles, granules, spines, teeth,* and similar structures (Fig. 24).

Fig. 24.   Types of Sculpturing

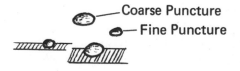

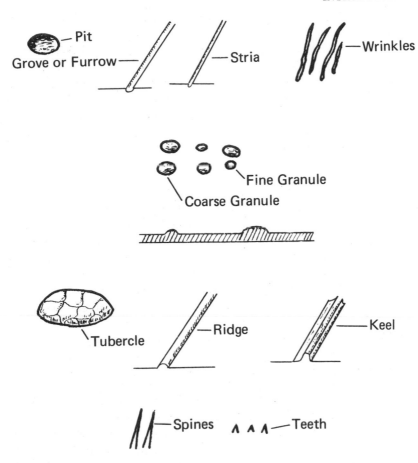

The Habitats of Insects (Beetles)

Beetles are found in a great many different kinds of habitats: fields, pastures, meadows, marshes, swamps, woodlands, forests, ponds, lakes, streams, bogs, alpine peaks, deserts, sand dunes, seashores, hot springs, and caves. The only place where beetles are not present are the oceans, though other insects may be found there.

The Habits of Insects (Beetles)

Food

Any matter of organic origin may serve as food for the beetles. This means, of course, plants and animals, but beetles will not eat anything simply because it is a plant or an animal. They have their individual preferences. In other words, a beetle that eats the green leaves of a tree will not feed on the insides of a twig and a beetle that lives on other animals will not attack a plant, though there are exceptions.

All insects, and beetles are no exception, depend directly or indirectly upon plants for their existence. Those that depend directly on plants feed upon green plants, nongreen plants, dried plants, and decayed plants. They eat buds, leaves, shoots, branches, bark, wood, roots, flowers, pollen, seeds, fruit, or sip nectar, fruit juices, and sap. Those that live indirectly on plants are those that live on animals either as predators, scavengers, or parasites.

Eggs

All insects develop from eggs. Generally they are laid in places where the young may have access to food, but in some instances, for example in aphids and in some flies, the eggs hatch within the female body. An insect egg is usually surrounded by a shell or *chorion;* immediately beneath the chorion is a delicate lining, the *vitelline membrane,* that encloses the contents of the egg: the nutritive matter or *yolk,* the *nucleus,* and the accompanying *cytoplasm.*

The eggs differ greatly in size but all are comparatively small and, contrary to popular misconception, most of them can be seen with the naked eye, though there are some that tax our vision. And they are anything but egg shaped. Thus the eggs may be spherical, long and curved, cylindrical, conical, and even flat. A few are ribbed, some have a circle of spines, others have a cap that is ornamented with raylike extensions, and still others are furnished with long filaments. The egg of the poultry louse is covered with glasslike spines and at one end has a lid that bears at its apex a long, lashlike whip.

Almost every color and color combination may occur in the eggs: brown, dark green, pale yellow, red, white, orange, pink, and black. Some eggs are deposited singly, others in rows, and still others on top of one another. They may also be laid in clusters and covered with a varnishlike coating, in masses overlaid with a hard covering of silk or hairs, or beneath a waxy coating. Indeed, they are covered with all sorts of materials, including fecula and regurgitated food, all for the purpose of protecting them against winter conditions or to make them less conspicuous to enemies.

Many beetles lay their eggs in open places such as branches, tree trunks, fences, and the like; the eggs are deposited with a viscous substance that, upon drying, forms a cement that holds them firmly in place. Other beetles lay their eggs in places where the eggs are completely hidden from view, as in stems, tree trunks, fruit, seeds, roots, and in the ground making incisions, punctures, scars, and holes for the reception of the eggs by means of an ovipositer or a prolonged beak.

Hatching and Development

The eggs of insects usually hatch a few days after they are laid, except in species that spend the winter in the egg stage; these eggs will not hatch for five or six months. From the egg to the adult, the insect goes through a series of dramatic changes called *metamorphosis,* a word derived from the Greek words, *meta,* change, and *morphe,* form. Thus metamorphosis actually means *a change in form.* In the life of an insect there are developmental periods that are sometimes conspicuously different from other periods. These periods are termed *stages*

In some insects the immature forms resemble the adults both in form and in food habits; in other words, there is no distinct change in form between the egg and the adult. These insects are said to have *no metamorphosis,* though, strictly speaking, there are no insects without metamorphosis. In a large number of insects the immature stage, exclusive of the egg, consists of a number of active, feeding periods that differ little from one another except in the gradual development of the wings and reproductive organs. All these species are terrestrial, there is no change in food habits, and there is no resting stage before they become adults. These insects are said to have *gradual metamorphosis* and the young are known as *nymphs.*

In still other insects the adults are terrestrial, but the young are aquatic and breathe by means of gills. There is a change in food habits and there is also a more or less distinct resting period before the adult stage is reached. These insects are said to have *incomplete metamorphosis* and the young are known as *naiads.*

Finally there are the insects in which the immature forms are strikingly different from the adults and in which there is a distinct resting period before the adult stage. These insects, such as the beetles, have four stages in their development—egg, larva, pupa, and adult—and are said to have *complete metamorphosis.* The larvae of beetles are known as *grubs.*

Molting

As the outer covering or *integument* of insects is hard and inelastic, it must be shed periodically to allow the young insects to grow and to increase in size. The process is called *molting.* Just before the outer covering or "skin" is shed, a new one is formed beneath it from a liquid secreted by certain glands called *hypodermal glands.* The new "skin" is soft and elastic and can easily accommodate an increase in size, but it soon hardens and after a while it, too, has to be shed, and still again, until the insect matures. The number of molts varies with different insects.

The cast "skin" is known as *exuviae* and the periods between molts as *stadia* (singular, *stadium*). The form of an insect during a stadium is known as an *instar*. In describing the growth or development of an insect, both the stadia and instars are numbered. The first stadium is the period between hatching and the first molt, and the first instar is the form of the insect between hatching and the first molt. The second stadium is the period between the first and second molts, the second instar the form during this same period, and so on.

Parental Care

Although the vast majority of insects simply lay their eggs and completely forget about them, leaving their young to fend for themselves and to find their own food, a few species take care of their young in varying degrees. For instance, some store food for their young so that when the young emerge from the eggs, they have a supply right at hand; others feed their young day by day. A few guard their eggs until they hatch, and one species not only guards its young, but also assists them in the construction of the cocoons.

Solitary Insects

From the viewpoint of food supply, insects can conveniently be grouped into three classes: the *nonsolitary* or *nonsocial,* the *solitary* (some entomologists prefer the word *subsocial*), and the *social*. In the first class belong the insects that do not provide food for their young; in the second class are those that store food for their young (a method of feeding called *mass provisioning*); and in the third class belong those that feed their young each day (called *progressive provisioning*).

There are several other characteristics that serve to distinguish these classes. The free feeders (nonsolitary or nonsocial) do not construct a nest as both the solitary and social insects do. There is no caste system or division of labor and no exercise of any parental care, such as is found among the social insects, in either the free feeders or the solitary insects. It must be said that many insects have habits that approximate those of these three classes and, because they represent indeterminate forms, it is apparent that the three groups intergrade with one another and that no sharp or distinct line can be drawn between them.

Social Insects

The social insects live in organized groups or communities in which there is a caste system, division of labor, provisioning, and parental care that involves day-to-day feeding of the young. They all construct more or less elaborate nests and frequently build up large populations. Ants, honey bees, and termites are well-known examples of social insects.

The Color of Insects

A glass prism placed in a ray of light produces a rainbow effect; a puddle in the road will do the same. The rainbow effect or light spectrum is a band of colors with red at one end and purple at the other. Actually, the colors we see are sensations produced in our brain by light waves when they strike certain nerve areas on the retina of the eye. Without going into the physics of color, we can say that each color is a light wave of a definite length and frequency. The light waves that produce the color of the spectrum collectively compose the light we get from the sun or an electric light bulb, and if the light falls on an object, the light waves are collectively absorbed, reflected, or separated so that some may be absorbed and others reflected. If all are absorbed, the object appears black; if all are reflected, the object appears white; if all are absorbed except the red wave and this is reflected, the object appears red; if all are absorbed but the green wave and this is reflected, the object appears green; if two waves are reflected, a color combination is the result. There is more involved, but this is basically the idea.

Now, as color is due to the absorption or reflection of various wave lengths, the colors of insects must be due to structural peculiarities or to substances present in the outer covering that either absorb or reflect the waves that make up the light that falls on them. Accordingly, the colors of insects may be either *structural* or *pigmental*.

A pigmental color is the green of many caterpillars that is due largely to the ingestion of chlorophyll, the green colored matter found in the leaves they eat; similarly, insects that feed on the blood of higher animals become red because of the ingested hemoglobin. Such colored matter or substances are known as *pigments*. The red and yellow colors of many insects are due to *carotene* and *xanthophyll*, pigments that give autumn leaves their beautiful coloring. A substance known as *anthocyanin*, which produces the blue, red, and purple colors in flowers, fruits, leaves, and stems, is also responsible for the reds, purples, and possibly blues in many insects. Thus the pigments found in insects may be taken directly from the food, be manufactured indirectly from the food, or be excretory products. The brown and black colors of insects are by-products of metabolism. They are nitrogenous substances known as *melanins* and are diffused in the cuticle.

We are all familiar with the brilliant iridescent colors of a butterfly's wing. Such colors are due to the *diffraction* or breaking up of light by fine, closely parallel grooves or *striae* on the scales of the wings that act much the same as a prism forms a spectrum; these are known as *structural colors*. The brilliant colors of various tropical butterflies are due to the scales being both pigmented and striated. Sometimes the colors of butterflies may be due not only to surface markings, but also to the lamination of the scales and to the overlapping of two or more scales.

The brilliant blues and greens and iridescence in general of certain beetles are due partly to minute lines or pits that diffract the light. The pits alone, however, do not produce any color; it is only when they are combined with a reflecting or refracting surface and a pigment layer that iridescence results.

The metallic sheen of many beetles is produced in much the same way as the metallic luster of metals like gold, silver, or copper, which are extremely opaque and reflect practically all the light that falls on them, resulting in the characteristic brilliant reflection. The distance to which light can penetrate the opaque surface of these metals is only a small fraction of a light wave. Now, the depth to which different wave lengths can penetrate varies and so some colors are transmitted more freely than others. What this amounts to is that the transmitted light is perceived as colored and the reflected light is complementary to the transmitted color. In gold the reflected light is yellow, the transmitted light is blue. The greenish sheen of certain tiger beetles and wood-boring buprestids is of this nature. It is all rather complicated, but so is the subject of color anyway.

Sexual Color Dimorphism

In many insects the sexes show a difference in color or color pattern by which they may be distinguished. This difference is known as *sexual color dimorphism* and may be slight or quite marked. Thus in the familiar white cabbage butterfly, the male has a conspicuous black spot on the upper side of each front wing and the female has two; a difference that may not be readily detected by the casual observer. On the other hand, the wings of the male peach-tree borer are colorless and transparent; in the female the forewings are violet and opaque. Sometimes the same sex may show two kinds of coloration, like the tiger swallowtail. In the Northern States, the female is yellow with black markings; in the Southern States, she is blackish brown with black markings. Sexual color differences are not common in the *Coleoptera,* although there are some examples, as in *Hoplia trifasciata* where the male is grayish in color and the female is reddish.

Winter Life

In regions where the temperature becomes so low at certain times of the year that normal activities are impossible, animals seek a secluded place and pass into a condition of dormancy or semidormancy that is known as *hibernation.* Beetles, like other insects, are no exception.

Beetles hibernate in all stages of development: as eggs, larvae, pupae, and adults. The method is usually constant for a given species, though some may hibernate in any one of the stages.

All sorts of places are utilized as winter retreats: grass roots and tussocks, burrows and passageways in trees and shrubs, the leaf cover of the woodland floor, logs, the soil, and buildings. Few beetles, or any insects for that matter, spend the winter beneath stones that are small enough to be turned over easily and fewer still beneath boulders, because such places offer relatively little protection and little food and in low places may be submerged by soil water.

Migration

We usually think of migration as movements of animals over long distances, whether they occur occasionally, as the hordes of lemmings that every now and then overrun the highlands and go down to the sea in Scandinavia, or seasonally, as the annual departure of the birds for the South to escape the rigors of northern winters. But a migration may take place over a short distance as well. Thus when temperatures begin to fall, insects that have spent the summer on trees and shrubs or in bushy, weedy hedges move downward to the ground where they spend the winter beneath the leaf cover and those that have lived on the surface of the ground dig into the soil. And when spring comes there is a general emergence from their resting places. Migration may also occur when a pond dries up and the water insects are compelled to seek a new one or when food becomes scarce, as when grasshoppers and cutworms have exhausted a crop in a field and must find another one elsewhere. If a beehive becomes crowded, some bees leave and locate new quarters. Though most insects migrate only a short distance, a few cover distances that rival those of the birds. Thus the common milkweed or monarch butterfly gathers by the thousands in the fall and goes southward, where it passes the winter, to return the following spring. The painted lady also migrates to the Southland.

Protection and Defense

Insects in general and beetles in particular have developed a variety of ways as a defense against their enemies, though the latter succeed in attacking and destroying them in vast numbers. No protective device is foolproof and though it may be ineffective against one kind of enemy, it is usually effective against another. Thus a hairy caterpillar may be eaten by one species of bird and left alone by others, which is better than being eaten by all.

The hard covering of insects and especially of the beetles is a defense against some enemies and so is the noise some of them make. When handled, many insects make a sound that may be faint to human ears, but exceedingly loud to other animals, which causes them to be dropped.

Many insects when disturbed or attacked, give off an ill-smelling or pungent and often corrosive fluid that is a potent weapon in many instances. Hairs are probably more effective, however, since many birds will eat ill-flavored insects, whereas they usually leave hairy caterpillars alone. Venomous spines and stings are generally a successful deterrent against a would-be aggressor, as are the jaws of some insects.

Insects not only defend themselves against their enemies by various aggressive means, but also in a passive way by resembling some object of their surroundings (*protective resemblance*) or by blending with their background (*protective coloration*).

The Economic Importance of Insects (Beetles)

All of us know that insects can be quite destructive and that the damage they do to various crops, forests, and our household possessions runs into millions of dollars each year. Indeed, there is hardly anything that we grow, manufacture, or borrow from nature that is not subject to their ravages. And many beetles are among our worst pests.

Insects are also dangerous as vectors of disease: malaria, the plague, and sleeping sickness. And many are pestiferous or annoying by attacking us directly by biting, stinging, and so on. All of these belong to the debit side of the ledger. Few beetles are in this category, though some are vectors of plant diseases.

On the credit side are the many species that are useful and beneficial. Among the foremost of these insects are the predacious and parasitic forms that control or keep in check the injurious kinds, plus those that transport pollen. As cross-pollination is necessary for the fertility and vigor of plants, the value of insects in this respect can hardly be measured in dollars and cents.

Insects also serve as food for birds, lizards, frogs, fish, and other animals, including man, since some primitive people consume insects in great quantities and often consider them a luxury. Many insects provide us with useful products: honey and wax; lac from which shellac is made; dyes; tannin, used in the process of tanning; and silk, which has now been largely superseded by synthetics. A few are even of value in medicine, like the blister beetles.

The Beetles of America

Key to Families of Beetles

How To Use the Key

The key to the families of beetles is merely a means of determining to which family an unidentified beetle belongs. Thus to use the key, begin with the first couplet and decide by examining the unidentified beetle whether its head is prolonged into a snout or beak or is not prolonged into a snout or beak. If its head is not prolonged into a snout or beak, proceed to couplet 8. Here a decision has to be made as to whether the beetle's hind legs are modified for swimming. If they are not modified for swimming, go on to triplet 12, where the tarsal segments have to be counted. If they are five in number, the next step is to go on to couplet 13. Couplet 13 offers two alternatives. If the antennae are threadlike, couplet 14 is next in order. On examining the head of the beetle and finding that the antennae are inserted above the bases of the mandibles, it becomes apparent that the beetle belongs to the family *Cicindelidae*. Continue now to the first page of the Families of Beetles and, after reading a description of the family, compare the beetle with the descriptions of the various tiger beetles until the unidentified beetle matches one of them. In this respect the illustrations should help. The striae and intervals are counted left and right from the suture.

It must be said that the key is not infallible and is merely an aid to the identification of an unknown beetle and should be so considered.

1a. Head prolonged into a snout or
　　beak (Fig. 25) 2

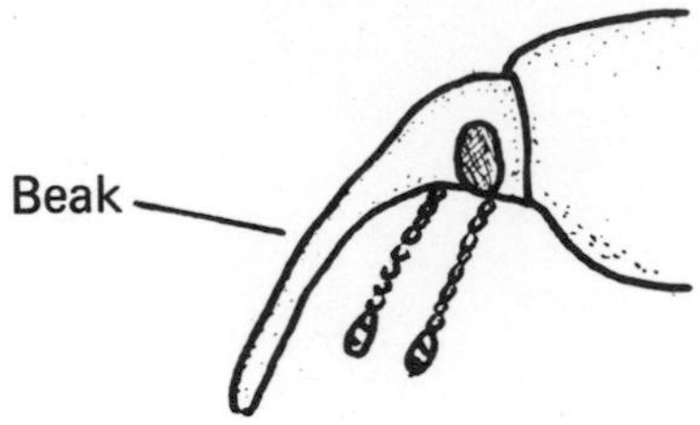

Fig. 25.　Side View of a Snout Beetle

1b. Head nót prolonged into a snout or
　　beak 8
2a. Beak small, much shorter than
　　wide, tibiae with teeth (Fig. 26) ...3

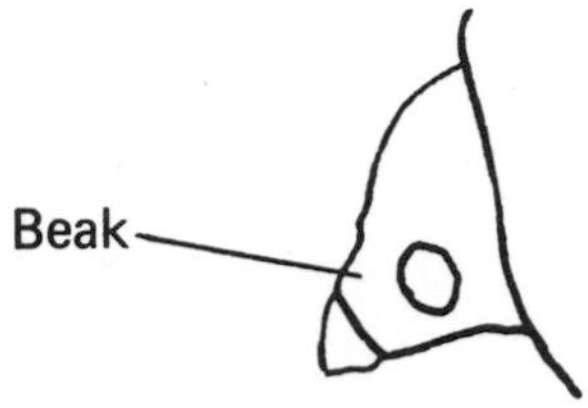

Fig. 26.　Beak Small, Shorter than Wide

2b. Beak longer than broad, tibiae
　　　without teeth 4
3a. First tarsal segment of front leg
　　longer than next three combined ....*Platypodidae,* **Page 454**
3b. First tarsal segment of front leg
　　shorter than next three combined ...*Scolytidae,* **Page 455**
4a. Antenna with a distinct club
　　(Fig. 8) 5
4b. Antenna without a distinct club ....*Brentidae,* **Page 420**
5a. Stout gray-and-black checkered
　　beetles ....*Belidae,* **Page 424**
5b. Not stout gray-and-black checkered
　　beetles 6
6a. Maxillary and labial palpi flexible,
　　labrum present ....*Anthribidae,* **Page 422**
6b. Maxillary and labial palpi rigid,
　　labrum not present 7
7a. Last dorsal abdominal segment
　　exposed (Fig. 27) ....*Rhynchophoridae,* **Page 449**

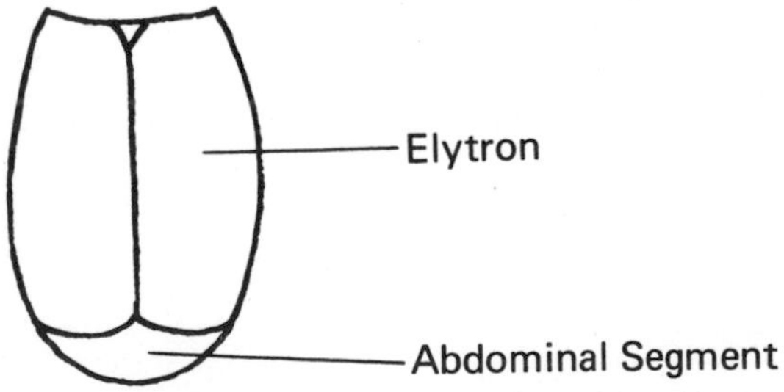

Fig. 27.　Last Dorsal Abdominal Segment Exposed

7b. Last dorsal abdominal segment
　　covered ....*Curculionidae,* **Page 425**
8a. Hind legs modified for swimming,

that is, flattened with fringes of long
hair (Fig. 28) 9

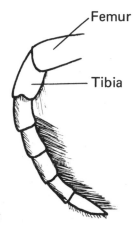

Fig. 28. Hind Leg Modified for Swimming

8b. Hind legs not modified for swimming, that is, not flattened with
fringes of long hair 12
9a. Eyes divided (Fig. 29) .... *Gyrinidae,* Page 95

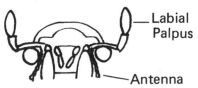

Fig. 29. Side View of Head of Whirligig Beetle Showing Divided Eye

9b. Eyes not divided 10
10a. Legs with large spurs and small
claws 11
10b. Legs with short bristles only .... *Haliplidae,* Page 84
11a. Antenna with a knob at apex (Fig.
9) labial palpi very long and easily
mistaken for antennae (Fig. 30) .... *Hydrophilidae,* Page 98

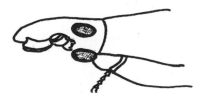

Fig. 30. Labial Palpi Long

11b. Antenna threadlike, without a
knob, labial palpi normal (Fig. 6) .. *Dytiscidae,* Page 87
12a. Tarsi of all legs with five segments
each (Fig. 31) 13

Fig. 31. Tarsus with Five Segments

12b. Tarsi of front legs with five seg-
     ments each, tarsi of hind legs with
     four segments each 56
12c. Tarsi of all legs with less than five
     segments each . . . . .67[1]
13a. Antennae threadlike 14
13b. Antennae usually not threadlike . .17
14a. Antennae inserted above the bases
     of the mandibles (Fig. 32) ; head,
     including eyes, wider than
     pronotum . . . . *Cicindelidae,* Page 48

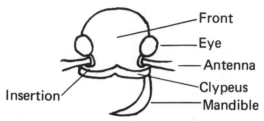

Fig. 32.   Antennae Inserted above the Base of the Mandibles

14b. Antennae inserted between eyes
     and bases of mandibles (Fig. 33) ;
     head, including eyes, narrower than
     pronotum 15

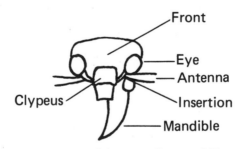

Fig. 33.   Antennae Inserted between Eyes and Base of Mandibles

15a. Body covered with scales . . . .*Cupesidae,* Page 172
15b. Body not covered with scales 16
16a. Scutellum visible or exposed
     (Fig. 1) . . . .*Carabidae,* Page 54
16b. Scutellum not visible or exposed . .*Omophronidae,* Page 82
17a. Antennae with distal segments
     expanded laterally to form leaflike
     or platelike structures (Fig. 10) . .18
17b. Antennae with distal segments not

---

[1] The following families actually have tarsi with five segments each but the fourth is so
small and hidden that the tarsi appear to have only four segments: *Cerambycidae,
Phalacridae, Mylabridae,* and *Chrysomelidae.*

expanded laterally to form leaflike
or platelike structures 21
18a. Distal segments capable of being
closely folded together 19
18b. Distal segments not capable of
being closely folded together 20
19a. Abdomen with five visible segments.. *Trogidae,* Page 339
19b. Abdomen with six visible segments
or, if only five are present, coxae of
middle legs are transverse
(Fig. 34) ....*Scarabaeidae,* Page 319

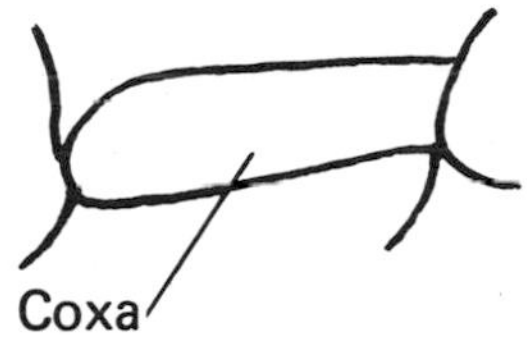

Coxa   **Fig. 34. Transverse Coxa**

20a. Antennae elbowed (Fig. 14),
mentum not notched ....*Lucanidae,* Page 341
20b. Antennae straight, mentum deeply
notched (Fig. 35) ....*Passalidae,* Page 344

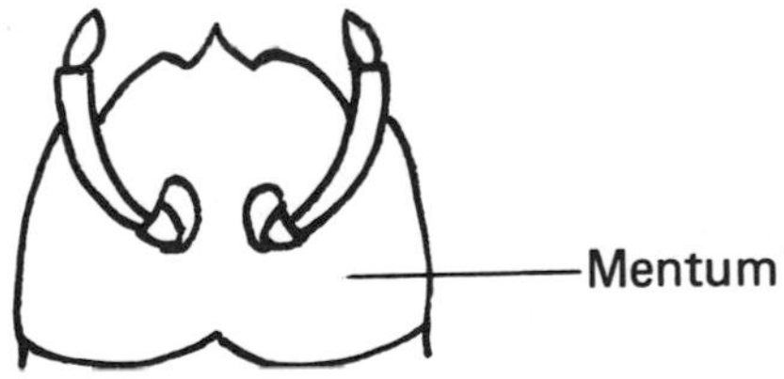

Mentum

Fig. 35. Notched Mentum

21a. Elytra abbreviated, covering less
than half the length of the abdomen 22
21b. Elytra covering whole abdomen or
exposing only one or two dorsal
segments 24
22a. Abdomen flexible, with seven or
eight visible ventral segments ......*Staphylinidae,* Page 112
22b. Abdomen not flexible, with only
five or six visible ventral segments 23
23a. Antennae each with only two
segments ....*Clavigeridae,* Page 133
23b. Antennae each with ten or eleven
segments ....*Pselaphidae,* Page 128
24a. Elytra square cut, abdomen
conical ....*Scaphidiidae,* Page 134
24b. Elytra not square cut, abdomen not
conical 25

25a. Abdomen with seven or eight
visible segments 26
25b. Abdomen with less than seven
visible segments 28
26a. Coxae of middle legs separated ....*Lycidae,* Page 144
26b. Coxae of middle legs touching 27
27a. Head completely or largely exposed
or at most one-half covered by
pronotum ....*Cantharidae,* Page 153
27b. Head completely covered by pro-
notum or at least more than one-
half covered ....*Lampyridae,* Page 147
27c. Head completely exposed, antennae
well separated at their bases ....*Phengodidae,* Page 157
28a. First three ventral segments of
abdomen fused and immovable ...29
28b. First three ventral segments of
abdomen not fused and not
immovable 31
29a. Abdomen with six visible segments..*Psephenidae,* Page 229
29b. Abdomen with five visible seg-
ments 30
30a. Coxae of front legs transverse,
densely pubescent ....*Dryopidae,* Page 230
30b. Coxae of front legs rounded,
sparsely pubescent ....*Elmidae,* Page 231
31a. Abdomen with six ventral seg-
ments 32
31b. Abdomen with five ventral segments 39
32a. Very small, flattened beetles with
rudimentary eyes or none at all ....*Leptinidae,* Page 111
32b. Very small, oval beetles with
eyes 33
33a. With erect hairs ....*Scydmaeniidae,* Page 109
33b. Not with erect hairs 34
34a. Elytra leaving tip of abdomen
exposed ....*Silphidae,* Page 104
34b. Elytra completely covering abdo-
men 35
35a. Small and oval beetles ....*Leiodidae,* Page 108
35b. Not small and oval beetles 36
36a. First segment of abdomen cut into
three parts by coxae of hind legs
(Fig. 36) ....*Rhysodidae,* Page 241

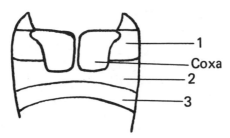

Fig. 36. First Segment of Abdomen Cut into Three Parts by Coxae of Hind Legs

36b. First segment of abdomen not cut
into three parts by coxae of hind
legs 37
37a. Coxae of hind legs conical ....*Melyridae,* Page 158
37b. Coxae of hind legs flat 38
38a. Each fourth tarsal segment about
size of third ....*Cleridae,* Page 161
38b. Each fourth tarsal segment very
small, usually indistinct ....*Corynetidae,* Page 168
39a. Antennae bent at an angle or
elbowed ....*Histeridae,* Page 137
39b. Antennae not bent at an angle or
elbowed 40
40a. Femur attached to tip or near tip
of trochanter (Fig. 37) 41

Fig. 37. Femur Attached to Tip of Trochanter

40b. Femur attached to side of trochanter (Fig. 38) 44

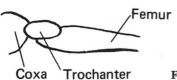

Fig. 38. Femur Attached to Side of Trochanter

41a. Each first tarsal segment shorter
than second 42
41b. Each first tarsal segment equal to
or longer than second 43
42a. Antennae inserted on front of head
between eyes (Fig. 39) ....*Ptinidae,* Page 308

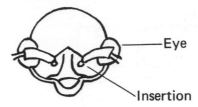

Fig. 39. Antennae Inserted on Front of Head between Eyes

42b. Antennae inserted directly in front
of eyes (Fig. 40) ....*Anobiidae,* Page 310

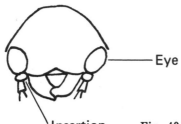

Fig. 40. Antennae Inserted Directly in Front of Eyes

43a. First abdominal segment much
longer than second ....*Lyctidae,* Page 316
43b. First abdominal segment not longer
than second ....*Bostrichidae,* Page 313
44a. Coxae of front legs conical 45
44b. Coxae of front legs transverse 46
44c. Coxae of front legs spherical 50
44d. Coxae of front legs oval ....*Cryptophagidae,* Page 262
45a. Antennae each with a three-seg-
mented club ....*Dermistidae,* Page 235
45b. Antennae usually sawlike or fan-
like (Figs. 11, 13) ....*Rhipiceridae,* Page 198
46a. Elytra leaving tip of abdomen
exposed ....*Nitidulidae,* Page 243
46b. Elytra completely covering abdo-
men 47
47a. Soft-bodied beetles, antennae
usually sawlike ....*Helodidae,* Page 234
47b. Hard-bodied beetles, antennae each
usually with a small club 48
48a. Head deeply impressed with a
small, smooth tubercle on each side
inside the eye ....*Derodontidae,* Page 265
48b. Head not deeply impressed with
a small, smooth tubercle on each
side inside the eye 49
49a. Each femora of hind legs, when at
rest, fits into a groove in the coxa ...*Byrrhidae,* Page 240

49b. Each femora of hind legs, when at
     rest, does not fit into a groove in the
     coxa ....*Ostomidae,* Page 241
50a. Area between the coxae of front
     legs with a spine (Fig. 41) 51

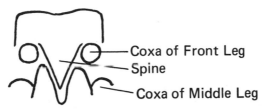

Fig. 41.   **Area between the Coxae of Front Legs with a Spine**

50b. Area between the coxae of front
     legs without a spine 54
51a. First two abdominal segments
     united ....*Buprestidae,* Page 219
51b. First two abdominal segments not
     united 52
52a. Prothorax solidly attached to meso-
     thorax ....*Throscidae,* Page 217
52b. Prothorax not solidly attached to
     mesothorax 53
53a. Labrum visible ....*Elateridae,* Page 200
53b. Labrum not visible ....*Melasidae,* Page 216
54a. Antennae each with a club 55
54b. Antennae each without a club ......*Cucujidae,* Page 250
55a. Cavities in which coxae of front legs
     are attached closed behind
     (Fig. 42) ....*Erotylidae,* Page 258

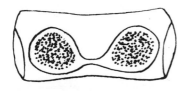

Fig. 42.

Coxal Cavities of Front Legs Closed Behind

55b. Cavities in which coxae of front legs
     are attached open behind (Fig. 43) .. *Languriidae,* Page 256
56a. Cavities in which coxae of front legs
     are attached closed behind
     (Fig. 42) 57
56b. Cavities in which coxae of front legs
     are attached open behind
     (Fig. 43) 59

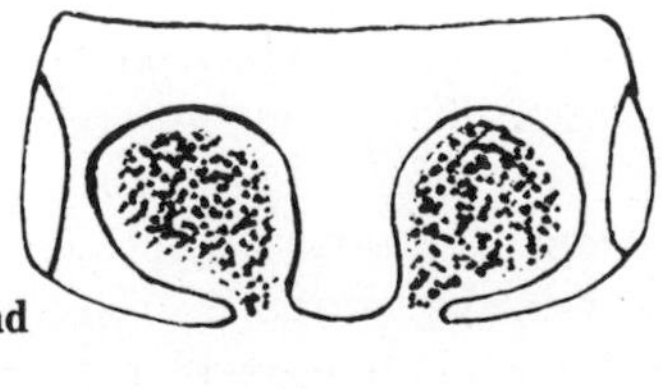

Fig. 43.   **Coxal Cavities of Front Legs Open Behind**

57a. Tarsal claws comblike (Fig. 44) ....*Alleculidae,* Page 288

Fig. 44.   Tarsal Claw Comblike

57b. Tarsal claws not comblike 58
58a. Next to last segment of each tarsi
spongy beneath ....*Lagriidae,* Page 302
58b. Next to last segment of each tarsi
not spongy beneath ....*Tenebrionidae,* Page 291
59a. Head strongly and suddenly con-
stricted behind the eyes 60
59b. Head not strongly and suddenly
constricted behind the eyes ....*Oedemeridae,* Page 172
60a. Base of pronotum as wide as
combined elytra 61
60b. Base of pronotum narrower than
combined elytra 63
61a. Antennae threadlike 62
61b. Antennae with long, flat processes,
which fold like a fan (male) or
somewhat sawlike (female) ....*Rhipiphoridae,* Page 182
62a. Coxae of hind legs with plates
(Fig. 45), abdomen usually ending
in a pointed process ....*Mordellidae,* Page 175

Coxa

Plate   Fig. 45.   Coxa of Hind Leg with Plates

62b. Coxae of hind legs without plates,
abdomen not ending in a pointed
process ....*Melandryidae,* Page 303
63a. Coxae of hind legs large and
prominent 64
63b. Coxae of hind legs not large and
prominent 65
64a. Tarsal claws simple (Fig. 18) ......*Pyrochroidae,* Page 190
64b. Tarsal claws cleft or toothed
(Fig. 21) ....*Meloidae,* Page 183
65a. Eyes notched ....*Pedilidae,* Page 197
65b. Eyes not notched 66
66a. Each second tarsal segment lobed
beneath ....*Euglenidae,* Page 198

66b. Each second tarsal segment not
     lobed beneath .... *Anthicidae,* Page 193
67a. Tarsi each with four segments
     (Fig. 46) 68

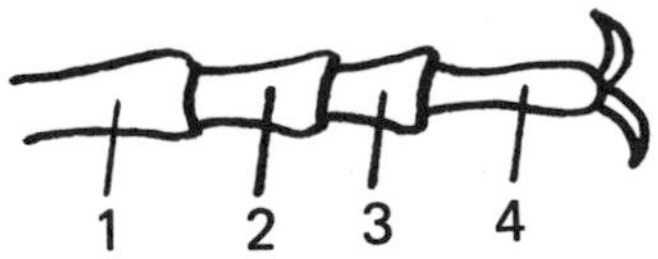

Fig. 46. Tarsus with Four Segments

67b. Tarsi each with apparently four
     segments, for the fifth is small and
     concealed (Fig. 47) 73

Fig. 47. Tarsus with Apparently only Four Segments but Actually with Five

67c. Tarsi each with apparently three
     segments, though some actually
     have four segments but with the
     third so small that the tarsus seems
     to be composed of only three seg-
     ments 76
68a. First four ventral segments of abdo-
     men fused together, only the fifth
     being movable 69
68b. First four ventral segments of abdo-
     men not fused together 71
69a. Tibia enlarged and armed with
     spines .... *Heteroceridae,* Page 232
69b. Tibia not enlarged and armed
     with spines 70
70a. Antennae inserted under the
     margin of the frontal region .... *Colydiidae,* Page 267
70b. Antennae inserted on the frontal
     region .... *Mycetaeidae,* Page 270
71a. Coxae of front legs spherical 72
71b. Coxae of front legs oval .... *Mycetophagidae,* Page 265
72a. Head covered at least in part by
     pronotum .... *Cisidae,* Page 318
72b. Head not at all covered by pro-
     notum .... *Endomychidae,* Page 273
73a. Body elongate, antennae long ...... *Cerambycidae,* Page 245
73b. Body short, more or less oval,
     antennae short 74
74a. Antennae each with a three-seg-
     mented club .... *Phalacridae,* Page 275
74b. Antennae each without a club 75
75a. Frontal region prolonged into a
     short, quadrate beak .... *Mylabridae,* Page 417

75b. Frontal region not prolonged into
a short, quadrate beak .... *Chrysomelidae,* Page 385
76a. Wings with a fringe of long hairs. .77
76b. Wings without a fringe of long
hairs 78
77a. Tarsi actually with four segments
each, the third very small and concealed within a notch of the second,
wings broad (Fig. 49) .... *Orthoperidae,* Page 110
77b. Tarsi with three segments each,
wings narrow (Fig. 48) ....*Ptilidae,* Page 133

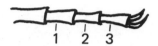

1 2 3   **Fig. 48.   Tarsus with Three Segments**

78a. Tarsi actually with four segments
each, the third being very small and
not easily seen (Fig. 49) .... *Coccinellidae,* Page 278

1 2 3   4

**Fig. 49.   Tarsus Actually with Four Segments, the Third Being Very Small
and not Easily Seen**

78b. Tarsi with only three segments
each 79
79a. Elytra exposing the last abdominal
segment .... *Monotomidae,* Page 250
79b. Elytra completely covering the ab-
domen .... *Lathridiidae,* Page 270

The Families of Beetles

The placing of plants and animals into two great groups such as the plant and animal kingdoms and the further placing of plants and animals into various divisions of each kingdom such as orders, families, and genera is an artificial or man-made device created by taxonomists for the purpose of more readily identifying the many different kinds of plants and animals. Certainly, as far as the plants and animals themselves are concerned such groupings except for species do not exist in nature.

The basis for grouping plants and animals into the various divisions is structure. Thus, in the present book, the tiger beetles, which are placed in the family *Cicindelidae,* have certain structural features in common, the ground beetles, which are placed in the family *Carabidae,* have certain structural features in common, and so on. But among the tiger beetles and ground beetles there are many that differ in minor ways from the others and they are therefore grouped in genera. And again those that are placed in a genus differ slightly from one another and hence we have species.

Taxonomy, or the science of classifying plants and animals, is in a constant state of flux and orders and families and genera are constantly undergoing revisions. Thus a family of beetles today may tomorrow be divided into one or more families or several families may be combined into one; and the same goes for genera and even species. Moreover, entomologists are not always in agreement as to a particular classification.

The following families of beetles are those that are generally recognized as of the moment and the sequence in which they appear is that which is commonly followed in most books.

In the descriptions of the beetles an attempt has been made to make the format as uniform as possible. First the length in millimeters is given. Then the color of the beetle, followed by the shape and sculpturing of the head (when necessary), pronotum, elytra, and other structural characteristics that may be helpful in identifying a species. Finally, the habitat and the range or area where the beetle occurs are mentioned whenever they may serve in the determination of a species.

The Tiger Beetles

Family Cicindelidae

The tiger beetles (Fig. 50) are long legged, rather slender, ac-

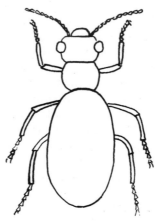

Fig. 50. Tiger Beetle

tive insects that run swiftly over the ground and fly readily when disturbed. Although many are dull colored on the upper surface, some species are a brilliant blue or green or bronze and all have bright metallic colors on the underparts. Because of their predatory habits and the stripes with which many of them are marked, they are known as the *tiger beetles*. They are graceful and beautiful in form and appearance and are common from early spring until fall along country roads, woodland paths, beaches, and the shores of ponds and streams.

These beetles have a fairly large head and prominent eyes except in *Amblycheila*. The antennae have eleven segments each, with at least the six outer segments pubescent (Fig. 51), are filiform or

Fig. 51. Antennae with Pubescence

threadlike in appearance, and are inserted on the front of the head, above the base of the jaws or mandibles instead of between the eyes. The legs are long and slender with tarsi five segmented each. The adults are provided with recumbent hairs and erect bristles. The sexes may be distinguished by the fact that in the male seven abdominal segments are visible, whereas only six can be seen in the female, and that in the male the first three segments of each anterior tarsus are usually dilated and densely clothed with hair on the lower surface.

The tiger beetles are diurnal in habit and on bright sunny days may be seen on dusty roads, well-beaten paths, and in sandy places. When approached, they remain still until one gets fairly close to them and then they suddenly fly up and away, alighting some distance ahead. Before alighting they usually turn so that when they land on the ground they face the direction from which they came. They hide in cloudy or rainy weather and by night in holes in the ground or beneath stones, logs, and rubbish. Each beetle hibernates in a separate burrow.

The eggs are usually laid in holes excavated by the females in sandy ground and hatch into long, whitish, grublike larvae. Unlike the adults, the larvae are ugly looking and anything but graceful, with a large head and prominent curving jaws. They live in vertical burrows that they usually excavate in sandy soil or in beaten paths and that are sometimes a foot or more deep. The burrows may be recognized by the smooth circular depression worn by the larva's feet surrounding the mouth of the burrow. The larva takes up a position at the opening of the burrow where it remains alert for an unwary victim to come within reach of its rapacious jaws that are extended upward and wide open to seize instantly the unsuspecting prey, which, when caught, is taken to the bottom of the burrow and there devoured.

The larva has a hump on the fifth abdominal segment that is provided with two curved hooks that point forward. The hooks serve to anchor the larva in its burrow should it succeed in capturing a large insect that might otherwise drag the larva out of its burrow and so make an escape. By inserting a straw down the burrow and then withdrawing it gently, it is often possible to secure a larva that will likely be found chewing savagely at the end of the straw.

The tiger beetles, as we know them, belong to the genus Cicindela. *They have prominent eyes with the third segment of the maxillary palpus shorter than the fourth (Fig. 52) and with the hind coxae touching each other (Fig. 53).*

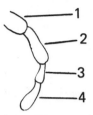

Fig. 52. Third Segment of Maxillary Palpus Shorter than Fourth

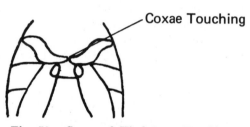

Fig. 53. Coxae of Hind Legs Touching

Cicindela dorsalis Length: 13–15mm. Dull brown with metallic green or bronze; elytra white or cream colored with variable black or brown markings (Fig. 54).
Sandy beaches and along the seashore.
Common throughout the Northeast.

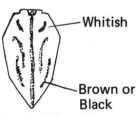

Fig. 54. Cicindela

Cicindela formosa generosa   Length: 16–18mm. Dull brown or dull red, greenish bronze or brownish bronze above, metallic green below; elytral markings whitish (Fig. 55). This is the largest of our tiger beetles.
Bare, sandy situations and along paths and roads.
Eastern half of the United States west to Colorado.

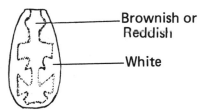

Fig. 55.   Cicindela formosa generosa

Cicindela repanda   Length: 12–13mm. Brownish bronze with a coppery reflection, abdomen metallic green; each elytron with three white markings.
Sandy banks of streams and ponds.
A common and widely distributed species throughout the United States.

Cicindela hirticollis   Length: 13–14mm. Bronze above, green below, densely covered with long, white hairs; elytra with white markings.
Edges of fresh-water bodies.
Eastern United States.

Cicindela tranquebarica   Length: 13–16mm. Brown with a bronze sheen above, dark green beneath; elytra with white markings, one of which is a crescent-shaped mark at each shoulder.
Sandy roads and pathways; also sandy or muddy flats near running water.
Eastern United States.

Cicindela punctulata   Length: 11–14mm. Black, dark brown, or greenish bronze above, greenish or greenish blue beneath; each elytron with a row of green punctures along the suture and with indistinct, scattered white dots, which are sometimes absent.
Roads, garden paths, and even city streets in the summer.
Throughout the United States except extreme West and North.

Cicindela sexguttata   Length: 10–16mm.   Bright metallic green

above, sometimes with a bluish cast, green beneath with a few scattered white hairs; each elytron with two white dots and a crescent-shaped mark, both of which are sometimes obscure or absent (Fig. 56). One of our most conspicuous species.
Sunny woodland paths.
Eastern United States west of the Rockies.

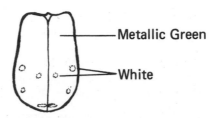

Fig. 56. Cicindela sexguttata

Cicindela purpurea Length: 14–16mm. Purplish to coppery, abdomen metallic green; margins and suture of elytra green, each elytron with a short, median band, a dot near the apex, and the apex tipped with cream.
Meadow paths and roadsides.
Eastern United States.

Cicindela rufiventris Length: 9–12mm. Dull, dark brown, varied with metallic green and bronze above, bluish green beneath, abdomen red; elytra with white spots. This species is easily recognized by its red abdomen.
Roads and paths on the slopes of wooded hills.
Eastern United States.

Cicindela scutellaris lecontei Length: 12–13mm. Greenish and purplish bronze, sides of thorax with long, white hairs; elytra brilliant purplish with cream white spots (Fig. 57). Two varieties of *scutel-*

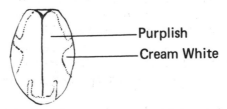

Fig. 57. Cicindela scutellaris lecontei

laris are *modesta,* which is black, and *rugifrons,* which is green. Each has three large white spots; one at the apex of the elytra and one on each elytral margin. The varieties are found in pine barrens. Open, rather dry, sandy situations.
Type species and two subspecies all Eastern United States.

Cicindela unipunctata Length: 14–15mm. Dull brown above, metallic green and blue beneath; elytra with green pits and punctures and one triangular white spot is common to the apices of the two elytra and one spot on the outer margin of each elytron (Fig. 58). Shaded woodland paths.
New York and New Jersey west to Iowa and Missouri and south to Georgia and North Carolina.

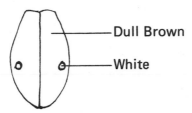

Dull Brown

White

Fig. 58. Cicindela unipunctata

In the species of the genus Tetracha *the hind coxae touch each other, the eyes are prominent, and the third segment of the maxillary palpus is longer than the fourth. The members of this genus are nocturnal in habit, hiding by day and coming out at night to feed.*

Tetracha carolina Length: 15–17mm. Metallic green, shining; antennae, mouthparts, legs, and apex of abdomen pale yellow; each elytron purplish bronze with a large comma-shaped, pale yellowish spot at the apex (Fig. 59).
Beneath stones, logs, debris, etc.
Southern United States.

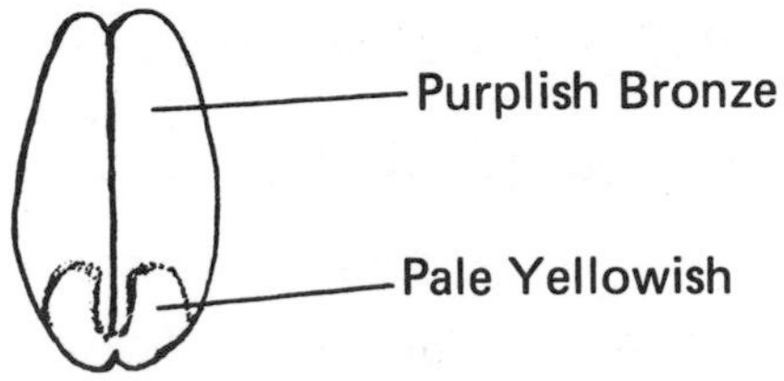

Purplish Bronze

Pale Yellowish

Fig. 59. Tetracha carolina

Tetracha virginica   Length: 20–24mm. Dark yellow green; antennae, legs, and last ventral segment of abdomen brownish yellow or a rusty brown; elytra blackish at middle, sides with a broad metallic green stripe.
Beneath stones, logs, and debris, especially near water.
Pennsylvania south to Florida and west to Nebraska and Texas.

In the genus Amblycheila *the hind coxae are separated* (Fig. 60), *the eyes are small, and the sides of the elytra are widely inflexed.*

Fig. 60.   Coxae of Hind Legs Separated

Amblycheila cylindriformis   Length: 30–38mm. Brown or blackish; elytra pale brown. Nocturnal in habit.
In holes in clay banks.
Kansas, Colorado, Arizona, and New Mexico.

In the genus Omus *the hind coxae are separated* (Fig. 60), *the eyes are small, and the sides of the elytra are narrowly inflexed. The members of this genus are nocturnal insects, hiding under rubbish during the daytime. They are western in range, occurring along the Pacific Coast.*

Omus dejeani   Length: 15–21mm. Black, the elytra with conspicuous pits.

Omus californicus   Length: 14–17mm. Black, shining, the elytra without distinct pits.

Omus laevis   Length: 13–16mm. Black, the elytra smooth.

The Ground Beetles

Family Carabidae
   The family *Carabidae* is one of the largest families of insects. The members, which are common and in abundance, live essen-

tially on the surface of the ground and hence are known as the *ground beetles* (Figs. 61, 62). They are more or less nocturnal in

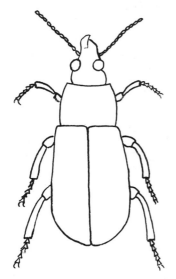

Fig. 61. Ground Beetle

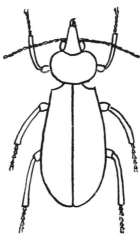

Fig. 62. Ground Beetle

habit, hiding by day beneath stones, logs, rubbish, and loose bark and coming out at night to search for food. For the most part predatory, feeding on other insects that they spring upon or pursue, ground beetles include among their prey some of our worst economic pests such as gypsy moths, cankerworms, and cutworms. A few species, however, are plant eaters and occasionally do considerable damage to various crops.

Most species of ground beetles are black or dull brownish in color but some are yellow, metallic blue, green, or purple. A few are spotted. The elytra or wing covers are generally ornamented with longitudinal ridges and rows of punctures.

The head is narrower than the pronotum and is directed forward. The antennae, which are threadlike and have eleven segments each with at least the six outer segments pubescent (Fig. 51), taper gradually toward the tips and are inserted between the bases of the mandibles and the eyes (Fig. 33). There are six abdominal sternites present. The legs are usually slender and adapted for running. The tarsi have five segments each (Fig. 31).

The larvae of the ground beetles are relatively long and flat. They have sharp projecting mandibles and a pair of bristly appendages at the hind end of the body. Like the adults, they are predaceous and occur in the same situations but, being rather shy, are less often seen. They live for the most part in underground burrows and pupate in small earthen cells.

Scaphinotus elevatus   Length: 18–19mm. Pitchy black with a coppery, greenish, or violet reflex; antennae and legs pitchy black. Hind coxae separated (Fig. 60) ; pronotum nearly as wide as elytra, the sides turned up or elevated, the hind angles prolonged over the elytra; the first segments of each antenna longer than the third and with four basal segments smooth; labrum deeply forked (Fig. 63) ;

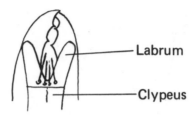

Fig. 63.   Labrum Deeply Forked

labial palpi shaped like a long-handled spoon. This beetle feeds on snails, the head and mandibles being especially adapted for reaching into the shell.
Under stones, logs, and leaves in moist woods where snails are plentiful.
Central and Eastern United States.

Sphaeroderus lecontei   Length: 12–14mm. Black, shining; elytra violet with metallic violet margins. Hind coxae separated; labrum deeply forked; labial palpi each with more than two setae; elytra finely striate.
Beneath stones, logs, and moss in low-lying woods.
Eastern half of United States.

The beetles of the genus Carabus *are of large or moderate size. The hind coxae touch each other (Fig. 53), the mandibles are distinctly curved, and the third segment of each antenna is cylindrical.*

Carabus serratus   Length: 20–24mm. Black, shining; margins of pronotum and elytra blue or bright violet. Elytra finely striate, each elytron with three series of very large punctures and with two to

four fine teeth on each margin; sides of pronotum rounded.
Beneath stones and logs in wooded areas and in damp places.
Eastern half of United States.

Carabus limbatus   Length: 17–26mm. Black, somewhat shining, margins of pronotum and elytra bluish. Elytra deeply striate and each with three series of coarse punctures; sides of pronotum rounded (Fig. 64).
Beneath logs and stones in moist woodlands.
Eastern half of United States.

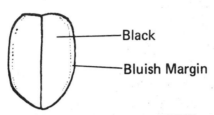

Fig. 64.   Carabus limbatus

Carabus vinctus   Length: 20–25mm. Black, somewhat shining, bronzed; pronotum with greenish tinge at borders. Elytra finely striate, striae finely punctured; sides of pronotum rounded.
Under bark in low moist woods; often found with the species *limbatus*.
Throughout the United States.

Carabus sylvosus   Length: 27–30mm. Black; margins of pronotum and elytra blue. Each elytron with three rows of pits, striae very fine; margins of pronotum upturned.
Sandy woods.
Eastern and Southern States.

The species of the genus Calosoma *are large with the third segment of each antenna compressed or flattened; mandibles distinctly curved.*

Calosoma scrutator   The Caterpillar Hunter   Length: 25–35mm. Head, legs, and pronotum deep blue or purple; margins of pronotum gold, green, or metallic red; elytra metallic green with margins of red or gold; abdomen green and red. Elytra with many fine punctured striae; sides of pronotum sharply curved, base and apex equal in width (Fig. 65). Male with a dense brush of hairs on inner

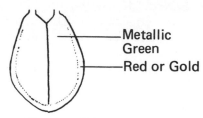

Fig. 65. Calosoma scrutator

surface of each curved middle tibia. This is a very useful species, destroying large numbers of harmful caterpillars, often climbing trees in search of them, hence called *The Searcher* or *Caterpillar Hunter*.
Gardens, fields, and open woods.
Throughout the United States.

Calosoma calidum The Fiery Hunter Length: 21–27mm. Black, shining; pronotum and elytra sometimes with a narrow border of green; each elytron with three rows of bright yellow, copper, or red pits or impressions. Elytra deeply striate and finely punctured; sides of pronotum rounded (Fig. 66). Both the adult and larva, the latter called

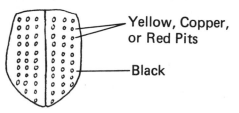

Fig. 66. Calosoma calidum

the *cutworm lion,* feed on large numbers of cutworms each year.
Meadows and open woodlands.
Throughout the United States.

Calosoma frigidum Length: 20–23mm. Black above, greenish black below; pronotum and elytra narrowly edged with green; each elytron with three rows of green punctures. Elytral striae punctured; sides of pronotum rounded.

Gardens, fields, and open woods.

Eastern half of United States.

Calosoma willcoxi Length: 17–20mm. Head, legs, and pronotum deep blue or purple, the pronotum with a margin of gold, green, or red; elytra metallic green or blue green and with a margin of green, gold, or red. Elytra with fine, punctured striae; sides of pronotum rounded with base of pronotum slightly narrower than the apex.

Fields and open woods.

Throughout the United States.

Calosoma externum Length: 28–32mm. Black; margins of pronotum and elytra blue. Elytral striae distinctly punctured; sides of pronotum rounded, flattened, and turned up behind.

Fields and open woodlands.

Eastern United States west to the Missouri River.

Calosoma sycophanta Length: 25–30mm. Pronotum blue; green elytra. This is a European species that was introduced near Boston to combat the gypsy moth and the brown-tail moth.

Found in parts of the Northeast.

The following two species of the genus Elaphrus *resemble in general appearance small tiger beetles. But in these beetles the head is wider than the pronotum, the eyes are prominent, and the elytra lack striae but have, instead, rows of many large, shallow pits. Also the bases of the elytra and pronotum touch each other. The base of the antennae are not covered.*

Elaphrus ruscarius Length: 8–10mm. Dull brown brassy above, metallic green below; legs reddish brown; impressions or pits on elytra purplish or violet (Fig. 67).

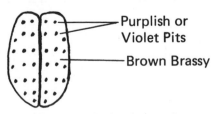

Purplish or
Violet Pits

Brown Brassy

Fig. 67. Elaphrus ruscarius

Margins of ponds and lakes, especially common in spring.
Northern half of the United States.

Elaphrus cicatricosus   Length: 6–7.5mm. Brown brassy, lower surface
sometimes bluish; impressions on elytra greenish.
Sand flats.
Eastern half of the United States.

Nebria pallipes   Length: 10–12mm. Dark reddish brown to black,
shining; antennae and legs reddish brown. Antennae about two-thirds
as long as the body; head with one seta above each eye; and the
mandibles each with a bristle-bearing puncture (Fig. 68). Elytral
striae deep.
Beneath stones, logs, and debris near water.
Eastern half of the United States.

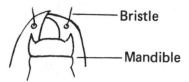

Fig. 68.   Mandible with a Bristle-bearing Puncture

The beetles of the genus Pasimachus *have the basal segment of
each antenna as long as the following three combined; the head has
a bristle-bearing puncture above each eye* (Fig. 69) ; *the base of each*

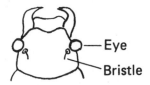

Fig. 69.   Head with But One Bristle-bearing Puncture above the Eye

*antenna is covered with a frontal plate; the hind angles of the pro-
notum are quite distinct; and the elytra have a ridge at the shoulders.*

Pasimachus depressus   Length: 24–30mm.   Black,   usually   with   a blue margin; male shining, female dull. Elytra smooth with apices rounded (Fig. 70).

Beneath stones, logs, and debris along the borders of cultivated fields. Central and Southern States.

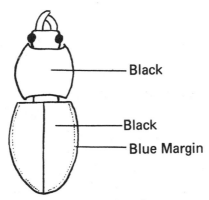

Fig. 70.   Pasimachus depressus

Pasimachus sublaevis   Length: 21–28mm. Similar in color to the species *depressus,* but differs from it in having the elytra striate. This species, as well as the preceding one, is extremely predaceous and feeds on caterpillars and other larvae, especially those of the army worm.

Beneath stones, logs, and debris in open woods, pastures, and along the borders of cultivated fields.

Eastern states west to the Mississippi River.

Scarites subterraneus   Length: 15–20mm. Black, shining. The head with two deeply indented, parallel lines, and a bristle-bearing puncture above each eye; the base of each antenna covered with a frontal plate; the pronotum squarish with sides nearly straight and separated from the elytra by a neck: elytra distinctly striate and rounded at apices; each antenna with first segment as long as the following three combined; and each tibia of front legs with three teeth preceded by a smaller tooth. A Southern species, *substriatus,* is similar but somewhat larger; it also differs in having each tibia of the front legs with three large teeth preceded by two or three smaller teeth.

Beneath stones, logs, and leaves in the vicinity of cultivated areas.

Common in gardens.

Central and Eastern States.

The beetles of the following two genera, Dyschirius *and* Clivina, *are small in size and similar in habits, often being found together. The first segment of each antenna is about as long as the second one; there are two bristle-bearing punctures above each eye and at the hind angles of the pronotum (Fig. 71); and the base of each anten-*

Fig. 71.   Head with Two Bristle-bearing Punctures above the Eye

na is covered with a frontal plate. The two genera differ in that the pronotum of Dyschirius *is globular or oval, while that of* Clivinia *is squarish. The beetles live in burrows in wet, sandy places, especially shady or muddy banks, and may be collected by throwing or pouring water over their burrows.*

Dyschirius globulus   Length: 2.5–3mm. Black, dark brown, or reddish brown; antennae and legs light reddish brown or yellowish brown. Elytra coarsely punctured at bases but not at apices; pronotum broader than long.
Beneath the loose bark of logs in damp ground; also in burrows.
Eastern half of the United States.

Dyschirius sphaericollis   Length: 5.5–6mm. Bronzed black; antennae and legs dark red. Elytra deeply striate; pronotum oval.
In habits similar to the species *globulus*.
Eastern half of the United States.

Clivinia dentipes   Length: 7.5–9mm. Black, shining; legs pitchy black; antennae and tarsi reddish brown. Elytral striae with fine punctures; pronotum squarish; each tibia of the middle legs with a spur near outer tip.
Eastern half of the United States.

Clivinia impressifrons   Length: 6–6.5mm. Reddish brown. Elytral striae with fine impressed dots; pronotum slightly longer than wide, sides rather wavy, hind angles rounded; each tibia of the middle legs with a spur; sometimes eats sprouting corn grains.
Underneath stones in the vincinity of water and also in low, damp fields.
Eastern half of the United States.

Clivinia americana Length: 5mm. Black; pronotum with a narrow margin of reddish brown; antennae pale brown; legs reddish brown; elytra with narrow margins of reddish brown. Pronotum squarish, sides slightly curved or rounded; elytral striae with fine, deeply impressed dots.
Eastern half of the United States.

Clivinia bipustulata Length: 6–8mm. Black; antennae and legs reddish brown; each elytron with a somewhat indistinct red spot near the base and another one near the apex. Elytral striae coarsely punctured; pronotum squarish, hind angles somewhat rounded (Fig. 72).
Often attracted to lights.
Eastern half of the United States.

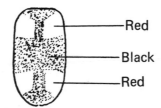

Fig. 72.   Clivinia bipustulata

Aspidoglossa subangulata Length: 7.5–8mm. Black, shining; antennae and legs reddish brown or dull brownish orange. First segment of each antenna shorter than the second; head with two bristle-bearing punctures above each eye and two at hind angles of pronotum; base of each antenna covered with a frontal plate; sides and base of pronotum rounded into a continued arc; elytra deeply striate and coarsely punctured with a reddish spot near the apices.
Beneath stones, logs, and debris in moist woods; also under stones in the vicinity of water.
Eastern half of the United States.

The following two species of the genus Schizogenius *are small, oblong, slender beetles. The first segment of each antenna is shorter than the second; the head has several fine, longitudinal grooves; the head also has two bristle-bearing punctures above each eye and two at the hind angles of the pronotum; the base of each antenna is covered with a frontal plate; and the mentum is deeply notched.*

Schizogenius lineolatus Length: 3.5–5mm. Blackish, shining; dark

reddish brown beneath. Sides of pronotum narrowed to apex, hind angles rounded; elytra deeply striate.
Beneath stones, logs, and debris in damp places.
Eastern half of the United States.

Schizogenius ferrugineus   Length: 3–4mm. Light yellowish brown to dark brown or reddish brown. Elytra deeply striate; pronotum slightly longer than broad with hind angles rounded.
Beneath stones, logs and debris in moist situations.
Eastern half of the United States.

The species of the genus Bembidion *are small, oval beetles that are flattened vertically. Each antenna is slender with the first two segments smooth; two bristle-bearing punctures are above each eye; the mandibles have a bristle-bearing puncture in the groove on the outer side; the eyes are prominent; the last segment of each labial palpus is short, sharp, and needlelike. These beetles are usually found along the shores of ponds and streams and on mud flats.*

Bembidion inaequale   Length: 4.5–5.5mm. Black, bronzed, shining; antennae pitchy, basal segment of each pale reddish; legs dark green, tibia and basal segment of each femur dull yellow. Each elytron has two dorsal punctures on third interval with fourth striae wavy.
Eastern United States.

Bembidion versicolor   Length: 2.5–3.5mm. Bronzed, greenish black, shining; legs light brown; elytra blackish with yellowish or reddish brown markings. Each elytron with two dorsal punctures on third stria; base of pronotum narrower than apex (Fig. 73).
Eastern United States.

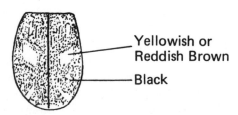

Yellowish or Reddish Brown

Black

Fig. 73.   Bembidion versicolor

Bembidion quadrimaculatum   Length: 2.7–3.7mm. Head and pronotum dark bronze or blackish bronze, shining; antennae pitch colored, basal segment of each dull yellow; legs dull yellow or yellow brown; elytra brown or black, with two conspicuous yellow spots on each. Base of pronotum much narrower than apex; third striae of each elytron with two dorsal punctures (Fig. 74). Throughout the United States.

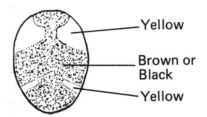

Fig. 74. Bembidion quadrimaculatum

Bembidion patruele Length: 3.5–4.7mm. Deep brown or black, somewhat shining; antennae pitch colored; legs yellow brown or red brown; elytra black with dull yellow markings. Each elytron with two dorsal punctures on third interval.
Northeastern United States.

Bembidion americanum Length: 5–6mm. Black or blackish bronze, shining; antennae pitch colored with first and second segments dark reddish brown; tibiae of legs reddish brown. Pronotum with sides rounded and apex slightly wider than base; each elytron with two dorsal punctures on the third stria.
Eastern half of the United States.

Bembidion variegatum Length: 5–6mm. Black, rather shining; antennae pitch colored with three basal segments dull yellowish; legs dull yellowish; elytra dull pale yellow with dark brown bands. Each elytron with two dorsal punctures on the third interval.
Eastern half of the United States.

The beetles belonging to the genus Tachys *are small with slender antennae and prominent eyes. The head has two bristle-bearing punctures above each eye; the mandibles have a bristle-bearing puncture in the groove on the outer side (Fig. 68); and the last segment of the labial palpus is short, sharp, and needlelike.*

Tachys incurvus Length: 1.5–2.5mm. Dark orange brown or reddish brown to nearly black, shining; antennae brownish except bas-

al segments, which are dull yellow; legs dull yellow; each elytron with a pale yellowish stripe from humerus or shoulder nearly to apex. Elytra distinctly wider than pronotum; striae on elytra only near suture (Fig. 75).
Beneath stones in open woods; also in ants' nests.
Throughout the United States.

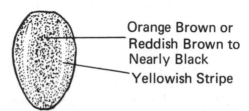

Fig. 75.   Tachys incurvus

Tachys scitulus   Length: 2.5–3mm. Brownish yellow, head darker; antennae brownish black, basal segments yellowish; legs yellowish; elytra with an indistinct darker crossband behind their middle. Elytra with four or five fine, distinct striae.
Beneath stones and rubbish in damp places and on mud flats.
Eastern half of the United States.

Patrobus longicornis   Length: 12–14mm. Black, pitchy black beneath, shining; antennae reddish brown; legs paler. Head with two bristle-bearing punctures above each eye; mandibles with a bristle-bearing puncture in the groove on the outer side; last segment of labial palpus slender, elongate, or subcylindrical; pronotum slightly broader than long with a median-impressed line and a transverse impression at the apex; elytra deeply striate, the striae punctured.
Beneath stones and rubbish and along streams and lakes.
Northeastern United States.

Pterostichus adoxus   Length: 13–15mm. Black, shining; antennae, legs, and margins of elytra dark reddish brown or brown. Head with two bristle-bearing punctures above each eye; margin of each elytron interrupted at hind third and with a distinct, internal fold; next to last segment of each labial palpus with two setae (Fig. 76); base of pronotum narrower than apex; elytral striae not punctured.
Beneath stones, logs, and debris in woodlands.
Eastern half of the United States.

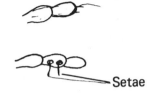

Setae

Fig. 76.   Next to Last Segment of Labial Palpus with Two Setae

Gastrellarius honestus   Length: 8mm. Black, shining; antennae and legs dark reddish brown. Head with two bristle-bearing punctures above each eye; margin of each elytron interrupted at hind third and with a distinct, internal fold; pronotum with sides curved and constricted at base; elytra wider than pronotum, deeply striate, and with a single dorsal puncture on the third interval of each elytron. Beneath stones and logs in wooded areas.
Northeastern United States.

Eumolops sodalis   Length: 15–17mm. Black; apical half of each antenna reddish brown; tarsi reddish brown. Margin of each elytron interrupted at hind third and with a distinct, internal fold; head with two bristle-bearing punctures above each eye; base of pronotum distinctly narrower than apex; elytra deeply striate, the striae finely punctured and with a single dorsal puncture on third interval of each.
Eastern half of the United States.

Euferonia coracina   Length: 15–18mm. Blackish, shining; antennae and tarsi somewhat paler. Margin of each elytron interrupted at hind third and with a distinct, internal fold; head with two bristle-bearing punctures above each eye; pronotum narrower at base than at apex and with a ridge on the hind angles; elytral striae deep and with two dorsal punctures on third interval of each.
Eastern United States.

Abacidus permundus   Length: 12–14mm. Black or purplish, often with an iridescent sheen; antennae dark brown. Margin of each elytron interrupted at hind third and with a distinct, internal fold; head with two bristle-bearing punctures above each eye; pronotum squarish with base wider than apex; each elytron with three dorsal punctures, the first on the third stria, the others on the second.
Beneath logs in open woods.
North Central States.

Poecilus lucublandus   Length: 10–14mm. Green or purplish, slightly shining; legs brown or reddish brown. Margin of each elytron interrupted at hind third and with a distinct, internal fold; head with two bristle-bearing punctures above each eye; three basal segments of antennae with a ridge; sides of pronotum rounded, apex more constricted than the base; two large dorsal punctures on the third interval of each elytron (Fig. 77).
Cultivated fields.
Throughout the United States. Probably the most common of the ground beetles in the Northeast.

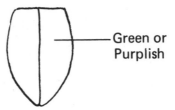

Fig. 77.   Poecilus lucubandus

Poecilus chalcites   Length: 10–14mm. Metallic green or bronzed, or black green, very shining; black legs with two large dorsal punctures on the third interval of each elytron.
It may be found under rocks and logs.
Throughout the United States.

The following species of the genus Melanius *are of moderate size with the margin of the elytra interrupted at the hind end and with a distinct, internal fold. The head has two bristle-bearing punctures above each eye and the pronotum has two basal impressions on each side and has hind angles that are somewhat right angles.*

Melanius ebeninus   Length: 14–16mm. Black shining; antennae and legs pitch colored. Pronotum distinctly narrowed at base, hind angles with a ridge; elytra finely striate, one dorsal puncture on the third stria of each elytron, two on the third interval of each elytron.
Beneath stones and logs, usually in the vicinity of water.
Eastern half of the United States.

Melanius caudicalis   Length: 10–11.5mm. Black; antennae and legs pitch colored. Pronotum with base much narrower than apex, hind

angles with a ridge; elytra deeply striate, one dorsal puncture on the third stria of each elytron, two on the third interval of each elytron.
Eastern half of the United States.

Melanius luctuosus Length: 8–9mm. Brownish black to black, shining; antennae and legs pitch colored. Pronotum with base slightly narrower than apex, hind angles with a ridge; elytra deeply striate, one dorsal puncture on the third stria, two on the third interval of each elytron.
Eastern half of the United States.

Dysidius mutus Length: 10–12.5mm. Black, shining; antennae and legs pitch colored. Margin of each elytron interrupted at hind end and with a distinct, internal fold; the head with two bristle-bearing punctures above each eye; pronotum with a single basal impression on each side and the hind angles broadly rounded; elytra deeply striate, one dorsal puncture on the third stria, two on the second, of each elytron. Another species found in the Northcentral States is *Dysidius purpurarus;* it is purplish and 13–14mm long.
Eastern half of the United States.

Pseudargutor erythropus Length: 8–8.5mm. Black, shining; antennae and legs reddish brown. Margin of each elytron interrupted at hind end and with a distinct, internal fold; the head with two bristle-bearing punctures above each eye; pronotum with a single basal impression on each side, hind angles rounded; elytra deeply striate, three dorsal punctures on the third interval of each elytron; last segment of labial palpi elongate and oval.
Under debris in the vicinity of water.
Eastern and Central United States.

The following species of the genus Amara *are of small or moderate size with the next to the last segment of the labial palpus shorter than the apical segment and with more than two setae. The basal two or three segments of each antenna have a ridge; the margin of each elytron is interrupted at the hind end and with a distinct, internal fold; the head has two bristle-bearing punctures above each eye; the base of the pronotum is wider than the apex; and the elytra are without dorsal punctures.*

Amara impuncticollis Length: 7–9mm. Brownish black to black or dark bronze; tibiae and tarsi dark reddish brown. Elytral striae shallow, a large puncture where the scutellar stria joins the second stria.
Throughout the United States.

Amara cupreolata Length: 6–7mm. Blackish or purplish black with a brassy reflex; antennae and legs dark reddish brown. Distinguished from *impuncticollis* by the absence of the large puncture at the end of the scutellar stria.
Northcentral States, where it is quite common.

Amara angustata Length: 6–7.5mm. Black, shining, somewhat bronzed; bases of antennae and legs reddish yellow. Pronotum with hind angles rounded; elytra as wide as pronotum and deeply striate; apical spur of each tibia of the front legs three pronged.
At the bases of trees and stumps in open woods.
Eastern half of the United States.

Rembus laticollis Length: 13–15mm. Black, slightly shining; antennae and tarsi dark brown. Head with two bristle-bearing punctures above each eye; basal three segments of antennae smooth; pronotum wider at the base than at the apex, hind angles of pronotum right angles; elytral striae shallow, elytra each with one dorsal puncture on the third interval; coxae of hind legs touching.
Beneath stones and debris in damp or wet places.
Eastern half of the United States.

The beetles of the genus Dicaelus *are large stout species: the head has two bristle-bearing punctures over each eye; the three basal segments of the antennae are smooth or without hairs; the base of the pronotum is prolonged over the elytra; the elytra are deeply striate; and the coxae of the hind legs are touching.*

Dicaelus elongatus Length: 15–18mm. Black, shining. Pronotum squarish, hind angles broadly rounded, with two bristle-bearing punctures on the margin; elytra with humeral or shoulder ridge reaching halfway to tips (Fig. 78), eighth and ninth striae of each elytron well separated.
Under stones.
Central and Eastern States.

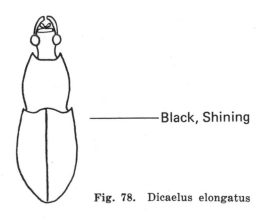

————Black, Shining

Fig. 78. Dicaelus elongatus

Dicaelus dilatatus Length: 20–25mm. Black. Pronotum distinctly narrower at apex than at base, hind angles narrowly rounded, and with one bristle-bearing puncture on the margin; elytra with shoulder ridge reaching two-thirds of the way to tips, eighth and ninth striae well separated.
Eastern and Central States.

Dicaelus purpuratus Length: 20–25mm. Purplish; antennae pitch colored at bases but becoming paler toward apices; legs black. Pronotum distinctly narrower at apex than at base, sides broadly rounded; elytra with shoulder ridge reaching two-thirds of the way to tips, eighth and ninth striae well separated.
Sometimes rather common.
Eastern and Central States.

Badister pulchellus Length: 5.5–6.5mm. Dull brownish yellow; head black; antennae dusky with first segment of each yellow; elytra with black iridescent markings. Head with two bristle-bearing punctures over each eye; antennae with two basal segments smooth; base of pronotum narrower than apex; elytral striae shallow with two dorsal punctures on the third interval of each elytron; coxae of hind legs touching.
Eastern and Central States.

Calathus opaculus Length 8.5–10mm. Head and pronotum reddish brown to pitch colored; antennae and legs slightly paler; elytra dull pitch colored or brownish black. Head with two bristle-bearing punctures above each eye; three basal segments of antennae smooth; pronotum with two bristle-bearing punctures on each side; elytra obliquely wavy at apices; tarsal claws with notched edges like the teeth of a saw; coxae of hind legs touching.
Under stones, logs, and leaves in dry woods.
Throughout the United States.

Calathus gregarious Length: 10–11mm. Shining reddish brown upper surface. A larger species and gregarious in hibernation.
It is widely distributed throughout the United States.

The species of the genus Platynus *are of small or medium size with long and slender antennae each covered with soft hairs from the fourth segment. The pronotum narrows toward the base and the apex, with the angles at the apex acute. There are two bristle-bearing punctures on each side; the elytra are much wider than the pronotum; the coxae of the hind legs are touching; and the next to last segment of the labial palpus has two setae.*

Platynus hypolithos Length: 13–15mm. Black, shining; undersurface dark reddish brown; antennae and legs pale reddish brown.

Pronotum constricted at base, hind angles rounded; elytra without shoulder angles and deeply striate with fairly large punctures on sides of alternating intervals.
New York west to Indiana.

Platynus decorus Length: 7.5–8.5mm. Head green or greenish bronze; pronotum, scutellum, legs, and bases of antennae reddish yellow; elytra bluish often tinged with green at margins. Pronotum slightly elongate and narrowed at the base; elytra with broadly rounded shoulder angles and shallow striae; all tarsi with distinct grooves on the sides (Fig. 79).
Eastern United States west to the Rockies.

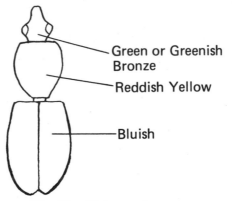

Green or Greenish Bronze

Reddish Yellow

Bluish

Fig. 79. Platynus decorus

Platynus extensicollis Length: 8–9.5mm. Head and pronotum metallic green or bronzed, shining; undersurface black; antennae and legs yellowish brown; elytra greenish or purplish. Pronotum slightly elongate, constricted at base, with angles at apex or those near the head acute; elytra with broadly rounded shoulder angles, third interval of each with four or five small punctures; all tarsi with distinct grooves on the sides.
Eastern half of the United States.

Platynus sinuatus Length: 10.5–11mm. Black, shining; antennae, legs, and margin of pronotum pitch colored. Pronotum elongate, constricted at base, hind angles are right angles; elytra deeply striate and finely punctured; only the tarsi of the middle and hind legs with grooves on the sides, tarsi of front legs smooth.
Northeast United States.

Platynus cincticollis   Length: 9.5–11mm. Black. Pronotum constricted both at apex and base; elytra deeply striate, intervals with fine
wrinkles; only the tarsi of the middle and hind legs with grooves on
the sides, tarsi of the front legs smooth.
Eastern half of the United States.

Platynus picipennis   Length: 6–7mm. Head and pronotum dark reddish brown to black; antennae, legs, and elytra brownish yellow. Pronotum as long as wide, hind angles rounded, lateral margins wider
toward the base and bent backward; elytral striae fine, third interval of each with four to six dorsal punctures; all tarsi with distinct
grooves on the sides.
Northcentral and Middle States.

Colliuris pennsylvanicus   Length: 7–8mm.   Head   and   pronotum
black; antennae brownish black with three basal segments reddish;
legs pale yellowish brown; elytra brownish orange, each with two
black marks forming an interrupted transverse band at the middle
and a small transverse one at the apex. Head with two bristle-bearing punctures above each eye, elongate and prolonged behind eyes;
neck constricted and dilated into a semiglobular knob; next to last
segment of labial palpus with two setae; first segment of each antenna nearly as long as next two combined; pronotum cylindrical,
broader at base than at apex; elytra squarish at apices, striae of each
elytron with large punctures on basal half (Fig. 80); *Colliuris* looks
very much like an ant.
Beneath stones, logs, and rubbish.
Throughout the United States.

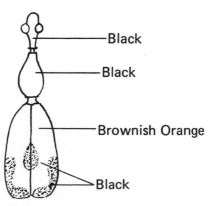

Fig. 80.   Colliuris pennsylvanicus

Galeritula janus Length: 17–22mm. Black or bluish black and densely covered with short pale yellowish hairs; pronotum, labial and maxillary palpi, bases of antennae, and legs reddish brown; elytra bluish black. Head with two bristle-bearing punctures above each eye; next to last segment of labial palpus with a number of setae and always longer than the terminal segment; first segment of each antenna elongate; lateral margins of pronotum flattened and bent backward at hind angles; elytra squarish at apices, striae fine (Fig. 81).

Beneath stones and leaves in open woods; often attracted to lights. Eastern half of the United States.

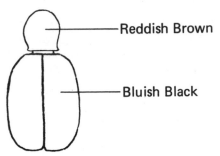

Fig. 81. Galeritula janus

Galeritula bicolor Length: 17–21mm. Similar to *janus* but the sides of the head are longer and less rounded behind the eyes; also the hairs near the scutellum stand erect, and the pronotum is more distinctly longer than wide.

Fence rows and woodlands.

Eastern half of the United States.

The beetles of the genus Lebia *are small or moderately small, oval in shape, and with the head constricted into a neck behind the eyes. The head has two bristle-bearing punctures above each eye; the next to the last segment of labial palpus has two setae; the mandibles each have a distinct groove; the mentum is notched at the margin; the pronotum is somewhat wider than the head but much narrower than the elytra; the elytra are squarish at the apices; the coxae of the hind legs are touching; and the tarsal claws are comb-like, a feature which doubtless helps the beetles to climb plants to feed.*

Lebia grandis Length: 4.5–5.5mm. Head and pronotum reddish yellow; abdomen black; antennae pale yellowish; elytra dark blue or green. Pronotum almost twice as wide as long, hind angles obtuse; elytra deeply striate, intervals with fine wrinkles (Fig. 82).
Beneath stones and leaves.
Throughout the United States.

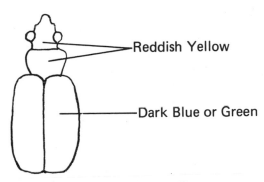

Reddish Yellow

Dark Blue or Green

Fig. 82. Lebia grandis

Lebia atreventris Length: 6–7mm. Head, pronotum, legs (except tarsi), and basal segments of antennae reddish yellow; elytra dark purplish blue. Pronotum nearly twice as wide as long, hind angles nearly right angles; elytra finely striate with fine punctures.
Beneath stones, logs, and leaves.
Throughout the United States.

Lebia ornata Length: 4.5–5mm. Head and pronotum pitch colored, the pronotum with pale yellowish margins; antennae yellowish brown, the three basal segments paler; legs and undersurface yellowish brown; elytra pitch colored, each with a dull spot at the apex and base. Mentum with a distinct tooth; elytra deeply striate.
Beneath stones, logs, and leaves.
Throughout the United States.

Lebia viridis Length: 4.5–5.5mm. Green or purplish blue, shining; antennae pitch colored, basal segments greenish; legs black. Mentum with a distinct tooth; elytral striae shallow.
Often found on flowers.
Throughout the United States.

Lebia scapularis Length: 4.5–5.5mm. Head, pronotum, and legs pale

reddish yellow; antennae brownish black, three basal segments paler; elytra brownish black with yellowish stripes. Pronotum broadly margined; elytra deeply striate (Fig. 83).
On various plants.
Eastern half of the United States.

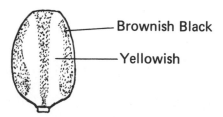

Fig. 83.   Lebia scapularis

The species of the genus Brachinus *are small to medium-sized beetles with narrow heads and pronoti; the head narrows behind the eyes into a neck. The head has one bristle-bearing puncture above each eye; the elytra are squarish at the bases; the mandibles each have a bristle-bearing puncture in the outer groove; the two basal segments of each antenna are smooth; and the coxae of the hind legs are not touching, but are separated. These beetles have little sacs at the hind end of the body in which is secreted an evil-smelling fluid that serves as a means of defense. When disturbed or attacked by an enemy, this fluid is discharged with a distinct popping sound and, on contact with the air, changes to a gas that looks very much like smoke. When a larger insect attempts to capture one of these beetles,* Brachinus *discharges its "gun" into the face of its enemy who is surprised by the noise and is temporarily blinded by the smoke; on recovering, the intended victim is at a safe distance. By reason of this defensive device, the beetles are known as the* bombardier beetles.

There are about thirty species of bombardier beetles and, except for size, are all much alike in general appearance.

Brachinus cordicollis   Length: 7.5–9mm. Head, pronotum, and first pairs of legs brownish yellow; antennae, abdomen, and often the hind legs darker; and elytra blackish blue.

Brachinus americanus   Length: 10–12mm. Head, pronotum, and first two pairs of legs brownish yellow; antennae, abdomen, and often the hind legs darker; and elytra bluish black.

Brachinus fumans   Length: 11.5–12mm. Head, pronotum and first two pairs of legs brownish yellow or brown orange; antennae, abdomen, and often hind legs darker; elytra dull blue or black violet (Fig. 84).

Generally found under stones, logs, and dead leaves usually in damp places.

Throughout the United States.

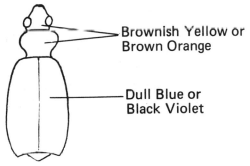

Brownish Yellow or Brown Orange

Dull Blue or Black Violet

Fig. 84.   Brachinus fumans

Members of the genus Chlaenius *are medium-sized or large beetles. The antennae each have three smooth basal segments, each elytron has the margin more or less interrupted and with an internal fold, the head has one bristle-bearing puncture above each eye, the coxae of the hind legs are touching, and the mentum is toothed. They are often found under stones and logs in damp places and have a strong, musky odor, particularly when they are disturbed.*

Chlaenius tricolor   Length: 11.5–13mm. Head and pronotum green somewhat bronzed; antennae and legs orange brown; elytra bluish black. Pronotum with sides somewhat wavy; elytra deeply striate and finely punctured (Fig. 85).

Throughout the United States.

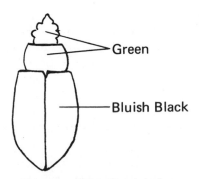

Green

Bluish Black

Fig. 85.   Chlaenius tricolor

Chlaenius tomentosus Length: 13–15mm. Blackish, bluish, or greenish, somewhat bronzed above, shining beneath; antennae black, each with two basal segments paler; elytra with fine yellowish pubescence. Pronotum gradually wider from apex to base, hind angles right angles; elytral striae moderately deep with coarse punctures.
Often attracted to lights.
Throughout the United States east of the Rockies.

Chlaenius sericeus Length: 12.5–17mm. Bright green sometimes with a bluish tinge, undersurface black; antennae and legs pale brownish yellow; elytra with fine, yellowish pubescence. Pronotum with base wider than apex, hind angles slightly obtuse; elytral striae fine with small distant punctures, intervals flat finely punctured; third segment of each antenna distinctly longer than the fourth.
Usually in the vicinity of water, as along the margins of lakes and streams.
Throughout the United States.

Chlaenius cordicollis Length: 12.5–16mm. Dark violet blue or brilliant green; antennae and legs reddish brown; elytra with short yellowish pubescence. Pronotum with base as wide as apex, sides rounded anteriorly, wavy posteriorly, hind angles somewhat obtuse; elytral striae finely punctured, intervals densely punctured; third segment of each antenna distinctly longer than the fourth.
Along creeks and rivers.
Eastern half of the United States.

Anomolossus emarginatus Length: 12–14mm. Head bright green; pronotum green and bronzed; antennae and legs pale orange brown; elytra dark blue. The head with one bristle-bearing puncture above each eye; margin of each elytron more or less interrupted and with an internal fold; antennae each with three, smooth basal segments; coxae of hind legs touching. Pronotum wider at base than at apex, hind angles obtuse; elytral striae fine and moderately punctured, intervals densely and coarsely punctured.
Beneath stones and debris in moist situations.
Eastern half of the United States.

The beetles of the following and remaining genera of the Family Carabidae *have one bristle-bearing puncture on the head above the eye and the two basal segments of each antenna are smooth. that is, without hairs.* (This taxonomic fact refers only to those beetles marked with an *.)

*Cratacanthus dubius Length: 8–10mm. Black, shining; antennae

and legs red brown or brown orange. Next to last segment of labial palpus has many setae and is longer than the following segment; first segment of each tarsus of the hind legs not as long as the three following combined; submentum with tooth equal to lateral lobes; pronotum with base narrower than apex and hind angles are right angles; elytra deeply striate.
Cultivated fields; often attracted to light.
Eastern half of the United States.

The beetles of the genus Harpalus *are large or medium sized with the next to the last segment of the labial palpus having several setae and being longer than the last segment; the first segment of each tarsus of the hind legs is not as long as the following two combined.*

The genus Harpalus *is a large one with over one hundred species described from the United States. The three described are among the more common ones.*

Harpalus caliginosus Length: 21–25mm. Black, shining; legs black; antennae and tarsi reddish brown. Pronotum wider than long, as wide as elytra at base, hind angles are right angles; elytra deeply striate (Fig. 86).
Common about dry fields; often attracted to light. Destroys large numbers of cutworms each year, but since it also eats seeds, its value might be questioned.
Throughout the United States.

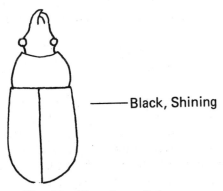

Black, Shining

Fig. 86. Harpalus caliginosus

Harpalus pennsylvanicus Length: 13–15.5mm. Black, shining; antennae and legs pale yellowish or reddish yellow; lower surface black or reddish brown. Pronotum wider at base than at apex, as wide as elytra at base, sides rounded, hind angles obtuse; elytra deeply striate; submentum toothed.

Fields and cultivated areas. Like *caliginosus,* also feeds on cutworms and seeds.

Throughout the United States.

Harpalus herbivagus   Length: 8–10mm. Black, shining; lateral margins of pronotum and elytra reddish; antennae and legs yellowish brown; lower surface black. Pronotum wider than long, hind angles rounded; elytral striae deep, third interval of each elytron with a dorsal puncture.

Throughout the United States.

Selenophorus opalinus   Length: 9–10mm. Black; antennae and legs yellowish brown. Pronotum wider than long with base as wide as apex, sides somewhat rounded; elytra deeply striate; labial palpus with next to last segment bearing several setae; first segment of each of the tarsi of the hind legs as long as the following three combined. Often found beneath bark.

Eastern half of the United States.

Triplectrus rusticus   Length: 9–14mm. Brownish black; bases of antennae and part of hind pronotal angles reddish brown; legs pitch colored. Pronotum wider than long, as broad at base as elytra, hind angles obtuse; elytra deeply striate, third interval of each elytron with one to four dorsal punctures; next to last segment of labial palpus with many setae and longer than the following segment; basal segment of each of the tarsi of the hind legs as long as next two combined; terminal spur of each tibia of the front legs three pronged.

Common in newly plowed fields.

Central and Eastern States.

Anisodactylus harrisii   Length: 11–11.5mm. Black, shining; antennae and tarsi dark reddish brown. Pronotum slightly wider than long, hind angles obtuse; elytra deeply striate; next to last segment of labial palpus with many setae and longer than the next; first segment of each of the tarsi of the hind legs not as long as three following combined; terminal spur of each tibia of the front legs simple or nearly so.

Eastern half of the United States.

Amphasia interstitialis   Length: 9.5–10mm. Head, pronotum, antennae, and legs red yellow or orange brown; elytra pitch colored. Pro-

notum wider than long, sides and apex with broad margins, hind angles rounded; elytra deeply striate, intervals coarsely punctured; next to last segment of labial palpus with many setae and longer than the following segment; first segment of each of the tarsi of the hind legs as long as the two following combined; abdomen punctured over whole surface.
Northcentral States eastward to Atlantic Coast.

Stenocellus rupestris Length: 4.5–5mm. Reddish brown, shining; head pitch colored; antennae brownish black, the two basal segments and the legs brownish yellow. Pronotum wider than long, hind angles obtuse; striae of elytra deep, a dorsal puncture near second stria of each elytron; each second labial palpal segment with two setae and shorter than the third; the first segment of each of the tarsi of the hind legs shorter than the next two combined; mentum with a large tooth.
Throughout the United States, rather common in the Southern States.

The beetles of the genus Stenolophus *are small in size with the next to the last segment of the labial palpus having two setae and being shorter than the following segment; the fourth segment of each of the tarsi of the front legs has two lobes; the tarsi of the hind legs are threadlike; and the submentum is toothed.*

Stenolophus ochropezus Length: 5.5–6mm. Black or pitch colored; bases of antennae and legs yellowish or brown orange; elytra frequently iridescent. Pronotum only slightly wider than long, hind angles obtuse; elytra deeply striate, intervals minutely punctured.
Throughout the United States.

Stenolophus plebjus Length: 4.5–5mm. Blackish, shining; narrow margins of pronotum, bases of antennae, and legs brownish-yellow. Pronotum slightly narrowed toward the base, hind angles rounded; sutural striae short and not joining the first dorsal striae.
United States east of the Rockies.

Stenolophus conjunctus Length: 3.5–4.5mm. Blackish, shining; bases of antennae and legs yellowish brown. Pronotum wider than long, sides so rounded that hind angles are lacking; elytral striae deep, intervals densely punctured.
Common in sandy places; often attracted to lights.
Throughout the United States.

The beetles of the genus Agonderus *are small in size with the next to the last segment of labial palpus having two setae and being shorter than the following segment; the tarsi of the hind legs taper to the apices, the first segment of each being shorter than the next two combined. The two species described often feed on germinating corn seed during cold, wet weather; they are often attracted by lights.*

*Agonderus pallipes Length: 5.5–7mm. Yellowish brown with an indefinitely wide blackish stripe on each elytron, though sometimes this stripe is faint or absent completely; head blackish (Fig. 87).
Under stones and rubbish about gardens and plowed fields.
Central and Southern States.

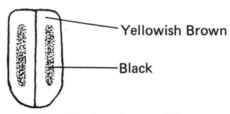

Fig. 87.   Agonderus pallipes

*Agonderus comma Length: 6–7mm. Head and lower surface black; pronotum and elytra yellowish brown or reddish brown, pronotum with a large black spot, and each elytron with a blackish stripe, which is wider than in *pallipes*.
Beneath stones and debris in gardens and plowed fields.
Eastern half of the United States.

The Hemispherical Savage Beetles

Family Omophronidae
    The beetles of this family are distinctive because of their round form and the fact that the scutellum is not exposed but wholly concealed (Fig. 88). They are of small size, ranging from 5 to 8 millimeters in length, and their color varies from a pale brownish yellow to nearly black or a dark bronzed green.
    The head is narrower than the pronotum; antennae are threadlike, each with eleven segments, and are inserted between the eyes and the bases of the mandibles; the four basal segments are smooth, that is, without hairs. The elytra are slightly shortened so that a part

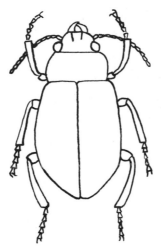

Fig. 88.   The Hemispherical Savage Beetle

of the last abdominal segment is exposed; and the tarsi each have five segments.

These beetles live in burrows in the wet margins of ponds, streams, and lakes, in openings between the roots of plants, or beneath stones and debris along the water's edge and come out only at night to feed. To see or collect them is merely a matter of pouring water over the banks, which drives them out of their burrows.

Omophron americanum   Length: 6–7mm. Bronzed or greenish black; head largely green; pronotum and elytra with narrow, paler margins; lower surface reddish brown; legs paler.
At times under debris at some distance from water.
Northeast United States.

Omophron labiatum   Length: 6mm. Dark brown, dull yellow, or nearly black, shining; sides margins of pronotum and elytra paler; legs paler.
United States east of the Rockies.

Omophron tessellatum   Length: 6–7mm. Pale brownish yellow; head with a green band across the base; pronotum with a central green spot; elytra with metallic green cross markings; lower surface rusty red brown; legs paler (Fig. 89).
Middle United States.

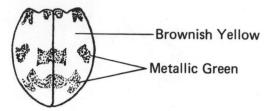

Fig. 89.   Omophron tessellatum

The Crawling Water Beetles

Family Haliplidae

This family includes a number of aquatic beetles that are oval in form, very convex, and more or less pointed at each end (Fig. 90). They are brown or yellow and somewhat spotted with black.

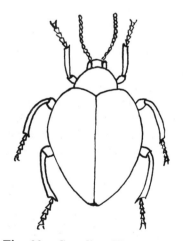

Fig. 90.   Crawling Water Beetle

Our larger species measure from 3.5 to 5 millimeters in length, but some are much smaller.

The antennae are threadlike, without hairs, and each has ten segments; the coxae of the hind legs are so enlarged that they cover part of the hind femora and three to six abdominal segments.

As their name implies, the beetles of this family crawl among the water plants and along the bottom of the pond or stream rather than swim, since they are not well equipped for swimming. They can

swim, however, but poorly, preferring to move leisurely, if somewhat awkwardly, over the plants and bottom mud. They are adapted for this kind of life by having slender legs that are not flattened
or fringed with hairs, which they would be were they used for propelling the insects through the water. The legs are not, however,
completely devoid of hairs: the tibiae of the first and middle pairs
and the tarsi of all are provided with short bristles.

The larvae are also aquatic and live in the same situations as
the adults. They are slender creatures with each of the body segments, except the head, being furnished on the back with fleshy
lobes having spiny tips that vary greatly in size in the different
species.

Both the larvae and adults are omnivorous in food habits. Although insects and other small animals that they can capture are
eaten, plants form the larger part of their diet, the larvae, especially, feeding on filamentous algae. When the larvae mature, they leave
the water and each makes a cell in the damp earth in which the
pupal state is passed.

Most of the crawling water beetles belong to the two genera *Haliplus* and *Peltodytes*. Those of *Haliplus* have only the first three
segments of the abdomen covered by the coxae of the hind legs
(Fig. 91); those of *Peltodytes* have all but the last segment of the
abdomen covered by the coxae (Fig. 92). In the former, the last seg-

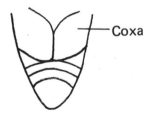

Fig. 91. Only First Three Abdominal Segments Covered by Coxae of Hind

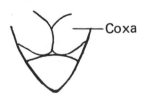

Fig. 92. All but Last Abdominal Segment Covered by Coxae of Hind Legs

ment of each of the labial and maxillary palpi is smaller than the preceding one and awl shaped; in the latter it is longer than the preceding segment and conical.

Haliplus triopsis   Length: 2.5–3mm. Pale dull yellow or dull orange; pronotum with a black spot at middle of apex; legs pale yellow; elytra with a number of black spots (Fig. 93).
Quiet fresh water.
Maine west to Wisconsin and Colorado and south to Georgia and New Mexico.

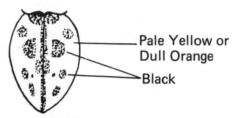

Fig. 93.   Halipus triopsis

Haliplus fasciatus   Length: 3–3.5mm. Brownish yellow to orange brown or dull orange to yellow; elytra each with irregular black markings that form three more or less oblique rows (Fig. 94).
Ponds.
Eastern half of the United States.

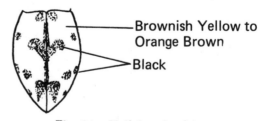

Fig. 94.   Haliplus fasciatus

Peltodytes duodecimpunctatus   Length: 3.5–4mm. Dull yellow or dull orange; each elytron with six well-defined, black spots on last two-thirds of apex (Fig. 95).
Quiet water.
Eastern half of the United States.

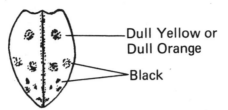

Dull Yellow or
Dull Orange

Black

Fig. 95.   Peltodytes duodecimpunctatus

Peltodytes muticus   Length: 3.5–4mm. Dull yellow or dull orange; each elytron with four small black spots and with a large common one; femora of hind legs dark or almost black.
Eastern half of the United States.

The Predaceous Diving Beetles

Family Dytiscidae
The *predaceous diving beetles* are eminently adapted to living in the water: their streamlined form is designed to minimize the resistance of the water and their long hind legs are effective propelling organs (Fig. 96). They are usually shining black or brown-

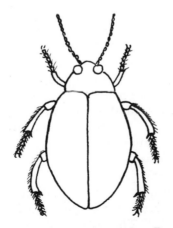

Fig. 96.   Predaceous Diving Beetle

ish, often marked with dull yellow, with threadlike antenna of eleven segments, and long hind legs that are more or less flattened and fringed with long hairs, though these hairs may be appressed against the legs and difficult to see. The tarsi have five segments, though the fourth segment of each of the tarsi of the front and middle legs may be obsolete in some of the smaller species. The middle and hind pairs of legs are widely separated and in the males of certain genera the first three segments of the tarsi are dilated to form a circular disk upon the under side of which are little cuplike suckers that function as clasping organs while mating. In some species the females may either have smooth elytra or have them deeply furrowed, an interesting instance of dimorphism.

The females deposit their eggs singly in punctures that they make in the tissues of living plants from which hatch elongated, spindle-shaped grubs called *water tigers* because of their blood thirstiness. The larvae have a large, flattened, and oval or rounded head; six well-developed legs; and large, sickle-shaped mandibles that have a slitlike opening near the tip from which a canal extends to the mouth making them admirably fitted for holding prey and sucking its body juices. The tip of the abdomen is provided with a pair of appendages that are fringed with hairs, as are the last two segments of the abdomen. These abdominal appendages are used to buoy up the tip of the abdomen when the larvae protrude it into the air in order to breathe; two large spiracles at the tip serve this purpose.

The larvae may either swim in the water or creep about on the bottom mud or on the submerged vegetation, to which they often cling when resting or lying in ambush. Upon reaching maturity, they leave the water and each one burrows into the ground and makes a round cell in which it pupates.

The predaceous diving beetles are familiar inhabitants of our ponds and streams, though they seem to be found more often in standing water. Here they are usually found hanging head downward with the tip of the abdomen projecting above the water. The spiracles, or the external openings to the internal air tubes, are located on the dorsal side of the abdomen beneath the elytra. When the beetles prepare to dive, they lift the elytra slightly thus forming a reservoir of air that they breathe when below the surface. When this air becomes impure, they rise to the surface, force it out, and take in a fresh supply.

Both the adults and larvae are very voracious and destroy large numbers of other insects. They also attack other animals such as tadpoles and small fish. The adults often fly from pond to pond and toward lights at night. Many species are capable of producing sounds, both underwater and in the air. In some instances the sounds are made by rubbing the abdominal segments upon the elytra, or in others by rubbing the hind legs upon a rough spot on the lower side of the abdomen.

Hydrocanthus iricolor   Length: 4–5mm. Head, pronotum, and un-

derparts reddish yellow; elytra dark reddish brown, iridescent. Last segment of labial palpus large and triangular; each tarsus of hind legs with two slender claws of equal length; each tibia of front legs with a strong spur.
Eastern half of the United States.

In the species of the genus Laccophilus, *the scutellum is practically hidden from view and each tarsus of the hind legs has a single, thick, straight claw.*

Laccophilus fasciatus   Length: 4.5–5.5mm. Dull brownish yellow; elytra greenish yellow with a broad black bar (Fig 97).
Eastern half of the United States.

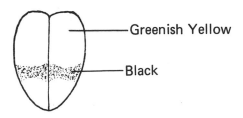

Fig. 97.   Laccophilus fasciatus

Laccophilus maculosus   Length: 5.5–6.5mm. Reddish yellow; elytra blackish with greenish yellow spots.
Eastern half of the United States.

Desmopachria convexa   Length: 1.5–2.5mm. Brownish red, shining. Form rounded and convex; scutellum hidden; elytra tapering and obtuse at apices (Fig. 98).
Beneath grass roots along the water's edge of stagnant pools.
Throughout the United States east of the Rockies.

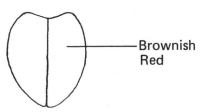

Fig. 98.   Desmopachria convexa

Bidessus affinis   Length: 1.5–2mm. Head, pronotum, and legs yellowish or dull yellow; elytra and lower surface dark yellowish brown, elytra sometimes with paler margins. Oval; scutellum hidden; elytra rather coarsely and densely punctured.
Eastern half of the United States.

Hygrotus nubilus   Length: 4–4.5mm. Head, pronotum, and legs dull yellow or orange; elytra yellow with brown or blackish markings that sometimes form a dark blotch. Oval; scutellum hidden; lower part of body very convex (Fig. 99).
Eastern half of the United States.

Yellow

Brown or
Black

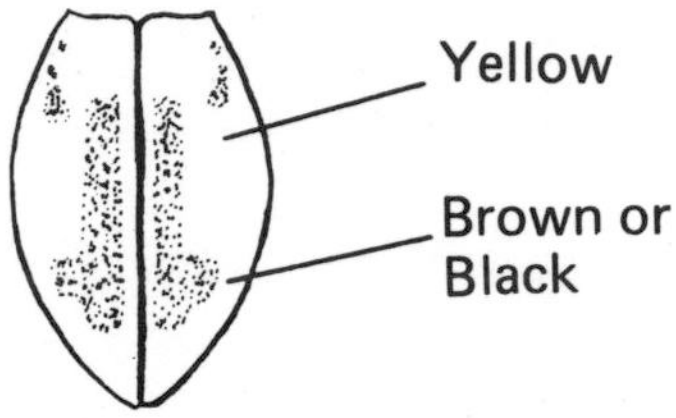

Fig. 99.   Hygrotus nubilus

The beetles of the genus Hydroporus *are small with the scutellum hidden and the coxae of the hind legs extended over the trochanters (Fig. 100). They are difficult to identify at best.*

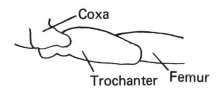

Coxa

Trochanter   Femur

Fig. 100.   Coxa of Hind Leg Produced over Base of Trochanter

Hydroporus wickhami   Length: 3–4mm. Pale yellow to reddish brown or dull orange; elytra paler with dark brown or reddish brown crossbands.
Eastern half of the United States.

Hydroporus niger   Length: 4–5mm. Black or nearly so with some reddish brown spots on head, pronotum, and elytra.
Eastern half of the United States.

Hydroporus undulatus   Length: 4–4.5mm. Head and pronotum reddish brown or yellowish brown; elytra blackish each with reddish brown markings that are somewhat variable.
Eastern half of the United States.

Hydroporus consimilis   Length: 4–5mm. Head, pronotum, undersurface, and legs reddish yellow; elytra blackish each with three irregular, reddish brown spots (Fig. 101).
Northern United States.

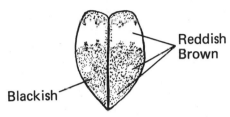

Reddish
Brown

Blackish

Fig. 101.   Hydroporus consimilis

The species of the three genera, Agabus, Ilybiosoma, *and* Ilybius, *have a notch in the margin of the head in front of each eye and each femur of the hind legs has a more or less thick group of cilia or long hairs on the inner half of the inner apical angle.*

Agabus disintergatus   Length: 7.5–8.5mm. Head and pronotum dull reddish or reddish yellow; elytra dull yellow each with three or four narrow black stripes (Fig. 102).
Beneath stones in wet, grassy situations.
Throughout the United States.

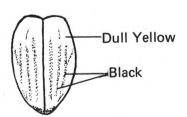

Dull Yellow

Black

Fig. 102.   Agabus disintergatus

Agabus confinis Length: 8.5–9.5mm. Head, pronotum, and undersurface black; antennae and legs reddish brown; elytra dark brown with margins reddish brown.
Beneath stones in wet, grassy situations.
Throughout the United States.

Ilybiosoma bifarius Length: 6–7mm. Black, shining; head with indistinct, reddish marks; antennae, legs, and side margins of thorax reddish brown. First segment of the tarsus of each of the hind legs shorter than the tibial spur and only twice as long as second segment.
Eastern half of the United States.

Ilybius fenestralis Length: 10–11mm. Black, slightly bronzed; antennae and front and middle legs reddish brown; hind legs and undersurface blackish; elytra with reddish margins. Tarsal claws of hind legs unequal; tibiae of hind legs each with a line of long hairs on the inner half of the apical angle.
Northeastern United States.

Agabetes acuductus Length: 7–7.5mm. Blackish or dull orange, somewhat shining; head, side margins of pronotum, and shoulders of elytra reddish. Notch in the margin of the head in front of each eye.
Woodland pools.
Eastern half of the United States.

Copelatus glyphicus Length: 5–6mm. Dark reddish brown; antennae and legs paler; elytra darker. Notch in the margin of the head in front of each eye; each elytron with ten deeply impressed striae; under stones and logs along the margins of brooks and pools.
Eastern half of the United States.

Coptotomus interrogatus Length: 6.5–7.5mm. Head, pronotum, and underparts reddish brown, tip of head black; pronotum black at base and apex; elytra pitch brown each with very small, pale yellowish markings. Notch in margin of head in front of each eye; last segment of each palpus notched at tip; last segment of each tarsus of hind legs equal to the fourth.
Throughout the United States east of the Rockies.

Rhantus binotatus Length: 11.5–12.5mm. Dull yellow or dull orange, rather shining; tip of head black, front with a pair of blackish spots; pronotum with two black spots; elytra dull, densely covered with black dots and with several series of indistinct black marks. Notch in the margin of the head in front of each eye; tarsal claws of hind legs unequal in length.

Colymbetes sculptilis Length: 15.5–16.5mm. Front of head, pronotum, and margins of elytra dull yellow; top of head black, with two small dull orange spots; pronotum with a transverse black bar; legs reddish brown. Notch in the margin of the head in front of each eye; tarsal claws of hind legs unequal in length (Fig. 103).

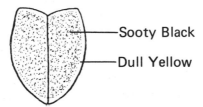

Fig. 103.   Colymbetes sculptilis

To the genus Dytiscus *belong the largest of our diving beetles. The tibiae of the hind legs are distinctly longer than broad; the outer apical spur on each is slender; and each of the tarsi of the hind legs is not fringed on the outer margin.*

Dytiscus fasciventris Length: 25–28mm. Greenish black above; undersurface and legs pale reddish brown; pronotum margined with yellow only on the sides or with a faint trace of yellow at base and apex; elytra with yellow margins. Each elytron of female with ten grooves reaching beyond the middle (Fig. 104).
Eastern half of the United States.

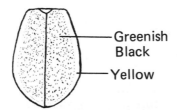

Fig. 104.   Dytiscus fasciventris

Dytiscus hybridus Length: 26–28mm. Olive brown; pronotum with apex narrowly yellow and sometimes with a faint yellow line at the base; underparts, hind legs, and tibiae of middle legs orange brown,

remaining legs pale yellowish; elytra with pale yellow margins. Each elytron with three rows of fine punctures.
Eastern half of the United States.

Dytiscus verticalis   Length: 33–35mm. Olive brown; pronotum with yellow side margins only; abdominal segments uniformly black; undersurface and legs reddish brown; marginal yellow line on each elytron narrowed toward apex; narrow, oblique, yellow crosbar near apex of each elytron often indistinct. Each elytron with three rows of fine punctures.
Eastern half of the United States.

Dytiscus harrisii   Length: 38–40mm. Olive brown; all edges of the pronotum distinctly margined with yellow; elytra each with a narrow crossbar near apex and marginal line narrowed only near apex. Each elytron with three rows of fine punctures.
Eastern half of the United States.

The beetles of the three genera Acilius, Thermonetus, *and* Graphoderus *have each of the tarsi of the hind legs fringed on the outer margin with golden yellow flattened hairs.*

Acilius semisulcatus   Length: 12–14mm. Brownish yellow above, black beneath; base of head and an M-shaped mark at top black; pronotum with two transverse black lines; elytra covered with many black dots, except a rounded area at apices; abdomen yellowish at the sides and at extreme apex. Femora of middle legs with setae on posterior margins equal in length to width of each femur.
Northern United States.

Acilius fraternus   Length: 13–15mm. Pale yellowish to yellowish brown; pronotum with two transverse black bands; elytra with many black dots, except a rounded area at apices. Femora of middle legs with setae on posterior margins equal in length to width of each femur.
Eastern half of the United States.

Thermonetus basillaris   Length: 9–10mm. Black; front of head and a transverse line on top dull yellow; pronotum on sides and a narrow bar on disk dull yellow; elytra with margins, crossbar near each base, and some faint markings on sides yellowish; first two pairs of legs dull yellow, third pair brownish black. Femora of middle legs with setae one and one-half to twice as long as width of each femur.
Eastern half of the United States.

Graphoderus liberus   Length: 11–12mm. Dull reddish yellow or orange; undersurface reddish brown; legs pale brownish yellow; ely-

tra blackish brown with many yellowish marks that are united along sides to form a yellowish margin. Femora of middle legs with setae not more than one-third as long as width of each femur.
Eastern half of the United States.

Cybister fimbriolatus Length: 30–33mm. Brown with a faint greenish tinge; pronotum and elytra broadly margined with yellow; front of head, first two pairs of legs, and spots at sides of the third to sixth abdominal segments, inclusive, yellow. Tibiae of hind legs almost as broad as long, apical spur of each very much expanded; tarsal claws of hind legs unequal; pronotum and elytra of female with many fine, short grooves, except along the suture (Fig. 105).
Eastern half of the United States.

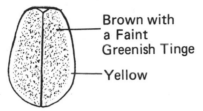

Fig. 105. Cybister fimbriolatus

The Whirligig Beetles

Family Gyrinidae

Most of us have seen the *whirligig beetles*. They are the somewhat small, oval or elliptical bluish black insects that swim about on the surface of pools and quiet ponds, swiftly moving about tracing graceful curves on the water, which vanish almost as soon as they are made (Fig. 106).

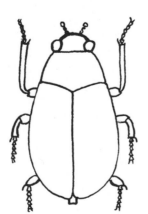

Fig. 106. Whirligig Beetle

They are not always in motion, though they may seem to be, but often bask like turtles on logs and stones. Most of their time is spent on the water but they can fly fairly well, if they can climb out of the water onto some kind of support so as to get a start; they also dive freely, especially when disturbed, and at such times they carry a bubble of air down with them at the tips of and under the elytra. An unusual feature of these insects is that their eyes are divided by the margin of the head so that they appear to have four eyes, one pair for looking up into the air and another for looking down into the water (Fig. 29). Extremely agile, they can be captured most easily with a net. Many of them when caught exhale a milky fluid that has a disagreeable odor.

Other family characteristics, in addition to those already mentioned, are short, thick antennae that are inserted behind the mandibles with the third segment of each enlarged and the following segments broad and united forming a sort of spindle-shaped structure; long and slender front legs that are adapted for grasping; middle and hind legs that are short, broad, and strongly flattened; the hind legs also fringed with long hairs that are used oarlike in rapid sculling movements; and tarsi that are each five segmented.

The eggs of the whirligig beetles are oval and white and are laid end to end in parallel rows on submerged leaves of water plants. The larvae are pale, slender creatures that crawl over the bottom trash or swim through the water with a sinuous motion of their bodies, doubtless aided by the eight heavily fringed gills that hang from each side of the abdomen. The elongated form of the body and the conspicuous gills make the larvae resemble small centipedes. When the larvae have matured, they leave the water and each spins a gray, paperlike cocoon that is attached to some object near the water.

Both the larvae and adults are predaceous in their food habits; the larvae feeding on such insects as mayflies and dragonflies, the adults on such insects as may fall on the water, such as flies and other forms.

The two principal genera are Gyrinus *and* Dineutes. *They may be distinguished by the fact that in* Dineutus *the scutellum is concealed or hidden, but in* Gyrinus *it is distinct and visible.*

Dineutus discolor Length: 11.5–13mm. Upper surface, black, bronzed, shining; lower surface brownish to straw color or yellowish (Fig. 107).
Eastern half of the United States.

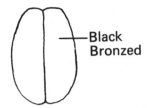

Fig. 107. Dineutus discolor

Dineutus ciliatus Length: 12–15mm. Bronzed black; pronotal and elytral sides with a bronze, curved stripe.
In ditches and streams.
Atlantic and Southern States.

Dineutus americanus Length: 10–12mm. Black, strongly bronzed above, black and shining beneath; abdominal segments often tinged with brown; legs brownish yellow.
More often found in small streams than in ponds.
Eastern half of the United States.

Gyrinus analis Length: 5–6mm. Black, somewhat bronzed; legs reddish yellow.
Maine west to Kansas and south to Florida and Louisiana.

Gyrinus minutus Length: 3.5–4.5mm. Upper surface black; sides dull bronze; lower surface brownish yellow; abdomen black.
Throughout the United States.

Gyrinus borealis Length: 6.5–7.5mm. Black, shining; legs brownish yellow; margins of elytra bronzed (Fig. 108).
Probably the most common species of *Gyrinidae*.
Throughout the United States.

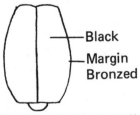

Fig. 108. Gyrinus borealis

The Water Scavenger Beetles

Family Hydrophilidae

In the same situations that we find the diving beetles, we also often see large black beetles that look and act very much like them (Fig. 109). These beetles, known as the *hydrophilids* or *water scav-*

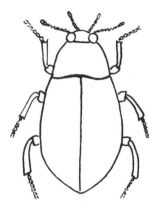

Fig. 109.   Water Scavenger Beetle

enger beetles, differ, in a number of ways from the diving beetles, though they may at first glance be mistaken for them. Water scavenger beetles are more convex, have short, club-shaped antennae (unlike the threadlike antennae of the diving beetles), and have very long labial and maxillary palpi that may easily be mistaken for antennae, especially by anyone inexperienced (Fig. 30). Moreover, they hang at the surface of the water with heads up (the diving beetles hang with heads down) and, when they come to the surface, the water scavenger beetles project their antennae into the air and pull back a bubble of air that spreads like a silver blanket over the lower surface of the body, which they use to breathe while submerged.

Though most of the water scavenger beetles are wholly aquatic in habits, there are a few species that live in dung or moist earth. They are rather common in quiet ponds and pools where they may be seen swimming through the water or crawling among the plants growing on the bottom. They are usually black in color, but sometimes they have yellow, orange, or red markings along the margins. The surface is usually smooth and polished; the eyes are large; each antenna has six to nine segments and each is inserted under the sides of the frontal region behind the mandibles; the last segment of the sternum is usually large, often keeled, and often produced into a long spine behind; and each of the tarsi has five segments, the first segment of each often very small and inconspicuous.

The hydrophilids are generally supposed to live chiefly on decaying vegetation, but the adults also eat living water plants; some species catch and eat living animals. The larvae are largely predaceous.

The females lay their eggs in beautiful silken cases or cocoons. In some instances they are fastened beneath the leaves of water plants; in others they are provided with floats and let loose in the water; and in still others the cases are carried by the females underneath their bodies. The cases are completely waterproof and contain about a hundred eggs, but frequently some of the young larvae devour their companions so that by the time they all leave the egg case, their number has been reduced. The larvae are much like those of the diving beetles but they are clumsier and each of their tarsi never have more than a single claw, whereas those of the diving beetles and whirligigs have two. Pupation takes place in moist earth near the water's edge, the pupa being kept from touching the cell bottom by projecting hooklike spines.

The species of the genus Helophorus *have the first segment of each of the tarsi of the hind legs shorter than the second, the second about equal to the third, and the last shorter than the preceding segments combined; the pronotum is rough and with five longitudinal grooves; and the elytra have ten rows of punctures or striae.*

Helophorus lineatus Length: 3–4mm. Light brown with greenish tinge; antennae and legs paler; elytra sometimes with a brownish black inverted V on the suture and with two spots on each side (Fig. 110).
United States east of the Rockies.

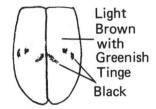

Light
Brown
with
Greenish
Tinge
Black

Fig. 110. Helophorus lineatus

Helophorus lacustris Length: 4–5mm. Blackish brown, slightly

bronzed; head and pronotum tinged with green; may be distinguished from *lineatus* by the obtuse hind angles of the pronotum. Brooks.
United States east of the Rockies.

The species of the genus Hydrochus *have the first segment of each of the tarsi of the hind legs shorter than the second, the second about equal to the third, and the last as long or longer than the preceding segments combined; the pronotum is much narrower than the elytra; and the antennae each have seven segments.*

Hydrochus squamifer   Length: 3.5–4mm. Grayish bronze or coppery; head and pronotum darker than elytra and tinged with green.
Northcentral States.

Hydrochus subcupreus   Length: 3.5–4mm. Brown, tinged with a brassy hue; legs reddish brown (Fig. 111).
Eastern half of the United States.

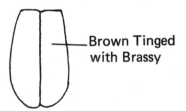

Brown Tinged
with Brassy

Fig. 111.   Hydrochus subcupreus

The beetles of the following species up to but not including Sphaeridium scarabaeoides *have the first segment of each of the tarsi of the hind legs shorter than the second, the second longer than the third, and the last shorter than the preceding segments combined.* (This taxonomic fact refers only to those beetles marked with an *.)

*Berosus pantherinus   Length: 3.5–4.5mm. Pale dull yellow; head blackish; pronotum with two black spots; abdomen reddish brown; and each elytron with ten distinct black spots. Antennae each with seven segments; tibiae each of middle and hind legs with long swimming hairs on the inner side; and five abdominal segments visible.
Eastern half of the United States.

Hydrophilus triangularis Length: 34–37mm. Black, shining with an olive tinge; dark brown beneath; sides of abdomen with pale reddish, triangular spots. Last segment of maxillary palpus shorter than preceding; elytra with six rows of coarse punctures (Fig. 112).
Ponds and streams.
Throughout the United States.

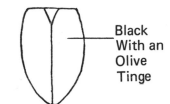

Black
With an
Olive
Tinge

Fig. 112.   Hydrophilus triangularis

Dibolocelus ovatus Length: 31–33mm. Black with an olive tinge; blackish beneath; legs dark reddish brown. Last segment of maxillary palpus shorter than the preceding; abdominal segments pubescent, last three each with an indistinct reddish spot on the side; elytra with six rows of coarse punctures.
Eastern third of the United States.

Hydrochara obtusata Length: 13–16mm. Black, shining; dark reddish brown beneath. Tibiae of middle and hind legs each fringed on inner side; elytra with four rows of distinct punctures.
Beneath stones and logs in the vicinity of water; often abundant about lights.
Eastern and Central States.

Tropisternus lateralis Length: 8.5–9mm. Bronze black or olive black, shining; undersurface black; legs yellow, each femur black at base; pronotum and elytra with margins of pale yellow. Maxillary palpus with last segment equal to or longer than one preceding; elytra with a few scattered coarse punctures (Fig. 113).
Lakes and slow-flowing streams.
Throughout the United States.

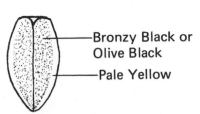

Bronzy Black or
Olive Black

Pale Yellow

Fig. 113.   Tropisternus lateralis

Tropisternus glaber Length: 9.5–11mm. Black, slightly bronzed. Found beneath rubbish along the edges of ponds and lakes. Throughout the United States.

Hydrobius melaenum Length: 7–8mm. Black, shining. Antennae each with nine segments; last segment of maxillary palpus longer than third; elytra with rows of distinct punctures. Beneath stones in fresh-running water. Northeast United States.

Hydrobius fuscipes Length: 6.5–8mm. Colored much like *melaenum* but having the elytra striate. In ponds and bogs. Northeast United States.

Anacaena limbata Length: 2–2.5mm. Dark brownish yellow or reddish; margins of pronotum and elytra paler. Femora of middle and hind legs densely pubescent; pronotum finely punctured; elytra coarsely but less densely punctured than pronotum. Brooks, ponds, and bogs. Eastern half of the United States.

Paracymus subcupreus Length: 1.5–2mm. Blackish above, dark reddish black beneath. Ponds and bogs. Throughout the United States.

Enochrus ochraceus Length: 3.5–4mm. Dull smoky brown, shining; head darker, a paler spot before each eye; pronotum and elytra with paler margins. Last segment of maxillary palpus shorter than the one preceding it; pronotum and elytra rather densely punctured (Fig. 114). Margins of ponds. Eastern half of the United States.

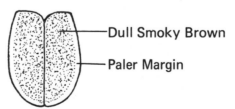

Dull Smoky Brown

Paler Margin

Fig. 114.   Enochrus ochraceus

Enochrus perplexus   Length: 4–5.5mm. Black, shining; pronotum and elytra with narrow, pale borders; pronotum densely, finely punctured; elytra more coarsely punctured.
In fresh-water pools.
Eastern half of the United States.

Cymbiodyta fimbriata   Length: 4.5–6mm. Black; pronotum and elytra paler on sides. Sides of pronotum rounded to apex; elytra with rows of distinct punctures; last segment of maxillary palpus shorter than third; tarsi of middle and hind legs each with only four segments.
Eastern half of the United States.

Helocombus bifidus   Length: 5.5–7mm. Blackish, shining; margins of elytra paler. Last segment of maxillary palpus distinctly shorter than preceding one; elytra with many distinct striae.
Eastern half of the United States.

Laccobius agilis   Length: 2–3mm. Head and pronotum blackish with greenish reflex; lower surface brownish black; legs orange brown; elytra pale yellow with dark brown punctures. Maxillary palpus rather stout, last segment longer than preceding one; elytra with rows of punctures; six segments of abdomen visible.
Eastern half of the United States.

Sphaeridium scarabaeoides   Length: 5.5–7mm. Black, shining; elytra each with a dark red basal spot and yellowish tip. First segment of each of the tarsi of the middle and hind legs longer than second; scutellum elongate; antennae each with eight segments; last dorsal abdominal segment visible; elytra punctured (Fig. 115).
This is a European species and is common in cow dung.
Throughout the United States.

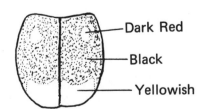

Fig. 115.   Sphaeridium scarabaeoides

Cercyon praetextatus   Length: 2.5–3mm. Blackish, shining; front angles of pronotum and margins and tips of elytra yellowish. First segment of each of the tarsi of the middle and hind legs longer than second; scutellum equilateral; antennae each with nine segments; last dorsal segment of abdomen covered.

In cow dung and dead fish.

United States east of the Rockies.

Cercyon navicularis   Length: 1.5mm. Very small black species. Occurs in damp leaves near pools of water.

Throughout the United States.

The Carrion Beetles

Family Silphidae

The *carrion beetles* are for the most part medium or large-sized insects though some are rather small, minute in fact. They vary considerably in shape and many are attractively marked making them collectors' favorites in spite of what seems to us their unpleasant food habits (Figs. 116, 117).

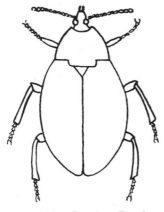

Fig. 116.   Carrion Beetle

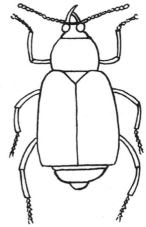

Fig. 117.   Burying Beetle

Their antennae each have eleven segments, though sometimes there are only nine or ten, and are gradually or suddenly thickened, usually each one forming a club at the apex; however, at times they are nearly filiform. The front coxae are large, conical, and touching; the legs are variable, sometimes slender, at other times adapted for digging; the tibiae have large terminal spurs; the tarsi each usually have five segments; and sometimes the elytra are a little shorter than the abdomen, which has five or six visible ventral segments.

The carrion beetles feed largely on decaying animal matter (dead birds, mice, etc), though some feed on fungi, while still others live on vegetables. A few species, when pressed by hunger, become predaceous and attack living snails and other insects; a few occur only in the nests of ants.

We have over a hundred species of carrion beetles in the United States, the larger and more familiar species representing two genera: *Necrophorus* and *Silpha*. The species of *Necrophorus* are called *burying beetles,* because they bury the bodies of dead animals and feed on them underground. They are large, longer than wide, thick-bodied beetles with elytra having red spots; each antenna is apparently ten segmented, the second segment being very short and more or less hidden in the tip of the first and the last four segments forming a distinct club; and the elytra are short with the tips more or less squarish.

The species of the genus *Silpha* are extremely flattened, very egg shaped or almost round; each antenna is distinctly eleven segmented and slender or gradually thickened toward the tip; and the elytra are not shortened, the tips rounded together or prolonged at the suture.

Necrophorus americanus   Length: 27–35mm. Black, shining; orange red on vertex of head, central part of pronotum, two irregular spots on each elytron, and clubs of antennae (Fig. 118). Tibiae of hind legs curved.
Usually found on larger decaying animals, especially reptiles.
Eastern half of the United States.

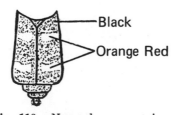

Fig. 118.   Necrophorus americanus

Necrophorus sayi   Length: 16–18mm. Black, shining; a crossbar near the base and a spot near apex of each elytron orange red; antennal clubs and sometimes tarsi of front legs reddish brown. Hind tibiae curved.
Eastern half of the United States.

Necrophorus marginatus　Length: 20–27mm. Black, shining; the orange red elytral spots are sometimes connected along the margin, the basal spot sometimes divided; tibiae of hind legs curved.
Usually on dead snakes.
Throughout the United States.

Necrophorus orbicollis　Length: 20–25mm. Black, shining; a crossbar near base and a spot near apex of each elytron orange red; antennal clubs and sometimes tarsi of front legs reddish brown. Tibiae of hind legs straight.
All kinds of carrion.
Eastern half of the United States.

Necrophorus pustulatus　Length: 17–18mm. Black, shining; a small basal spot and double spots at apex of each elytron and antennal clubs orange red. Tibiae of hind legs straight.
Throughout the United States.

Necrophorus tomentosus　Length: 15–20mm. Black, shining; two crossbars on each elytron orange red. Central part of pronotum densely covered with silky, yellow hairs (Fig. 119). Tibiae of hind legs straight.
All kinds of carrion.
Eastern half of the United States.

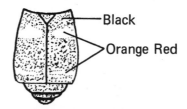

Fig. 119.　Necrophorus tomentosus

Silpha surinamensis　Length: 15–25mm. Black; elytra with an orange red crossbar near apices, often broken into spots and sometimes absent altogether. Longer than wide, eyes prominent (Fig. 120).
United States east of the Rockies.

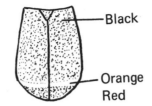

Fig. 120.   Silpha surinamensis

Silpha inaequalis   Length: 10–14mm. Black. Pronotum twice as wide as long with a broad, depressed, squarish lobe in the middle; elytra rounded at apices, each with three distinct ridges.
Abundant on carrion.
Throughout the United States.

Silpha noveboracensis   Length: 13–14mm. Brownish; head and pronotum blackish, the latter with a reddish yellow margin; elytra brownish to blackish. Pronotum one-half wider than long, squarish at middle of base, sides wavy; elytra rounded at apices with three ridges.
Sometimes on fungi but usually on carrion.
Throughout the United States.

Silpha americana   Length: 16–20mm. Pronotum yellow with a black central spot; elytra brownish with crinkly elevations somewhat darker; pronotum nearly twice as wide as long and much narrower in front (Fig. 121).

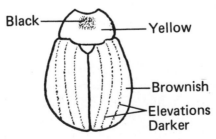

Fig. 121.   Silpha americana

A black western species, *Silpha bituberosa,* found from Kansas westward damages spinach, squash, beets, pumpkins and other cultivated plants.

On toadstools, decaying fungi, in dung and on carrion.
Eastern half of the United States.

*Some authors have included the following small beetles in the.
family* Leptodiridae.

Catops basillaris   Length: 3–4mm. Head and pronotum pitch colored; elytra dark brown. Head narrowed behind the eyes; abdomen with six segments.
Eastern and Central States.

Pinodytes cryptophagoides   Length: 2–3mm. Chestnut brown, shining. In rotten wood.
Throughout the United States.

Colon magnicolle   Length: 2.5–3mm. Pitch colored, somewhat dull; finely pubescent. Antennae each with eleven segments; abdomen with five segments though sometimes four.
Central United States.

The Round Fungus Beetles

Family Leiodidae
The beetles of the family *Leiodidae* are small and oval in form, the antennae each have nine to eleven segments that gradually thicken toward the apex; and the tibiae have large terminal spurs. These beetles occur in decaying fungi and other kinds of decaying vegetable matter, under stumps, in logs, and in the nests of ants. They have the habit of rolling themselves into a ball when disturbed and playing dead.

Colensis impunctata   Length: 1.5–2mm. Pale reddish brown, shining. Pronotum much wider than long, sides rounded, narrowed toward apex; elytra with fine transverse lines; last segment of maxillary palpus cylindrical; antennae each with eleven segments, each club with three segments; each of the tarsi of front legs with five segments, those of the middle and hind legs with four (Fig. 122). This species does not contract itself into a ball when disturbed.
In fungi.
Eastern half of the United States.

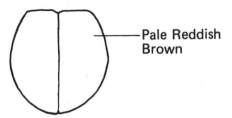

Fig. 122.   Colensis impunctata

Agathidium oniscoides Length: 3.5–4mm. Black, smooth, shining. Head and pronotum together and the elytra each form a sphere, which are united; pronotum wider than long, front and hind angles rounded; elytra together almost circular; antennae each with fourth to eighth segments small and gradually widening, each ninth to eleventh segments forming an oblong club; each of the tarsi of the hind legs with four segments, each of those of the front and middle legs with five (Fig. 123); rolls itself into a tiny ball when disturbed.
Beneath the bark of logs that have fungi growing on them.
Eastern half of the United States.

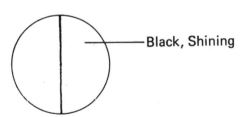

Fig. 123.   Agathidium oniscoides

The Antlike Stone Beetles

Family Scydmaenidae
    The *antlike stone beetles* are a small species—some only a fraction of a millimeter in length—shining, oval in shape, and usually of a brownish or blackish color (Fig. 124). They occur under bark, in damp places, and in the nests of ants.

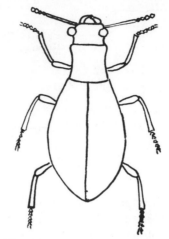

Fig. 124.   Antlike Stone Beetle

Pycnophus rasus   Length: 1.6–1.8mm. Shining; pale reddish brown. Pronotum with well-defined small pit at each basal angle; fourth segment of maxillary palpus awl shaped; neck narrow; eyes in front of middle of the head (Fig. 125).
Under logs and in the nests of ants.
Eastern half of the United States.

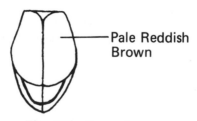

Fig. 125.   Pycnophus rasus

Scydmaenus motschulskyanus   Length: 1.7mm. Dark chestnut brown with yellowish pubescence. Fourth segment of maxillary palpus obtuse; coxae of hind legs oval; elytra very convex.
Eastern half of the United States.

The Fringed-Winged Fungus Beetles

Family Orthoperidae
This family includes very small beetles found under bark and in

decaying fungi and other vegetable matter. The body is oval or rounded, in many species covered with a grayish pubescence, and the wings are wide and fringed with long hairs.

Molamba ornata   Length: 1.3–1.5mm. Blackish; pronotum reddish yellow with a dark spot; elytra each with a spot and edge of tip dull yellow; antennae and legs yellowish (Fig. 126).
Central United States.

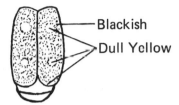

Fig. 126.   *Molamba ornata*

The Nest-Dwelling Beetles

Family Leptinidae

The family *Leptinidae* is a small family of beetles that are generally found in the nests of various mammals as well as birds and bumblebees. It is not known just what is their relationship to their hosts but it has been suggested that they prey on the fleas and mites that live on the mammals. They are not especially common but are worth looking for.

Leptimus testaceus   Length: 2–2.5mm. Pale yellow. Eyes absent; fine regular punctures thickly covered with golden hairs; flattened (Fig. 127).
Throughout the United States.

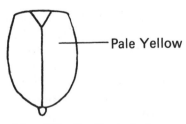

Fig. 127.   *Leptimus testaceus*

The Rove Beetles

Family Staphylinidae

The family of *rove beetles* is a large one, some twenty thousand species having already been described and there are probably many more. They are for the most part small insects, though a few species are of larger size measuring twelve millimeters or more in length (Figs. 128, 129).

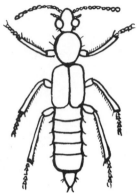

Fig. 128. Rove Beetle

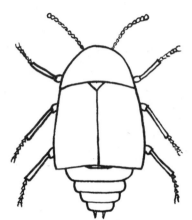

Fig. 129. Rove Beetle

The rove beetles are very common about decaying animal and vegetable matter, in excrement, fungi and fermenting sap and are often found upon the ground beneath stones and other objects; sometimes they may be seen on flowers. They are long and slender, dull in color, black predominating, though some are brilliantly ornamented; they have very short wing covers or elytra, thus exposing most of the abdomen. The wings, however, are fully developed and when not in use are folded beneath the wing covers.

The rove beetles can run quite swiftly and have the curious habit, when disturbed, of raising the tip of the abdomen as if about to sting. This habit, together with their short elytra, make them fairly easy to be recognized.

The larvae resemble the adults in body form and occur in the same places, that is, about decaying animal and plant matter, beneath stones and bark, and in fungi.

Anthobium hornii   Length: 2–2.5mm. Brownish orange or dull reddish yellow, shining; male with blackish abdomen, female with abdomen blackish only at apex. Antennae shorter than head and pronotum together, segments seven to ten forming a loose club; pronotum twice as wide as long, sides rounded; elytra more than twice the length of the pronotum; coxae of hind legs touching or nearly so; an ocellus on each side of the front of the head; last segment of maxillary palpus longer than third; tibiae with short hairs; tarsi each five segmented (Fig. 130).
Often found on flowers in spring.
Eastern half of the United States.

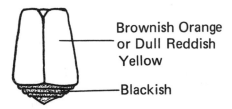

Brownish Orange or Dull Reddish Yellow

Blackish

Fig. 130.   Anthobium hornii

Platysethus americanus   Length: 2.5–3.5mm. Black, shining; elytra and abdomen brownish black; tibiae and tarsi paler. Pronotum slightly wider than long; elytra slightly wider than pronotum; antennae each with eleven segments; tibiae of front and middle legs each with a single row of spines on outer margin; tarsi each with three segments.
In decaying fungi and cow dung.
Eastern half of the United States.

The beetles of the genus Stenus *are small, rather stout species with eleven-segmented antennae inserted between the eyes, the last three segments larger than the preceding ones; the elytra are much shorter than the abdomen; the abdomen gradually tapers toward the apex; and the coxae of the hind legs are small, spherical, and widely separated.*

Stenus bipunctatus   Length: 4–4.5mm. Black, shining; each elytron with a small, rounded orange spot. Pronotum finely and densely punctured; elytra coarsely and evenly punctured (Fig. 131).
Eastern half of the United States.

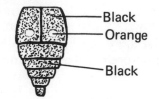

Fig. 131.   Stenus bipunctatus

Stenus flavicornis   Length: 4.5–5mm. Black, shining with a few gray-ish, short hairs; antennae and legs yellowish. Third segment of each antenna almost twice as long as fourth; pronotum slightly longer than wide, coarsely and densely punctured; elytra slightly longer than wide, deeply and sparsely punctured.
Eastern half of the United States

Stenus punctatus   Length: 3–3.5mm. Black, shining, rather densely covered with gray, short hairs. Third segment of each antenna one-third longer than fourth; pronotum almost squarish with fine dense punctures; elytra as wide at base as the head, longer than pronotum, with dense coarse punctures; abdomen narrower than elytra at base.
Eastern half of the United States.

The following species of Homaeotarsus *have the neck of the head distinctly constricted; the coxae of the hind legs are conical, the inner faces of the mandibles each have three teeth; the basal segment of each of the antennae is much longer than wide and rather strongly elbowed; and the last segment of the maxillary palpus is very small and awl shaped.*

Homaeotarsus bicolor   Length: 7.5–10mm. Head black; labrum, antennae, pronotum, elytra, and last two segments of abdomen pale reddish brown; legs pale yellow. Head somewhat oblong; pronotum narrower than head, wider than long, and with sides parallel; elytra one-third wider and longer than pronotum, surface densely and coarsely punctured (Fig. 132) .

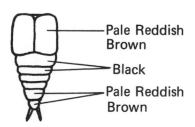

Fig. 132.   Homaeotarsus bicolor

Under stones, debris, and leaves as well as on fungi; more often in wooded pasture areas.
Eastern and Central States.

Homaeotarsus pallipes Length: 8–11mm. Black or blackish, shining; antennae dusky; legs dull yellow. Head oval; pronotum slightly narrower than head, sides slightly rounded; elytra one-third wider and slightly longer than pronotum, finely, coarsely, and densely punctured; abdomen as wide as elytra; head with distinct hind angles.
Under stones and rubbish on sandy banks of ponds and streams.
Eastern half of the United States.

Homaeotarsus cribatus Length: 8.5–10mm. Black, shining; antentennae, mouthparts, and elytra reddish yellow; legs dull yellow. Head somewhat oval; pronotum longer than wide, sides nearly straight; elytra one-third wider and slightly longer than pronotum, each elytron with nine irregular rows of coarse punctures.
Eastern half of the United States.

Homaeotarsus badius Length: 10–13mm. Uniformly reddish brown with the head slightly darker.
Common throughout much of the eastern one-third of the United States.

Homaeotarsus pimerianus Length: 8–11mm. Reddish brown to blackish.
Occurs from Indiana westward to California.

Paederus littorarius Length: 4–5.5mm. Reddish yellow or dull orange, shining; head black; last two segments of abdomen black; antennae dark at middle, paler at each end; elytra dark blue. Head slightly longer than wide; pronotum slightly longer than wide, sides slightly rounded; elytra slightly wider than pronotum; coxae of hind legs conical; head constricted into a neck behind eyes; last segment of maxillary palpus obtuse; fourth segment of each of the tarsi of hind legs with two lobes beneath (Fig. 133).
Under stones in damp places.
Eastern and Central United States.

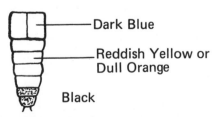

Fig. 133. Paederus littorarius

Lathrobium simile Length: 7.5–9mm. Black, shining; antennae reddish brown; legs paler; elytra and abdomen pitch colored. Head constricted into a distinct neck; labrum with two lobes; fourth segment of maxillary palpus conical, pointed at apex; pronotum slightly longer than wide; elytra slightly wider than pronotum; coxae of hind legs conical.
Eastern half of the United States.

Lobrathium collare Length: 4.5–6mm. Head black; pronotum reddish brown; abdomen blackish; elytra dark brown or blackish. Head small and constricted into a distinct neck; labrum with two lobes; fourth segment of maxillary palpus conical, sharply pointed at apex; pronotum slightly longer than wide, wider than head, and with sides slightly rounded; elytra slightly wider than pronotum and coarsely punctured; coxae of hind legs conical.
Eastern half of the United States.

Sunius confluentus Length: 3–4mm. Dark brown; bases of antennae, legs, and elytra at apices usually lighter brown. Pronotum narrower than head, wider than long; elytra slightly wider than pronotum, densely and roughly punctured; third segment of each antenna distinctly longer than second, outer segments beadlike.
Beneath bark, on decaying vegetable matter, and on fungi.
Eastern half of the United States.

Nudobius cephalus Length: 6–7.5mm. Black, shining; antennae and undersurface deep reddish brown to blackish; legs and elytra brownish yellow. Coxae of hind legs triangular and touching or nearly so; fourth segment of maxillary palpus longer than third; elytra overlapping along suture; pronotum longer than wide; elytra slightly wider than pronotum and sparsely punctured (Fig. 134).
Throughout the United States.

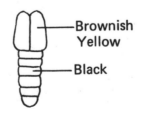

Fig. 134. Nudobius cephalus

Gyrohypnus hamatus Length: 5–6mm. Head black, shining; pronotum reddish brown; abdomen deep brown; antennae, legs, and elytra brownish yellow. Head somewhat oblong; pronotum slightly longer than wide, sides parallel; elytra slightly wider than pronotum, each with four or five rows of fine punctures; coxae of hind legs triangular and touching or almost so; fourth segment of maxillary palpus much longer than third and acutely conical (Fig. 135).
Eastern half of the United States.

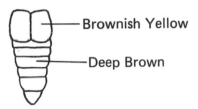

Fig. 135.   Gyrohypnus hamatus

The species of the following two genera, Philonthus *and* Staphlinus, *have the coxae of the hind legs touching or nearly so and the fourth segment of the maxillary palpus equal to or longer than the third.*

Philonthus politus Length: 10–13mm. Black, shining; antennae pitch colored; elytra bronzed with some pubescence. Pronotum slightly wider than long, rounded into base; elytra slightly wider than pronotum and finely punctured; first segment of each of the tarsi of hind legs as long or longer than the fifth.
In fungi.
Eastern half of the United States.

Philonthus cyanipennis Length: 12–15mm. Black, shining; antennae and tarsi pitch colored; elytra metallic blue or green. Head square, pronotum slightly longer than wide, sides rather rounded; elytra wider than pronotum, coarsely and rather densely punctured; first segment of each of the tarsi of the hind legs as long or longer than the fifth (Fig. 136).
In fleshy fungi.
Eastern half of the United States.

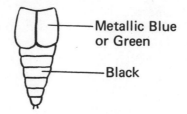

Fig. 136.   Philonthus cyanipennis

Philonthus fusiformis   Length: 5–6mm. Black, shining; legs brownish yellow; elytra brownish red or red. Antennal segments longer than wide; elytra slightly wider than pronotum and coarsely and densely punctured; first segment of each of the tarsi of the hind legs as long or longer than the fifth (Fig. 137).
Eastern half of the United States.

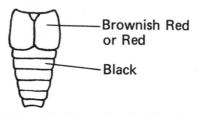

Fig. 137.   Philonthus fusiformis

Staphlinus maculosus   Length: 18–25mm. Dark reddish brown; antennae, tibiae, tarsi, and apex of abdomen pale reddish brown; femora pitch colored; elytra and upper part of abdomen with deep brown spots. Head as wide as or wider than pronotum; pronotum pubescent; abdomen more or less tapering toward tip; coxae of middle legs separated, sometimes slightly so (Fig. 138).
On carrion, dung, and decaying fungi.
Throughout the United States.

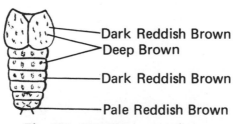

Fig. 138.   Staphlinus maculosus

Staphylinus cinnamopterus Length: 12–14mm.   Head,   pronotum, tibiae, tarsi, apical margins and whole last segment of abdomen, and elytra brownish red; antennae, femora, and much of abdomen pitch colored. Pronotum densely and coarsely punctured; elytra slightly wider than pronotum and densely punctured; abdomen more or less tapering toward tip; coxae of middle legs separated, sometimes slightly so.
Beneath bark and on fungi.
Throughout the United States.

Staphylinus violaceus Length: 12–14mm. Head, pronotum, and elytra deep violet blue or coppery; antennae pitch colored; abdomen and legs black. Much like *Staphlinus cinnamopterus* in shape and size. A very attractive species.
Beneath bark and logs and on fungi and carrion.
Eastern half of the United States.

Ontholestes cingulatus Length: 13–18mm. Dark brown or pitch colored; densely covered with yellowish, brownish, and blackish pubescence, the black hairs forming irregular spots on head, pronotum, and abdomen; antennae dark; basal segments of tibiae and tarsi reddish brown; tip of abdomen golden. Head wider than pronotum; pronotum squarish, sides rounded, densely punctured; elytra slightly wider than pronotum and covered with many small flattened elevations.
On carrion and fungi.
Throughout the United States.

Creophilus maxillosus Length: 10–21mm. Black, shining; second, third, and usually fourth segments of abdomen covered above with dull gray hairs; elytra each with a band of coarse, dull gray hairs. Last segment of each antenna longer but narrower than the one preceding it, notched at apex; fourth segment of maxillary palpus shorter than third; coxae of middle legs well separated; pronotum somewhat roundish; elytra wider than pronotum and very finely and sparsely punctured (Fig. 139).
On carrion and fungi.
Throughout the United States.

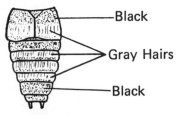

Fig. 139.   Creophilus maxillosus

The folowing species of Oxyporus have each of the antennae with eleven segments; the head is large and wider than pronotum; the eyes are small; and the coxae of the front legs are conical and those of the middle legs are separated.

Oxyporus femoralis   Length: 7–8mm. Black; tibiae, tarsi, and elytra paler, the latter with dull yellow markings (Fig. 140).
On fleshy fungi.
Eastern half of the United States.

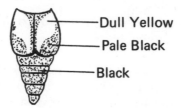

Fig. 140.   Oxyporus femoralis

Oxyporus major   Length: 10–14mm. Black; tibiae with golden brown hairs, tarsi pale yellowish, otherwise, legs black; elytra marked with golden yellow.
Eastern and Central States.

Oxyporus vittatus   Length: 6mm. Black; legs reddish yellow; elytra clay yellow with a black stripe on sides and at suture.
Eastern half of the United States.

The species of the following four genera have transverse coxae of the hind legs and the antennae inserted at the sides of the head.

Tachinus fimbriatus   Length: 7–9mm. Head and pronotum black, shining; antennae black, four basal and apical segments paler; abdomen and legs dark reddish brown to pitch colored; elytra light reddish brown. Maxillary palpi threadlike; tibiae each with a fringe of uneven small spines at apex; body somewhat tapered; head, pronotum, and elytra with many fine wrinkles; elytra together as wide as long (Fig. 141).
Eastern United States.

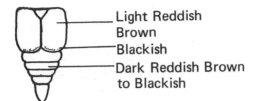

Light Reddish
Brown
Blackish
Dark Reddish Brown
to Blackish

Fig. 141. Tachinus fimbriatus

Tachinus pallipes Length: 5–6mm. Black; legs, margins of pronotum, bases and sides of elytra, and four basal segments of each antenna reddish yellow.
Throughout the United States.

Tachyporus jocosus Length: 3–4mm. Black, shining; pronotum, elytra, and legs yellowish brown; antennae dull yellow. Maxillary palpi
awl shaped; body abruptly tapered; pronotum wider than long,
hind angles rounded; elytra together as long as wide (Fig. 142).
Throughout the United States.

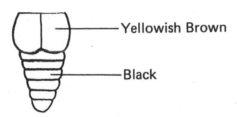

Yellowish Brown

Black

Fig. 142. Tachyporus jocosus

Tachyporus nitidulus Length: 2.5–3mm. Similar to *jocosus,* reddish
yellow with pitch colored head and dull yellow legs and antennae.
Throughout the United States.

Coproporus ventriculus Length: 2–2.5mm. Black, shining; antennae
and legs dark reddish brown; elytra and abdomen with a reddish,
pitch colored tinge. Pronotum wider than long, as wide as elytra
at base, finely and sparsely punctured; elytra covering more than
half of abdomen; abdomen tapering.
Beneath bark.
Throughout the United States.

Conosomus crassus Length: 3–5mm. Pitch colored with pale brown pubescence; antennae brownish black, apical segments paler; bases of pronotum and elytra with a reddish area. Pronotum slightly wider than elytra, sides rounded, hind angles rounded; elytra together as long as wide, densely punctured; apical fringes of tibiae with uniform spines; tibiae of middle legs each with one terminal spur. Beneath bark and on fungi.
Eastern half of the United States.

Bolitobius cinctus Length: 4.5–7mm. Reddish yellow; head, two large spots covering most of elytra, and last two segments of abdomen black; antennae pitch colored with apical and basal segments dull yellow; legs dull yellow. Head oval, sides margined beneath eyes; antennae inserted at sides of head; pronotum as wide as bases of both elytra together, hind angles rounded; elytra together about as wide as long, each with three rows of punctures; maxillary palpi threadlike; abdomen with six ventral segments; coxae of front legs conical; tibiae of middle and hind legs each fringed at apex with unequal, coarse, small spines (Fig. 143).
On fungi.
Throughout the United States.

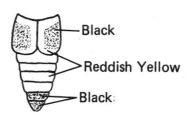

Fig. 143. Bolitobius cinctus

Gyrophaena vinula Length: 1.5–2.5mm. Light brownish yellow; head, apices of elytra, and fourth and fifth segments of abdomen blackish. Pronotum wider than long with two large punctures; elytra slightly wider than pronotum, sparsely punctured; antennae inserted between eyes; third segment of maxillary palpus stout; coxae of front legs conical, those of hind legs transverse; tarsi of front and middle legs each with four segments, each of those of the hind legs with five (Fig. 144).
On fleshy fungi.
Eastern half of the United States.

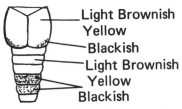

Light Brownish
Yellow
Blackish
Light Brownish
Yellow
Blackish

Fig. 144.   Gyrophaena vinula

Gyrophaena fasciata   Length: 1.5–2.5mm. Pale reddish yellow with the head, apical third of each elytron and fourth and fifth abdominal segments black.
Throughout the Eastern States.

Gyrophaena dissimilis   Length: 1.5–2.3mm. Pale dull yellow with head, apical angles of elytra and abdomen blackish.
Eastern and Central States.

Falagria dissecta   Length: 2–2.5mm. Black, shining, slightly pubescent; legs brownish yellow. Pronotum slightly wider than long, sides rounded toward apex and with a deep median groove; elytra distinctly wider than pronotum, sparsely punctured; head with a very narrow neck; antennae inserted between eyes; scutellum with sharp ridges; coxae of front legs conical, those of the hind legs transverse, tarsi of the front legs each with four segments, each of those of the middle and hind legs with five segments.
Throughout the United States.

Aleochara lata   Length: 5–7mm. Black, shining, covered with scattered gray pubescence; tarsi reddish brown. Pronotum wider than long, base rounded, sides slightly so; elytra slightly wider than pronotum; head small, distinctly narrower than pronotum; antennae inserted between the eyes; coxae of front legs conical, those of hind legs transverse; tarsi each with five segments.
On decaying logs and carrion.
Throughout the United States.

Baryodma bimaculata   Length: 4–7mm. Black, shining; elytra paler near apices; tibiae, tarsi, and tips of posterior abdominal segments dull brownish red. Head small; antennae inserted between eyes; eyes large; pronotum wider than long, sides and hind angles rounded; elytra not as wide as pronotum, densely and coarsely punctured;

coxae of front legs conical, those of hind legs transverse; tarsi each with five segments.
In horse dung and fungi.
Throughout the United States.

Micropeplus cribratus   Length: 2mm. Blackish; sides of thorax orange brown. Coxae of hind legs widely separated and round; antennae each with nine segments and knob at end, inserted at sides of head; next to last abdominal segment with an elevated ridge; elytra with wavy ridges; tarsi each with three segments.
Southeast United States.

Euaesthetus americanus   Length: 1.2–1.5mm. Dark reddish brown, antennae and legs paler. Coxae of hind legs touching or nearly so, those of hind legs conical; abdomen as wide at base as elytra and punctured, with margin; tarsi each with four segments.
Eastern third of the United States.

Palaminus testaceus   Length: 3.5–4mm. Pale reddish yellow, shining; antennae and legs pale yellow; abdomen reddish brown. Coxae of hind legs touching or nearly so, conical; last segment of maxillary palpus obliquely hatchet shaped and as long as preceding one; tarsi each with five segments.
Eastern half of the United States.

Lithocharis ochracea   Length: 3–4mm. Reddish brown, antennae and elytra paler; legs yellowish. Coxae of hind legs touching or nearly so and conical; last segment of maxillary palpus quite small and awl shaped; labrum toothed in the middle; tip of ligula densely fringed with hairs; tarsi each with five segments.
Throughout the United States.

Scopaeus exiguus   Length: 2–3mm. Head and elytra blackish; thorax dusky yellow; abdomen blackish, paler at tip; antennae and legs pale yellow. Coxae of hind legs touching or nearly so, conical; neck very slender; tarsi each with five segments, each of those of the hind legs short and thick with the basal segment as long or slightly longer than the second.
Eastern third of the United States.

Astenus longiusculus   Length: 3.5–4.5mm. Light reddish brown. Coxae of hind legs touching or nearly so, conical; tarsi each with five segments; last segment of maxillary palpus quite small and awl shaped; fourth segment of each tarsus of hind legs with two lobes; head, elytra and abdomen all wider than the oval pronotum.
Western United States.

THE FAMILIES OF BEETLES 125

Stilicus angularis Length: 3.8–4mm. Dark reddish brown, shining; tips of elytra paler; legs pale yellow; abdomen pitch colored. Coxae of hind legs touching or nearly so, conical; tarsi each with five segments; last segment of maxillary palpus quite small and awl shaped; antennae distinctly longer than head; neck very slender; pronotum almost round.
East and Southern States to Texas.

Acylophorus flavicollis Length: 5–6mm. Black, shining; pronotum and legs reddish yellow; antennae dusky, paler at the bases. Coxae of hind legs touching or nearly so and triangular; antennae elbowed; claws of tarsi of front legs longer than others; slight pubescence on elytra.
Pennsylvania west to Kansas and Texas.

Quedius capucinus Length: 6–9mm. Black; antennae, legs, and sometimes the elytra reddish brown. Coxae of hind legs touching or nearly so, triangular; maxillary palpi threadlike; pronotum longer than wide.
Throughout the United States.

Baptolinus macrocephalus Length: 6–7mm. Reddish brown, shining; legs and antennae yellowish brown; elytra reddish. Coxae of hind legs touching or nearly so, triangular; antennae with their bases close together; last segment of maxillary palpus much longer than the preceding one; head and elytra wider than pronotum; abdomen with prominent marginal ridges; elytra often overlapping.
Northeastern United States.

Ocypus ater Length: 15–16mm. Black, shining; tibiae, tarsi, and basal half of each antenna pitch colored. Coxae of hind legs touching or nearly so, triangular; bases of antennae widely separated; maxillary palpus with fourth segment equal to or longer than the third; ligula notched; sides of abdomen parallel.
Throughout the United States.

Belonuchus rufipennis Length: 6.5–7.5mm. Reddish yellow; head, pronotum, and last two segments of abdomen shining black. Coxae of hind legs touching or nearly so and triangular; bases of antennae widely separated; fourth segment of maxillary palpus equal to or longer than the third; femora each with a row of fine spines beneath.
Eastern States west to Arizona.

Thoracophorus costalis Length: 2–2.5mm. Dull, dark chestnut brown. Coxae of hind legs touching or nearly so and transverse; coxae of

front legs spherical; tarsi each with only three segments; each elytron with four ridges.
Throughout the United States.

Oligota parva   Length: 1mm. Pitch colored, tip of abdomen lighter, shining. Coxae of hind legs touching or nearly so and transverse, those of front legs conical; abdomen with six ventral segments; antennae inserted between the eyes; antennae each with ten segments, tarsi each with four; antennae each with a club; pronotum very widened behind; elytra widening even more from front to back.
Throughout the United States.

Myllaena dubia   Length: 1.5–2mm. Reddish brown; legs paler. Coxae of hind legs touching or nearly so and transverse, those of front legs conical; abdomen with six ventral segments; antennae inserted between the eyes and long and slender; tarsi of hind legs each with five segments, each of the others with four; labial palpi each with three segments; abdomen with scattered, long, coarse hairs.
Throughout the United States.

Myllaena minuta   Length: 2mm. Dark brown with legs and apical third of each antenna dull yellow.
Throughout the United States.

Xenodusa cava   Length: 5–6mm. Reddish brown, shining, with scattered pubescence. Coxae of hind legs touching or nearly so and transverse, those of front legs conical; abdomen with six ventral segments; antennae inserted between the eyes; tarsi of middle and hind legs each with five segments, each of those of the front legs with four; labial palpi each with four segments, maxillary palpi each with five; third segments of each antenna twice as long as second; abdominal segments with dense tufts of yellow hair.
Eastern and Central States.

Aleodorus bilobatus   Length: 3mm. Pitch colored or dark brown, shining; basal segment of each antenna and legs brownish yellow. Coxae of hind legs touching or nearly so and transverse, those of front legs conical; abdomen with six ventral segments; antennae inserted between the eyes; tarsi of front legs each with four segments, those of the middle and hind legs with five; labial palpi each with four segments, maxillary palpi each with five; head constricted into a narrow neck; pronotum heart shaped and slightly wider than head.
Eastern half of the United States.

Atheta dentata   Length: 3mm. Blackish, shining, with scattered fine

pubescence; legs dusky yellow; elytra dull clay yellow. Coxae of hind legs touching or nearly so and transverse, those of front legs conical; abdomen with six ventral segments; antennae inserted between the eyes; tarsi of front legs each with four segments, those of middle and hind legs with five; labial palpi each with three segments, maxillary palpi each with four; head if constricted behind only slightly so.
Throughout the United States.

Phloeopora sublaevis Length: 1.5–2mm. Dark brown; head and abdomen pitch colored; antennae brownish black, basal segment of each yellow; legs yellow. Coxae of hind legs touching or nearly so and transverse, those of front legs conical; abdomen with six ventral segments; antennae inserted between the eyes and each with eleven segments; tarsi of all legs each with five segments; maxillary palpi each with four segments; first segment of each of the tarsi of hind legs shorter than the following two taken together; head prominent, narrowed at base; pronotum as long as wide; elytra longer and wider than pronotum.
Eastern half of the United States.

Oxypoda amica Length: 2mm. Dull brownish yellow covered with long shaggy pubescence; legs paler. Coxae of front legs touching or nearly so and transverse, those of front legs conical; abdomen with six ventral segments; antennae inserted between the eyes and each with eleven segments; tarsi of all legs each with five segments; maxillary palpi each with four segments; head retracted; labial palpus gradually narrowing from base to apex.
Central States.

Megarthrus americanus Length: 2–2.5mm. Dusky yellow; head black; legs dull yellow. Coxae of hind legs touching or nearly so and transverse, those of front legs transverse; abdomen with six ventral segments; antennae inserted at sides of head; abdomen sparsely and coarsely punctured.
Throughout the United States.

Megalopsidia caelatus Length: 4–4.5mm. Black, shining; antennae and legs reddish brown; elytra each with an oblique reddish stripe from shoulder to suture at apex. Coxae of hind and middle legs touching; abdomen with seven segments; eyes very large; antennae each with ten segments and shorter than head; head wider than pronotum.
Florida north to Indiana.

Trogophloeus quadripunctatus Length: 3mm. Black, shining; anten-

nae and legs pitch colored, tarsi paler. Coxae of hind and middle legs touching; abdomen with seven segments; antennae each with eleven segments; tibia pubescent; scutellum invisible; pronotum wider than long.
Eastern half of the United States.

Bledius emarginatus   Length: 2mm. Black. Coxae of hind and middle legs touching; abdomen with seven segments; antennae each with eleven segments and elbowed; tibiae of front legs each with two rows of spines.
Along streams.
Eastern half of the United States.

Apocellus sphaericollis   Length: 2.5–3mm. Dark reddish brown, shining; head and abdomen usually darker; first three segments of antennae, and legs pale. Coxae of hind and middle legs touching; abdomen with seven segments; antennae each with eleven segments; tibia pubescent; head strongly constricted behind; eyes very small.
Throughout the United States.

Olophrum obtectum   Length: 5–6mm. Pitch colored, shining; antennae, legs, and narrow margin of pronotum reddish brown. Coxae of hind legs touching and transverse, those of front legs conical; ocelli on sides of head; antennae slender; tarsi of hind legs each with first two segments long and equal.
Eastern States.

Omalium hamatum   Length: 2mm. Dull reddish or dusky yellow, slightly pubescent; head and tips of elytra brownish black. Coxae of hind legs touching and transverse, those of front legs conical; ocelli on sides of head; tarsi of hind legs each with segments one to four very short and equal; tibiae each with fine spines, each of those of the hind legs deeply notched on the outer side.
Central States.

The Short-Winged Mold Beetles

Family Pselaphidae
   The species of the family *Pselaphidae* are known as the short-winged mold beetles because they apparently feed on mold. Some of them are found in the nests of ants, others live beneath leaves, stones, and bark, and a few live in caves. They are very small, even minute, less than 3.5mm in length, and are chestnut brown, dull yellow, or pitch colored and, as a rule, are slightly pubescent. They

resemble the rove beetles in the shortness of their elytra and in several other respects, but differ from them in that the abdomen has only five or six segments on the ventral side and is not flexible (Fig. 145).

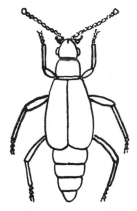

Fig. 145. Short-winged Mold Beetle

The head is equal or nearly equal in width to the pronotum and the mouthparts project forward; the antennae are generally gradually thickened toward the tips. Sometimes the antennae are threadlike and each usually has eleven segments, but in some genera they have only ten or even less. The pronotum is narrower than the elytra, which have squarish tips and are considerably shortened, thus exposing the abdomen; the coxae of the front legs are conical and touching; the legs are long and slender; and the tarsi each have two or three segments.

The short-winged mold beetles feed on mites and other small animals. The beetles that live in the nests of ants secrete a fluid, which the ants are fond of, from small tufts of hair. The ants caress the tufts of hair with their antennae, causing the fluid to flow, which they greedily swallow. In return for this favor the ants are said to feed the beetles.

Batrisodes globosus Length: 1.7–1.8mm. Reddish brown, shining; pubescent. Pronotum slightly wider than long, with a deep median groove ending in a deep pit near the base; elytra one-half longer than pronotum, each with three small, rounded pits on the base, striae shallow; antennae widely separated at bases and inserted on sides of head, each with a three-segmented club; last segment of maxillary palpus spindle shaped; legs long, femora each thickened toward the tip; tibiae of hind legs each with a slender terminal spur; tarsal claws unequal (Fig. 146).

In nests of ants and beneath stones on sloping hillsides; also in caves. Eastern half of the United States.

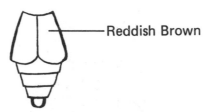

Fig. 146.   Batrisodes globosus

Batrisodes spretus   Length: 1.7mm. Pitch colored, with dark red elytra.
Throughout eastern half of United States.

Tychus minor   Length: 1.5mm. Dark reddish brown, shining; antennae and legs paler; pubescent. Eyes very small; pronotum wider than long and wider than head, five pits at the base, the middle one the largest; elytra with combined bases as wide as pronotum, squarish at apices, and each with two striae; antennae widely separated at bases and inserted on sides of head, each gradually thickened toward apex, last segment of each large and egg shaped; last segment of maxillary palpus long and hatchet shaped; second segment of each tarsus of hind legs equal to or longer than the third; only one claw on each tarsus.
Beneath stones on hillsides.
Eastern half of the United States.

Pilopius lacustris   Length: .7–1.8mm. Dark reddish brown; antennae, legs, and elytra paler. Head distinctly narrower than pronotum; two large pits on occiput between eyes; pronotum wider than long, with an oblong median pit at base, a smaller one at each side; elytra slightly wider at bases than pronotum and then widening toward the tips; antennae usually touching at bases, inserted on frontal region beneath two closely placed tubercles, last segments of each gradually becoming larger and forming a distinct club; maxillary palpi with long bristlelike appendages; tarsi short and slender (Fig. 147).
Beneath logs and bark.
Central States.

Fig. 147.   Pilopius lacustris

Ceophyllus monilis   Length: 3.3mm. Reddish brown; without punctures. Head as long and three-fourths as wide as pronotum; pronotum bell shaped with a fine impressed median line and two pits near base; elytra one-half wider at combined bases than pronotum, wider toward apices; antennae usually touching at bases, inserted on frontal region beneath two closely placed tubercles, beadlike, eleventh segment of each bluntly pointed; femora of front legs each with three strong spines near base; legs long and slender as are the tarsi; tarsal claws equal in length (Fig. 148).
In nests of ants.
Eastern and Central States.

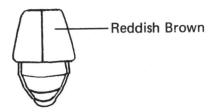

Fig. 148.   Ceophyllus monilis

Tmesiphorus costalis   Length: 3.3mm. Dark brown to pitch colored, shining; covered with short, fine yellowish hair. Head wider than long; eyes prominent; pronotum bell shaped with two shallow pits at the apex and two large ones at the base; each elytron with a long deep groove on the basal half; antennae usually touching at bases, inserted on front between two closely placed tubercles, each becoming thickened toward the apex; maxillary palpus with fourth segment triangular and notched, the last three segments with bristle-like appendages; abdomen with a keel or ridge on the upper surface of first and second segments; legs long and slender.
Beneath stones and bark and in the nests of ants.
Eastern half of the United States.

Tyrus humeralis   Length: 1.6mm. Pitch colored and covered with fine short hairs; antennae, legs, and palpi paler; elytra red. Head with two small pits between the eyes; pronotum bell shaped with a median rounded pit and a narrow transverse groove at base; elytra wider than pronotum, finely and sparsely punctured; abdomen slightly longer than elytra; antennae usually touching at bases, inserted on front between two closely placed tubercles, each becoming thickened toward apex; first segment of maxillary palpus minute, second long and curved, third short and inversely egg shaped, fourth with a needlelike spine at apex; femora of front legs each with a keel or ridge.
Beneath the bark of decayed stumps.
Eastern half of the United States.

Cylindrarctus longipalpis   Length: 2mm. Pale reddish brown with scattered long and somewhat erect hairs. Pronotum wider than long; elytra with sides rounded; antennae usually touching at bases, inserted on front between two closely placed tubercles; last segment of maxillary palpus long and hatchet shaped; tarsi each with but one claw.
Widely scattered throughout the United States.

Rhexius insculptus   Length: 1.2mm. Pale reddish brown, covered with short erect hairs. Head with ridge on top and with three pits on front; pronotum wider than long; sides of elytra somewhat rounded; antennae with bases wide apart and inserted on sides of head; coxae of hind legs conical and close together; antennae each elbowed and with segments three to eight transverse and equal; tarsi each with two unequal claws.
Eastern half of the United States.

Euplectus confluens   Length: 1.2–1.5mm. Reddish brown, covered with fine pubescence. Antennae with bases wide apart and inserted on sides of head; coxae of hind legs conical and close together; abdomen longer than elytra; tarsi each with but one claw.
Eastern and Central United States.

Decarthron brendeli   Length: 1.4mm. Pitch colored to brownish; antennae and legs pale brown; elytra dull red. Antennae with bases far apart and inserted on sides of head and each with ten segments, the last three forming a club; coxae of hind legs transverse and separated.
Central United States and the Southwest.

Reichenbachia propinqua   Length: 1.4mm. Pitch colored, blackish;

elytra dark red; pubescent. Antennae with bases far apart and inserted on sides of head and each with eleven segments; elytra each with three small pits on base; pronotum with one small and two large pits; coxae of hind legs transverse and separated; tarsi each with but one claw.
Massachusetts west to Minnesota.

Reichenbachia rubicunda Length: 1.5mm. Pitch colored to blackish, with antennae, legs, and elytra dull red.
Common throughout the eastern half of the United States.

The Ant-Loving Beetles

Family Clavigeridae
The members of this family are probably more ant-loving than those of the family *Pselaphidae,* which they resemble in structural characters and habits except that their antennae each have only two segments. Only a few species are known from the United States.

Fustiger fuchsi Length: 1.7mm. Dark brownish yellow. Head and pronotum somewhat deeply impressed with a netted pattern (Fig. 149).
Indiana and Tennessee.

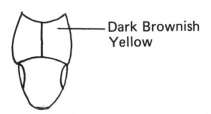

Dark Brownish Yellow

Fig. 149. Fustiger fuchsi

Adranes lecontei Length: 2.5mm. Brownish yellow and covered with a fine pubescence.
Indiana and Mississippi.

The Feather-Winged Beetles

Family Ptilidae
This family includes the smallest beetles that are known; most species are less than 1mm. in length. The wings of these beetles

are long, narrow, and fringed with long hairs, giving them a featherlike appearance, though in some species the wings are absent. Some species live in rotten wood, muck, manure, and other decaying organic matter; a few occur in ants' nests.

Nossidium americanum Length: 1mm. Head and pronotum blackish, shining; elytra reddish brown, covered with rather long yellowish hairs; antennae and legs yellow. (Fig. 150).
Throughout the United States.

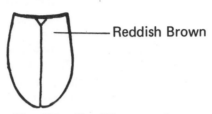

— Reddish Brown

Fig. 150. Nossidium americanum

Acratrichis moerens Length: .6–.7mm. Black, shining and widely distributed.

Limulodes paradoxus Length: 1mm. Reddish yellow and shining with grayish pubescence, and also widely distributed.

The Shining Fungus Beetles

Family Scaphidiidae
The beetles of this family live in fungi, rotten or decaying wood, dead leaves, and beneath the bark of dead trees and stumps. They are small, shining or polished, oval or boat shaped, with shortened elytra, and may readily be recognized by their strongly tapering or acute anal segment (Fig. 151). When disturbed they usually remain motionless but on occasion they will run rather swiftly with a characteristic uneven gait. The head is prolonged into something of a short beak; the antennae, inserted on the margin of the front of the head, are both threadlike or with a loose club; the coxae of the front legs are large and conical; and the tarsi, which are long and slender, each have five segments.

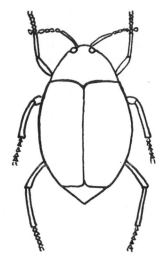

Fig. 151.   Shining Fungus Beetle

Scaphidium quadriguttatum   Length: 3.8–4.5mm.   Black,   shining; elytra each usually with two reddish transverse spots, one near the base, the other at the apex, and sometimes the spots may be yellowish; tarsi reddish. Pronotum with acute hind angles; elytra with sides broadly rounded, each with two or three short rows of punctures, and a basal row of coarse punctures that is continued along suture nearly to each apex; antennae each with a broad, somewhat flattened five-segmented club (Fig. 152).
Eastern and Central States.

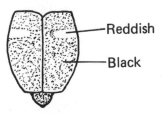

Fig. 152.   Scaphidium quadriguttatum

Scaphisoma convexum   Length: 2.2–2.7mm.   Dark chestnut brown to black; antennae, lower surface of body, and apices of elytra light-

er brown. Pronotum more than one-half as long as elytra with rounded sides; elytra each with a fine marginal line at base continuing along suture to apex, a row of coarse punctures between the line and suture, apices squarish; antennae each with the third segment very short, wedge shaped or triangular, threadlike, without a club; scutellum minute and triangular (Fig. 153).
Often found on fungi growing on logs.
Eastern half of the United States.

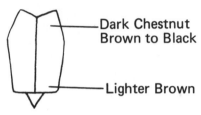

Fig. 153.   Scaphisoma convexum

Baeocera falsata   Length: 2.7mm. Black, shining; antennae, abdomen, legs, and apices of elytra brownish black. Pronotum wider than long with sides tapering to apex; elytra about as long as wide, with a deeply impressed line along each base and suture with a row of coarse punctures between the line and suture; antennae each with third segment elongate, cylindrical, and last three segments broadened into a sort of club; scutellum completely hidden (Fig. 154).
On various kinds of fungi.
Eastern and Central States.

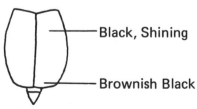

Fig. 154.   Baeocera falsata

The Hister Beetles

Family Histeridae

There is some doubt as to the origin of the name of the family *Histeridae*. It has been suggested that when Linnaeus named the type genus of the family *Hister*, he had in mind a person of that name mentioned in Juvenal's *Satires*, who was something of an unsavory character. If we judge some of the beetles of the family from our own standards, we must admit that many of them have rather filthy habits living as they do in excrement, carrion, and other decomposing substances. However, others live in a fairly clean manner beneath bark, in the nests of ants, and in the nests and burrows of birds and mammals.

The histerids are mostly small, short, rounded or squarish, hard, compact, shining black beetles and look not unlike black pills or seeds (Fig 155). The antennae are both elbowed each with a club;

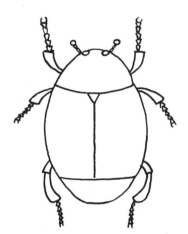

Fig. 155. Hister Beetle

the elytra are short with squarish apices, leaving two segments of the abdomen exposed, and are usually striate and punctured; the legs are short, each of the tibia of the hind legs often has long spines to provide traction in soft substances; and the tarsi each are five segmented.

These beetles are predaceous in feeding habits and for this reason it is believed they render a service in keeping in check the population of undesirable flies by destroying the larvae that live in excrement and those species that live beneath bark by eating the eggs and larvae of various destructive wood borers.

Hololepta fossularis Length: 7–10mm. Black, shining. Pronotum wider than long, apex notched; head stretched out; mandibles more or less long; elytra each with first dorsal stria short, the second shorter, the third merely a puncture; each of the tibia of front legs toothed on inner margin (Fig. 156).
Beneath the bark of trees.
Eastern half of the United States.

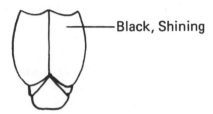

Fig. 156.   Hololepta fossularis

Teretrius americanus Length: 1.5–2.5mm. Pitch colored, shining; antennae, except basal segments, brownish orange; legs and sides of elytra dark reddish brown. Pronotum slightly longer than wide; elytra parallel without striae but densely punctured; head retracted and bent downward; tibiae of front legs each with five teeth (Fig. 157).
Beneath bark.
Eastern half of the United States.

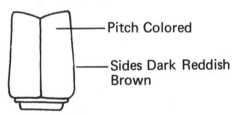

Fig. 157.   Teretrius americanus

Plegaderus transversus Length: 1.3–1.5mm. Brownish black, somewhat shining. Pronotum somewhat squarish; elytra each with elongate, confluent punctures and a short, oblique stria at each shoulder; head retracted; antennae inserted under lateral margin of frontal region; tibiae each with many fine teeth.
Eastern half of the United States.

Paromalus aequalis   Length: 2.5–3mm. Black, shining. Head retracted and bent downward; segment of sternum between coxae of front legs distinctly lobed in front; elytra with few or no striae.
Beneath the bark of logs.
Eastern half of the United States.

The following species of the genus Saprinus *have the head retracted and bent downward; the antennae inserted under lateral margin of the front of the head; and elytral striae more or less abbreviated, with the fourth stria of each elytron usually curved at the base to join the sutural stria.*

Saprinus pennsylvanicus   Length: 4–5mm. Bright metallic green to bronze. Pronotum with a few punctures along sides and basal margin; elytra each coarsely punctured on apical half between first dorsal stria and suture; tibiae of front legs each with coarse teeth (Fig. 158).
Beneath dung and carrion.
Eastern United States west to the Rockies.

Bright
Metallic
Green to
Bronze

Fig. 158.   Saprinus pennsylvanicus

Saprinus assimilis   Length: 4–5.5mm. Black, shining. Pronotal sides with coarse punctures, a distinct impression in front of scutellum; elytra each coarsely punctured on apical third; tibiae of front legs each with fine teeth.
On carrion of fish and reptiles.
Eastern half of the United States.

Saprinus conformis   Length: 3.5–5mm. Black, shining. Pronotum with dense, fine punctures on sides and apical margin, a single row of punctures along base, and a single larger one before the scutellum; elytra each with an irregular, triangular patch of coarse punctures on apical third.
Eastern half of the United States.

Pachylopus fraternus   Length: 3–4mm. Black, tinged with bronze, slightly shining. Pronotum rather densely punctured; elytra completely punctured except for a shining space near scutellum; front of head distinctly margined; antennae inserted under lateral margin of frontal region; tibiae of hind legs each with two rows of spinules (Fig. 159).

Beneath the carrion of fish and reptiles on sandy beaches.

Eastern half of the United States.

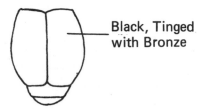

Black, Tinged with Bronze

Fig. 159.   Pachylopus fraternus

Platylomalus aequalis Length: 2.5–3mm. Black, shining. Head more or less retracted and bent downward; antennae inserted under lateral margin of frontal region; antennal grooves in middle of deflexed sides of pronotum; pronotum with small, dense punctures; elytra without striae though sometimes a stria is present at the shoulders, a few fine punctures.

Beneath bark and logs.

Eastern half of the United States.

Isolomalus bistriatus Length: 2mm. Dark reddish brown to pitch colored; shining; antennae and legs reddish brown. Head more or less retracted and bent downward; antennae inserted under lateral margin of front; antennal groove in middle of deflexed sides of pronotum; pronotum finely and densely punctured; elytra each more coarsely and sparsely punctured, except for first and second dorsal striae which are very short, other striae absent (Fig. 160).

Beneath bark of logs and in tree fungi.

Eastern half of the United States.

Dark Reddish Brown to Pitch-Colored

Fig. 160.   Isolomalus bistriatus

The following species of the genus Hister *have the head retracted and bent downward; the antennae are inserted under the lateral
margin of the frontal region; there is an antennal groove on anterior angle of each of the deflexed sides of the pronotum; and the
tarsal groove of each of the front tibiae is straight with a margin
only on the inner edge.*

Hister arcuatus   Length: 5–6mm. Black, shining; each elytron with
a curved red spot; clubs of antennae and femora of middle and hind
legs reddish. Pronotum with striae on margin converging at base;
first three striae of each elytron entire or unbroken, fourth stria
short; margin of pronotum with a fringe of short hairs; the last dorsal segment of the abdomen with a few fine punctures.
Eastern States and North Central States.

Hister abbreviatus   Length: 3.5–5.5mm. Black, shining; antennae
and legs pitch colored. Elytra each with four entire or unbroken
dorsal striae, fifth short, and two overlapping subhumerals (striae
from near the humerus) ; tibiae of front legs each with four small
teeth (Fig. 161).
On carrion of fish and reptiles; also in dung and fungi.
Eastern half of the United States.

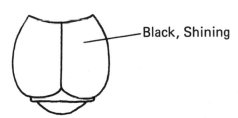

Black, Shining

Fig. 161.   Hister abbreviatus

Hister foedatus   Length: 4–6.5mm. Black, shining; clubs of antennae,
and tarsi dark reddish brown. Pronotum with outer marginal striae
very short; first three dorsal striae of each elytron entire, fourth
nearly so, and fifth short; last dorsal segment of abdomen densely and somewhat coarsely punctured; tibiae of front legs each with
four short teeth.
On carrion.
Throughout the United States.

Hister immunis   Length: 4.5–5.5mm. Black, shining; legs dark reddish brown. Marginal striae of pronotum entire, somewhat converging at base; first three dorsal striae of each elytron entire, fourth

slightly shortened at base, fifth very short; last dorsal segment of abdomen densely and finely punctured.
On carrion and dung.
Eastern half of the United States.

Hister depurator   Length: 5.5–6mm. Black, shining; antennae and spines of legs reddish brown. Outer marginal striae of pronotum variable in length, inner striae entire; first three dorsal striae of each elytron entire, fourth short, fifth a trace; last dorsal segment of abdomen densely and finely punctured; tibae of front legs each with three teeth.
Eastern half of the United States.

Atholus bimaculatus   Length: 4.5–5.5mm. Black, shining; each elytron with a large diagonal orange red spot. Pronotum with a single marginal stria; elytra each with five dorsal striae and each finely punctured; head retracted and bent downward; antennae inserted under lateral margin of frontal region; antennal groove on anterior angle of each of the deflexed sides of pronotum; tarsal groove of each of the tibiae of front legs straight and with margin only on inner edge, tibiae each with three teeth (Fig. 162).
In cow dung.
Throughout the United States.

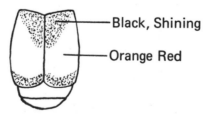

Fig. 162.   *Atholus bimaculatus*

Atholus americanus   Length: 3–4mm. Black, somewhat shining, with the outer pronotal marginal stria extremely variable, the inner one entire, and the elytra each with entire dorsal striae. The tibiae of the front legs each have three teeth, one at the tip prominent. In logs and beneath bark in moist woodlands.
Throughout the United States.

The following species of the genera Platysoma *and* Phelister *have the head retracted and bent downward; the antennae are in-*

serted under the lateral margin of the frontal region; and each antennal groove on the anterior angle of each of the deflexed sides of the pronotum.

Platysoma carolinum Length: 3–4mm. Black, shining; antennae, legs, and abdomen dark reddish brown. Pronotum with outer marginal stria entire and minutely punctured; first three dorsal striae entire, sutural stria extending anterior to middle; last dorsal segment of abdomen somewhat densely punctured; tibiae of front legs each with five fine teeth, each of those of the middle legs with four, and each of those of the hind legs with three short spines (Fig. 163) ; tarsal groove of each of the front tibiae S shaped. Eastern half of the United States.

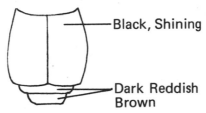

Fig. 163. Platysoma carolinum

Platysoma lecontei Length: 2.5–3mm. Black, shining; antennae and legs brownish black. Pronotum minutely punctured, stria along margin entire; elytra each with three entire dorsal striae; last dorsal segment of abdomen coarsely and densely punctured except at tip; tibiae of front legs each with four teeth, tibiae of middle legs with three spines, and each of those of the hind legs with two short spines; tarsal groove of each of the front tibiae S shaped. Beneath bark of logs and stumps and on fungi. Eastern half of the United States.

Phelister subrotundus Length: 2–3mm. Dark reddish brown with antennae and legs of the same color. Pronotum with only one marginal stria and with a small pit before scutellum; elytra each with five entire dorsal striae, finely and densely punctured; last dorsal segment of abdomen finely and densely punctured; tibiae of front legs each with many fine teeth and each with a straight tarsal groove (Fig. 164) . Beneath bark and on fungi. Throughout the United States.

Fig. 164.   Phelister subrotundus

Phelister vernus   Length: 2.5mm. Shining black, with antennae and legs reddish brown. The pronotum doesn't have any marginal stria, but each elytron has four entire dorsal ones.
Under bark and logs in damp places.
Throughout the United States.

The Net-Winged Beetles

Family Lycidae
   The beetles of the family *Lycidae* usually have the elytra covered with several longitudinal ribs and an intricate network of fine raised lines, hence their popular name. They are generally found in woodlands with a luxuriant growth of shrubs and here they may be seen either resting on the leaves or flying leisurely about with a mothlike flight. Many of them are brightly colored and are rather attractive insects; others, however, look much like some of the diurnal fireflies that are found in the same habitat and to which they are related (Fig. 165).

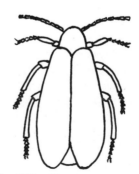

Fig. 165.   Net-winged Beetle

The head is sometimes prolonged into a long slender beak; the antennae are, as a rule, quite flattened; and the coxae of the middle legs are widely separated.

Both adults and larvae appear to be predaceous, though the adults often feed on the juices of decomposing plant material such as decaying wood.

Calopteron reticulatum Length: 9.5–18mm. Black; pronotum and elytra brownish yellow or dull orange yellow, the pronotum with a broad middle black stripe, the elytra each with the apical two-fifths black and usually with a premedian transverse black band; legs and. abdomen sometimes light yellowish brown. Head bent downward; scutellum notched at apex; underside of thorax with a prominent tubular spiracle behind and at the outer extremity of the coxae of the front legs; antennae each with the second segment transverse and inconspicuous; maxillary palpus with the last segment large and transverse; elytra widened posteriorly (Fig. 166).
On the leaves of shrubs but sometimes on flowers.
Eastern half of the United States.

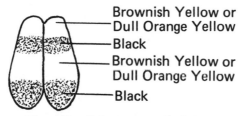

Fig. 166.   Calopteron reticulatum

Calopteron terminale Length: 11–17mm. Colored somewhat like *reticulatum* except that the apical third of each elytron is blue black.
Found on foliage and flowers.
Throughout the United States.

Celetes basalis Length: 6.5–9mm. Black or dark brown; sides of pronotum and bases of elytra yellowish or yellowish brown. Head small and bent downward; scutellum notched at apex; antennae each with second segment transverse and inconspicuous; last segment of maxillary palpus longer than wide; pronotum wider than long and with a ridge; elytra slightly widened towards the posterior (Fig. 167).
On the foliage of various plants, especially honey locust.
Eastern half of the United States.

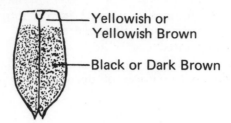

Fig. 167.   Celetes basalis

Dictopterus aurora   Length: 6.5–11mm. Pitch colored; sides of pronotum and elytra dull orange red; scutellum and legs blackish. Head
small and bent downward; scutellum notched at apex; second and
third segments of antennae about as long as fourth; pronotum with
two longitudinal ridges that run together at base and apex; elytra
pubescent (Fig. 168).
On old logs and decaying tree stumps.
Throughout the United States.

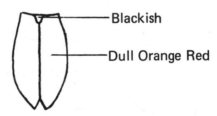

Fig. 168.   Dictopterus aurora

The following species of the genus Plateros *have the head bent
downward; the scutellum is notched at the apex; the coxae of the
front legs are touching or nearly so; distinct antennal prominences
are on the head; and the pronotum is widest at its base.*

Plateros canaliculatus   Length: 3.5–7.5mm. Black; pronotum orange
yellow with a black central area that reaches from base nearly to
apex. Eyes small; central part of pronotum minutely wrinkled; whole
surface of elytra minutely wrinkled.
About old stumps and logs in moist woods.
Eastern half of the United States.

Plateros lictor   Length: 3.5–8mm. Black; pronotum usually dull yellow with a black central spot that reaches base but not apex. Eyes

large; sides of pronotum broadly notched behind middle of pronotum, central part smooth but with more or less parallel, raised lines
or wrinkles toward the sides; total surface of elytra minutely wrinkled.
Throughout the United States.

Plateros sollicitus Length: 6–7.5mm. Dull black, the pronotum reddish yellow with a shining black center spot.
Throughout the eastern third of the United States.

Calochromus perfectus Length: 6–10.5mm. Black, somewhat shining;
sides of pronotum light yellowish brown; finely pubescent. Head
somewhat prolonged before eyes; antennae slender and well separated at bases; pronotum widest at base, sides nearly straight, and
with an oblique elevation on each side; elytra finely punctured.
On foliage and on flowers.
Eastern half of the United States.

Lycostomus lateralis Length: 8–10mm. Black; apex and sides of pronotum dull yellow; the side of each elytron to middle of each is also
dull yellow. Head prolonged into a beak; third segment of each antenna scarcely as long as fourth.
Eastern half of the United States.

Caeniella dimidiata Length: 10mm. Resembles *Calopteron terminale*,
but has comblike antennae and a black scutellar spot.
Found throughout the Atlantic States.

The Fireflies

Family Lampyridae
The name of the *fireflies* is a misnomer on two counts: they are
not flies, nor are they on fire or produce fire either for that matter.
But why quibble over a name? We know these little "torchbearers"
as *fireflies* and we shall continue to know them as such. And who
has not seen their flashes on a summer's evening as they wing their
way hither and thither among the shadows of the woodland, in the
gloom of the marsh or meadow, or in the semilight that veils the
banks of ponds and streams.
The fireflies are unique among the luminescent insects in that
they are able to produce their light at will, whereas the others glow
continuously. Both adults and larvae are able to emit light; the
larvae and the wingless females of certain species are known as *glow-
worms*. The light they produce is a "cold light," that is, light without any sensible heat; the light is the result of the oxidation of a

complex organic compound known as *luciferin* by the use of an enzyme, *luciferase,* in the presence of oxygen, magnesium ions, and adenosine triphosphate. The light-producing organs of the winged adults are located on the lower side of one or more of the abdominal segments.

The fireflies are nocturnal in habits, being rather sluggish by day, and are predaceous in both adult and larval stages, feeding on other insects, snails, and the like. At one time it was believed that their light served as a warning to nocturnal birds, bats, and other insectivorous animals—a theory supported by the fact that fireflies are refused by birds in general—but it is now believed that their light is a signal to their mates. Whatever the reason may be, each species has its own characteristic light pattern so that by a little effort we can learn to identify the various species by the color of their light, the number of flashes, the intervals between the flashes, and the flight levels.

The fireflies are soft-bodied beetles of small or medium size; the antennae are each slender, eleven segmented, and sawlike; the pronotum is expanded into a thin, projecting margin that in most cases completely covers the head; the elytra are rather soft, with broad margins, and never embrace the sides of the abdomen, which has eight segments; the coxae of the middle legs touch, those of the hind legs are conical and prominent; and the tarsi each have five segments (Fig. 169).

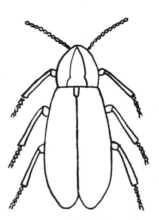

Fig. 169.   Firefly Beetle

Lucidota atra   Length: 8–11mm. Black; sides of pronotum and apex dull yellow; pronotum with two reddish or orange spots and yellowish margins. Head completely covered by pronotum; eyes small; antennae strongly compressed, second segment of each minute, transverse, not sawlike; elytra with many small, flattened elevations (Fig. 170).

On leaves and trunks of trees in open woods.

Eastern half of the United States.

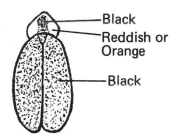

Fig. 171.   Ellychnia corrusca

Lucidota punctata   5.5–6mm. Black, with few grayish short hairs; middle and basal margin of pronotum black, remainder reddish yellow. Elytra with coarse elevations; other characters similar to those of *Lucidota atra*.

On low herbaceous plants.

Eastern half of the United States.

Ellychnia corrusca   Length: 10–14mm. Black, sometimes rusty; pronotum with reddish and yellow markings; elytra with fine yellowish pubescence. Head completely covered by pronotum; eyes small; second segment of each antenna at least one-third as long as third, third shorter than fourth; last segment of maxillary palpus triangular; last dorsal segment of abdomen squarish at apex; fourth segment of each tarsus long and lobed (Fig. 171).

On trunks of trees in open woods and on asters and goldenrod.

Generally throughout the United States.

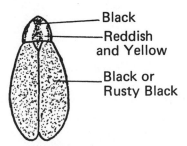

Fig. 170.   Lucidota atra

Pyropyga decipiens   Length: 5–7mm. Black, sometimes rusty; margins of pronotum pale reddish yellow. Head completely covered by pronotum; eyes small; second antennal segment of each antenna at least one-third as long as third, third as long as or slightly longer than fourth; last dorsal segment of abdomen squarish; pronotum rounded at the apex, squarish at the base; elytra appear covered with small grains.
Eastern half of the United States.

Pyractonema angulata   Length: 8–15mm. Blackish brown; pronotum yellowish with a dark middle area and margins, the yellow areas tinged with rose; lateral margins of elytra pale yellowish. Head completely covered by pronotum; eyes large; pronotum with a low middle ridge; antennae not sawlike, second segment of each antenna more than one-half as long as third, third as long as fourth; pronotum with anterior margin bluntly angular; elytra with fine elevations and each with two or three distinct ridges (Fig. 172).
Eastern third of the United States.

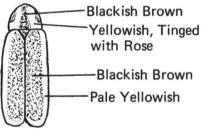

Fig. 172.   Pyractonema angulata

The following species of the genus Photinus have the head completely covered by the pronotum; the eyes are large; the antennae are slender, the second segment of each is one-half to one-third as long as the third; and the anterior margin of the pronotum is bluntly rounded.

Photinus consanguineus   Length: 8–12.5mm. Dusky or pitch colored; pronotum yellowish with a broad, elongate black spot, the spot bordered with rose; suture and side margins of elytra pale yellow; fourth ventral abdominal segment deep brown (Fig. 173).
Eastern half of the United States.

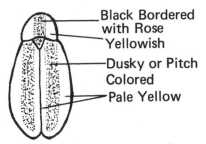

Black Bordered
with Rose
Yellowish
Dusky or Pitch
Colored
Pale Yellow

Fig. 173.   Photinus consanguineus

Photinus pyralis Length: 10–14mm. Pitch colored to brown; margins of pronotum dull yellowish, central area reddish with a black spot; margins and suture of elytra pale yellow; fourth ventral abdominal segment more or less yellowish (Fig. 174).
Eastern half of the United States.

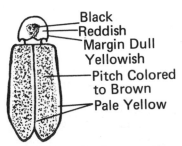

Black
Reddish
Margin Dull
Yellowish
Pitch Colored
to Brown
Pale Yellow

Fig. 174.   Photinus pyralis

Photinus marginellas Length: 6–9mm. Dull brownish; middle of pronotum reddish, with or without a brownish spot; antennae and legs dusky; fourth ventral abdominal segment more or less yellowish.
Eastern half of the United States.

Photinus scintillans Length: 5.5–8mm. Dusky brown; pronotum reddish, with yellowish margin and a central dark brown spot; suture and side margins of elytra pale yellowish (Fig. 175). One of our more common species.
Eastern half of the United States.

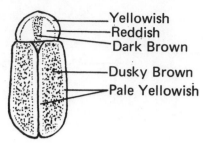

Fig. 175.   Photinus scintillans

Photurus pennsylvanicus   Length: 11–15mm. Head and pronotum dull yellowish; central part of pronotum reddish with a median black spot; elytra brownish, suture, side margins, and a narrow oblique stripe pale yellowish. Head not completely covered by pronotum; eyes large, convex, and widely separated; antennae slender, threadlike, second and third segments of each about equal and together as long as each of the succeeding segments; anterior margin of pronotum broadly rounded; both pronotum and elytra densely punctured (Fig. 176) ; this is one of our common species. Eastern half of the United States.

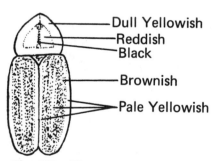

Fig. 176.   Photurus pennsylvanicus

Phausis splendicula   Length: 8–9mm. Segmented, needle-shaped appendage on the last antennal segment.
A European species found in the Eastern States.

Calyptocephalus bifaria   Length: 9–10mm. Black, with front and sides of pronotum reddish yellow; antennae have comblike projections on each side. A rare but interesting species.
Ohio and Indiana.

The Soldier Beetles

Family Cantharidae

The beetles of the family *Cantharidae,* usually known as the *soldier beetles* but sometimes called the *leather-winged* beetles, are of small to moderate size with a head that is either large and prominent and extending far beyond the anterior margin of the pronotum, or with a head that is almost completely hidden by the pronotum. The antennae are widely separated; the coxae of the middle legs touch, those of the hind legs are conical and prominent; and the fourth segment of each tarsus is lobed (Fig. 177).

The adults of many species may be found on foliage, others feed on the pollen of such plants as milkweed, goldenrod, and hydrangea, but the larvae, which are predaceous, occur for the most part beneath bark and rubbish.

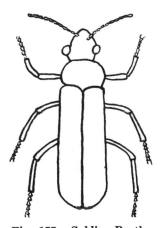

Fig. 177.   Soldier Beetle

Chauliognathus pennsylvanicus The Soldier Beetle   Length: 9–12mm. Head, lower surface, and legs black; pronotum and elytra yellow or dull orange yellow with black markings. Head prolonged before and behind eyes; mentum very long, wider in front; maxillae with a threadlike, pubescent process; maxillary palpi long and slightly dilated; pronotum wider than long (Fig. 178).
Very common especially on goldenrod in autumn.
Eastern half of the United States.

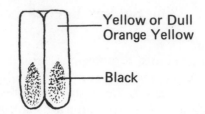

Fig. 178.   Chauliognathus pennsylvanicus

Chauliognathus marginatus   Length: 8–11mm. Dull orange yellow; head partially blackish; pronotum with a mid-dorsal black stripe; each elytron with a highly variable black spot. Except for the pronotum, which is longer than wide, other characters similar to *pennsylvanicus* (Fig. 179).

Abundant on the flowers of such plants as the hydrangea, new jersey tea, and linden; often very common but appearing earlier than *pennsylvanicus*.

Eastern half of the United States.

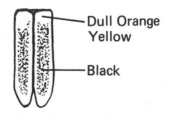

Fig. 179.   Chauliognathus marginatus

In the following species of the genus Podabrus *the head is completely exposed; the mentum is small and square shaped; the margin of the pronotum at the apex is squarish; and the elytra completely cover the wings.*

Podabrus rugulosus   Length: 7–8mm. Black; front of head and sides of pronotum yellow. Head coarsely punctured; pronotum less so; elytra coarsely wrinkled (Fig. 180); fairly common.

On leaves and flowers of various shrubs.

Eastern half of the United States.

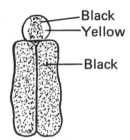

Black
Yellow

Black

Fig. 180.   Podabrus rugulosus

Podabrus modesta   Length: 9–13mm. Black or grayish black; front of head, margins of pronotum, and femora yellow. Pronotum rather wider than long, hind angles rectangular, front ones rounded, sparsely punctured; elytra densely and finely wrinkled.
Eastern half of the United States.

Podabrus tomentosus   Length: 9–12mm. Head, first segment of thorax, two basal segments of antennae, most of abdomen, and femora dull reddish yellow; rest of antennae, tibiae and tarsi blackish; elytra black with fine, grayish pubescence. Pronotum squarish, anterior angles rounded, finely and sparsely punctured; elytra rather coarsely wrinkled.
On giant ragweed; sometimes quite abundant.
Throughout the United States.

In the species of the genus Cantharis *the head is partly covered by the pronotum; the last segment of the maxillary palpus is dilated and hatchet shaped; the mentum is small and square shaped; the anterior margin of the pronotum is squarish, the hind angles are rounded; and the elytra completely cover the wings.*

Cantharis dentiger   Length: 8–9mm. Grayish black, covered with a fine grayish pubescence; pronotum yellowish, with a large transverse black spot; mouthparts, side margins of abdomen, and sometimes margins of elytra dull yellow. Pronotum sparsely and coarsely punctured; head and elytra densely and roughly punctured.
Eastern half of the United States.

Cantharis excavatus   Length: 5–6mm. Black; pronotum reddish yellow with a narrow, median black stripe, which is sometimes absent; basal third of each antenna, tibiae, tarsi, and lateral margins of elytra dull yellow. Pronotum about as long as wide, almost smooth; elytra slightly punctured.
Eastern half of the United States.

Cantharis carolinus   Length: 9–11mm. Black with a fine pubescence; pronotum reddish yellow with a large median black spot; mouthparts, three basal segments of antennae, and side margin of abdomen dull yellow. Pronotum wider than long, anterior angles rounded, posterior somewhat acute; elytra coarsely wrinkled.
On the leaves and flowers of various shrubs.
Eastern half of the United States.

Cantharis rotunicollis   Length: 12–14mm. Brownish yellow or dull reddish yellow; elytra dark gray or grayish brown. Pronotum about as wide as long, anterior angles rounded, posterior ones rectangular; elytra moderately granulate, that is, appearing as if covered with small grains (Fig. 181).
Eastern half of United States.

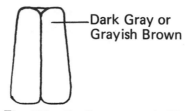

Fig. 181.   Cantharus rotunicollis

Cantharis bilineatus   Length: 6–8mm. Dull reddish yellow; back of head, elytra, spots on pronotum, tibiae, tarsi, and all but two basal segments of antennae black. Pronotum slightly wider than long, anterior angles rounded, posterior ones somewhat angular, rather coarsely punctured; elytra coarsely punctured.
Eastern half of the United States.

Cantharis lineola   Length: 4–6.5mm. Black with some grayish pubescence; pronotum orange yellow with a black stripe. Pronotum wider than long, anterior and posterior angles rounded, with minute cracks or wrinkles; elytra with apices squarish, coarsely and densely punctured.
On the foliage of a variety of shrubs and herbaceous plants and on blackberry flowers.
Eastern half of the United States.

Cantharis impressus   Length: 5–7mm. Black, shining; pronotum yellowish with a broad black stripe. Pronotum with a median, deeply

impressed line and a transverse impression on each side, anterior angles rounded; elytra coarsely and rather deeply wrinkled.
On various shrubs, such as alder, along borders of marshes.
Eastern half of the United States.

Trypherus latipennis   Length: 6–7mm. Pitch colored above, dull yellow below; antennae blackish; margins of pronotum and tips of elytra dull yellow. Mentum small and square shaped; last segment of maxillary palpus elongate and hatchet shaped; third segment of each antenna equal to second and slightly shorter than fourth; pronotum slightly wider than long, anterior margin rounded, posterior squarish; elytra short exposing the wings, apices rounded, and punctured; claws with an appendage.
On the foliage of various plants, often on catnip.
Eastern United States.

Silis latilobus   Length: 4.5–5.5mm. Black or pitch colored, slightly shining; pronotum reddish yellow. Mentum small and square shaped; head short; pronotum rounded in front and partly covering the head, hind angles notched; second antennal segment of each antenna rounded, less than one-fourth the length of the third, the third equal to the fourth.
Northcentral States.

The Pseudofireflies

Family Phengodidae
    This family includes a small number of species that were formerly included in the firefly family. In the beetles of this family, the pronotum, though rounded in front, does not cover the head, which is exposed. The antennae are usually feathery and platelike in the males. The females of some species are photogenic (Fig. 182).

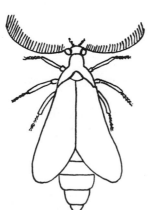

Fig. 182.   Pseudofirefly

Phengodes plumosa   Length: 11–12mm. Dull yellow with fine pubescence. Elytra small and diverging; female elongate and wormlike.
Eastern half of the United States.

The Soft-Winged Flower Beetles

Family Melyridae

The members of the family *Melyridae* are small or very small
beetles that resemble the *Lampyridae,* but they are not as elongate in form nor do they have any light-producing organs. They
have soft wing covers; the antennae each have eleven segments, are
sometimes sawlike (those of some males being curiously knotted),
and are inserted on the front of the head at the sides, usually before the eyes; the head is prolonged into a short, broad beak; the
mentum is small and square shaped; the elytra are entire and more
or less squarish at the apices; the abdomen has five or six visible
segments; the coxae of the front legs touch and are conical; and
each tarsus is threadlike and five segmented, the claws each usually with a membranous lobe (Fig. 183).

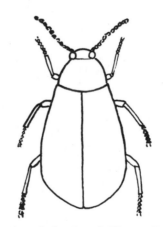

Fig. 183.   Soft-winged Flower Beetle

The adults of many of the *soft-winged flower beetles* are found
on flowers and herbage, others only on the ground in low, moist
places. In some species the adults are provided with soft, orange
colored vesicles that they can protrude from the sides of the abdomen, which are supposed to be scent organs for defense. The larvae occur generally beneath the bark on tree trunks and on dead
animals, and feed, as do the adults, on insect eggs, larvae, and soft-
bodied insects.

The following species of the genus Collops *seemingly have only ten segments in each antenna, the second segment being very small and hidden.*

Collops tricolor Length: 4–5mm. Head and legs black; antennae dark reddish brown; pronotum and abdomen reddish yellow; elytra a uniformly deep blue or bluish black (Fig. 184).
Eastern half of the United States.

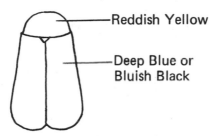

—Reddish Yellow

—Deep Blue or Bluish Black

Fig. 184. Collops tricolor

Collops vittatus The Striped Collops Length: 4–5mm. Black; pronotum, suture and sides of elytra, and underparts of body reddish yellow; pronotum sometimes with a central black spot, and each elytron with a broad blue stripe (Fig. 185).
Throughout much of the United States.

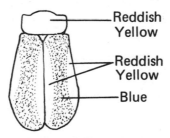

—Reddish Yellow

—Reddish Yellow

—Blue

Fig. 185. Collops vittatus

Collops quadrimaculatus Length: 4–6mm. Head and abdomen black; pronotum and elytra reddish yellow, each elytron with a blue or bluish black spot at the base and near the apex (Fig. 186). On grasses and herbaceous plants in damp places.

Throughout much of the United States, especially east of the Rockies.

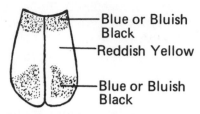

Fig. 186.   Collops quadrimaculatus

Collops nigriceps   Length: 6–8mm. Head black; lower surface black except abdominal segments which are rellowish brown; antennae and femora yellowish; pronotum dull yellow with a black spot in the middle; elytra blue or bluish black.
On herbaceous plants and various flowers.
Eastern half of the United States.

Malachius aeneus   Length: 6–7mm. Metallic green, shining; pronotum with anterior angles reddish; elytra brownish red or brown orange, with bases and a stripe along suture metallic green. Pronotum somewhat square shaped, slightly wider than long, minutely wrinkled; elytra densely wrinkled; antennae inserted on front of head nearly between the eyes; last segment of each tarsus with two membranous appendages beneath each claw (Fig. 187).
Eastern half of the United States.

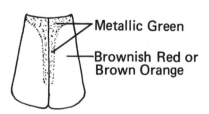

Fig. 187.   Malachius aeneus

Pseudebaeus oblitus   Length: 1.5–2mm. Pitch colored to bluish black, shining; antennae and legs pale yellowish. Antennae inserted at anterior edge of front of head near sides; pronotum wider than

long and densely, finely punctured; elytra broadened posteriorly and densely wrinkled.
Canadian border to Florida.

The species of the genus Attalus *have the antennae inserted at the anterior edge of the front of the head near the sides and have the labrum as long as the clypeus, with the pronotum slightly wider than long.*

Attalus terminalis Length: 2–3mm. Black, shining; slightly pubescent; tips of elytra in male pale yellowish, in female black. Pronotum sparsely and finely punctured; elytra coarsely and rather densely punctured.
Eastern half of the United States.

Attalus scinctus Length: 2.5–3mm. Dull yellow; back of head, a median stripe on pronotum, scutellum, and a sutural stripe on elytra blackish; antennae, legs, and lower surface of body yellowish. Pronotum finely and sparsely punctured; elytra densely wrinkled (Fig. 188).
On the flowers of dogwood, haw, wild rose, and viburnum.
Eastern half of the United States.

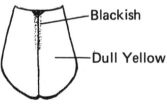

Blackish

Dull Yellow

Fig. 188. Attalus scinctus

The Checkered Beetles

Family Cleridae
The *checkered beetles* are for the most part small, active, and attractive, many of them being beautifully marked with strongly contrasting colors that have suggested the common name for them. Some of them are more or less antlike in form and in such cases the prothorax is narrower than either the head or the wing covers. Each antenna, ten or eleven segmented, is either thickened gradually toward the tip or has a knob at the end, is usually sawlike, and is inserted at the sides of the frontal region; the elytra are usually

entire or nearly so and rather soft; the abdomen has either five or six ventral segments; the coxae of the front legs are conical, prominent, and usually touch, those of the hind legs are transverse and not prominent; the legs are slender; and the tarsi are each five segmented, the first and fourth each often being minute, first to fourth each with membranous lobes (Fig. 189).

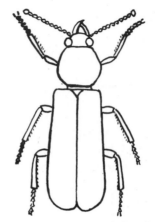

Fig. 189.   Checkered Beetle

The adult beetles, which are usually pubescent, are found on flowers, foliage, trunks of trees, and about flowing sap. They are predaceous as are the larvae, which live within the burrows of wood borers and under bark; the larvae are especially useful in keeping wood borers and bark beetles in check.

The species of the genus Phyllobaenus *have the maxillary palpi cylindrical, the last segment of each tapering slightly; the labial palpi are elongate, the last segment of each dilated; each antenna is threadlike, with the club somewhat spherical and two segmented; the tarsi are each seemingly four segmented, the fourth about the same size as the third; and the tarsal claws are toothed.*

Phyllobaenus humeralis   Length: 3.5–5.5mm. Violet or bluish black; elytra dark blue, shoulder angles usually reddish orange; antennae and legs generally reddish. Pronotum wider than long and constricted near the base and apex; elytra densely and coarsely punctured. Eastern half of the United States.

Phyllobaenus verticalis   Length: 3.5–5mm. Head mostly pale yellow and usually with a black spot on the vertex; antennae and legs pale yellowish; pronotum brownish yellow sometimes with a white spot or stripe on each side; elytra dull yellow at the bases but frequently completely black. Pronotum cylindrical and coarsely punctured; elytra narrowed to tips and coarsely, densely punctured.
Eastern half of the United States.

Phyllobaenus pallipennis Length: 3.5–5mm. Black, somewhat bronzed; mouthparts, antennae, legs, and elytra brownish yellow; each elytron with blackish markings on the sides, at the apex, along the suture, and across its middle. Pronotum slightly wider than long and constricted at the base and apex, sparsely punctured; elytra shorter than abdomen, widest at the bases, and coarsely, densely punctured (Fig. 190).
Eastern half of the United States.

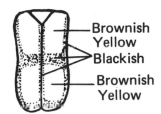

Fig. 190.   Phyllobaenus pallipennis

Zenodosus sanguineus Length: 4.5–6.5mm. Head, pronotum, and lower surface brown or brownish black; apical segments of antennae, legs, and abdomen usually dull red; elytra bright orange red or crimson, rather dull. Head and pronotum densely punctured; elytra coarsely and deeply punctured; maxillary palpi compressed, last segment of each tapering; labial palpi triangular, last segment of each dilated; club of each antenna three segmented; tarsi each apparently four segmented, last segment as long as preceding combined (Fig. 191).
A beautiful species; found under bark and sometimes in moss.
Northeastern half of the United States.

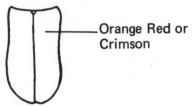

Fig. 191.   Zenodosus sanguineus

Placopterus thoracicus Length: 5–7mm. Black, sometimes tinged with bluish or violet; pronotum and occasionally front of head reddish yellow, the pronotum with a large black spot. Pronotum much wider than head, constricted at base, with scattered fine punctures; elytra coarsely and densely punctured; eyes deeply notched; last segment of maxillary palpus elongate and cylindrical; last segment of each labial palpus longer than the other, dilated and triangular; club of each antenna three segmented; tarsi each with apparently four segments, tarsal claws toothed.
On foliage in damp meadows.
Eastern half of the United States.

Thanasimus dubuis Length: 7–9mm. Reddish brown or dull orange; elytra largely black except at the bases, with two white cross bands; antennae and legs varying from red to black. Pronotum slightly wider than long, constricted at base and apex, and with a deep, transverse groove, densely and finely punctured; elytra coarsely punctured at the bases, finely and densely punctured at the apices; eyes notched (Fig. 192); maxillary palpi threadlike, last segment of each

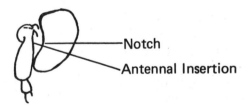

Fig. 192.   Eye of Thanasimus

tapering; last segment of each labial palpus elongate and triangular; club of each antenna three segmented; tarsi each apparently four segmented, the fourth about equal in size to the third; tarsal claws each with a broad tooth (Fig. 193).

On flowers and herbage.

Eastern half of the United States.

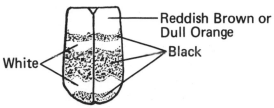

Fig. 193.   Thanasimus dubuis

Enoclerus nigripes   Length: 5–7mm. Dull red or reddish brown; apical two-thirds of each elytron black and each with white bands; antennae and legs dark brown. Pronotum somewhat square shaped, constricted at base, finely and densely punctured; elytra coarsely and densely punctured at the bases. Eyes notched; maxillary palpi slender; labial palpi dilated; club of each antenna three segmented, last segment of each sickle shaped; tarsi each seemingly four segmented, fourth segment of each equal in size to third, third and fourth segments of tarsi of hind legs dilated; tarsal claws toothed (Fig. 194).

One of the most common of the checkered beetles; found on various trees in late spring and early summer.

Throughout the eastern half of the United States.

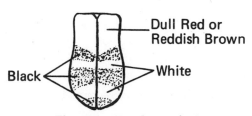

Fig. 194.   Enoclerus nigripes

Enoclerus rosmarus   Length: 4–7mm. Brownish orange or yellowish brown; elytra each with two black crossbands separated by a curved

white one; abdomen black and shining; apices of elytra usually yellowish white (Fig. 195).
Usually found on horseweed.
Throughout the eastern half of the United States.

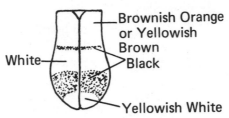

White—
Brownish Orange or Yellowish Brown
Black
Yellowish White

Fig. 195. Enoclerus rosmarus

Trichodes nutalli Length: 8–11mm. Dark blue, purplish, or greenish blue; elytra blue black each with three yellow or reddish yellow crossbands, antennae and mouthparts brown. Pronotum bell shaped, sparsely and coarsely punctured; elytra coarse and irregularly punctured; eyes notched; club of each antenna three segmented and triangular; last segment of maxillary palpus longer and somewhat wider than preceding; labial palpi dilated; tarsi each seemingly four segmented (Fig. 196).
On flowers and foliage.
Eastern half of the United States.

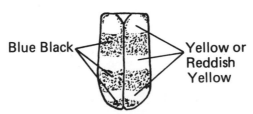

Blue Black
Yellow or Reddish Yellow

Fig. 196. Trichodes nutalli

Trichodes ornatus Length: 6–7mm. Metallic blue with three yellow bars across each elytron; structural characters similar to *T. nutalli*.
Throughout most of the Western States.

Monophylla terminata   Length: 4–7mm. Black, somewhat shining; pronotum and elytra marked with yellow; abdomen of male wholly yellow, last segment in female black. Last segment of each antenna more than half the length of the whole antenna; elytra with scattered punctures.
Southern States.

Cymatodera bicolor   Length: 6–10mm. Black, rather dull; pronotum, legs, and first two segments of antennae reddish yellow marked with black. Elytra with punctures in rows.
Eastern half of the United States.

Priocera castanea   Length: 6.5–10mm. Head, pronotum, and legs chestnut brown, shining; elytra reddish brown with black and yellow markings. Eyes notched; antennae sawlike; tarsi each seemingly with only four segments; tarsal claws toothed.
Eastern half of the United States.

Clerus ichneumoneus   Length: 8–11mm. Head, pronotum, and elytra brick red; elytra with a median band of yellowish margined with black; antennae, legs, and much of underparts black. Eyes notched; club of each antenna three segmented; last segment of maxillary palpus slender; tarsi each seemingly with only four segments; tarsi of hind legs each dilated (Fig. 197).
Eastern half of the United States.

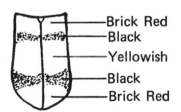

Fig. 197.   Clerus ichneumoneus

Hydnocera unifasciata   Length: 3.4–4.5mm. Bluish black; each elytron with a white crossband. Club of each antenna small, spherical and two segmented; tarsi each seemingly with only four segments; tarsal claws toothed (Fig. 198).
Throughout the United States.

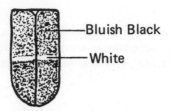

Fig. 198.　Hydnocera unifasciata

The Bone Beetles

Family Corynetidae

The members of this family are known as *bone beetles* because they are usually found on carrion after most of the flesh has been removed, presumably feeding on other insects rather than on the carrion itself. They were at one time members of the *Cleridae,* which they closely resemble, but were separated and placed in a family of their own. However, there are authors who would like to return them to the *Cleridae* and, as a matter of fact, some have already done so. The characteristic distinguishing the bone beetles from the checkered beetles is that the fourth segment of each tarsus in the bone beetles is atrophied or rudimentary (Fig. 199).

The bone beetles feed not only on drying carrion and bones but also on fish, cheese, and cereals, and hence often become pests.

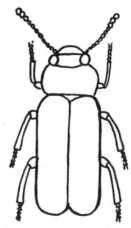

Fig. 199.　Bone Beetle

The following three species of the genus Necrobia *are known as* ham beetles *because they are often found on that staple; they also occur on other substances like those mentioned. All three are found throughout the United States.*

Necrobia ruficollis   Red-Shouldered Ham Beetle   Length: 4–5mm. Front of head and three-fourths of elytra metallic blue or green; base and lower surface of head, pronotum, legs, and bases of elytra red or brownish red. Club of each antenna small, compact, and three segmented; last segment of maxillary palpus oval; tarsal claws toothed (Fig. 200).

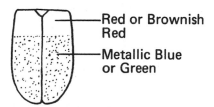

Fig. 200.   Necrobia ruficollis

Necrobia rufipes   Red-legged Ham Beetle   Length: 3.5–6mm. Metallic blue or green, shining; antennae dark brown; legs reddish brown (Fig. 201).

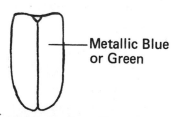

Fig. 201.   Necrobia rufipes

Necrobia violacea   Violet Ham Beetle   Length: 3–4.5mm. Metallic dark blue or green; antennae black; legs bluish black.

Phlogistoternus dislocatus   Length: 3.5–6mm. Dark brown to black;

antennae and legs yellowish brown; elytra variable, but each usually with an oblique pale yellow stripe that extends from shoulder to suture, then along suture to just behind the middle where it connects with a yellow crossband. Last three segments of antennae large, flat, and dilated; eyes notched; pronotum somewhat cylindrical, widest at base, rather densely and finely punctured; elytra with rows of densely placed coarse punctures; tarsal claws toothed (Fig. 202).
On flowering shrubs and on the dead branches of ash, butternut, and hickory.
Eastern half of the United States.

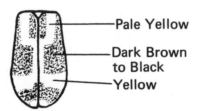

Fig. 202. Phlogistoternus disclocatus

Orthopleura damicornis Length: 4–9mm. Black; pronotum reddish yellow; elytra sometimes with an indistinct, pale crossbar. Last three segments of antennae large, flat, and dilated; eyes notched; first segment of each antenna small and concealed from above by overlapping second segment, each antenna eleven segmented; elytra with many coarse punctures (Fig. 203).
Throughout the United States.

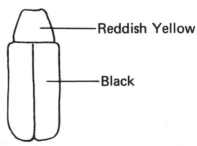

Fig. 203. Orthopleura damicornis

Cregya oculatus   Length: 4–6.5mm. Black, shining; pronotum and elytra yellow with black markings; legs yellow. Last three segments of antennae large, flat, and dilated; eyes notched; pronotum widest behind its middle, then abruptly constricted.
Eastern half of the United States.

Pelonides quadripunctata   Length: 5–7mm. Black; elytra bright red, each with two black spots. Last three segments of each antenna large, flat, and dilated, each antenna ten segmented; eyes notched; pronotum widest behind its middle, then abruptly constricted (Fig. 204)
Throughout the Central States.

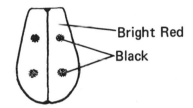

Fig. 204.   Pelonides quadripunctata

Chariessa pilosa   Length: 7–13mm. Black; pronotum reddish with black markings. Last three segments of each antenna large, flat, and dilated; eyes notched; elytra widening toward apices, then abruptly rounded, densely and finely punctured (Fig. 205).
Eastern half of the United States.

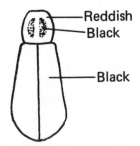

Fig. 205.   Chariessa pilosa

The Reticulated Beetles

Family Cupesidae

This is a small family and one of the lesser known, with only one species, which is widely distributed.

The beetles are small, flattened insects covered with scales. The head is furnished with tubercles and constricted, forming a distinct neck; the pronotum is small and square shaped; the elytra have rows of large square punctures, the intervals are ridged; and the tarsi each are five segmented, with a spongy pad.

The adult beetles occur mostly beneath the bark of decaying trees and in old frame houses; the larvae live mostly in dead or decaying wood.

Cupes concolor   Length: 7–11mm. Pale brownish or ashy gray, densely covered with small scales, the elytra beautifully sculptured in sunken rows separated by ridges. Head with four tubercles; pronotum wider than long; with a median longitudinal ridge, and a deep impression on each side (Fig. 206).
Eastern half of the United States.

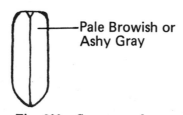
Pale Browish or Ashy Gray

Fig. 206.   Cupes concolor

The Oedemerid Beetles

Family Oedemeridae

The beetles of this family are of moderate size, elongate and narrow in form, and soft bodied. The head is prolonged; the antennae are long and slender, threadlike, each with eleven to twelve segments, sometimes sawlike; the palpi are each four segmented, the last segment of each is dilated; the pronotum is narrower than the elytra, which are soft in texture and smooth or with fine punctures and silky hair; the coxae of the front legs are large, conical, and touching, and those of the middle legs are prominent; each of the

tarsi has the next to last segment dilated and with a dense brush
of hairs, each of those of the front and middle legs are five segmented, and those of the hind legs are each four segmented; and
the tarsal claws are toothed (Fig. 207).

The adult beetles are generally found on flowers and foliage but
some live on the ground near water, others beneath debris, and
still others on decaying stumps and logs. The larvae occur in decaying wood.

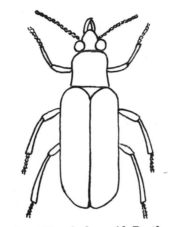

Fig. 207.   Oedemerid Beetle

Nacerda melanura Length: 8–12mm. Dull yellow above; legs and
lower surface largely pitch colored; elytra deep purple at apices
(Fig. 208). Pronotum narrowed posteriorly and coarsely and dense-

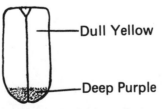

Fig. 208.   Nacerda melanura

ly punctured; each elytron with four elevated lines, finely and densely punctured; fourth segment of maxillary palpus elongate and triangular; tibiae of front legs each with a single spur (Fig. 209). Common in cellars, woodsheds, and lumberyards.

A cosmopolitan species, originally European, and now found throughout the United States.

Spur

Fig. 209.   Tibia of Front Leg of Nacerda Showing One Spur

Alloxacis dorsalis   Length: 10–13mm. Pale yellowish white to dull yellow; pronotum with a dark median stripe and another on side margins; each elytron with two longitudinal stripes uniting near apex, sometimes these stripes are broken or absent altogether (Fig. 210). Pronotum with two pits on each side on anterior half, dense-

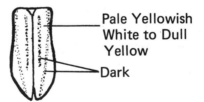

Pale Yellowish
White to Dull
Yellow

Dark

Fig. 210.   Alloxacis dorsalis

ly and finely punctured; elytra with wrinkles, densely finely punctured; right mandible with two equal lobes; maxillary palpi threadlike, last segment of each tapering; tibiae of front legs each with two spurs; tarsal claws toothed (Fig 211).

Rather common beneath or in wet boards, timber, and the like. Eastern half of the United States.

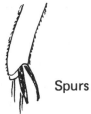

Spurs

Fig. 211. Tibia of Front Leg of Alloxacis Showing Two Spurs

Asclera ruficollis Length: 5–6.5mm. Black; pronotum completely red. Pronotum wider than long, sides narrowed toward the apex, oblique towards the base, with three pits; each elytron with three distinct longitudinal ridges; both mandibles each with two equal lobes; last segment of maxillary palpus triangular; tibiae of front legs each with two spurs; tarsal claws toothed (Fig. 212).
Common on dogtooth violet, wild plum, willow catkins, and other plants.
Central States.

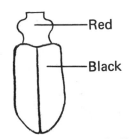

Red

Black

Fig. 212. Asclera ruficollis

Copidita thoracica Length: 5–7mm. Reddish yellow pronotum and purplish or blue elytra.
Throughout the Central and Southern States.

The Tumbling Flower Beetles

Family Mordellidae
    The common name of the members of this family is quite descriptive of their behavior, for when disturbed on the flowers on which they occur they fly, run, tumble, or jump off the flowers in

their efforts to escape. They are small, arched, wedge or spindle shaped, with the head bent downward, with the body usually ending in a conical or pointed process, and with long, flattened, spiny hind legs that are admirably fitted for leaping. The body is densely covered with fine silky hairs and is usually black but sometimes brown, often spotted or banded with yellow or silver; the maxillary palpi are each four segmented; the antennae each have eleven segments, are slender, somewhat thickened toward the tips, and are inserted at the sides of the frontal region before the eyes; the pronotum is narrowed anteriorly and is as wide as the elytra at its base; the elytra are narrowed and pointed at the apices; the coxae of the front legs are large, conical, and touch, those of the hind legs are flat, usually very large, and also touch; the tarsi of the front and middle legs are each five segmented, each of those of the hind legs are four segmented; and the tarsal claws may be either simple or cleft (Fig. 213).

The adult beetles occur on flowers or on dead trees and are very active. The larvae live in old wood or in the pith of plants, some, it is believed, being carnivorous in habit.

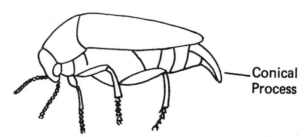

Conical
Process

Fig. 213.   Tumbling Flower Beetle

Tomoxia bidentata   Length: 10–13mm. Brown; pronotum with four ashy gray stripes radiating from middle of front margin; each elytron with three or four stripes basally, a broken band behind its middle, and an apex ashy gray with a large brown spot. Abdomen with last segment prolonged, cone shaped; claws cleft and comblike; antennae sawlike; last segment of maxillary palpus more or less elongate and triangular; scutellum notched; anal style short and blunt (Fig. 214). On dead trees.
Throughout the United States.

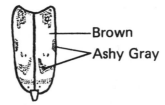

Fig. 214.   Tomoxia bidentata

Tomoxia lineela   Length: 5–7mm. Brown with markings of ashy gray. Throughout much of the United States.

The species of the genus Mordella *have the last segment of the abdomen prolonged and conical; the tarsal claws are cleft and comb-like; each of the tibiae of the hind legs has a small ridge; the scutellum is triangular; the anal style is long and slender; and the femora of the hind legs are stout and flat.*

Mordella octopunctata   Length: 6–7mm. Black or dark grayish; pronotum with a network of grayish yellow hairs; each elytron with four yellowish spots (Fig. 215).
Throughout the United States.

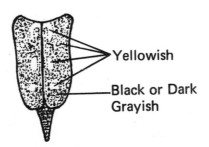

Fig. 215.   Mordella octopunctata

Mordella marginata   Length: 3–4.5mm. Black or dark gray; pronotum with margins and stripes of silvery or ashy gray; elytra with small silvery spots (Fig. 216).
On the flowers of various shrubs such as new jersey tea, wild hydrangea, and dogwood.
Throughout the United States.

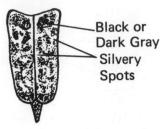

Fig. 216.   Mordella marginata ·

Mordella melaena   Length: 5–7mm. Deep velvety black; bases of elytra and lower surface of body with pubescence that is more or less iridescent.
On the flowers of the wild rose.
Eastern half of the United States.

Mordella atrata   Length: 3–6mm. Black with brownish pubescence.
On various composites, such as asters, sunflowers, dandelions, and goldenrod.
Eastern half of the United States.

Mordella discoidea   Length: 2–3mm. Black; pronotum yellow with a black central spot; elytra each with a large shoulder spot, a band in back of the middle, and each tip all yellow; antennae, legs, and top of head yellow.
Central and Southern States.

Mordella serval   Length: 4–4.5mm. Blackish brown; pronotum and elytra mottled with yellowish pubescence; antennae and front legs yellow.
Eastern half of the United States.

The species of the genus Mordellistena *have the last segment of the abdomen prolonged and conical; the tarsal claws are cleft and comblike; the tibiae and the tarsi of the hind legs have oblique ridges; the scutellum is rounded; and the anal style is long and slender.*

Mordellistena scapularis   Length: 3.5–5mm. Black; elytra each with a reddish orange shoulder spot; apex of abdomen bright reddish (Fig. 217).
Western two-thirds of the United States.

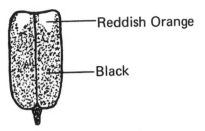

Fig. 217.   Mordellistena scapularis

Mordellistena pubescens   Length: 2.5–3mm. Black, with brownish pubescence; pronotum black or reddish yellow with a black spot; elytra each with a yellow spot on the shoulder and two yellowish crossbands (Fig. 218).
On various flowering herbaceous plants.
Throughout the United States.

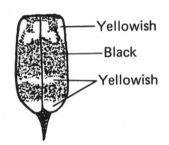

Fig. 218.   Mordellistena pubescens

Mordellistena marginalis   Length: 3–4mm. Black; head and pronotum reddish yellow, head usually spotted with black and pronotum with some black markings.
On various flowering herbaceous plants.
Throughout the United States.

Mordellistena comata   Length: 2.8–3.2mm. Black; head mostly or wholly reddish; pronotum brick red, usually with an oblong black spot near the base; front and middle legs dull yellow in part.
Throughout the United States.

Mordellistena aspera   Length: 2–3mm. Black, with brownish gray pubescence.
Throughout the United States.

Mordellistena trifasciata   Length: 2.3–2.8mm. Black; pronotum with margin at base and sides dull yellow; head dull yellow; legs and abdomen tinged with yellow; elytra each with two yellowish crossbands (Fig. 219).
Eastern half of the United States.

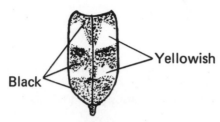

Fig. 219.   Mordellistena trifasciata

Mordellistena andreae   Length: 2.5–3mm. Yellow; pronotum sometimes black at base; front legs yellow; tibiae and tarsi of hind legs dull yellow; elytra each with base, apex, suture, and a large marginal spot all black (Fig. 220).
Eastern half of the United States.

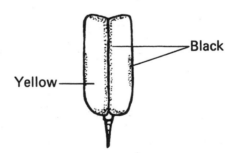

Fig. 220.   Mordellistena andreae

Pentaria trifasciatus   Length: 3–4mm. Head, pronotum, legs, and bases of antennae dull reddish yellow; elytra yellow, each with base, apex, and a broad band behind its middle dark brown, the band sometimes absent. Complete upper surface finely wrinkled and covered with short prostrate hairs. Eyes notched; anal style absent;

fourth tarsal segment of each hind leg slightly shorter than third; tarsal claws not cleft (Fig. 221).
Eastern half of the United States.

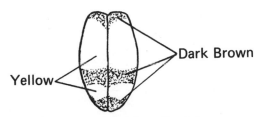

Fig. 221. Pentaria trifasciatus

Anaspis rufa. Length: 3–4mm. Head yellow or blackish; antennae and abdomen brownish black or yellow; elytra dull reddish yellow. Anal style absent; fourth segment of each of the tarsi of front and middle legs small; tarsal claws not cleft (Fig. 222).
On the flowers of spiraea, maple, sour gum.
Throughout the United States.

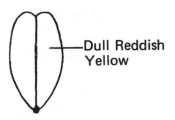

Fig. 222. Anaspis rufa

Anaspis flavipennis Length: 3–4mm. Black; tibiae, tarsi, and mouthparts brownish yellow; elytra pale brownish yellow (Fig. 223).
On viburnum, haw, and huckleberry.
Throughout the eastern half of the United States.

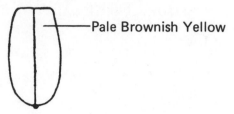

Fig. 223.   Anaspis flavipennis

The Rhipiphorid Beetles

Family Rhipiphoridae

This is a small family whose members resemble the tumbling flower beetles in general appearance. They are wedge shaped, the antennae are comblike or fan shaped in the males, usually sawlike in the females, and the elytra are usually shorter than the abdomen and narrowed behind (Fig. 224).

The adult beetles are found on flowers and under bark or dead logs. The larvae are parasites on bees, wasps, and cockroaches.

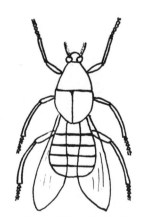

Fig. 224.   Rhipiphorid Beetle

Rhipiphorus fasciatus   Length: 4–6mm. Black; legs and elytra yellowish. Vertex with a median ridge; pronotum conical with a median impressed line and densely punctured; elytra widely separated and only one-third as long as abdomen.

Central and Northeastern States.

Macrosiagon limbatum   Length: 6–10mm. Head, pronotum, lower surface, femora and tibiae of middle and hind legs reddish yellow; pronotum with oval black spot and elytra each either completely black or with pale yellow in its middle. Elytra not much shorter than abdomen (Fig. 225).
Eastern half of the United States.

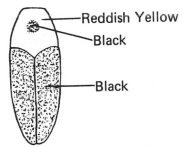

Fig. 225.   Macrosiagon limbatum

Macrosiagon dimidiatum   Length: 6–10mm. Black with pale yellow elytra, which are blackened at the tips.
Often found on the flowers of mountain mint.
Eastern half of the United States.

The Blister Beetles

Family Meloidae

The members of the family *Meloidae* are known as *blister beetles* because they were once used in making blister plasters. The beetles were killed, dried, and pulverized, and the powder that resulted was made into a paste that produced a blister when applied to the skin. The species most generally used was a European one and known as the "Spanish fly." The active substance, *cantharidin*, used as a counterirritant, occurs chiefly in the elytra. Some of our species are able to cause blisters when they come in contact with the skin.

The blister beetles are of moderate to large size, elongate and slender with the body and the elytra comparatively soft in texture. The head is broad, vertical, and abruptly narrowed into a neck; the antennae are each eleven segmented and are inserted at the sides of the frontal region; the pronotum is narrower than the elytra; the elytra are sometimes shortened; the legs are long and slender; the coxae of the front and middle legs are large, conical, and touching; the tarsi of the front and middle legs have five segments, those of the hind legs four segments; and the tarsal claws each usually has a long appendage (Fig. 226).

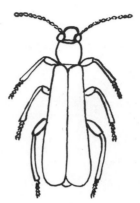

Fig. 226.　Blister Beetle

The adult beetles occur on foliage and flowers on which they feed, sometimes being quite destructive; the *old-fashioned potato bug* is one of the more destructive members of the family and often does considerable damage to various crops. The larvae, on the other hand, feed on the eggs of various insects and are especially useful in keeping grasshoppers under control.

The species of the genus Epicauta *have a silky pubescent patch beneath the apex of each of the femora of the front legs; the first antennal segment is usually shorter than the third; and the next to last segment of each of the tarsi is cylindrical.*

Epicauta vittata Striped Blister Beetle Length: 12–18mm. Upper surface dull yellow, underparts and legs black; head and pronotum with two brownish black stripes; each elytron with two stripes of brownish black. Head wider than pronotum; head and pronotum finely and somewhat densely punctured; elytra densely and finely granulate (Fig. 227).
This species is a serious pest to gardens.
Central and Northeastern United States.

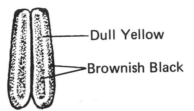

Fig. 227.   Epicauta vittata

Striped Blister Beetle; Epicauta vittata

Epicauta pennsylvanica Black Blister Beetle Length: 7–15mm. Dull black; sparsely covered with black pubescence. Pronotum square shaped, anterior angles rounded, a distinct median impressed line; scutellum very small; complete surface densely and finely punctured;

tibiae of front legs each with two spinelike spurs (Fig. 228).
Very common on goldenrod and other fall plants.
Throughout the United States.

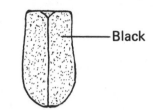

Fig. 228.   Epicauta pennsylvanica

Epicauta ferruginea   Length: 4–9mm. Black, moderately shining; elytra covered with dense gray or grayish yellow pubescence. Pronotum as wide as long, coarsely and densely punctured; antennal segments of equal thickness throughout; each tarsal claw cleft to base.
Throughout the United States but principally in the West.

Epicauta trichrus   Length: 8–11mm. Black, covered with short, rather dense, black or gray pubescence, which often forms a marginal stripe and, rarely, one on the suture of the elytra; usually red behind the eyes or there may be a small red spot in front; antennae threadlike; each tarsal claw cleft to base.
On various plants especially members of the morning glory family.
Atlantic States to Texas.

Epicauta cinera   Gray Blister Beetle   Length: 10–18mm. Black, covered with gray hairs throughout. Antennae each with segments on apical half slender, loosely united, and more or less compressed; a serious garden pest being found on potatoes and other plants.
Northeastern and Central United States.

Epicauta marginata   Margined Blister Beetle   Length: 10–18mm. Black elytra having gray margins and suture and with a black spot on the pronotum; may be merely a variety of *cinera*, though there are some authors that regard it as a distinct species. However it may be, it is a serious garden pest being found on potatoes and other plants (Fig. 229).
Northeastern and Central United States.

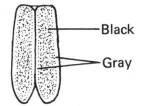

Fig. 229.   Epicauta marginata

Margined Blister Beetle; Epicauta marginata

Epicauta maculata   Spotted Blister Beetle   Length: 10–14mm. Black, but so covered with ashy gray hairs that elytra appear as if with numerous black spots (Fig. 230).
On potato, clover, and other plants.
Eastern half of the United States.

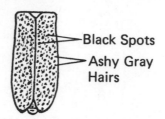

Fig. 230.   Epicauta maculata

Epicauta murina   Ash Gray Blister Beetle   Length: 8–15mm. Black, densely covered with grayish hairs. First segment of each antenna much enlarged; pronotum somewhat longer than broad.
A common pest of gardens.
Eastern half of the United States.

Epicauta albida   Two-spotted Blister Beetle   Length: 14–20mm. Gray or yellowish, the pronotum with two nearly parallel lines.
A serious pest of various garden crops.
Eastern half of the United States.

Pomphopoea sayi   Length: 13–19mm.   Uniformly   dark   metallic green; antennae pitch colored; legs brownish orange, each femur and tibia at apex and base with black rings. Pronotum bell shaped, with scattered fine punctures and with a slight impression in the middle at its base; elytra extremely long, about five times as long as pronotum and coarsely and densely wrinkled with dense fine punctures interspersed; labrum with deep notch.
On the flowers of various trees like shadbush and apple.
Eastern half of the United States.

Pomphopoea aena   Length: 10–16mm. This species is somewhat similar to *sayi* being metallic green, with pitch colored antennae, and bright yellow legs (Fig. 231).
On blossoms of apple and related plants.
Eastern half of the United States.

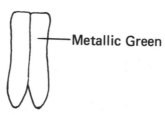

Fig. 231.   Pomphopoea aena

The species of the genus Meloe *have the elytra short, with one elytron overlapping the other, thus exposing much of the soft abdomen; there are no hind wings. The head is wider than the pronotum; the legs are rather short; the tibial spurs are long; and the tarsal claws are cleft.*

These beetles are called oil beetles *because they give off a disagreeable oily fluid when disturbed. They are usually found in early spring or late autumn.*

Meloe angusticollis Length: 12–15mm. Head and pronotum dark blue; elytra and abdomen violet or violet tinted. Pronotum longer than wide (Fig. 232); elytra shallowly wrinkled.
Eastern half of the United States.

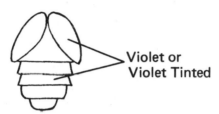

Fig. 232. Meloe angusticollis

Meloe americanus Length: 15–24mm. Bluish black, shining. Pronotum densely punctured; elytra roughly sculptured.
Eastern half of the United States.

Meloe impressus Somewhat smaller than *americanus* and dull black, the pronotum with an impression on basal half of median line.
Eastern half of the United States.

The species of the genus Zonitis *have the mandibles projecting beyond the labrum and acute at the tips.*

Zonitis vittigera Length: 9–11mm. Reddish yellow; antennae, tibiae, and tarsi blackish; each elytron with a black stripe; outer lobe of each of the maxilla bristlelike and prolonged (Fig. 233).
Central and Western States.

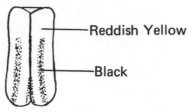

Fig. 233.   Zonitis vittigera

Zonitis punctalata flavipennis   8–11mm. Orange yellow, thinly covered with yellow hairs; much of the lower surface and much of the antennae and tarsi are blackish; outer lobe of each of the maxilla bristlelike and prolonged.
Eastern half of the United States.

Zonitis bilineata   Length: 7–9mm. Dull brownish yellow; elytra yellowish white, each one with a median blackish stripe not fully reaching either base or apex; does not have outer lobe of each of the maxilla prolonged (Fig. 234).
Eastern half of the United States.

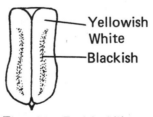

Fig. 234.   Zonitis bilineata

The Fire Colored Beetles

Family Pyrochroidae
The beetles of this family are called the *fire colored beetles* because they usually have some "fire color" on them. They are of moderate size, flattened, with soft elytra; the head is constricted behind the eyes into a distinct neck; the eyes are notched; the antennae each have eleven segments and are inserted at the sides of the frontal region just anterior to the eyes; the antennae are also sawlike or somewhat comblike in the females and fanlike in the males; the elytra are wider than the pronotum at their bases; the coxae of the

front legs are large, conical, and touching; and the tarsi each have next to last segment dilated (Fig. 235).

These beeles are found about dead or decaying trees and often come to lights. The larvae are found beneath the bark of the same trees.

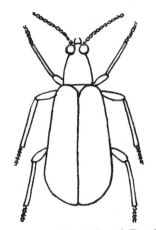

Fig. 235.   Fire Colored Beetle

Neopyrochroa flabellata   Length: 15–17mm. Reddish or reddish yellow, except the elytra and most of the antennae which are black. Last segment of maxillary palpus broad and square shaped; eyes occupying almost whole side of head; pronotum wider than long with rounded sides and angles and with a broad median impression at the base; elytra each wider behind its middle, finely punctured (Fig. 236), with sparse pubescence.
On foliage in open woodlands and sometimes beneath bark.
Eastern half of the United States.

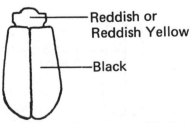

Reddish or
Reddish Yellow

Black

Fig. 236.   Neopyrochroa flabellata

Neopyrochroa femoralis   Length: 14–17mm. Head and pronotum yellowish red; elytra bluish black with scattered pubesecnce; lower surface, tibiae, tarsi, and palpi blackish.
Throughout the United States.

Schizotus cervicalis   Length: 6–8mm. Blackish, covered with fine yellowish hairs; front of head, pronotum, and sutural and marginal lines on elytra reddish. Pronotum one-half wider than long with rounded sides and angles and a broad median groove, finely and densely punctured; elytra densely punctured; last segment of maxillary palpus oval (Fig. 237).
Eastern half of the United States.

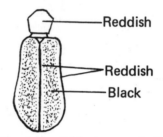

Fig. 237.   Schizotus cervicalis

Dendroides concolor   Length: 9–13mm. Uniformly pale brownish yellow. Pronotum longer than wide with a median impression at base and sparsely, minutely punctured; elytra coarsely, rather densely punctured and each one has three indistinct ridges; eyes very large; last segment of maxillary palpus rounded at apex (Fig. 238).
Beneath bark.
Eastern half of the United States.

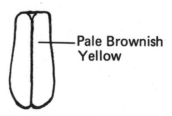

Fig. 238.   Dendroides concolor

Dendroides cyanipennis Length: 9–13mm. Reddish yellow; head and elytra pitch colored. Structural characters somewhat similar to *concolor*.

Also found beneath bark.

Eastern half of the United States.

The Antlike Flower Beetles

Family Anthicidae

Many members of this family resemble ants in the form of the body and in being able to run about rapidly, but others are quite different in body form and have a peculiar hornlike structure projecting forward on the pronotum (Fig. 239). They are small to me-

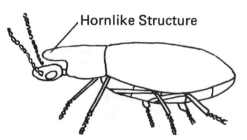

Fig. 239.   Antlike Flower Beetle

dium size with a head constricted into a slender neck; the antennae each usually have eleven, rounded segments and are inserted before the eyes on the front of the head; the pronotum is narrower than the elytra, which are rounded at the apices; the coxae of the front legs are conical, prominent, and touching, those of hind legs are transverse; and the tarsi each have the next to last segment usually notched.

The adult beetles occur in spring and summer on the flowers and foliage of various trees and shrubs and under stones, logs, and debris, as well as in burrows, usually in moist and sandy places. The larvae live in decaying plant material and fruit. Some of them are predaceous and it is believed that the adults are too.

The species of the genus Notoxus *have the pronotum near the apex prolonged into a hornlike process; the mandibles are notched; the antennae are threadlike; the coxae of the middle legs are touching; and the next to last segment of each of the tarsi is somewhat dilated.*

Notoxus talpa Length: 3.5–4mm. Antennae, pronotum, and legs dull reddish brown; head, undersurface, and elytra pitch colored; each elytron with an oblique, pinkish spot extending from shoulder to middle of suture and another of same color on apical third. Pronotum oval, somewhat wider than long; horn broad and sawlike, crest strongly elevated and slightly scalloped; elytra finely punctured (Fig. 240).

Frequently found on the foliage of oak and hazel.

Eastward from the Rockies.

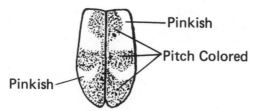

Fig. 240. Notoxus talpa

Notoxus bifasciatus Length: 3–3.8mm. Pitch colored, shining; antennae and legs usually reddish brown; elytra each with two pale yellowish or pinkish crossbands; slightly pubescent. Pronotum sphere shaped, slightly wider than long; horn distinctly margined and slightly sawlike, crest abruptly elevated; elytra sparsely punctured, apices rounded (Fig. 241).

On the flowers of dogwood and wild cherry.

Eastern States westward to Arizona.

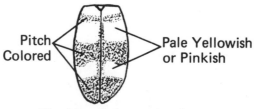

Fig. 242. Notoxus monodon

Notoxus monodon Length: 2.5–4mm. Dull brownish yellow; elytra each with a crossband, one spot at the base of each, and sometimes

with a spot at the apex all blackish. Pronotum oval, slightly wider than long, sparsely and finely punctured; horn broad, margined, and sawlike, crest elevated and granulate; elytra coarsely and densely punctured with both long and short grayish hairs (Fig. 242).
On foliage and beneath stones and rubbish in sandy situations. Throughout the United States.

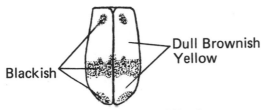

Fig. 241.   Notoxus bifasciatus

Notoxus murinipennis   Length: 3.5mm. Head brownish black; pronotum, legs, and undersurface reddish yellow; elytra purplish black with fine, prostrate grayish pubescence. Pronotum oval, slightly wider than long; horn broad, obtuse at apex, coarsely toothed, crest finely sawlike; elytra finely punctured with apices rounded.
Eastern half of the United States.

Tomoderus constrictus   Length: 2.5–3mm. Dark reddish brown to pitch colored, shining; sparsely pubescent; antennae dark reddish brown, legs somewhat paler; basal half of each elytron reddish brown. Pronotum longer than wide, constricted behind middle; elytra each finely punctured on apical half, more coarsely toward base, apex rounded; antennae made up of beadlike segments; next to last segment of each tarsus with two lobes (Fig. 243).
Eastern half of the United States.

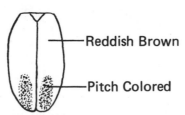

Fig. 243.   Tomoderus constrictus

The species of the genus Anthicus *have the last segment of the maxillary palpus hatchet shaped; the antennae are threadlike with the apical segments more or less beadlike; and the next to last segment of each tarsus has two lobes.*

Anthicus cervinus   Length: 2.4–2.7mm. Reddish brown, slightly shining, sparsely and finely pubescent; antennae and legs dull yellow; elytra each with two pitch colored bands on apical half enclosing a rounded, pale yellow spot on apical third (Fig. 244).
Beneath stones and rubbish in sandy places.
Eastern half of the United States.

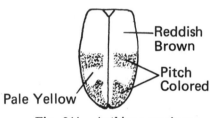

Fig. 244.   Anthicus cervinus

Anthicus sturmii   Length: 2.5–3mm. Dark reddish brown, covered with fine pubescence; elytra each pitch colored, the basal third reddish and with a crossband of longer gray hairs.
Connecticut west to Iowa.

Anthicus floralis   Length: 3–3.5mm. Reddish brown, shining; head, abdomen, and apical two-thirds of elytra pitch colored.
A European species found throughout the United States.

Anthicus pubescens   Length: 2.7–3mm. Black or dark brown with yellowish hairs.
Eastern half of the United States.

Anthicus cinctus   Length: 3–4mm. Dark reddish brown, shining; elytra black each with a reddish base and a pale transverse band in front of each middle broken at the suture.
Central States.

The Pedilid Beetles

Family Pedilidae

The *pedilid beetles* are rather small, usually black, elongate, cylindrical forms that were once included in the *Anthicidae*. In this family the head is constricted behind the eyes into a neck; the eyes are large and usually notched; the base of the pronotum is narrower than the elytra; the coxae of the front legs are conical and prominent, those of hind legs are touching or very close together; and the tarsi each have the next to the last segment lobed (Fig. 245).

These beetles may often be found on the flowers of various plants, but sometimes under leaves.

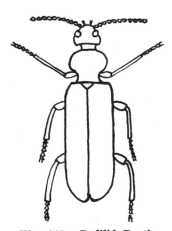

Fig. 245.   Pedilid Beetle

Pedilus labiatus Length: 6–8mm. Pitch colored to black, slightly shining; palpi, labrum, and first two segments of each antenna pale yellow; pronotum marked with reddish yellow (Fig. 246). Eastern two-thirds of the United States.

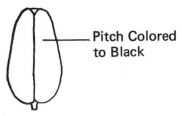

Pitch Colored to Black

Fig. 246.   Pedilus labiatus

Pedilus lugubris   Length: 6–8mm. Black; first two segments of each antenna and labrum reddish brown.
Throughout the United States.

Macratria confusa   Length: 4–4.5mm. Dark gray, thickly covered with silky, yellowish hairs; antennae and legs dull yellow.
Connecticut west to Iowa.

The Euglenid Beetles

Family Euglenidae
   The members of this family are small or minute beetles that resemble those of the families *Pedilidae* and *Anthicidae*. In these beetles the head is constricted behind the eyes into a neck; the pronotum is narrower at its pronotal base than the elytra; the coxae of the front legs are conical and prominent; and the second to last segment of each tarsus is bilobed.
   The beetles are found on leaves and flowers.

Zonantes fasciatus   Length: 2–2.5mm. Black; antennae, labial and maxillary palpi, legs, and tips of elytra dull yellow; elytra marked with reddish yellow (Fig. 247).
Eastern half of the United States.

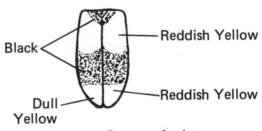

Fig. 247.   Zonantes fasciatus

Phomalis brunnipennis   Length: 2mm. Dark brown; head, pronotum, and middle and hind legs pitch colored with short, dense, yellowish gray pubescence.
Throughout the United States.

The Cedar Beetles

Family Rhipiceridae
   The beetles of this family are called *cedar beetles* because they

are most commonly found on cedars. The pronotum is as wide at its base as the elytra; the antennae are threadlike, sawlike in the females and often fan shaped in the males; the coxae of the front legs are conical and prominent, the coxae of the hind legs are transverse and dilated into a small plate that partly covers the femora (Fig. 248).

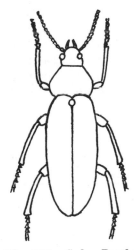

Fig. 248.   Cedar Beetle

Zenoa picea Length: 11–15mm. Dark reddish or blackish brown. Each elytron with four raised lines and a short oblique one on each side of the scutellum (Fig. 249).
Throughout the eastern half of the United States.

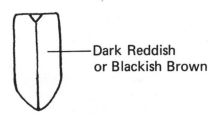

Fig. 249.   Zenoa picea

Sandalus niger Length: 21–24mm. Black, slightly shining. Elytra with faint ridges.
Throughout the Central States.

The Click Beetles

Family Elateridae

The *click beetles* are mostly small or of medium size and most of them are of a uniform brownish color, though others are black or grayish, and still others are conspicuously spotted or rather brilliantly colored. Some Southern species have luminous spots.

The beetles are called *click beetles* because they have the singular ability of springing into the air with a clicking sound if placed on their backs. When a beetle finds itself on its back or in an upside-down position, it bends itself up on a loose hinge between the pro and mesothorax. Then with a sudden snap it bends itself in the opposite direction with such force that it is tossed several inches into the air, making a clicking sound as it does so, and at the same time turning over several times so that when it lands it invariably lands on its feet.

The "clicking" device is a simple one and consists essentially of a long spine on the posterior end of the prosternum that fits into a groove on the mesosternum (Fig. 250). When in action the spine

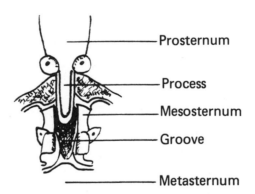

— Prosternum

— Process

— Mesosternum

— Groove

— Metasternum

Fig. 250.   **Part of Lower Surface of a Click Beetle Showing Long Process that fits into a Groove**

is inserted into the groove by the lifting of the prothorax and by its sudden release, the insect is propelled into the air. This unique trick has won for the beetles various names such as *skipjacks, spring beetles, snapping bugs,* as well as the more familiar *click beetles.*

The body of the click beetles is elongated, somewhat flattened, and tapers more or less toward each end. The antennae each have eleven segments, are more or less sawlike, and are inserted into pits before the eyes; the legs are slender; the tarsi each have five segments; and the coxae of the front legs are small and rounded, while those of the hind legs are transverse and touching (Fig. 251).

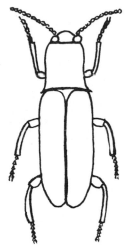

Fig. 251.   Click Beetle

The adult beetles are found on leaves and flowers of herbaccous plants and on the leaves of trees and shrubs; quite frequently they are found in decaying logs. Most species are plant feeders but some species are carnivorous.

The larvae are long, narrow, and cylindrical, have a very hard cuticula, are brownish or yellowish in color, and are called *wireworms* because of their appearance. Some of the wireworms live under the bark of trees and in rotten wood, but many of them are found in the ground where they feed on the seeds and the roots of grass and grain. Indeed, there is hardly a cultivated plant that they do not attack and, moreover, they attack them at the most susceptible time, when the plants have not grown to a sufficient size and strength to withstand them. Many fields of corn or other grain have been destroyed even before the seeds have had a chance to germinate; potatoes and other root crops have been damaged by the insects eating holes in them.

The family is a large one and includes some 8,000 species of which more than 500 have been described from North America alone.

The species of the genus Lepidotus *have deep grooves on the underside of the prothorax for the reception of the antennae when not in use.*

Lepidotus obtectus Length: 14–16mm. Dark reddish brown to pitch colored. Pronotum oblong with sides gradually curved from base to apex and deeply and broadly grooved in the middle; elytra each with two indistinctly raised lines at the base.
Beneath bark.
Eastern half of the United States.

Lepidotus marmoratus Length: 15–17.5mm. Dark reddish brown, sparsely covered with dull yellow and black scales; elytra with irregular spots of brown and yellow scales. Pronotum somewhat square shaped with a deep median groove, posterior angles acute, densely and coarsely punctured; elytra each gradually but slightly narrowed from base to apex, densely and rather coarsely punctured; deep grooves on the underside of prothorax for reception of front tarsi when at rest (Fig. 252).
Under bark of logs in moist woods.
Eastern half of the United States.

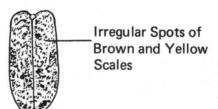

Irregular Spots of Brown and Yellow Scales

Fig. 252. Lepidotus marmoratus

Lepidotus discoideus Length: 8–11mm. Black, somewhat shining; head and margins of pronotum covered with golden scales. Pronotum oblong, sides nearly straight, with a deep median groove, densely and coarsely punctured; elytra densely covered with coarse punctures; grooves on the underside of prothorax for reception of front tarsi shallow.
Under bark and in dead logs.
Eastern half of the United States.

Alaus oculatus The Eyed Click Beetle Length: 25–45mm. Black, shining, with many small irregular spots of silvery scales. Pronotum with two large, velvety black spots (eyespots) surrounded by a ring of gray scales; scutellum oval; elytra distinctly striate, intervals finely and sparsely punctured; tarsal claws each with one or more bristles at the base (Fig. 253).

In decaying logs in open wooded areas or orchards. Eastern United States west to the Rockies.

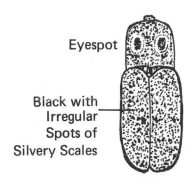

Fig. 253. Alaus oculatus

The Eyed Elater; Alaus oculatus
(Courtesy of Henry B. Kane, the Massachusetts Audubon Society)

Alaus myops   Length: 24–38mm. Similar to *oculatus* but somewhat smaller; eyespots also smaller and narrower and only indistinctly margined with grayish scales.
Usually beneath the bark of dead pine trees.
Southern States.

In the species of the genus Conoderus *the first segment of each antenna is rather elongate; the coxae of the hind legs are strongly expanded at the middle; the margin of the front of the head is elevated; the femora are toothed; and the fourth segment of each tarsus is lobed.*

Conoderus lividus   Length: 11–17mm. Dull brown, densely covered with short prostrate pubescence; antennae reddish brown; legs yellowish. Pronotum slightly longer than broad, widest at middle, tapering to apex, sides undulate, densely coarsely punctured; elytra with deep striae and oblong punctures; lobe of fourth segment of each tarsus very broad (Fig. 254).
On trees and shrubs, especially walnut and hickory.
Central and Southern States.

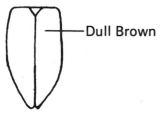

Fig. 254.   Conoderus lividus

Conoderus vespertinus   Tobacco Wireworm   Length: 7–10mm. Color variable but usually dark reddish brown or yellowish to pitch colored above; head with a black spot; pronotum yellow in the center and on the sides; elytra each with a broad yellow stripe extending from shoulder to beyond its middle, with a yellow spot at the apex, these markings sometimes reduced to small spots; scutellum yellowish. Pronotum slightly longer than wide, sides slightly curved, posterior angles acute, coarsely punctured; elytral striae and intervals indistinctly punctured (Fig. 255).
Adults found on mullein; larvae injurious to tobacco, beans, cotton, and other crops.
Throughout the United States.

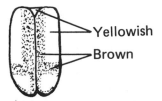

Yellowish

Brown

Fig. 255. Conoderus vespertinus

Tobacco Wireworm, adult; Conoderus vespertinus

Tobacco Wireworm, larva; Conoderus vespertinus

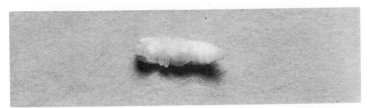

Tobacco Wireworm, pupa; Conoderus vespertinus

Conoderus auritus Length: 5–7mm. Color varying from uniformly pitch colored to red or brownish red, with black margins on pronotum and elytra; two basal segments of each antenna and legs yellow. Pronotum slightly longer than wide, sides slightly curved, densely and rather coarsely punctured; elytral striae and intervals punctured (Fig. 256).

In mullein leaves and beneath logs and dead leaves.
Eastern half of the United States.

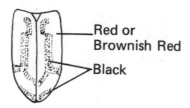

Red or
Brownish Red
Black

Fig. 256. Conoderus auritus

Conoderus bellus Length: 3.5–4.5mm. Black, sparsely covered with yellow pubescence; hind angles and a median line of pronotum reddish; elytra dull red, each irregularly marked with two or three crossbars; antennae and legs yellow. Pronotum slightly longer than wide, narrow towards the apex, sides slightly curved, hind angles obtuse, sparsely and rather coarsely punctured; elytra tapering to apices, striae punctured.

Under rubbish in moist places.
Eastern half of the United States.

Aeolus dorsalis Length: 4–4.5mm. Reddish brown; head, scutellum, a median, diamond-shaped spot on pronotum, a spot before the middle of each elytron, and an apical crossband on each elytron all black. Pronotum slightly longer than wide, coarsely punctured; elytral striae and intervals punctured; coxae of hind legs dilated near middle (Fig. 257).

Throughout the United States.

Reddish Brown

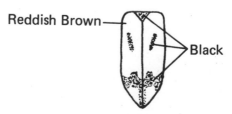

Black

Fig. 257. Aeolus dorsalis

The species of the genus Limonius *have the front of the head margined and elevated above the labrum and have the tarsal segments gradually getting shorter beginning with the first segment.*

Limonius griseus   Length: 10–14mm. Dark brown or grayish, densely covered with grayish yellow pubescence on head and pronotum, elytra less so. Pronotum slightly longer than wide, narrowed towards the apex; elytral striae coarsely punctured.
On various herbaceous plants as well as on the flowers of rhubarb.
Eastern half of the United States.

Limonius interstitialis   Length: 13–18mm. Blackish brown, somewhat bronzed with sparse yellow pubescence. Pronotum square shaped, hind angles acute, densely and coarsely punctured; elytral striae finely punctured, intervals more coarsely punctured.
Under stones and debris as well as on foliage.
Eastern half of the United States.

Limonius basillaris   Length: 4–5.5mm. Black, with some grayish pubescence; hind angles of pronotum and legs reddish yellow. Pronotum slightly longer than wide, sides slightly curved; elytrae striae deeply punctured; clypeus notched.
On oaks.
Eastern half of the United States.

Athous cucullatus   Length: 10–12mm. Dark brown or dark reddish brown; antennae and legs somewhat paler. Pronotum longer than wide, hind angles rounded, densely and coarsely punctured; elytral striae and intervals sparsely punctured; front of head margined and elevated behind labrum; coxae of hind legs dilated near middle; first segment of each of the tarsi of hind legs elongate and as long as second and third together; second and third tarsal segments lobed (Fig. 258).
Eastern half of the United States.

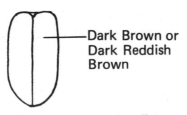

Dark Brown or Dark Reddish Brown

Fig. 258.   Athous cucullatus

Athous scapularis   Length: 9–11mm. Dull black with fine scattered pubescence; pronotum and thorax marked with reddish yellow.
Throughout the eastern half of the United States.

Athous brightwelli   Length: 11–18mm. Pale, dull brown with scattered yellowish hairs.
Throughout the eastern half of the United States, but as far west as the Rockies.

Denticollis denticornis   Length: 11–13mm. Dark brown with long, yellow pubescence; part of head, lateral and apical margins and median line of pronotum, and side margins of elytra yellow or reddish. Pronotum wider than long, hind angles acute, coarsely and densely punctured; elytra strongly wrinkled; tarsi of hind legs with first segment of each elongate; second segment of each antenna spherical.
On herbaceous plants in damp situations.
Eastern half of the United States.

The species of the genus Ctenicera *have the front of the head somewhat flattened; the coxae of the hind legs are dilated near the middle; and the tarsal segments are pubescent.*

Ctenicera cylindriformis   Length: 11.5–19mm. Blackish brown with some gray pubescence, slightly bronzed and shining; antennae, front and hind margins of pronotum, and sutural stripe of elytra reddish. Pronotum of male longer than wide, densely punctured; pronotum of female square shaped, sparsely punctured; elytral striae sparsely punctured, intervals densely punctured; each third antennal segment three times as long as second and triangular, antennae sawlike.
On various plants usually close to the ground and under stones in fields.
Eastern half of the United States.

Ctenicera hieroglyphica   Length: 11–13mm. Dark brown with grayish yellow pubescence; hind angles of pronotum and legs dull yellow; elytra yellowish, each with two crossbands and a longitudinal stripe of black. Pronotum slightly longer than wide, sides curved or rounded, coarsely and densely punctured; elytral striae and intervals coarsely punctured; antennae sawlike, third segment of each cylindrical (Fig. 259).
On foliage of trees and shrubs.
Eastern half of the United States.

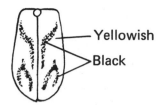

Fig. 259. Ctenicera hieroglyphica

Ctenicera tarsalis Length: 9–12mm. Black, shining, sparsely pubescent; legs yellowish; elytra dull yellow, suture and lateral margins edged with black. Pronotum longer than wide, densely and rather coarsely punctured along the sides, less so in the middle, hind angles obtuse; elytral striae coarsely punctured, intervals finely so; second segment of each antenna very small, third triangular (Fig. 260). On blossoms of fruit trees.
Eastern half of the United States.

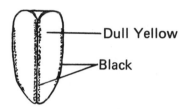

Fig. 260. Ctenicera tarsalis

Ctenicera pyrrhos Length: 18–23mm. Dark reddish brown, elytra somewhat paler, with sparse, pale yellowish pubescence. Pronotum longer than wide, coarsely and densely punctured along the sides, less so in the middle; elytral striae deep and coarsely punctured; intervals nearly flat and finely punctured; third segment of each antenna equal to fourth and nearly three times as long as second.
On various trees, especially walnut and hickory.
Eastern half of the United States.

Ctenicera inflata Length: 8–12mm. Black, with dense yellowish pubescence. Pronotum somewhat square shaped, sides rounded, coarsely and densely punctured; elytral striae moderately deep and finely punctured, intervals flat and finely punctured; third segment of each antenna more than twice as long as second.
On foliage in open woods.
Throughout the United States.

Hemicrepidius decoloratus Length: 9–15mm.   Black,   sometimes bronzed, shining, with yellow pubescence; base of pronotum some-times reddish; elytra often dark reddish brown. Pronotum longer than wide, rather sparsely and finely punctured, hind angles with a ridge; elytral striae and intervals finely punctured; second and third segments of tarsi with prominent lobes.
On leaves of various plants; sometimes on asparagus.
Throughout the United States.

Hemicrepidius memnonius Length: 12–22mm.   Pale   brown   to blackish, with sparse yellow pubescence; antennae and legs some-what paler. Pronotum square shaped, rather densely and coarsely punctured, hind angles with a ridge; elytral striae coarsely punc-tured, intervals more densely punctured; second and third seg-ments of tarsi with prominent lobes (Fig. 261).
On leaves of various plants.
Eastern half of the United States.

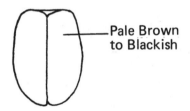

Pale Brown to Blackish

Fig. 261.   Hemicrepidius memnonius

Hemicrepidius bilobatus Length: 13–16mm. Chestnut brown, shin-ing; antennae and legs paler. Elytra with coarsely punctured striae, intervals with two rows of fine punctures.
Throughout the Central States.

Hypolithus obliquatulus Length: 2.3–4mm. Dark orange brown to pitch colored; antennae and legs yellowish; each elytron with a me-dian crossband of yellow and an oval spot of the same color at the apex. Pronotum wider than long, sides rounded, posterior angles acute, sparsely punctured; elytra without striae and more finely punctured than pronotum; margin of front of head elevated behind labrum; tarsal segments with stiff hairs (Fig. 262).
Beneath stones and logs in sandy areas.
From Iowa eastward.

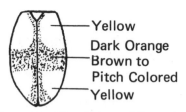

Fig. 262. Hypolithus obliquatulus

Hypolithus choris Length: 3–5mm. Black with scattered yellow hairs and elytra marked with yellow.
Sandy areas.
Throughout the eastern half of the United States.

Melanactes piceus Length: 23–32mm. Black, smooth, shining. Pronotum slightly longer than wide, narrowed at base and apex, sides densely punctured, middle less so; elytra without striae but with rows of punctures; antennae sawlike, third segment of each usually slightly longer than fourth; tarsal segments each with a dense brush of hairs.
Beneath stones and debris in dry situations.
Throughout the United States.

Dalopius lateralis Length: 5–8mm. Pitch colored or brownish black, with yellow pubescence; legs and basal segments of antennae yellowish; apex and hind angles of pronotum yellowish; elytra with yellowish longitudinal stripes. Pronotum square shaped, hind angles acute; elytral striae punctured, intervals flat and finely and densely punctured; front of head convex and bent downward at nearly a right angle; antennae slender and somewhat sawlike (Fig. 263).
On the foliage of trees and on various flowers.
Eastern half of the United States.

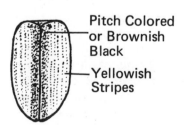

Fig. 263. Dalopius lateralis

The species of the genus Agriotes *have the front of the head very convex and bent downward at nearly a right angle; the an-*

tennae are slender and somewhat sawlike; the pronotum has side margins bent downward toward the apex; and the coxae of the hind legs are toothed above the insertion of each femur.

Agriotes mancus The Wheat Wireworm   Length: 7–9mm. Yellowish brown with scattered short yellow pubescence; antennae and legs slightly paler. Pronotum slightly wider than long, sides rounded, coarsely and densely punctured with a slight median impressed line at the base; elytral striae with large, deep punctures, intervals finely punctured (Fig. 264).
The larva is a serious pest of wheat, corn, potatoes, and other crops. Eastern half of the United States.

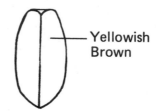

Fig. 264.   Agriotes mancus

Agriotes oblongicollis   Length: 6–9mm. Dark reddish brown with yellowish pubescence; antennae and legs somewhat paler. Pronotum longer than wide, hind angles with a ridge, coarsely and densely punctured; striae of elytra deep with oblong punctures, intervals minutely punctured.
On the foliage of various plants.
Eastern half of the United States.

Agriotes pubescens   Length: 8–10mm. Sooty brown, densely covered with grayish yellow pubescence. Striae of elytra with fine punctures, intervals with fine wrinkles.
Eastern and Central United States.

The species of the genus Ampedus *are more or less wedge shaped; the margin of the front of the head is elevated behind the labrum; the hind angles of the pronotum have a distinct ridge; the scutellum is rounded; and the tarsi are as long as the tibiae.*

Ampedus nigricollis   Length: 8–12mm. Black, with some yellow pubescence; antennae pale reddish brown; legs reddish; elytra dull yellow. Pronotum longer than wide, hind angles acute, coarsely and densely punctured; elytral striae with large punctures, each interval with a double row of setal punctures; antennae comblike with second segment of each antenna globular, third triangular (Fig. 265).

Beneath bark in decayed logs in moist woodlands.

Eastern half of the United States.

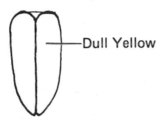

Fig. 265.   Ampedus nigricollis

Ampedus linteus Length: 7.5-11mm. Black, with some yellow pubescence; antennae and legs pitch colored; elytra grayish yellow with apices and suture black. Pronotum with acute hind angles and coarsely punctured; elytral striae coarsely punctured, intervals minutely punctured; antennae sawlike, second segment of each antenna globular (Fig. 266).

Beneath the bark of logs in dry, sandy places.

Eastern half of the United States.

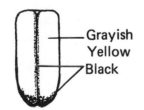

Fig. 266.   Ampedus linteus

Ampedus rubricus Length: 7-9mm. Black, with a few yellow hairs; part of pronotum red. Pronotum slightly wider than long, sides slightly rounded, hind angles acute, coarsely but sparsely punctured; striae of elytra deep and coarsely punctured, intervals with few fine punctures; antennae sawlike, fourth segment of each antenna triangular.

On the flowers and foliage of various shrubs such as viburnums.

Eastern half of the United States.

Ampedus sanguinipennis   Length: 7–8.5mm. Black, with brown pubescence; elytra scarlet to dull red. Pronotum with acute hind angles, coarsely and sparsely punctured; striae of elytra with coarse, deep punctures, intervals minutely punctured; antennae sawlike, second segment of each antenna globular, fourth triangular (Fig. 267). Beneath loose bark in moist woodlands.
Eastern half of the United States.

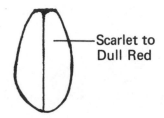

Fig. 267.   Ampedus sanguinipennis

Ampedus collaris   Length: 8–9mm. Black, shining, with sparse yellow pubescence; pronotum red. Pronotum slightly longer than wide, hind angles acute, finely and sparsely punctured; elytral striae deeply and coarsely punctured, intervals finely and sparsely punctured; antennae sawlike, third segment of each shorter than fourth. On foliage.
Eastern half of the United States.

The species of the genus Melanotus *have the margin of the front of the head elevated behind the labrum; the antennae are sawlike, the coxae of the hind legs are toothed above the insertion of each femur, and the tarsal claws are comblike.*

Melanotus fissilis   Length: 13–17mm. Dark smoky brown with scattered pubescence. Pronotum square shaped, sides rounded, hind angles acute and ridged; elytra narrowed to apices; elytral striae punctured, intervals sparsely so; third segment of each antenna at least twice as long as second.
Beneath loose bark and rubbish.
Throughout the United States.

Melanotus castanipes   Length: 15–21mm. Dark reddish brown with scattered pubescence. Pronotum somewhat square shaped, sides slightly rounded, hind angles acute and ridged, coarsely and densely punctured; elytra with parallel sides and with rows of punctures.
Beneath the bark of pine.
Throughout the United States.

Melanotus communis Length: 11–15mm. Reddish brown, with some pubescence. Pronotum somewhat square shaped, sides rounded, hind angles acute and ridged, rather finely punctured; elytra gradually tapering to apices, striae punctured, intervals finely so; third segment of each antenna twice as long as second (Fig. 268).
Larvae very destructive to corn and potatoes.
Eastern half of the United States.

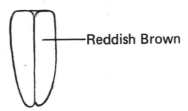

Fig. 268.   Melanotus communis

The heart-shaped scutellum distinguishes the species of the genus Cardiophorus *from other click beetles.*

Cardiophorus cardisce Length: 5.5–8mm. Black, with rather dense, short, yellow hairs; each elytron with two yellow spots (Fig. 269).
Eastern half of the United States.

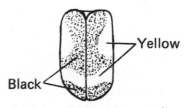

Fig. 269.   Cardiophorus cardisce

Cardiphorus convexus Length: 8–10mm. Black, shining, with dense yellow pubescence; basal segments of antennae, hind angles of pronotum, and legs reddish.
On foliage and beneath stones.
Eastern half of the United States.

Cardiophorus gagates Length: 5–8mm. Black and shining with some grayish yellow pubescence.
Throughout the eastern half of the United States.

The Melasid Beetles

Family Melasidae

The *melasid beetles,* also known as the *cross-wood borers,* were once members of the *Elateridae* but they differ from the click beetles in having the labrum concealed and the antennae somewhat farther from the eyes (Fig. 270). The adults are found on the leaves of plants or under bark, the larvae in wood that is just beginning to decay. The larvae excavate burrows across the grain of the wood, hence their common name of cross-wood borers. Most species of this family are rather rare.

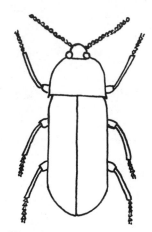

Fig. 270. Melasid Beetle

Melasis pectinicornis Length: 6–8mm. Dull black and thinly covered with short gray pubescence; antennae reddish brown. Pronotum wider than long, sides wavy, hind angles acute, a distinct impressed line in the middle, coarsely punctured; elytra with deep punctured striae and acute apices; last segment of maxillary palpus acute (Fig. 271).

Beneath the bark of various hardwoods.

Connecticut south to Florida and west to Texas.

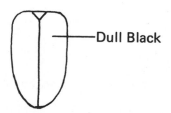

Fig. 271. Melasis pectinicornis

Melasis rufipennis Length: 8–12mm. Black with reddish elytra and antennae.
Very destructive to trees in the Pacific Coast States.

Microrhagus pectinatus Length: 4.5–5mm. Pitch colored, somewhat shining; legs brownish with paler tibiae and tarsi. Pronotum wider than long, sides parallel, hind angles with a ridge, coarsely punctured; elytra same width as pronotum at its base, densely and coarsely punctured; last segment of maxillary palpus dilated.
In decayed logs, especially those of elm.
Eastern half of the United States.

Microrhagus triangularis Length: 3–4mm. Black with brownish legs and antennae.
From the Canadian border south to Georgia.

Sarpedon scabrosus Length: 6–8mm. Black with the front margins of the pronotum reddish. Antennae of male each with two comblike teeth, that of female each with two sawlike teeth; last segment of maxillary palpus dilated.
Throughout the United States.

Isorhipis obliqua Length: 4–7mm. Black with reddish brown antennae; legs and the elytra marked with hellow. Elytral striae densely and roughly punctured; last segment of maxillary palpus pointed.
Throughout the United States.

The Pseudo Click Beetles

Family Throscidae
This family includes a few small, oblong, black or brownish beetles that resemble the click beetles in form and in having the prosternum prolonged behind into a spine, which fits into a cavity in the mesosternum. They differ, however, in having the prothorax firmly fixed to the mesothorax so that they do not have the ability of leaping and snapping.

In these beetles the antennae each have eleven segments, are inserted in the front of the head, and, in repose, are received into grooves along the inner margins of the prosternum; the head is retracted to the eyes in the pronotum; the mouthparts when in rest are covered by an anterior rounded lobe of the prosternum; the coxae of the front and middle legs are small and rounded, those of the hind legs are transverse and dilated into a plate partly covering the femora; and the tarsi are short each with five segments, the first four segments of each with long lobes. The larvae occur in worm-eaten wood and are probably predaceous.

The adults are usually found on flowers and on dead wood and are not easily seen because of their small size.

Drapetes geminatus   Length: 4mm. Black, shining, with very sparse pubescence; elytra each with a crossbar or dot of red on basal half. Pronotum as wide at base as long, narrowing to apex, sparsely and coarsely punctured; elytra not striate but finely punctured; antennae sawlike (Fig. 272).
On various flowers such as those of milkweed.
Eastern half of the United States.

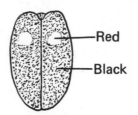

Fig. 272.   Drapetes geminatus

Throscus chevrolati   Length: 2.5–2.8mm. Reddish brown, densely covered with coarse yellowish pubescence. Pronotum nearly twice as wide as long, narrow toward the apex, rather finely and sparsely punctured; elytra narrowed behind their middle, stria distinctly impressed and punctured, each interval with two rows of fine punctures; antennae each ending in a three-segmented club (Fig. 273). Eastern and Central United States.

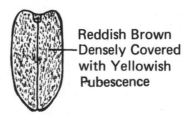

Fig. 273.   Throscus chevrolati

The Metallic Wood-Boring Beetles

Family Buprestidae

The *metallic wood-boring beetles* or *buprestids* vary greatly in size and shape. The larger species are usually elliptical and somewhat flattened, the smaller are either elongate-cylindrical or broadly ovate. Many of them are bronzed and metallic in color or reflection, others are rather gaudily marked with red or yellow bands or spots. Their bodies are hard and inflexible and many of them have the upper surface deeply grooved or pitted.

The antennae each have eleven segments, are short and rather slender, with fine sawlike teeth; the head is retracted into the prothorax, which is rigidly attached to the remainder of the body so that the wood-boring beetles, unlike the click beetles, are unable to leap into the air; the elytra cover the abdomen or nearly so, leaving one segment exposed; the coxae of the hind legs are expanded into a plate that partially covers the femora; and the tarsi each have five segments (Fig. 274).

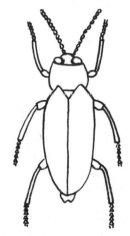

Fig. 274. Metallic Wood-boring Beetle

The adults delight to bask in the hot sunshine and may be found on tree trunks, flowers, leaves, and branches. Most of them are active and fly readily when disturbed, others drop to the ground and feign death.

The larvae are wood borers, usually living under bark and making rather shallow burrows, galleries, or chambers. They are very elongated in shape and somewhat flattened with the anterior segments so enlarged as apparently to form part of the head, thus giving rise to the common names of *flat-headed borers* or *hammerheads*. They are very destructive to orchard and forest trees.

Acmaeodera pulchella Length: 5.5–12mm. Deep brown, shining, slightly bronzed; pronotum with an orange or yellow spot near the hind angles; elytra black, reflexed with metallic colors and variable orange yellow markings. Pronotum wider than long, apex and base squarish, a basal pit on each side, densely and coarsely punctured; side margins of elytra sawlike, striae finely punctured, each interval with a row of punctures bearing short, brownish hairs; each antenna sawlike from fifth segment; tarsal claws toothed (Fig. 275).
On flowers, especially those of the new jersey tea.
Throughout the United States.

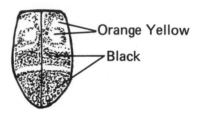

Fig. 275.   Acmaeodera pulchella

Acmaeodera tubulus Length: 5–7.5mm. Black, shining, bronzed with some white, erect pubescence; elytra with irregular spots of yellow or orange. Pronotum wider than long with three pits at base, densely punctured; elytral striae deeply and coarsely punctured, side of each elytron sawlike on apical third; each antenna sawlike from fifth segment; tarsal claws toothed.
On flowers and leaves, especially hawthorns; larvae in white oak, hickory, and redbud.
Throughout the United States east of the Rockies.

Chalcophora virginiensis The Larger Flat-Headed Pine Borer Length: 20–30mm. Dull black, shining, slightly bronzed; impressions of pronotum and elytra often brassy. Pronotum wider than long, roughly sculptured; elytra roughly sculptured, with irregular, smooth, connected ridges, separated by irregular punctured striae, sides parallel; each antenna thickened toward the end, second segment of each globular; tarsi of hind legs each with first segment as long as next two combined (Fig. 276).
On pines.
Eastern half of the United States.

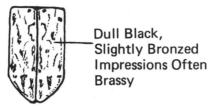

Dull Black,
Slightly Bronzed
Impressions Often
Brassy

Fig. 276. Chalcophora virginiensis

Chalcophora liberta The Smaller Flat-Headed Pine Borer Length: 19–24mm. Bright coppery or brassy, shining; antennae, legs, and raised lines on pronotum and elytra dark brown. Pronotum wider than long, sides rounded towards the apex, with a median impression and two others on each side, coarsely and irregularly punctured; elytra roughly sculptured, each with four irregular, smooth, connected ridges, separated by irregular punctured striae, sides parallel, converging towards the apices; each antenna thickened toward the end, each segment globular; tarsi of hind legs each with first segment as long as next two combined.
Adults on the buds and leaves of pine, larvae in the decaying wood. Throughout the United States.

The species of the genus Dicerca *have the meso and metasternum separated by a suture; the mentum is completely hornlike; the fourth segment of each antenna is longer than the third, the remaining segments are triangular and toothed; the tarsi of the hind legs each have the first segment equal in length to the second; and the elytra are irregularly sculptured, the apices being more or less prolonged.*

Dicerca divaricata Length: 16–21mm. Brown or gray, with a coppery, brassy, or greenish bronze; undersurface coppery, shining. Pronotum wider than long, roughly and coarsely punctured; elytra coarsely punctured and with scattered, smooth, elevated spaces (Fig. 277).

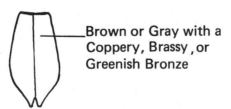

Brown or Gray with a
Coppery, Brassy, or
Greenish Bronze

Fig. 277. Dicerca divaricata

Adults on various trees such as apple, peach, pear, cherry, birch, ironwood, ash, and maple.
Throughout the United States, in the West known as the *Flat-Headed Cherry Tree Borer*.

Dicerca punctulata   Length: 12–15mm. Grayish brown, slightly shining; pronotum and elytra with smooth, deep brown streaks and spaces. Pronotum wider than long, sides curving to apex, densely and coarsely punctured except for four smooth, longitudinal, raised ridges, the two center ones broader; elytra densely and coarsely punctured with a few scattered, smooth, raised lines and with several rows of coarser punctures (Fig. 278).
On pitch pine.
Eastern half of the United States.

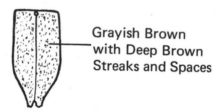

Grayish Brown
with Deep Brown
Streaks and Spaces

Fig. 278.   Dicerca punctulata

Dicerca lurida   Length: 14–19mm. Dark brown, with coppery and greenish bronze, shining; upper surface and sides covered with gray pubescence, under surface coppery. Pronotum wider than long, curved behind middle, slightly so to apex, irregularly and densely punctured; apex of each elytron with two teeth, stria punctured, intervals coarsely punctured.
On hickory and alder.
Eastern half of the United States.

Dicerca tuberculata   Length: 13–18mm. Dark brown, brassy and greenish bronze, shining; lower surface coppery. Pronotum wider than long, with four smooth, elevated spaces, the two at middle broad, the two at sides short, densely punctured; elytra densely punctured, with many raised spaces, each apex with two teeth.
On various fruit trees as well as in hemlock, pine, and arborvitae.
Eastern half of the United States.

The species of the genus Buprestis *have the meso- and metasternum separated by a suture; the mentum has a membranous front margin; the first segment of each antenna is elongate, and more or less thickened, the third is twice as long as the second, and the remaining segments are triangular and toothed; the scutellum is small and rounded; and the tarsi of the hind legs each have the first segment longer than the second.*

Buprestis lineata Length: 11–15mm. Metallic black above with a brassy tinge, beneath dull orange or dull bronze; head yellowish; each elytron with four yellowish spots that sometimes form two broad longitudinal stripes (Fig. 279).
Eastern half of the United States.

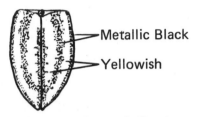

Fig. 279. Buprestis lineata

Buprestis maculativentris Length: 17–20mm. Black, slightly brassy or greenish bronze; parts of head, anterior angles of pronotum (sometimes), and a row of spots on sides of abdomen yellow or reddish yellow.
On spruce and balsam.
Throughout the United States.

Buprestis fasciata Length: 12–18mm. Metallic green or blue, shining; each elytron in the male with three yellow spots, in the female with two (Fig. 280).
On maple, poplar, and pine.
Throughout the United States.

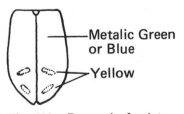

Fig. 280. Buprestis fasciata

Buprestis adjecta Length: 13–18mm. Completely metallic green. Western United States.

Buprestis laeviventris Length: 14–20mm. Dark brown or black; a marginal line at the anterior of the pronotum and front of head yellow orange; elytra with spots or broken spots of yellow or orange. Western mountains.

The species of the genus Melanophila *have the front margin of the mentum horny; the first segment of each of the antenna is elongate, the third is slightly longer than the second, and the following segments are triangular and toothed; the pronotum is wavy at its base; and the tarsi of the hind legs each have the first segment longer than the second.*

Melanophila fulvoguttata The Hemlock Borer Length: 9–12mm. Blackish bronze, with dull green or coppery reflections; elytra each with three or four small orange yellow spots. Head densely and deeply punctured; pronotum wider than long, apex narrower than base, punctured; elytra with rounded apices and coarsely punctured (Fig. 281).
On hemlock, spruce, and white pine.
Middle and Northern United States.

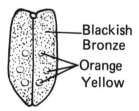

Fig. 281. Melanophila fulvoguttata

Melanophila aeneola Length: 5–6.5mm. Black, with a brassy, greenish, or purple bronze. Head and pronotum finely netted; pronotum slightly wider than long and apex slightly narrower than base; elytra with rounded apices and densely but finely punctured. On pine.
Eastern half of the United States.

Anthaxia viridifrons The Hickory Twig Borer Length: 4–6mm. Pitch colored, somewhat bronzed; head and side margins of pronotum sometimes green. Pronotum wider than long, sides rounded, netted, and usually with two broad, shallow impressions on each side; elytra tapered toward the apices and wrinkled; mentum completely horny; segments four to eleven of each antenna with pits at each apex.

Adults on various plants, larvae in hickory and American elm.

Eastern half of the United States.

Anthaxia viridicornis Length: 5–6.5mm. Pitch colored and purplish bronze with the complete front of head and sides of pronotum bright coppery and undersurface bluish and shining.

Adults may be found on vegetation and the larvae in willow, hickory, and elm.

Rather scarce in the Eastern States but fairly common in the Central States.

Anthaxia quercata Length: 4–6mm. Bluish or purplish, sometimes green shining, with the pronotum and each elytron with a median brown stripe.

Adults on oak leaves; the larvae on redbud, white pine, and American larch.

Throughout eastern half of the United States.

The species of the genus Chrysobothris *have the front of the head narrowed by the insertion of the antennae; the mentum is membranous at the apex; each antenna has the first segment elongated and thickened, the second short and globular, the third elongate, and the remaining short and triangular; the scutellum is large and pointed; the femora of the front legs are toothed; and the tarsi of the hind legs each has the first segment as long as or longer than the next three combined.*

Chrysobothris femorata *The Flat-Headed Apple Tree Borer* Length: 7–16mm. Dark bronze with sheens of green, copper, or brass. Pronotum wider than long, densely and coarsely punctured; elytra tapering toward apices, sides sawlike, sculpturing variable, each usually with two side, elevated ridges, coarsely and densely punctured; clypeus deeply notched (Fig. 282).

Adults on trunks of trees; larvae in various hardwoods, sometimes quite destructive, frequently to apple and other orchard trees.

Throughout the United States.

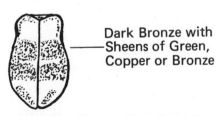

Dark Bronze with Sheens of Green, Copper or Bronze

Fig. 282. Chrysobothris femorata

Chrysobothris sexsignata   Length: 7–11mm. Black, slightly bronzed. shining; each elytron with three impressed metallic spots; undersurface green. Pronotum wider than long, hind angles obtuse, densely and coarsely punctured; elytra with obtuse apices and slight ridges, densely and coarsely punctured; clypeus triangularly notched.
Adults on trunks of trees; larvae in dead branches of such trees as hickory, birch, oak, beech, ash, and hemlock.
Eastern half of the United States.

Chrysobothris pusilla   Length: 5–7.5mm. Uniformly coppery bronze. Pronotum wider than long, sides more or less parallel, coarsely punctured; elytra each with three irregular, broad pits, coarsely punctured; clypeus triangularly notched.
Adults on pine; larvae in pine, hemlock, and spruce.
Eastern half of the United States.

Chrysobothris scitula   Length: 6–7.5mm. Usually purplish bronze, shining; elytra each with three bright blue or green impressed spots. Pronotum wider than long, densely and coarsely punctured; elytra rather coarsely and densely punctured, side margins sawlike, apices rounded, each elytron with three pits; clypeus with a triangular notch (Fig. 283).
Adults on trunks of trees; larvae in alder, white birch, and oak.
Eastern half of the United States.

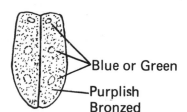

Fig. 283.   Chrysobothris scitula

Actenodes acornis   Length: 10–13mm. Black, with a bronze or green tinge; undersurface coppery. Pronotum wider than long, hind angles toothed, coarsely and densely punctured; elytra with many fine, closely set lines, sides sawlike; antennae each toothed from fourth segment; tarsi each with third segment having two long spines.
Adults on foliage; larvae in the dead wood of red maple, birch, beech, hickory, and black oak.
Eastern half of the United States.

The species of the genus Agrilus *have the front of the head*

*narrowed by the insertion of the antennae; the antennae are each
sawlike from the fourth or fifth segment and are pitted at the apices; and the scutellum is wider than long and is pointed.*

Agrilus bilineatus The Two-Lined Chestnut Borer Length: 5–9.5mm.
Black, sometimes tinged with green or blue; a narrow line of
brown yellow along lateral edges of pronotum; each elytron with a
wavy line of brown yellow reaching to extreme apex; undersurface
greenish black. Pronotum wider than long, narrower at base, sides
slightly rounded, hind angles rectangular; elytra densely granulate,
sides wavy, apices rounded, slightly sawlike (Fig. 284).
On oak, honey locust, and chestnut.
East of the Rockies.

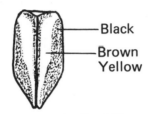

Fig. 284. Agrilus bilineatus

Agrilus anxius The Bronze Birch Borer Length: 6–13mm. Olive
bronze, sometimes with a coppery tinge. Pronotum slightly wider
than long, base narrower than apex, sides somewhat rounded, hind
angles acute, with many closely set transverse lines; elytra densely
granulate, apices rounded and sawlike.
On willow, poplar, and birch.
Central and Eastern United States.

Agrilus ruficollis The Red-necked Cane Borer Length: 4–7mm.
Black or bluish black, slightly shining; head and pronotum coppery
red. Pronotum slightly wider than long, sides slightly rounded, hind
angles rectangular; elytra densely and finely granulate, apices rounded and sawlike.
A serious pest on blackberry and raspberry. The adults girdle the
tips of the tender stems or canes and cause the ends to wilt and
fall over. The larvae bore down the center of the canes and eventually kill them.
East of the Rockies.

Agrilus egenus Length: 3.5–5mm. Black, slightly shining, bronze
or greenish bronze; head sometimes light green. Pronotum slightly

wider than long, finely punctured, ridged near hind angles; elytra granulate or with many small flattened elevations, apices rounded and sawlike.
On locust and hickory.
Eastern half of the United States.

Agrilus arcuatus   Length: 5–9mm. Brown; head and pronotum coppery or brassy; elytra blue or black. Pronotum wider than long, sides rounded, finely punctured; elytra widened behind middle, densely granulate, apices rounded and sawlike.
On hickory, hazel, beech, and white oak.
Eastern half of the United States.

Pachyschelus purpureus   Length: 3–3.5mm. Black, shining; elytra purple or blue. Pronotum wider than long, sparsely and finely punctured; elytra with rows of coarse punctures, each elytron with a basal impression and one behind each shoulder, sides sawlike posteriorly; scutellum large and triangular; antennae received into grooves on underside of prothorax; front of head narrowed by insertion of antennae; tibiae dilated (Fig. 285).
On leaves and various kinds of vegetation.
Eastern half of the United States.

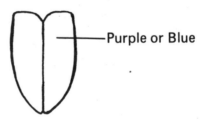

Fig. 285.   Pachyschelus purpureus

Brachys ovatus   Length: 5–7mm. Black or blue black, slightly shining; irregularly covered with white and golden hairs, those on elytra arranged in three irregular transverse bands on each elytron. Pronotum wider than long, sparsely and coarsely punctured; elytra with rows of rather coarse punctures, with a ridge from each shoulder to apex; antennae received into grooves on underside of prothorax; front of head narrowed by insertion of antennae.
On oak; adults are found on the leaves, the larvae mine in the leaves.
Throughout the United States.

Brachys aerosus Length: 4–4.5mm. Black or blue black, slightly shining, and covered irregularly with light yellowish brown hairs; these hairs on the elytra forming three irregular transverse bands on each elytron.
Adults found on the leaves of oak, hickory, and elm; the larvae are leaf miners in oak.
Throughout the eastern half of the United States.

Brachys aeruginosus Length: 3.5–4mm. Black or blue black and somewhat shining; the elytra with three transverse bands of white and light yellowish brown hairs on each elytron, the white predominating.
Adults on various deciduous trees; the larvae are miners in the leaves.
Throughout the eastern half of the United States.

Taphrocerus gracilis Length: 3–5mm. Black, shining, slightly bronzed; elytra usually with indistinct spots of whitish pubescence. Pronotum wider than long, finely and densely punctured; elytra coarsely punctured, impressed at bases, sides wavy, apices rounded and sawlike; antennae received into grooves on under side of prothorax; front of head narrowed by insertion of antennae; tibiae grooved for reception of tarsi.
On grasses and herbaceous plants in moist places.
Eastern half of the United States.

The Long-Toed Water Beetles

Family Psephenidae
  The beetles of this family are usually found in the vicinity of water and during the heat of the day often collect on stones that project from the water. They fly swiftly when disturbed. The body is oval, narrowed in front, and covered with fine silken hairs that retain a film of air when the insects go beneath the water. The maxillary palpi are elongate, the last segment of each is hatchet shaped; the antennae are widely separated, sawlike, and each has eleven segments; the abdomen of the male has seven ventral segments, the first and the second are united, the fifth is notched, the sixth is bilobed, and the seventh is rounded; and the female has the segment corresponding to the sixth in the male absent.
  The larvae are flat and circular, and are known as *water pennies*. They cling tightly to stones usually in rapid streams. When mature, they leave the water and pupate underneath the last larval skin, beneath a stone or other object in a damp situation.

The eggs are laid on the underside of submerged stones in running water.

Psephenus lecontei Length: 4–6mm. Black, often tinged with dull brown and with a fine pubescence; head and pronotum darkest. Pronotum with sides rounded posteriorly, narrowed anteriorly, base twice as broad as apex, finely punctured; elytra finely, densely punctured (Fig. 286).

Of the only four species known for this family, the other three are confined solely to California.

Eastern half of the United States.

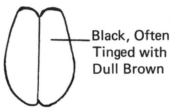

Black, Often
Tinged with
Dull Brown

Fig. 286.   Psephenus lecontei

The Hairy Water Beetles

Family Dryopidae

This family is a small one and includes small water beetles in which the legs are not fitted for swimming. They are found most often in swift-running water where the adults cling either to the upper surfaces of partially submerged stones, logs, or debris, or to the undersides completely under water. Their bodies are clothed with fine silken hairs that retain a film of air when they are beneath the water. The head is retractile; the antennae are short and each has six or eleven segments; only five abdominal segments are visible; and the tarsi each have five segments, each of those of the hind legs being long and having very long claws.

The larvae are flattened and live on the undersides of stones, plants, and the like in swift-running streams and feed on decayed plant matter.

Helichus lithophilus Length: 5–6mm. Dark reddish brown, body clothed completely with fine, silky pubescence, which gives the insect a bronzy sheen. Pronotum wider than long, narrowed anteriorly, both front and hind angles acute, densely and finely punctured; elytra coarsely, sparsely punctured, each with four rows of punc-

tures, sides strongly tapering behind middle, apices acute; antennae widely separated at bases, segments four to eleven on each antenna leaflike; last segment of each tarsus of hind legs nearly as long as four preceding (Fig. 287).
Eastern half of the United States.

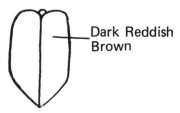

Fig. 287.   Helichus lithophilus

The Marl Water Beetles

Family Elmidae
Both the larvae and adults of this family are for the most part aquatic, or, at least, semiaquatic. Generally they may be found clinging to stones or beneath rocks in swiftly-flowing streams but many of them are found associated with the marl deposits in lakes, a fact which has led to the common name of the family. Like the psephenids and dryopids, the *Elmidae* have extremely long tarsi and long, stout, tarsal claws. They can be distinguished from the others by the eyes being free of hair, by their slender threadlike antennae that are inserted on the front of the head near the eyes, and by the coxae of the front legs being round. Unlike the larvae of the psephenids and dryopids which are flattened and oval, those of the *marl water beetles* are long and slender, only occasionally being flattened in the region of the thorax.

Stenelmis crenata   Length: 3–3.5mm.   Brownish   black   to   black; pronotal margins, lower surface of body, and legs reddish brown; each elytron with two dull reddish spots, which are sometimes united to form a longitudinal stripe. Pronotum rounded and narrowed toward base which is wider than apex, with a median impressed line, finely and sparsely granulate; elytra with a number of striae of coarse punctures; head retractile; antennae each with eleven segments (Fig. 288).
Eastern half of the United States.

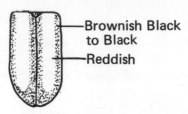

Fig. 288. Stenelmis crenata

Stenelmis quadrimaculata Length: 2.7–3.5mm. Black to pitch colored; the pronotum often largely dull yellowish gray; each elytron with two yellow spots; and the body beneath and the antennae dull reddish brown. (Fig. 289).
Eastern half of the United States.

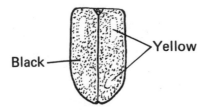

Fig. 289. Stenelmis quadrimaculata

Macronchyus glabratus Length: 3–3.5mm. Black; antennae and legs pitch colored; head covered with fine, matted hair. Pronotum with apical margin wavy each side behind eye, somewhat square shaped, apical angle obtuse; elytra with a number of rows of coarse punctures, seventh interval of each ridged; head retractile; antennae each with seven segments, first two segments of each cylindrical.
Eastern half of the United States.

The Variegated Mud-Loving Beetles

Family Heteroceridae
This is a small family of somewhat flattened beetles that live in galleries they excavate in sand or mud at the margins of ponds and streams. When disturbed, they run from their burrows and seek escape in flight.

They are somewhat oblong or elongated in shape and densely clothed with short, silky pubescence; they are very finely punctured and are a brown color, having their elytra variegated with wavy bands or spots of yellow. The first four abdominal segments are fused together on the ventral side; the tibiae are dilated and armed with rows of spines, hence fitted for digging; and the tarsi each have four segments (Fig. 290) .

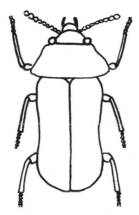

Fig. 290.   Variegated Mud-loving Beetle

Heterocerus auromicans Length: 3.5–4.5mm. Blackish, sparingly covered with golden, short, recumbent, scalelike hairs; elytra with yellow crossbands; pronotum with a pale median stripe; femora and tarsi reddish yellow, tibiae black (Fig. 291) .
Throughout the United States.

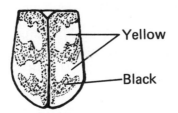

Fig. 291.   Heterocerus auromicans

Heterocerus collaris Length: 2.5–4mm. Sooty brown to black, clothed with brownish hairs; sides of pronotum and elytra marked with yellow; legs reddish yellow.
Throughout the United States.

Heterocerus pusillus Length: 2–2.5mm. Dull yellow marked with sooty brown or sometimes completely colored with one of these colors; legs paler.
Throughout the United States.

The Soft-Bodied Plant Beetles

Family Helodidae

The beetles of this family are small, usually oval in shape, and very soft. They occur on plants near water, in swamps, and sometimes in damp debris (Fig. 292).

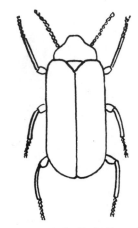

Fig. 292.   Soft-bodied Plant Beetle

Ptilodactyla serricollis   Length: 4–6mm. Chestnut brown to blackish with some pubescence; legs and antennae pale.
Eastern half of the United States.

Helodes pulchella   Length: 3.5–5mm. Yellow marked with black; pronotum finely punctured, elytra densely so (Fig. 293).
Throughout the eastern half of the United States.

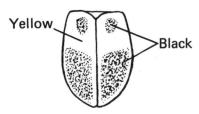

Fig. 293.   Helodes pulchella

Cyphon collaris   Length: 3.4–4mm. Black, shining, with fine pubescence; with reddish yellow markings.
Throughout the eastern half of the United States.

The Dermestid Beetles

Family Dermestidae

The *dermestid beetles* are generally small in size, although one of the common species measures 8mm. in length. They are usually oval, chunky beetles, with pale gray or brown markings, which are formed of minute scales, which can be rubbed off. When disturbed, they roll over on their backs with their legs folded and lie still as if they were dead. Many of them live in skins, fur, woolen materials, and dried animal matter, though some are occasionally found on flowers.

The head is small, rectractile up to the eyes, one median ocellus usually present (Fig. 294); antennae are short, each usually having

Fig. 294. **Head of** Attagenus **Showing One Median Ocellus**

eleven segments but sometimes only nine or ten segments, the last three segments forming a large club and usually fitting into a groove on the underside of the prothorax; the elytra, as a rule, cover the abdomen; the legs are short; the tibiae have spurs or spines; the tarsi each have five segments; and the coxae of the hind legs are grooved for the reception of the femora in repose (Figs. 295, 296).

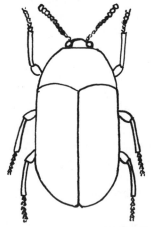

Fig. 295. **Dermestid Beetle**

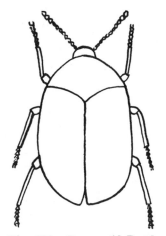

Fig. 296. **Dermestid Beetle**

Most of the larvae are brown, active grubs clothed with long hairs. They are much more destructive than the adults, and thrive in the same environment.

Byturus rubi   Length: 3.7–4.5mm. Dull brownish yellow; densely covered with pale yellowish, silky pubescence above, hairs whitish on undersurface. Pronotum wider than long, base wider than apex, sides rounded, coarsely and densely punctured; elytra coarsely, densely punctured with traces of numerous elevated lines; scutellum large and square shaped; second and third segments of tarsi with membranous lobe; tarsal claws toothed (Fig. 297).
The small white grub of this beetle infests the fruit of blackberries and raspberries and is known as the *raspberry fruit worm*. The adults are found on the flowers of both the blackberry and raspberry. Throughout the United States.

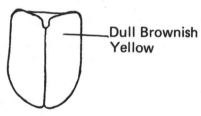

Dull Brownish Yellow

Fig. 297.   Byturus rubi

The species of the genus Dermestes *have no ocellus and the coxae of the front legs touch.*

Dermestes caninus   Length: 7–8.2mm. Black; pronotum with dense yellow and white pubescence; scutellum densely covered with long. yellow hairs; elytra with gray and black pubescence; undersurface with short, gray pubescence.
On dead animals. This beetle is used by vertebrate morphologists for cleaning the bony skeletons of specimens.
Throughout the United States.

Dermestes vulpinus   *The Leather Beetle*   Length: 6–9mm. Pitch colored, sparsely covered with black and yellowish hairs; last ventral abdominal segment brown with two white spots. Pronotum and elytra finely and densely punctured.
On improperly cooked meat and on hides and skins.
Throughout the United States.

Dermestes lardarius   *The Larder Beetle*   Length: 6–7.5mm. Black or

pitch colored; each elytron with basal half densely covered with coarse, yellowish hairs, with the exception of a spot at each shoulder and a transverse row of three spots near base, apical half with very fine sparse hairs; undersurface and legs black with a few yellowish hairs. Pronotum and elytra finely and densely punctured (Fig. 298). A commercial and household pest; feeds on smoked meats, cheese. hoofs, horn, skin, feathers, and hair.
Throughout the United States.

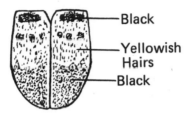

Fig. 298. Dermestes lardarius

Dermestes marmoratus Length: 7–11mm. Black with white markings at bases of elytra and yellowish hairs on underparts.
Western United States.

Dermestes talpinus Length: 5–7mm. Black above and covered with bluish gray, clay yellow, and black hairs with underparts mostly white.
Western United States.

Attagenus piceus *The Black Carpet Beetle* Length: 3.5–5mm. Head and pronotum black; elytra reddish brown covered with short, sparse pubescence. Pronotum coarsely punctured with a slight impression before scutellum; elytra finely and densely punctured; basal segment of each of the tarsi of the hind legs much shorter than second (Fig. 299).
A common museum and household pest. Larvae often destructive to rugs, carpets, upholstery, woolen materials, silks and feathers. A scourge of insect collections; feeds on the dried insect specimens destroying them.
Throughout the United States.

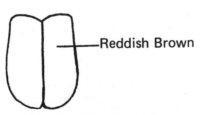

Fig. 299. Attagenus piceus

Trogoderma versicolor   Length: 2–3.5mm. Black; pronotum with lines of gray hairs; elytra with four more or less confluent reddish bands covered with gray pubescence. Pronotum wider than long, finely and sparsely punctured; elytra coarsely and densely punctured; basal segment of each of the tarsi of the hind legs elongate and a little shorter than second and third combined; eyes notched; antennae each with a club (Fig. 300).
Throughout the United States.

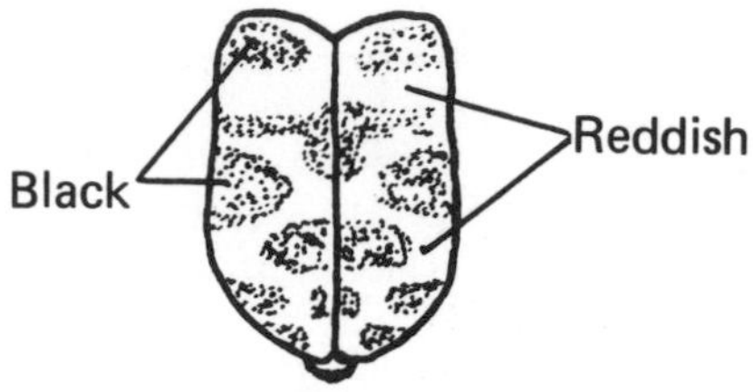

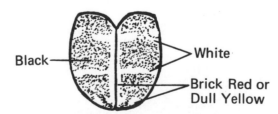

Fig. 300.   Trogoderma versicolor

Cryptorhopalum haemorrhoidale   Length: 2–2.5mm. Black, shining; pronotum and elytra deep reddish brown, each elytron dull yellow on apical third and each with two transverse bands of yellow pubescence; long sparse yellow hairs underneath. Head coarsely, densely punctured; pronotum finely punctured; club of each antenna two segmented, close fitting in repose within a deep groove on underside of prothorax.
On flowers.
Eastern half of the United States.

Anthrenus scrophulariae   *The Carpet Beetle*   Length: 2.2–3.5mm. Black; pronotal sides covered with white scales; elytra each with a sutural stripe, an apical spot of brick red or dull yellow, and white crossbands; body beneath covered with yellowish and white scales. Pronotum wider than long, finely and densely punctured; elytra also finely and densely punctured; eyes notched; antennal clubs oval (Fig. 301).
Adult beetles on flowers. Larvae, known as *buffalo bugs,* destructive to carpets, woolen materials, feathers, and fur. A museum pest.
Throughout the United States.

Fig. 301.   Anthrenus scrophulariae

Anthrenus verbasci   The Varied Carpet Beetle   Length: 2–3mm.
Black; pronotum with sparse yellow scales in the middle, sides with
white scales; elytra each with a large basal ring, and two transverse
zigzag bands of white scales bordered with yellow scales and a small
apical transverse band of white scales bordered with yellow; undersurface covered with pale yellow scales. Pronotum wider than long,
minutely punctured; elytra finely, densely punctured; antennal clubs
elongate (Fig. 302).
Adults on various flowers; larvae a museum pest, also destructive
to carpets, woolen materials, feathers, and fur.
Throughout the United States.

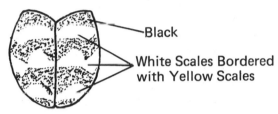

Fig. 302.   Anthrenus verbasci

*The following species eats like a dermestid but does not look
like one. It is usually placed in the Dermestidae but probably
should be in a family of its own.*

Thylodrias contractus Length: 2.5–3mm. Dull yellowish brown, rather densely covered with silky, whitish pubescence; elytra, antennae,
and legs pale brownish yellow. Pronotum wider than long, strongly
constricted at the apex, finely and densely punctured; elytra with
sides nearly parallel, apices together rounded, coarsely and rather
densely punctured; each antenna long, threadlike, eleven segmented;
head prominent; legs long and slender; tarsi threadlike, each five
segmented (Fig. 303).
A museum pest; also destructive to carpets, woolen materials, feathers, and fur.
Throughout the United States.

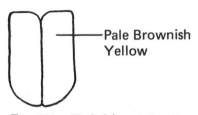

Fig. 303.   Thylodrias contractus

The Pill Beetles

Family Byrrhidae

The beetles of this family are called *pill beetles* because when disturbed they fold up their antennae and legs and form a compact ball.

They are for the most part small forms, very convex, and usually black with short hairs or minute scales that give them a silky sheen. They are slow moving, very hard bodied, and are found in the roots of trees and grasses, beneath logs, in crevices, and in sand along streams and lakes.

These beetles have retracted heads; the antennae are each eleven segmented, the apical segments of each forming an elongate club, and are inserted beneath the sides of the head; the legs are short and stout and so arranged that they can be folded so closely to the body as to be invisible; and the tarsi each have five segments, the last segment of each almost as long as the preceding ones combined.

Cytilus alternatus   Length: 4.5–5.5mm. Bronzy black, shining, with dense, fine pubescence; elytra metallic green. Pronotum densely punctured; elytra minutely wrinkled with many fine striae, which are sparsely and finely punctured (Fig. 304).
Among grass roots.
Eastern half of the United States.

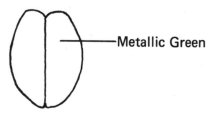

Metallic Green

Fig. 304.   Cytilus alternatus

Byrrhus americanus   Length: 8.5–9.5mm. Black, with fine, dense grayish pubescence; pronotum with indistinct gray markings; each elytron has three or four narrow, interrupted, black lines and a double narrow wavy gray band at its middle. Pronotum finely and densely punctured; elytral stria very fine, often with finely beaded edges and with fine, widely separated punctures.
Eastern half of the United States.

The Wrinkled Bark Beetles

Family Rhysodidae

This is a small family of elongated, somewhat flattened beetles with the head and prothorax deeply furrowed with longitudinal grooves. They occur under the bark of logs and trees of beech, oak, and elm.

Rhysodes americanus Length: 6–8mm. Dark reddish brown, shining. Elytral striae with large punctures; abdomen with six ventral segments, the first cut into three parts by coxae of hind legs (Fig. 305). Eastern half of the United States.

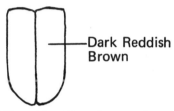

Dark Reddish Brown

Fig. 305. Rhysodes americanus

The Grain and Bark-Gnawing Beetles

Family Ostomidae

This is a family of oblong, somewhat flattened beetles of a black or reddish black color. They are small or of moderate size and most of them live under bark, though a few species are found in granaries and have been widely distributed by commerce.

The maxillae are two lobed; the antennae are short, each with eleven segments, and inserted under the sides of the head, the last three segments of each forming a club; all the coxae are transverse, those of the front and middle legs are separated, those of the hind legs are touching; the tarsi are slender and each has five segments, the first segment of each being very short; and the elytra cover the abdomen (Fig. 306).

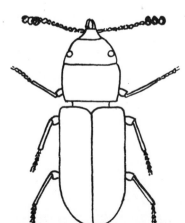

Fig. 306. Grain and Bark-gnawing Beetle

Tenebroides mauritanicus   The Cadelle   Length: 6–11mm. Deep brown to black, shining. Head large; pronotum wider than long, notched at apex, rather coarsely punctured; elytra with deeply impressed striae, each interval with two rows of punctures; last segment of each antennal club only slightly longer than wide (Fig. 307).
Both adults and larvae feed on grains, flour, and seeds, but are also predacious, feeding on other insects as well.
Throughout the United States.

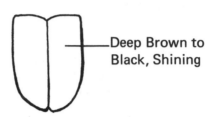
Deep Brown to Black, Shining

Fig. 307.   Tenebroides mauritanicus

Tenebroides americanus   Length: 9–11mm. Brownish black, shining; undersurface and legs dark reddish brown. Head and pronotum densely wrinkled, rather sparsely punctured; pronotum wider than long, sides wavy towards the base, hind angles acute; elytra ovate, striae shallow and finely punctured; last segment of each antennal club strongly elongate.
Throughout the United States.

Calitys scabra   Length: 9–10mm. Reddish. Pronotum with wide margins.
On fungi of logs.
Throughout the United States.

Ostoma quadrilineata   Length: 5–6mm. Black, slightly shining; antennae and legs lighter. Each elytron with four narrow ridges with three to four rows of punctures on each interval.
Central States.

Airora cylindrica   Length: 5–14mm. Dark reddish brown. Pronotum longer than wide, finely and sparsely punctured, hind angles obtuse; elytral striae finely punctured, intervals minutely so, elytral apices rounded together; all tibiae with distinct spines.
Beneath the bark of hickory, elm, and other hardwoods.
Eastern half of the United States.

The Sap-Feeding Beetles

Family Nitidulidae

The adult beetles of this family generally feed on the escaping sap of trees and on the juices of various fruits, though some are found on flowers where they probably feed on pollen and nectar, while a few are attracted to fungi. There are still others that occur under the bark of decaying logs or are pests in corn or in stored rice products; some species even live and breed on carrion.

The *sap-feeding beetles* are rather small forms, more or less flattened, usually black, but sometimes brightly colored or marked. The antennae are short, each with eleven segments and each with a round or oval club, and are inserted beneath the margin of the front of the head; the pronotum has margins usually expanded and thin; the elytra are usually short, cut off squarely at the tips so as to expose part of the abdomen, but they are often entire and cover the abdomen; the legs are short and stout and more or less retractile; the tarsi each usually have five segments and are often dilated, the last segment of each being elongate; and the abdomen has five free ventral segments (Fig. 308).

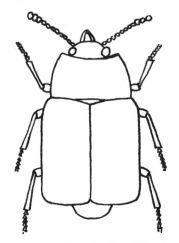

Fig. 308. Sap-feeding Beetle

Cateretes pennatus Length: 2.3–2.5mm. Yellowish brown to dark brown, somewhat shining, with few short hairs. Pronotum wider than long and densely punctured; elytra coarsely punctured; maxillae each with two lobes (Fig. 309).

On various flowers such as those of the hydrangea and elder.

Eastern half of the United States.

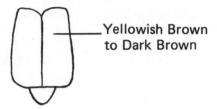

Fig. 309. Cateretes pennatus

Boreades abdominalis Length: 2–2.5mm. Metallic blue or greenish, shining; antennae reddish brown; abdomen and legs reddish. Pronotum slightly wider than long, hind angles rectangular, coarsely punctured; elytra coarsely and densely punctured, apices rounded; maxillae each with two lobes (Fig. 310).
On various flowers, as well as on the foliage of trees and shrubs in moist places.
Eastern half of the United States.

Fig. 310. Boreades abdominalis

Brachypterus urticae Length: 2mm. Black, slightly bronzed, shining, with few short hairs; antennae and legs reddish brown. Pronotum wider than long, sides rounded, coarsely and densely punctured; elytra obliquely cut off at apices, coarsely but less densely punctured than pronotum; tarsal claws toothed; maxillae each with two lobes.
On the flowers of elder.
Eastern half of the United States.

Colopterus truncatus Length: 2–2.5mm. Reddish brown, shining. Pronotum wider than long, rather densely punctured; elytra rather densely punctured, apices broadly cut off; maxillae each with one lobe; abdomen with two segments exposed above (Fig. 311).
About sap in the spring, on flowers in summer.
Eastern half of the United States.

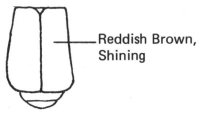

Reddish Brown,
Shining

Fig. 311. Colopterus truncatus

Conotelus obscurus Length: 3.5–4.5mm. Dull black, with scattered pubescence; antennae and legs brownish yellow, antennal clubs darker. Pronotum wider than long, sparsely punctured, hind angles obtusely rounded; elytra about twice as long as wide, apices rounded exposing at least three abdominal segments, finely granulate with irregular rows of indistinct punctures; first and second abdominal segments short, third and fourth longer, fifth longest. This species, elongate in form, resembles the rove beetles (Fig. 312).
On flowers of dogwood, hollyhock, dandelion, and wild morning glory.
Eastern half of the United States.

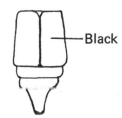

Black

Fig. 312. Conotelus obscurus

Carpophilus sayi Length: 3.5–4.2mm. Deep brown, with a few short hairs; legs reddish brown. Pronotum wider than long, sides rounded, hind angles rectangular, densely punctured; elytra densely punctured, apices obliquely cut off, exposing two dorsal segments of abdomen; labrum with two lobes; second and third ventral abdominal segments short—first, fourth, and fifth longer.
On flowers, sap, and sometimes beneath bark of decaying logs.
Eastern half of the United States.

Carpophilus hemipterus *The Dried Fruit Beetle* Length: 4mm. Black; legs paler; each elytron with a dull yellow shoulder spot and an irregular area of the same color covering the distal half (Fig. 313).
An introduced species found in grocery and bakery shops; also a serious pest in fruit drying areas.
Throughout the United States.

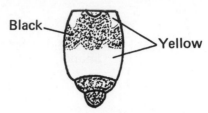

Fig. 313. Carpophilus hemipterus

Carpophilus dimidiatus The Corn Sap Beetle Length: 3.5–4mm.
Lighter in color, and somewhat smaller than *hemipterus* and also
differs from it in having a squarish pronotum with distinct front
angles.
A destructive pest of sweet corn, and also feeds on decaying fruits
and vegetation; often found swarming in rice mills.
Throughout the United States.

Carpophilus brachypterus Length: 2–3mm. Brownish black to black,
with antennae and legs reddish brown.
It is found on sap and on the flowers of various shrubs.
Eastern half of the United States.

Nitidula bipunctata Length: 4.5–6mm. Blackish, slightly shining,
finely pubescent; each elytron with a round reddish spot. Pronotum
wider than long, narrowed to apex, hind angles almost rectangular,
coarsely and densely punctured; elytra rather sparsely and finely
punctured, apices rounded; labrum slightly notched (Fig. 314).
On bones and skins.
Throughout the United States.

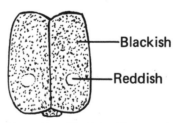

Fig. 314. Nitidula bipunctata

Omosita colon Length: 2–3mm. Blackish, rather shining; pronotum
with yellow margins; each elytron with three or four yellowish
spots on basal half and a large yellowish transverse band near apex.
Pronotum wider than long, coarsely punctured; elytra smooth, apices rounded; mentum not covering maxillae (Fig. 315).
On decaying animal and plant matter; often on greasy bones.
Throughout the United States.

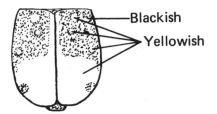

Blackish

Yellowish

Fig. 315.   Omosita colon

Epuraea helvola Length: 2.5–3.5mm. Dark reddish brown, slightly shining, with sparse pubescence. Pronotum wider than long, apex deeply notched, margins broadly flattened, rather densely punctured; elytra tapering toward apices, which are rounded, rather densely punctured; labrum with two lobes (Fig. 316).
On sap in spring, in decaying fleshy fungi in summer.
Eastern half of the United States.

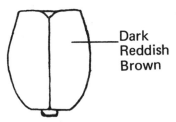

Dark
Reddish
Brown

Fig. 316.   Epuraea helvola

Epuraea duryi Length: 3.5–5mm. Shining pale yellow with scattered pubescence and somewhat flattened.
Eastern United States.

Epuraea obtusicollis Length: 2.5–3mm. Dark reddish brown to blackish with margins of pronotum and elytra paler.
Throughout the United States.

Stelidota geminata Length: 2–3.5mm. Dark brown or dark reddish brown, margins paler; elytra each with two indistinct crossbars of pale yellow. Pronotum wider than long, base wider than apex which is deeply notched, side margins broadly flattened, hind angles rectangular, coarsely and densely punctured; elytra narrowing to rounded apices, more or less ridged, each ridge with a single row of fine punctures bearing short hairs, intervals densely punctured; antennal grooves parallel (Fig. 317).
On sap in the spring, on decaying fruit in the fall.
Throughout the United States.

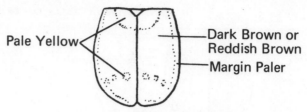

Pale Yellow — Dark Brown or Reddish Brown

Margin Paler

Fig. 317. Stelidota geminata

Prometopia sexmaculata Length: 5–6mm. Pitch colored with margins of reddish brown; undersurface of body grayish brown; elytra with a pale reddish brown band on shoulders and the same colored spot near apices. Pronotum wider than long, narrowed toward the apex, hind angles rectangular, sparsely and coarsely punctured; elytra coarsely, sparsely punctured with rounded apices; mentum covering the bases of the maxillae; mandibles with two equal lobes at apices (Fig. 318).
On sap in spring.
East of the Rockies.

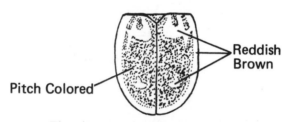

Reddish Brown

Pitch Colored

Fig. 318. Prometopia sexmaculata

Phenolia grossa Length: 6.5–8mm. Pitch colored, somewhat dull; each elytron with seven indistinct, reddish spots. Pronotum wider than long, slightly wider at base than at apex which is deeply notched, sides rounded, hind angles acute, coarsely and rather densely punctured; elytral apices separately, narrowly rounded, slightly ridged, each ridge finely punctured, each interval with three indistinct rows of punctures; mentum not covering the maxillae; apices of mandibles with two slight lobes; tarsi not dilated (Fig. 319).
Beneath bark and in fungi.
Eastern half of the United States.

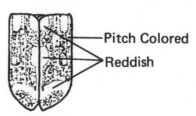

Pitch Colored

Reddish

Fig. 319. Phenolia grossa

Cryptarcha ampla   Length: 6–7mm. Dull brown to blackish, sparsely pubescent. Pronotum wider than long, apex slightly notched, hind angles obtuse, densely punctured; elytra with irregular rows of punctures, sides converging gradually toward apices, which are separately rounded; antennae each with a distinct head; labrum not distinct.
On sap in spring.
Eastern half of the United States.

The species of the genus Glischrochilus *have smooth bodies, that is, without hairs; there is also an indistinct labrum. Some of the most common and best-known species of the family belong to this genus.*

Glischrochilus fasciatus   Length: 4–7mm. Black, shining; each elytron with two transverse yellowish or reddish spots, one at the shoulder and one near the apex. Pronotum wider than long, finely punctured; elytra finely punctured (Fig. 320).
Beneath bark of decaying maple trees in spring, on sap and decaying vegetable matter in summer. Often abundant in and under garbage pails.
Throughout the United States.

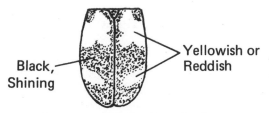

Black, Shining   Yellowish or Reddish

Fig. 320.   Glischrochilus fasciatus

Glischrochilus sanguinolentus   Length: 4–6mm. Black, shining; elytra red, each with a black spot at middle and at apex; largely reddish beneath. Pronotum wider than long, finely and sparsely punctured; elytra finely punctured (Fig. 321).
On sap and decaying vegetable matter.
Eastern half of the United States.

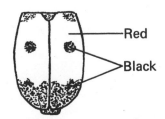

Red

Black

Fig. 321.   Glischrochilus sanquinolentus

The Monotomid Beetles

Family Monotomidae
The beetles of this family are small, depressed forms found mostly under the bark of trees, though some species live in the nests of ants. The elytra are cut off behind exposing the last abdominal segment; the first and fifth ventral abdominal segments are longer than the others.

Monotoma picipes Length: 2–2.3mm. Dull black or brownish; antennae and legs reddish brown. Pronotum coarsely, densely punctured; elytral striae with coarse punctures and yellowish hairs. (Fig. 322). Throughout the United States.

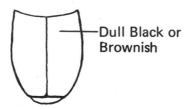

Dull Black or Brownish

Fig. 322. Monotoma picipes

The Flat Bark Beetles

Family Cucujidae
The *flat bark beetles* are somewhat elongate in form, rather flattened as their name suggests, mostly brown in color, though some are bright red, and live under loose but close-fitting bark of trees, an existence for which they are well adapted. Most of them are predaceous and feed on other insects, but a few are pests in stored grains.

The antennae are each eleven segmented and are inserted at the frontal margin of the head; the coxae of the front legs are rounded or somewhat spherical; the elytra are rounded at the apices and usually cover the abdomen; and the abdomen has five free ventral segments (Fig. 323).

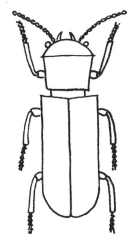

Fig. 323.   Flat Bark Beetle

Oryzaephilus surinamensis   *The Saw-Toothed Grain Beetle*   Length: 2.5mm. Dark reddish brown with paler pubescence. Pronotum longer than wide, with three longitudinal elevated lines and six distinct teeth on each edge; each elytron with four elevated lines; last three segments of each antenna forming a club (Fig. 324).
A pest in stored grains and dried fruits.
Throughout the United States.

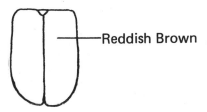

Reddish Brown

Fig. 324.   Oryzaephilus surinamensis

Silvanus bidentatus   *The Two-Toothed Grain Beetle*   Length: 2.7mm. .Dark reddish brown. Pronotum one-half longer than wide, each anterior angle with a sharp, divergent tooth, rough and densely punctured with traces of three raised longitudinal lines; elytra densely and coarsely punctured, punctures in close-set rows; segments nine to eleven of each antenna form a club (Fig. 325).
Under bark and in grains and cereals.
Throughout the United States.

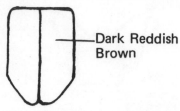

Fig. 325. Silvanus bidentatus

Catogenus rufus Length: 5–11mm. Dark reddish brown. Pronotum narrowed posteriorly, distinctly punctured; elytra deeply striate; head as wide as pronotum; antennae beaded, first segment of each the largest (Fig. 326).
Beneath bark.
Eastern half of the United States.

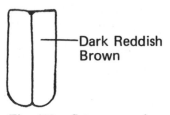

Fig. 326. Catogenus rufus

Cucujus clavipes Length: 10–14mm. Bright yellowish red or scarlet red above; dull red below; antennae and eyes black. Pronotum coarsely punctured with three slightly elevated ridges; elytra finely punctured; head widest behind eyes; antennae beadlike (Fig. 327); one of the largest and most brilliantly colored species of the family. Both adult and larva are beneficial as they feed on bark beetles and wood borers, entering the tunnels of these insects.
Common beneath the bark of ash and poplar.
Throughout the United States.

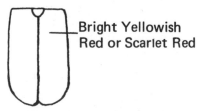

Fig. 327. Cucujus clavipes

Laemophloeus biguttatus Length: 3–4mm. Dark brown; antennae and legs slightly paler; each elytron with a yellowish spot. Pronotum wider than long, sides curved and slightly scalloped; elytra striate; head widest across eyes; labrum notched (Fig. 328).
Eastern half of the United States.

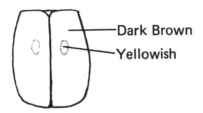

Fig. 328. Laemophloeus biguttatus

Laemophloeus adustus Length: 1.5–2.5mm. Head and pronotum reddish brown, densely and coarsely punctured; elytra darker, shining, smooth, and finely striate (Fig. 329).
Eastern half of the United States.

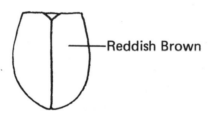

Fig. 329. Laemophloeus adustus

Laemophloeus minutus The Flat Grain Beetle Length: 1.5–2mm. Reddish brown. May be recognized by its small size and long antennae.
In dried fruit and cereals.
Throughout the United States.

Uleiota dubius Length: 4.5–5.5mm. Brownish black; head, pronotum, and sides of elytra usually paler. Pronotum wider than long, sides sawlike; elytra with both bases together broader than pronotum, a distinct elevated ridge on each extending from shoulder to apex, sides notched; first segment of each antenna elongate, about as long as head; head widest across eyes (Fig. 330).
Common beneath bark.
Throughout the United States.

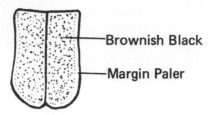

Fig. 330.   Uleiota dubius

Uleiota debilis   Length: 4–5mm. Pitch colored or black, with short yellowish hairs; antennae and legs brownish. Pronotum almost square shaped, anterior angles acute, posterior angles obtusely rounded, sides sawlike; each elytron with a distinct elevated ridge extending from shoulder to apex; each interval with a row of small granules; first segment of each antenna elongate, about as long as head; head widest across eyes.
In and beneath the litter of forest floor.
Throughout the United States.

Telephanus velox   Length: 3.5–4.5mm. Pale brownish yellow; head deep brown; apical half of each antenna dusky; each elytron sometimes with apical third brownish black. Pronotum one-half longer than wide; elytra broader than pronotum, with rounded apices; antennae slender and threadlike; third segment of each tarsus lobed; rather thickly covered with fairly long pubescence (Fig. 331). When exposed this beetle usually remains quiet, but when touched will run rapidly away.
Beneath stones, bark, and debris.
Eastern half of the United States.

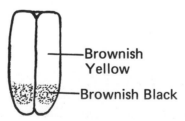

Fig. 331.   Telephanus velox

Cathartus quadricollis   The Square-Necked Grain Beetle   Length: 2–3mm. Reddish brown. Slightly punctured; last three segments of each antenna forming a club (Fig. 332). Pronotum straight edged and nearly square.

A common pest of grain products.
Throughout the United States.

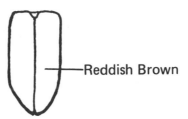

Fig. 332.   Cathartus quadricollis

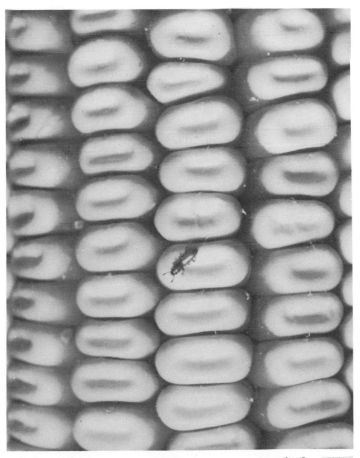

Square-necked Grain Beetle; Cathartus quadricollis

Cathartus advena   Length: 1.7–2mm. Pale reddish brown, shining; with fine pubescence. Elytra with rows of coarse punctures; last three or four segments of each antenna forming a club.
In stored grain and fruit products.
Throughout the United States.

The Slender Plant Beetles

Family Languriidae
    The beetles of this family are long and slender, ranging in size from small to large, and occur on the foliage and stems of plants. Sometimes the larvae, which live in the stems, are destructive to crop plants.
    The adults are either deep blue and red or black and red. The antennae are each eleven segmented, inserted close above the bases of the mandibles, and each has a club of three to six segments; the head is narrowed at the bases of the mandibles; the ligula has winglike, lateral lobes; and the tarsi each have five segments (Fig. 333).

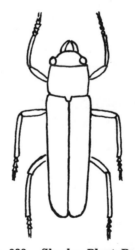

Fig. 333.   Slender Plant Beetle

Languaria mozardi   Length: 4–9mm. Head and pronotum red; elytra dark blue or bluish black; undersurface red; antennae and tarsi black. Pronotum square shaped, sides slightly rounded, sparsely punctured; elytra with regular rows of coarse, deep, elongate punctures; antennal clubs five segmented (Fig. 334); this is the most common and most widespread species of the family.
Adults on vegetation; the larva infests the stems of clover and is known as the *clover stem borer*.
Eastern half of the United States.

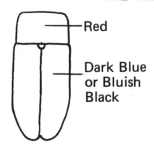

Fig. 334. Languaria mozardi

Languaria trifasciata Length: 6–7.5mm. Head and basal and apical third of each elytron blue black; pronotum, a broad median band on each elytron, and antennal segments two to six inclusive, reddish yellow; lower surface reddish yellow; last two abdominal segments black. Pronotum with rounded sides and finely and sparsely punctured; elytra with regular rows of coarse, deep, elongate punctures; antennal clubs each five segmented (Fig. 335).
On buttercups and wild lettuce.
Eastern half of the United States.

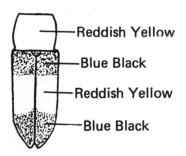

Fig. 335. Languaria trifasciata

Languaria bicolor Length: 7–13mm. Head and pronotum red, latter with a black spot; elytra very dark blue, shining; undersurface red; antennae, legs, and last abdominal segment black. Pronotum somewhat square shaped, sides rounded, with fine and sparse punctures; elytra with regular rows of deep, elongate punctures; antennal clubs each six segmented (Fig. 336).
On various kinds of herbaceous plants.
Eastern half of the United States.

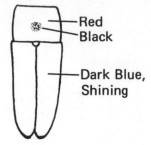

Fig. 336.   Languaria bicolor

Acropteroxys gracilis   Length: 6–12mm. Head in part or wholly red; pronotum red or yellowish red with a greenish black median stripe extending from apex almost to base; elytra and antennae black with a greenish tinge; undersurface of head and pronotum red; abdomen and legs greenish black. Pronotum punctured; elytra with rows of deep punctures; antennal clubs each five segmented; apices of elytra pointed (Fig. 337).
Adults on the flowers of new jersey tea, clover, wild rose, and willow; larvae in stems of ragweed and related plants.
Eastern half of the United States.

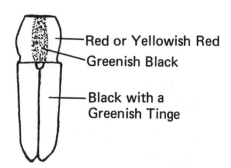

Fig. 337.   Acropteroxys gracilis

The Pleasing Fungus Beetles

Family Erotylidae
   The *pleasing fungus beetles* are usually of moderate or small size, though some are quite large and of an elongate-ovate form. They are usually yellow or brown with black or blue markings and many of them are shining. The antennae are each eleven segmented, inserted on the sides of the front of the head before the eyes, and each with a distinct club; the front of the head is more or less

prolonged into a short beak; the coxae of the front and middle legs are spherical, those of the hind legs are transverse; and the tarsi each have five segments, the fourth usually very small (Fig. 338).

The beetles and the larvae are common during the summer on fungus or under the bark of decaying logs. Some species may be seen about sap in the spring.

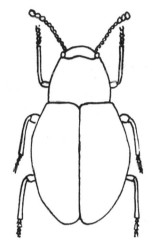

Fig. 338. Pleasing Fungus Beetle

Ischyrus quadripunctatus Length: 7–8mm. Head black; pronotum yellow with four black spots in a transverse row; elytra yellow, each with black markings as follows: a large common scutellar spot, a small round one on the shoulder, a deeply toothed median band, and an oblong spot on the apex; underparts black with sides of abdomen yellow; antennae and legs black. Pronotum more or less finely, sparsely punctured; elytra with regular rows of coarse, deep punctures; mentum triangular; last segment of maxillary palpus hatchet shaped; clubs of antennae each three segmented; tarsi each five segmented, but seemingly four segmented, the fourth being so small it will be missed unless closely examined (Fig. 339).
On fungi. Hibernates in large numbers under bark or beneath logs. Eastern half of the United States.

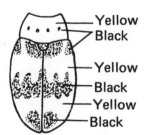

Yellow
Black

Yellow
Black
Yellow
Black

Fig. 339. Ischyrus quadripunctatus

The species of the genus Tritoma *have the last segment of the maxillary palpus broadly dilated and strongly transverse and have the first three tarsal segments widening from the first to the third; the mentum is triangular.*

Tritoma sanguinipennis Length: 4–5mm. Head and pronotum black; elytra dark reddish yellow or dark red; body black beneath; abdomen tipped with red. Pronotum finely and sparsely punctured; elytra with punctured striae (Fig. 340).
Throughout the United States.

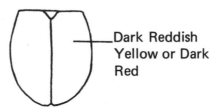

Fig. 340. Tritoma sanguinipennis

Tritoma humeralis Length: 3–4mm. Black, shining; elytra with a reddish yellow spot near each shoulder; lower surface black with tip of abdomen red. Pronotum finely, sparsely punctured; elytra with rows of fine punctures (Fig. 341).
Throughout the United States.

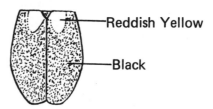

Fig. 341. Tritoma humeralis

Tritoma biguttata Length: 3–4mm. Black, shining; elytra with a large triangular reddish area at each base; body beneath pale red.
Eastern half of the United States.

Tritoma unicolor Length: 4–5mm. Black, shining. Pronotum sparsely and coarsely punctured; elytra with rows of distinct punctures.
Eastern half of the United States.

The species of the genus Triplax *have the last segment of the maxillary palpus transverse, the mentum is triangular, and the eyes have fine facets.*

Triplax thoracica   Length: 3.5–5mm. Head and pronotum reddish yellow; elytra and apical half of each antenna black; underparts and legs reddish yellow. Pronotum finely and closely punctured; elytral striae with fine close punctures.
Beneath bark and in fleshy fungi.
Throughout the United States.

Triplax festiva   Length: 5–6mm. Black, shining; pronotum, scutellum, and a broad band on middle of each elytron reddish yellow; body reddish yellow beneath. Pronotum finely, sparsely punctured; elytra with rows of rather deep punctures (Fig. 342).
A widely distributed species especially in the South.

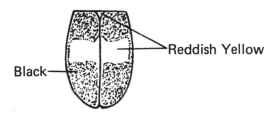

Black

Reddish Yellow

Fig. 342.   Triplax festiva

Triplax flavicollis   Length: 3–4mm. Pronotum, antennae with the exception of the clubs, and legs reddish yellow; antennal clubs, elytra, and lower parts of body shining black. Pronotum finely and closely punctured; elytral striae with coarse and somewhat close punctures.
Eastern half of the United States.

Dacne quadrimaculata   Length: 2.5–3.2mm. Black; each elytron with a round reddish yellow spot on shoulder and one at apex; pitch colored or dark reddish brown on underparts, antennae and legs paler. Pronotum finely and sparsely punctured; elytra with numerous irregular rows of fine punctures; mentum transverse; last segment of maxillary palpus bluntly pointed; tarsi each with five distinct segments (Fig. 343).
On fungi.
Eastern half of the United States; rather common in southern half of corn belt.

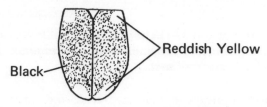

Fig. 343. Dacne quadrimaculata

Megalodacne heros Length: 18–21mm. Black, shining; elytra each with two reddish transverse bands. Pronotum wider than long; elytra with indistinct rows of fine punctures; mentum transverse; last segment of maxillary palpus hatchet shaped; tarsi each with five distinct segments, pubescence spongy (Fig. 344).
On fungi of tree trunks; also beneath bark of decaying logs.
Throughout the United States.

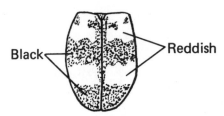

Fig. 344. Megalodacne heros

Megalodacne fasciata Length: 9–15mm. Colored and marked and otherwise much like *heros* though somewhat smaller.
In dry, rotten wood and beneath loose bark.
Throughout the United States.

The Silken Fungus Beetles

Family Cryptophagidae
The beetles of this family are of small size, rather variable in form, but never very flat. They are yellow or light yellowish brown to black in color, usually with coarse, short hairs and often with longer hairs on the elytra. The antennae are each eleven segmented, the last three segments of each form a loose club; the side margins of the pronotum are thickened into nodules or are sawlike; the elytra, completely covering the abdomen, are rounded posteriorly; the abdomen has five free ventral segments; the coxae of the front legs

are oval, sometimes transverse; and the tarsi each have five segments (Fig. 345).

The adult beetles and the larvae live on fungi and are found about wood-chip piles, in decaying logs, beneath dead leaves, and on flowers.

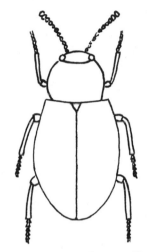

Fig. 345. Silken Fungus Beetle

Anchicera ephippiata Length: 1–2mm. Head and pronotum blackish, shining; elytra reddish yellow, each with a blackish transverse band that is sometimes broken into dots. Pronotum coarsely, sparsely punctured; elytra finely, irregularly, and distinctly punctured; antennae inserted on the front of the head and close together at bases; sparsely pubescent (Fig. 346).
Widely distributed throughout the United States.

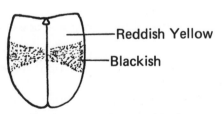

Fig. 346. Anchicera ephippiata

Tomarus pulchellus Length: 1.3–1.7mm. Brownish yellow to pitch colored; legs and basal half of each antenna paler; each elytron with a large yellow spot on the shoulder and a broad transverse band near the apex. Pronotum finely and distinctly punctured, as wide at base as at apex; elytra narrowed to acute apices, finely and sparsely punctured; second and third segments of each tarsi lobed, each third segment larger, and the fourth very small (Fig. 347).

Under dead leaves and stones in spring, on fungi in summer.

Eastern half of the United States.

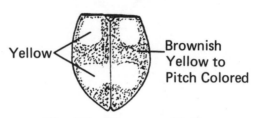

Fig. 347. Tomarus pulchellus

Antherophagus ochraceus Length: 4–4.5mm. Brownish yellow to bronze brown, slightly shining. Pronotum wider than long, sides somewhat rounded, finely and densely punctured; elytra densely, finely punctured; antennae widely separated at bases; tarsi threadlike (Fig. 348).

On flowers.

Eastern half of the United States.

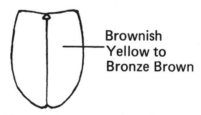

Fig. 348. Antherophagus ochraceus

Cryptophagus acutangulus Length: 2.5mm. Pale brownish yellow; head and pronotum darker.

Often found in cereals and sacked sugar.

Throughout the United States.

Telmatophilus americanus Length: 2.5–3mm. Reddish brown with yellowish to ash-gray pubescence.

Widely distributed throughout the United States.

The Tooth-Necked Fungus Beetles

Family Derodontidae
This is a small family of only five species, two being found in the East and three in the Far West. They are small, brown or dull brownish yellow beetles, with the head deeply impressed, and a small, smooth tubercle on each side of the head inside the eye; lateral margins of pronotum strongly toothed (hence their common name) or broadly flattened and bent upward. They occur on fungi.

Derodontus maculatus Length: 2.5–3mm. Dull brownish yellow; elytra with black markings (Fig. 349).
In fungi and beneath bark.
Eastern United States.

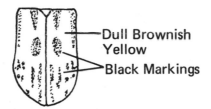

Fig. 349. Derodontus maculatus

The Hairy Fungus Beetles

Family Mycetophagidae
The *hairy fungus beetles* are small, oval insects that live under bark and in fungi. They are densely punctured and hairy and are usually attractively marked (Fig. 350).

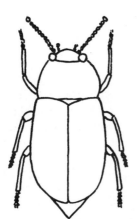

Fig. 350. Hairy Fungus Beetle

Mycetophagus punctatus Length: 4.5–5mm. Blackish above with reddish yellow markings; antennae reddish becoming blackish at apices. Eyes elongate; antennae gradually become larger at apices (Fig. 351). Eastern half of the United States.

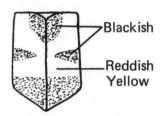

Fig. 351.   Mycetophagus punctatus

Mycetophagus flexuosus Length: 3–4mm. Blackish above with reddish yellow markings.
On sap and fungi.
Throughout the United States.

Typhaea stercorea Length: 2.5–3mm. Dull reddish yellow; elytra sometimes blackish. Eyes rounded; segments nine to eleven of each antenna abruptly enlarged (Fig. 352).
In cereal products.
Throughout the United States.

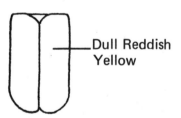

Fig. 352.   Typhaea stercorea

Lithargus didesmus Length: 2–2.2mm. Pitch colored, shining; each elytron with a yellow transverse band back of the middle and a yellow spot at the shoulder. Eyes rounded; segments nine to eleven of each antenna abruptly enlarged; pubescence in irregular patches. East of the Missouri River.

Thrimolus minutus Length: .7–.9mm. Dark brown or clay yellow.

Head large and transverse; pronotum wider than long, hind angles rounded.

Eastern half of the United States.

The Cylindrical Bark Beetles

Family Colydiidae

The beetles of this family are small insects that are usually elongate or cylindrical in form and that live under bark, in fungi, and in the earth. Some of the larvae and adults are carnivorous, feeding upon other small wood-boring species; others are parasitic; and still others live on decaying plant matter.

The antennae each have ten or eleven segments, are inserted under the margin of the frontal region, and usually have the last one or two segments of each enlarged to form a club; the coxae of the front and middle legs are small and globular, those of the hind legs are transverse; the elytra cover the abdomen; the legs are short; the tarsi are each four segmented; the abdomen has five ventral segments, the first four fused together (Fig. 353).

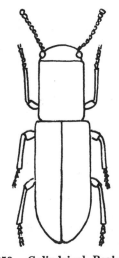

Fig. 353. Cylindrical Bark Beetle

Bitoma quadriguttata Length: 2.5–3mm. Black or blackish brown, slightly shining; each elytron with three dull reddish spots; antennae and legs reddish brown. Pronotum wider than long, with small grain-like elevations and four ridges; elytra slightly wider than pronotum, each with four ribs, the broader intervals with two rows of coarse punctures; first segment of each tarsus short.

Beneath bark and logs.
Throughout the United States.

Coxelus guttulatus   Length: 4–5mm. Black; antennae, legs, and margins of pronotum and elytra reddish brown. Pronotum wider than long, apex deeply notched, sides rounded, coarsely granulate, edges sawlike; elytra with rows of granules and spots of coarse, gray pubescence forming an interrupted wavy band on each; first segment of each tarsus short (Fig. 354).
Under bark of decaying hardwoods and in fungi.
Eastern half of the United States.

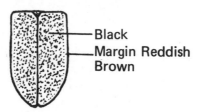

Fig. 354.   *Coxelus guttulatus*

Colydium lineola   Length: 4–6.5mm. Black, moderately shining; antennae and legs paler. Pronotum longer than wide, a strongly impressed line at middle and a shorter one either side, coarsely punctured; each alternate interval of elytra with fine ribs, others with two rows of punctures; first segment of each tarsus longer than second (Fig. 355).
Adults beneath bark, larvae in tunnels of ambrosia beetles.
Throughout the United States.

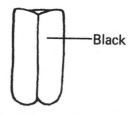

Fig. 355.   *Colydium lineola*

Bothrideres geminatus   Length: 3–4.5mm. Dark reddish brown, somewhat shining; slightly pubescent. Pronotum longer than wide, apex slightly notched, sides with small tubercle on middle of each margin,

coarsely and densely punctured; elytral striae finely punctured, intervals of each with a single row of punctures; all coxae widely separated; first segment of each tarsus longer than second or third. Beneath bark.
Eastern half of the United States.

Cerylon castaneum   Length: 2–3mm. Dark reddish brown, shining. Pronotum somewhat square shaped, hind angles rectangular, a feeble impression on each side, rather coarsely punctured; elytra with punctured striae; last segment of each of the labial and maxillary palpi needle shaped; tibiae each with small terminal spurs; combined length of first three tarsal segments shorter than fourth (Fig. 356). Beneath bark and under logs.
Throughout the United States.

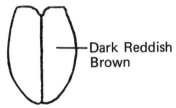

Fig. 356.   Cerylon castaneum

Philothermus glabriculus   Length: 2–3mm. Dark reddish brown, shining. Pronotum wider than long, sides rounded, finely and sparsely punctured; elytra with rows of coarse punctures; last segment of each of the labial and maxillary palpi needle shaped (Fig. 357). Beneath bark.
Eastern half of the United States.

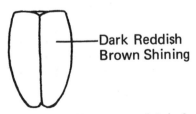

Fig. 357.   Philothermus glabriculus

The Mycetaeid Beetles

Family Mycetaeidae
   This is a small family of only four species that are found chiefly in fungi, beneath bark, and in decaying logs. The first four ventral abdominal segments are fused, only the fifth is free moving; the tarsi each have only four segments, and the antennae are inserted under a frontal ridge.

Phymaphora pulchella   Length: 3.5–4mm. Black with red markings (Fig. 358).
Eastern United States.

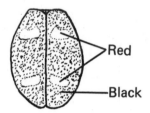

Fig. 358.   Phymaphora pulchella

The Minute Brown Scavenger Beetles

Family Lathridiidae
   As anyone might suppose from their common name, the beetles of this family are very small, hardly exceeding 2.5mm. in length. They occur, for the most part, in decaying leaves though some are found beneath bark and stones, on the flowers of viburnum, and in the nests of mammals. They are oblong in form with the elytra covering the abdomen and wider than the pronotum. The antennae each have nine or eleven segments, the club of each has two or three segments; the sides of the pronotum are often sawlike or scalloped, the hind angles each with a small tooth; the elytra each have six to eight rows of coarse punctures; the coxae of the front legs are conical and separated, those of the middle legs are rounded, and those of the hind legs are transverse; and the tarsi each have three segments, the third as long as the preceding two combined (Fig. 359).

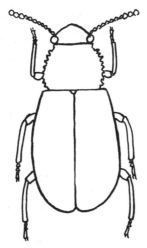

Fig. 359. Minute Brown Scavenger Beetle

Lathridius liratus   Length: 2 2.2mm. Dark reddish brown, shining; antennae and legs somewhat paler. Pronotum slightly longer than wide with two longitudinal ridges, coarsely and irregularly punctured; elytral striae coarsely, distinctly punctured; eyes on side of head; antennal clubs each three segmented; coxae of front legs spherical (Fig. 360).
Eastern half of the United States.

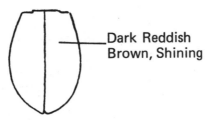

Dark Reddish
Brown, Shining

Fig. 360.   Lathridius liratus

Corticaria serrata   Length: 2–2.2mm. Dull reddish yellow to dark reddish brown; grayish pubescence. Pronotum wider than long, a short tooth at basal angle, coarsely and densely punctured, sides toothed; elytral sides rounded, apices obtusely rounded, striae slightly impressed, coarsely punctured .basally, finer apically; eyes large (Fig. 361).
In fungi.
Eastern half of the United States.

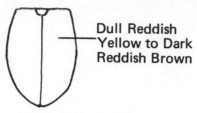

Fig. 361. Corticaria serrata

Corticaria elongata Length: 1.4–1.8mm. Light brownish or reddish yellow; elytra tinged with brownish black each side of scutellum; pubescence pale yellow. Pronotum wider than long, sides finely scalloped apically, toothed posteriorly, prominent tooth at each basal angle, finely and sparsely punctured; elytral sides rounded, apices obtusely rounded; striae finely punctured; eyes large (Fig. 362). In dead leaves and debris in damp situations.
Throughout the United States.

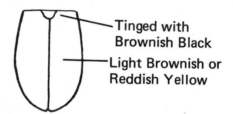

Fig. 362. Corticaria elongata

Melanophthalma distinguenda Length: 1.5–1.8mm. Dull brownish yellow; elytra usually darker, legs dull yellowish; long, conspicuous pubescence yellow. Pronotum wider than long, coarsely punctured, anterior and posterior angles rounded, transverse impression at base; elytra with coarse punctures on each basal half, finer apically; eyes very large (Fig. 363).
On various shrubs in summer; in debris in the spring.
Throughout the United States.

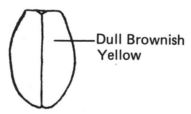

Fig. 363. Melanophthalma distinguenda

Melanophthalma cavicollis Length: 1.2–1.5mm. Head and pronotum dull reddish brown; elytra brownish black; bases of antennae, legs and apex of abdomen dull pale yellow. Pronotum wider than long, hind angles each with a small tooth, finely punctured, impression at base deep and transverse; elytra with moderate punctures, intervals finely punctured, apices rounded; eyes very large; second segment of each tarsus shorter than first.
In debris.
Eastern half of the United States.

Enicmus minutus Length: 1.5–2mm. Long, usually brown; no pubescence evident.
Throughout the United States.

Holoparamecus kunzei Length: 1mm. Long, dull reddish yellow; no pubescence evident.
Throughout the United States.

The Handsome Fungus Beetles

Family Endomychidae

This family includes a small number of species that are found for the most part in fungi, in decaying wood, or beneath logs and bark. They are moderately small beetles, oval or oblong in form, and many are strikingly colored, though some are completely black or brown.

The antennae are inserted on the frontal region and each have nine to eleven segments, the last three segments of each forming a distinct club; the pronotum is nearly square and usually has a wide, thin margin that is slightly turned upwards at the sides; the elytra are entire; the coxae of the front and middle legs are spherical, of the hind legs are transverse; and the tarsi each have four segments though they appear to have only three, the third being minute and fused to the last (Fig. 364).

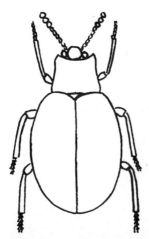

Fig. 364. Handsome Fungus Beetle

Endomychus biguttatus   Length: 3.5–5mm. Black, shining; elytra orange to reddish, each with two rounded black spots. Pronotum wider than long, finely and sparsely punctured; each elytron with a shallow impression near shoulder, finely and rather densely punctured; scutellum as long as wide, its apex rounded (Fig. 365).
Throughout the United States.

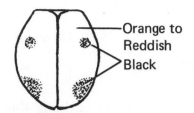

Fig. 365.   Endomychus biguttatus

Aphorista vittata   Length: 5.5–6.2mm. Dull orange to brownish red; pronotum edged with black and sometimes with an indistinct, brownish spot each side of its middle; elytra with a broad, tapering, common, black, longitudinal stripe on suture and each with another shorter one along the sides; antennae reddish. Pronotum wider than long, a distinct transverse impressed line at base, finely punctured; elytra with a broad, shallow impression near each shoulder, minutely and densely punctured; scutellum wider than long (Fig. 366).
In fungi.
Throughout the United States.

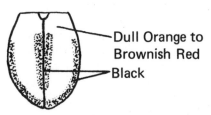

Fig. 366.   Aphorista vittata

Mycetina perpulchra   Length: 3.5–4mm. Black, shining; pronotum reddish yellow, occasionally with a blackish spot; each elytron with two reddish yellow spots. Pronotum wider than long, with a deep transverse impressed line at base, minutely and indistinctly punctured; each elytron with a deep impression at the middle of its base, finely leathery, and with fine, sparse punctures (Fig. 367).
Throughout the United States but probably more abundant on the Atlantic coastal region and in the South.

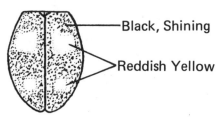

Black, Shining

Reddish Yellow

Fig. 367.   Mycetina perpulchra

Lycoperdina ferruginea   Length: 4.5–6mm. Dark brownish red to black; elytra often darker than rest of body. Pronotum wider than long, with a transverse impressed line at its base, finely and sparsely punctured; elytra sparsely, slightly punctured; scutellum wider than long (Fig. 368).

In fungi but more often in the mushroom *Lycoperdon pyriforme,* which is abundant on old fallen logs.

Eastern half of the United States.

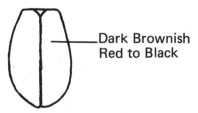

Dark Brownish
Red to Black

Fig. 368.   Lycoperdina ferruginea

The Shining Flower Beetles

Family Phalacridae

The beetles of this family are small, highly convex, and shining, with an oval or rounded body form. The adults and larvae live in the heads of various flowering plants, such as those of the *Compositae* (asters, sunflowers, dandelions, goldenrod) and various *umbelliferous plants* (carrots, celery, parsnip), but the adults also occur on leaves and in some species seem to live completely beneath the bark of logs.

The antennae are each eleven segmented, and are inserted under or on the sides of the frontal region, each with a three segmented, oval club; the elytra are entire and rounded apically; the coxae of the front legs are small and spherical, those of the middle legs are transverse and widely separated, and those of the hind legs also transverse but touching; and the tarsi are each five-segmented, the fourth small and may be difficult to find (Fig. 369).

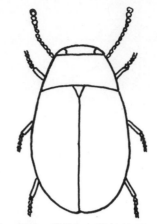

Fig. 369.   Shining Flower Beetle

Phalacrus politus   Length: 1.5–2.2mm. Black, shining; antennae and legs paler or brownish black. Head small; pronotum with lateral marginal line continued around prolonged anterior angles; elytra with a number of indefinite rows of coarse punctures; tarsi of hind legs equal in length to those of front legs; scutellum large, triangular.
Eastern half of the United States.

Olibrus semistriatus   Length: 1.7–2.3mm. Dark orange brown; body underneath, antennae and legs yellow brown to reddish brown. Eyes small; pronotum wider than long, coarsely and sparsely punctured; elytra each with two distinct, straight striae: one near suture, the second close to first; the remainder of elytral surface with rows of distinct punctures; scutellum large, triangular (Fig. 370).
Eastern half of the United States.

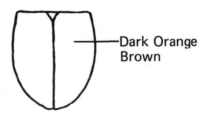

Dark Orange Brown

Fig. 370.   Olibrus semistriatus

Acylomus ergoti   Length: 1.6–1.8mm. Dark reddish brown to black, shining; body underneath and antennae often yellowish but usually light reddish brown. Eyes large; pronotum wider than long, sides rounded, lobed at base, sparsely punctured; elytra with indistinct rows of punctures, minutely and slightly wrinkled; scutellum triangular; tarsi of hind legs longer than those of front legs (Fig. 371). Eastern half of the United States.

Dark Reddish Brown to Black, Shining

Fig. 371. Acylomus ergoti

Stilbus apicalis Length: 1.2–1.4mm. Dark brown, shining; each elytron with an elongate spot of yellowish or yellowish brown at apex; body underneath, antennae, and legs light orange brown. Head about half as wide as pronotum, minutely punctured; pronotum finely leathery with minute, scattered punctures; elytra with sutural striae deep and with a number of rows of fine punctures; tarsi of hind legs longer than those of front legs; scutellum triangular (Fig. 372). Eastern half of the United States.

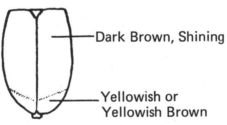

Dark Brown, Shining

Yellowish or Yellowish Brown

Fig. 372. Stilbus apicalis

Stilbus nitidus Length: 1.2–1.4mm. Orange brown, shining. Head more than half as wide as pronotum, minutely, sparsely punctured; pronotum wider than long with sparse, minute punctures; elytra broadly rounded, slightly wrinkled and with sparse, minute punctures; tarsi of hind legs longer than those of front legs; scutellum triangular (Fig. 373). Eastern half of the United States.

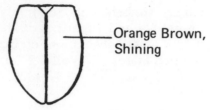

Orange Brown,
Shining

Fig. 373.   Stilbus nitidus

The Lady Beetles

Family Coccinellidae

All of us know the *lady beetles,* also called the *ladybugs* and *ladybird beetles,* as they occur frequently in our gardens and sometimes enter our houses. There are about 3,000 species. Some are very small, none are very large, and they are usually hemispherical in form, though some are more elongate-oval and less convex. They are generally red or yellow, sometimes with black spots, or black, sometimes with white, red, or yellow spots.

Both adults and larvae are found on the leaves and stems of plants and both are predaceous feeding on plant lice and other small insects. Two species, however, are herbivorous: the *squash beetle* and the notorious *Mexican bean beetle.* Some lady beetles, when handled, give off a yellowish fluid that has a rather disagreeable odor.

The antennae are each eleven segmented and are inserted at the inner margins of the eyes below the frontal region, each ending in a distinct three-segmented club; the last segment of the maxillary palpus is broad and hatchet shaped (Fig. 374); the pronotum is

Fig. 374.   Last Segment of Maxillary Palpus of Coccinella **Broad and Hatchet-Shaped**

wider than long, with its sides usually rounded and the anterior margin notched; the coxae of the front and hind legs are transverse and separated; and the tarsi are each three segmented, the second segment being dilated and padlike beneath (Fig. 375).

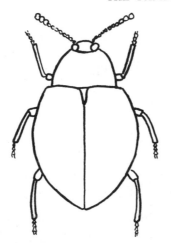

Fig. 375. Lady Beetle

The species of the genus Hyperaspis *have the coxae of the middle legs widely separated, the femora usually not extending beyond the sides of the body, the eyes partly covered by the pronotum, and the body usually oval.*

Hyperaspis undulata Length: 2–2.5mm. Black, shining; each elytron with a narrow marginal yellow stripe and a yellow oval spot near the center (Fig. 376).
Throughout the United States.

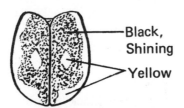

Fig. 376. Hyperaspis undulata

Hyperaspis signata Length: 2.5–3mm. Black, shining; each elytron with two reddish spots (Fig. 377).
Eastern half of the United States.

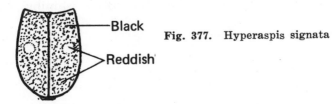

Fig. 377. Hyperaspis signata

Hyperaspis proba   Length: 2–3mm. Black, shining; pronotum with an orange spot on each side and each elytron with three spots of the same color (Fig. 378).
Eastern half of the United States.

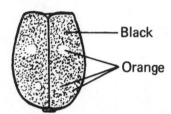

Fig. 378.   Hyperaspis proba

Hyperaspis lateralis   *The Lateral Lady Beetle*   Length: 3mm. Black, shining; pronotum with front margin yellow to red; each elytron with the shoulder margin and two spots yellow to red.
A western species, Montana to the Mexican border.

The species of the genus Brachyacantha *have characters similar to* Hyperaspis, *but the eyes are finely notched and the tibiae of the front legs each have strong spines on the outer edge.*

Brachyacantha ursina   Length: 2.5–3.5mm. Black, shining; each elytron with five yellow or orange spots; legs pale yellowish, each darker at its base (Fig. 379).
Eastern half of the United States.

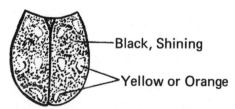

Fig. 379.   Brachyacantha ursina

Brachyacantha felina   Length: 1.8–2.3mm. Black, shining; each elytron with five orange or yellow spots.
Eastern half of the United States.

The species of the genus Scymnus *have characters similar to those of* Hyperaspis, *but the body is pubescent and not smooth as in* Hyperaspis.

Scymnus americanus Length: 2–2.5mm. Black; margins of pronotum and elytral apices broadly reddish; legs yellowish (Fig. 380). Eastern half of the United States.

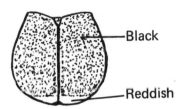

Fig. 380. Scymnus americanus

Scymnus puncticollis Length: 2–2.5mm. Dull black; pronotum usually with sides yellowish though sometimes only the apical angles are yellowish; apices of elytra reddish; tibiae and tarsi pale yellow; femora black.
Eastern half of the United States.

Scymnus terminatus Length: 1.5–1.8mm. Black; head, side margins of pronotum, legs, and apices of elytra reddish yellow; abdomen yellow except at base.
Eastern half of the United States.

Scymnus caudalis Length: 2–2.3mm. Black; head, sides of pronotum, tibiae and tarsi and sometimes a spot at tips of elytra, dull reddish; femora black.
Colorado castward.

Psyllobora vigintimaculata Length: 2–2.5mm. Pale yellowish; pronotum with five blackish spots; each elytron with nine spots; body beneath pale brownish yellow. Antennae slender, last segment of each elongate; scutellum very small; tarsal claws near apices with a large square tooth.
Eastern half of the United States.

Anisosticta strigata Length: 3–4mm. Yellow; base of head, two triangular spots on pronotum, a common, bilobed spot on elytra, and eight other spots on each of the elytra, black; body beneath

black; antennae, legs, and sides of abdomen yellow; on herbaceous plants and shrubs in swampy places.
Eastern half of the United States.

Naemia seriata   Length: 5–6mm. Head black; shining; pronotum and elytra yellow or orange, both with black spots; body beneath black.
Eastern half of the United States.

Coleomegilla fuscilabris   Length: 5–7mm. Head black with a red spot on front; pronotum and elytra reddish; pronotum with an oval black spot on each side of median line; elytra with two common black spots on suture, and each elytron with four black spots. Pronotum somewhat square shaped with anterior margin wavy; tarsal claws acutely pointed, each with a large, square-shaped basal tooth (Figs. 381, 382).
Eastern half of the United States.

Fig. 381.   Tarsal Claws of Coleomegilla

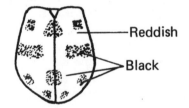

Fig. 382.   Coleomegilla fuscilabris

The species of the genus Hippodamia *have the coxae of the middle legs narrowly separated and the tarsal claws bilobed, the two lobes of unequal length* (Fig. 383).

Fig. 383.   Tarsal Claws of Hippodamia

Hippodamia tridecimpunctata tibialis   The Thirteen-Spotted Lady Beetle   Length: 4.5–5.2mm. Orange or reddish; base of head black; pronotum black, with broad, pale yellowish lateral margins, a small

black spot on each; each elytron with six small, round spots black and a common, scutellar, black one; femora and lower surface black; tibiae and tarsi pale yellowish (Fig. 384).
Throughout the United States.

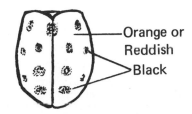

Orange or Reddish

Black

Fig. 384.   Hippodamia tridecimpunctata tibialis

Hippodamia parenthesis   The Parenthesis Lady Beetle   Length: 4–5mm. Yellowish red; head black at base and apex; pronotum black, with a narrow, white lateral margin, a small white spot at the middle of its base, and a short white line at apex; each elytron with a large, common, scutellar, black spot, a small black spot on each shoulder, and a crescent-shaped, black mark near each apex (Fig. 385).
Throughout the United States.

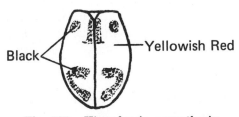

Black

Yellowish Red

Fig. 385.   Hippodamia parenthesis

Hippodamia convergens   The Convergent Lady Beetle   Length: 4–6mm. Head black, with a pale spot; pronotum black, lateral and apical margins, and two oblique, convergent bars white; elytra reddish or yellowish red, with a small common scutellar spot, and each with six small spots, all black; body beneath black (Fig. 386).
Throughout the United States.

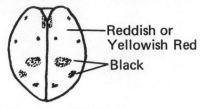

Fig. 386. Hippodamia convergens

Hippodamia glacialis Length: 6–7.5mm. Head black, with a yellow spot; pronotum black, with white apical margin and lateral margins; elytra red, each with a black oblique band and a large black spot near apex; body beneath black; abdominal segments each with a reddish spot on the sides (Fig. 387).
Eastern half of the United States.

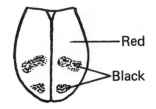

Fig. 387. Hippodamia glacialis

The species of the genus Coccinella *have the pronotum covering the greater part of the eyes; the apical segment of each antenna is cut squarely off at the tip; the coxae of the middle legs are widely separated; and the tarsal claws each have a large squarish tooth.*

Coccinella trifasciata Length: 4.5–5.5mm. Head black; pronotum black, with apical angles and margin white; elytra reddish orange, each with three black transverse bands; legs and lower surface black (Fig. 388).
Northern United States.

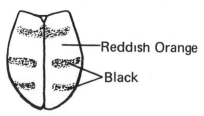

Fig. 388. Coccinella trifasciata

Coccinella novemnotata   Length: 5.5–7mm. Head black, with a yellowish white transverse band; pronotum black, with a pale yellowish apical margin and a large somewhat square-shaped spot at each apical angle of the same color; elytra yellow or orange with a common black scutellar spot and each with four other black spots; lower surface and legs black (Fig. 389).
Throughout the United States.

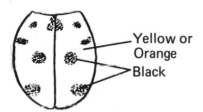

Fig. 389.   Coccinella novemnotata

Coccinella transversoguttata   Length: 6–7mm. Head black, with a white spot on each side; pronotum black, with a white spot on apical angles; elytra yellow or red, each with a transverse band near base, a very small spot near each external margin (often absent), a large transverse oval spot on each, and a transverse band near each apex, all black.
Eastern half of the United States.

Cycloneda sanguinea   Length: 4–5mm. Head black; pronotum, sides, and angles bordered with white; elytra dull reddish yellow; lower surface and legs black (Fig. 390); coxae of middle legs widely separated; tarsal claws each with a large squarish tooth.
Throughout the United States.

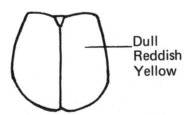

Fig. 390.   Cycloneda sanguinea

Cycloneda munda   The Red Lady Beetle   Length: 4–5.5mm. Highly similar to *sanguinea* but elytra sometimes very bright red.
Throughout the United States.

Adalia bipunctata   The Two-Spotted Lady Beetle   Length: 4–5.5mm.
Head black, with two yellowish spots; pronotum with a black, M-
shaped spot and pale whitish yellow side margins; elytra reddish,
each with a small round, black spot; lower surface black; tarsi and
sides of abdomen reddish brown. Pronotum covering large part of
eyes; coxae of middle legs widely separated (Fig. 391).
One of the most common of the species occurring in the Eastern
half of the United States; hibernates in houses.

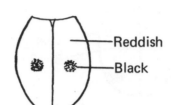

Fig. 391.   Adalia bipunctata

Mulsantina picta   Length: 4–5mm. Brownish yellow, shining; head
and pronotum both with black spots; each elytron with a longitudinal black stripe and several black spots, the spots sometimes forming transverse bands. Pronotum covering most of the eyes; coxae of
middle legs widely separated; tarsal claws each with a large, square
tooth.
Eastern half of the United States.

Anatis quindecimpunctata   The Fifteen-Spotted Lady Beetle   Length:
6.5–8.5mm. Head black, with two small yellow spots; pronotum
black, lateral margins pale with several black spots; elytra yellow or
reddish brown, with a common black spot and each with seven spots
of the same color; lower surface and femora black, tibiae and tarsi
pale yellowish or reddish brown. Pronotum covering a large part of
the eyes; coxae of middle legs widely separated; tarsal claws each
with a large squarish tooth (Fig. 392).
Eastern half of the United States.

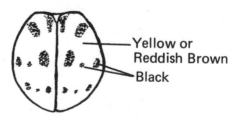

Fig. 392.   Anatis quindecimpunctata

Neomysia pullata Length: 6–7mm. Head black, with two brownish yellow spots; pronotum of male black, of female brown; elytra dull reddish brown. Pronotum covering a large part of the eyes; coxae of middle legs widely separated; tarsal claws cleft.
Eastern half of the United States.

Chilicorus stigma *The Twice-Stabbed Lady Beetle* Length: 4–5mm. Black, shining; each elytron with a round red spot. Antennae long, each with a loose club; pronotum covering large part of the eyes; coxae of middle legs widely separated; tarsal claws toothed (Fig. 393).
Throughout the United States.

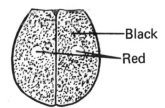

Fig. 393. Chilicorus stigma

Ceratomegilla maculata *The Spotted Lady Beetle* Length: 5–7mm. Bright red or pink; pronotum with two black spots; each elytron with six black spots. Pronotum with a narrow but distinct margin along the base, not covering the eyes; coxae of middle legs close together; tarsal claws each with a large square-shaped tooth.
A common species and quite destructive to several species of aphid pests; throughout the United States.

Rodolia cardinalis Length: 2.5–3.5mm. Red with variable black markings; upper surface pubescent. This is the famous ladybird beetle that was introduced from Australia to California for controlling the cottony cushion scale in 1888.
California and Florida.

Stethoris punctatum Length: 1.2–1.5mm. Black, shining; antennae and legs, except bases of femora, yellow. Pubescent; tarsal claws each with two lobes.
Eastern half of the United States.

Epilachna borealis *The Squash Ladybird Beetle* Length: 7–8mm. Pale orange yellow, somewhat shining; covered with short pubescence; pronotum with four black spots; each elytron with seven

black spots. Pronotum partially covering eyes; mandibles each with two lobes at each apex, with several teeth on each inner margin; tarsal claws cleft (Fig. 394). The larvae are injurious to squash, pumpkin, and related plants.
Eastern half of the United States.

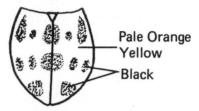

Fig. 394.   Epilachna borealis

Epilachna varivestis   The Mexican Bean Beetle   Length: 6–7mm. Yellow to coppery brown or brownish yellow, somewhat shining; each elytron with eight small, black spots (Fig. 395). Structural characters similar to those of *borealis;* both the adults and larvae very destructive to beans of all kinds.
Throughout the United States.

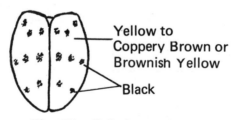

Fig. 395.   Epilachna varivestis

The Comb-Clawed Beetles

Family Alleculidae

The *comb-clawed beetles* are small to moderate-sized forms, are usually brownish or black, and, except for a few species in the genus *Mycetochara,* are without any markings. They are usually elongate, elliptical, quite convex, and clothed with minute hairs, which give a silky gloss to the upper surface. The adults are found on flowers and foliage or under bark, while the larvae, which resemble wireworms, are gregarious in burrows in dead or decaying stumps and logs.

The maxillary palpi are each four segmented and are some-times long and very dilated; the eyes are large, transverse, and notched; the antennae are long, more or less sawlike, and each are eleven segmented; the elytra are rounded at the apices; the coxae of the hind legs are transverse; the tarsi are slender, often lobed, those of the front and middle legs are each five segmented, those of the hind legs are each four segmented; and the tarsal claws are comblike (Fig. 396).

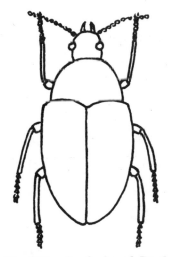

Fig. 396.   Comb-clawed Beetle

Hymenorus pilosus   Length: 7–8mm. Dark reddish brown to black-ish, shining; antennae, tibiae, and tarsi paler. Pronotum wider than long, sides rounded into apex, hind angles rectangular, coarsely and sparsely punctured; elytra nearly four times as long as pronotum, sides parallel, with rows of feebly impressed punctures; last seg-ment of maxillary palpus like a right-angled triangle (Fig. 397); tarsi lobed beneath (Figs. 398, 399) .
Central and Eastern States.

Fig. 397.   Last Segment of Maxillary Palpus of Hymenorus

Lobe

Fig. 398.   Metatarsus of Hymenorus Showing Lobe

Dark Reddish
Brown to
Blackish

Fig. 399.   Hymenorus pilosus

Hymenorus niger Length: 5.3–6mm. Black, shining, clothed with fine, ash gray pubescence. Pronotum wider than long, sides straight to middle, then rounded to apex, finely and sparsely punctured; elytra with sides nearly parallel, each with rows of small, deep punctures on basal half only; last segment of maxillary palpus shaped like a right-angled triangle; tarsi lobed beneath.
Eastern half of the United States.

Mycetochara foveata Length: 5–6mm. Dark reddish brown, shining; antennae and legs reddish brown; elytra with a small, pale reddish spot on each shoulder. Pronotum wider than long, sides rounded at middle, then converging to apex, hind angles rectangular, finely and sparsely punctured; elytra with rows of rather coarse punctures; intervals each with a single row of very fine punctures; pubescence fine and short; antennae short and heavy; last segment of maxillary palpus shaped like right-angled triangle; tarsi of front legs shorter than tibiae (Fig. 400).
Beneath bark of maple and walnut.
Central States.

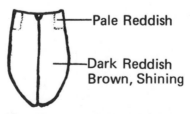

Pale Reddish

Dark Reddish
Brown, Shining

Fig. 400.   Mycetochara foveata

Mycetochara binotata   Length: 5.5–6.5mm. Shining black, with an elytral red spot about one-third of the way back on each elytron. Throughout the eastern half of the United States.

Isomira quadristriata   Length: 5–6.6mm. Dark reddish brown to black, somewhat shining; head and pronotum nearly black; antennae and tibiae usually paler. Pronotum wider than long, sides rounded on basal half, finely and densely punctured; elytra finely and sparsely but distinctly punctured, each with two striae on apical half; pubescence minute and dense; antennae slender and threadlike (Fig. 401).
On various shrubs along the borders of marshes.
Eastern half of the United States.

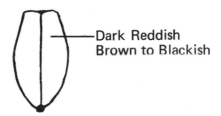
Dark Reddish
Brown to Blackish

Fig. 401.   Isomira quadristriata

Isomira sericea   Length: 5–5.5mm. Uniformly pale brownish yellow, somewhat shining, densely clothed with fine, short pubescence. Pronotum wider than long, sides straight and parallel to the middle then rounded to the apex, densely and finely punctured; elytra with two or three feebly impressed striae near the suture, more strongly marked near apices; fourth segment of maxillary palpus long and slender.
On the flowers of new jersey tea, wild hydrangea, and other shrubs. Eastern half of the United States.

Androchirus erythropus   Length: 9–10mm. Dull grayish black; antennae and legs pale reddish yellow. Eyes small and rather widely separated; antennae threadlike, third segment of each twice as long as second, shorter than fourth; mandibles sharply pointed at tips. Eastern half of the United States.

The Darkling Beetles

Family Tenebrionidae
   The *darkling beetles* are usually black or brown, though some are gray and a few are marked with bright colors. They vary great-

ly in size and in the form of the body. The adults and larvae are found under bark, in dead wood, in fungi, in dry vegetable matter, in dung, and in dead animal matter. The family is a large one and most of our species are western in their range, only a few occurring in the eastern half of the country.

The beetles are mostly oblong or oval in form; have beadlike antennae, each with eleven segments; the eyes are notched; the mandibles are short, stout, and each usually has a basal tooth; the coxae of the front legs are spherical, those of the hind legs are transverse; the tarsi of the front and middle legs each have five segments, each of those of the hind legs has four; and the first segment of each of the tarsi of the hind legs is always longer than the second (Figs. 402, 403).

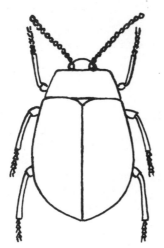

Fig. 402. Darkling Beetle

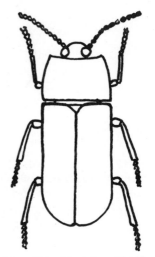

Fig. 403. Darkling Beetle

Phellopsis obcordata Length: 12–15mm. Yellow brown to deep brown. Roughly and densely sculptured; pronotum as long as wide, sides rounded, apical margin deeply notched, with small knoblike prominences; elytra each with two long elevated ridges and several rows of punctures; all ventral segments horny; mentum small, exposing maxillae and ligula; mandibles each with two lobes at apex; coxae of front legs separated (Fig. 404).
On fungi.
Eastern united States.

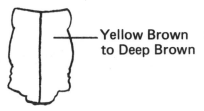

Yellow Brown
to Deep Brown

Fig. 404. Phellopsis obcordata

Blapstinus metallicus Length: 4–4.8mm. Bronzed, shining. Pronotum wider than long, apex notched, coarsely and deeply punctured; elytral punctures coarse and deep, in regular rows, intervals with fine, sparse punctures; antennal segments four to eight longer than broad.
Eastern half of the United States.

Blapstinus dilatus Length: 9–10mm. Black or dark brown. Pronotum wavy at base and with a thin cover of brownish hairs.
Under logs.
Arizona and California.

Bolitotherus cornutus Length: 10–11.5mm. Dark brown to black, dull. Pronotum wider than long, margin sawlike, with horns in male, tubercles in female; each elytron with four rows of large, irregular tubercles or knoblike prominences; surface roughly sculptured; antennae each ten segmented, third segment of each short; tarsi compressed, first segment of each short (Fig. 405).
In old fungi and on old logs; looks so much like pieces of the wood and fungi that it is hardly distinguishable.
Eastern half of the United States.

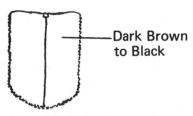

Dark Brown
to Black

Fig. 405. Bolitotherus cornutus

Diaperis maculata Length: 6–6.5mm. Black; head between eyes reddish; elytra dark orange red, each with a black sutural stripe and three black spots. Pronotum wider than long, finely and sparsely punctured; elytra with rows of fine, feebly impressed punctures;

eyes notched; antennae gradually broadened at apices; coxae of front legs transverse; first segment of each tarsus of hind legs not longer than second; tarsi pubescent (Fig. 406).
Under bark and in fungi.
Throughout the United States.

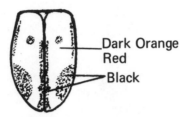

Fig. 406.   Diaperis maculata

Hoplocephala bicornis   Length: 3–4mm. Metallic bluish green, shining; pronotum occasionally brownish; lower surface black. Pronotum finely, sparsely punctured; elytral striae with coarse, deep punctures; eyes notched; antennae gradually broadened to apices; third and fourth abdominal segments with a leathery margin; first tarsal segment of each of the tarsi of hind legs longer than the second only.
On fungi of various kinds.
Throughout the United States.

Hoplocephala viridipennis   Length: 3–4mm. Differs from bicornis in having the pronotum, legs, and undersurface red, and the abdomen brownish red; elytra metallic green or blue (Fig. 407).
Beneath bark of fungus-covered logs.
Throughout the United States.

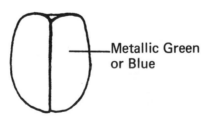

Fig. 407.   Hoplocephala viridipennis

Platydema excavatum   Length: 4.5–5.5mm. Black, shining; antennae dark reddish brown; legs the same color or black. Male with two prominent cylindrical horns between the eyes, female with tu-

bercles instead; pronotum wider than long, narrowed to apex, finely and sparsely punctured; elytral striae deep, coarsely and deeply punctured, intervals finely and sparsely punctured; last segment of maxillary palpus triangular; eyes notched; antennae gradually broadened to apices; first segment of each of the tarsi of hind legs longer than second and third together (Fig. 408).
Under bark.
Throughout the United States.

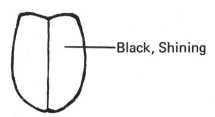

Black, Shining

Fig. 408. Platydema excavatum

The following species of the genus Platydema *have structural characteristics similar to* Platydema excavatum, *but differ slightly in size and in color and lack the horns and tubercles.*

Platydema ruficorne Length: 4–5.5mm. Dull black; lower surface and legs dark reddish brown; antennae pale reddish yellow.
Beneath bark and on fleshy fungi.
Eastern half of the United States.

Platydema ellipticum Length: 5.5–7mm. Dull black; each elytron with an oblique reddish spot extending from shoulder to suture; lower surface and legs dark reddish brown.
Beneath bark of fungus-covered logs.
Eastern half of the United States.

Platydema subcostatum Length: 5.5–6.5mm. Dark reddish brown or black, shining; antennae and legs reddish brown.
Under bark and in fungi.
Eastern half of the United States.

The species of the genus Uloma *have the last segment of the maxillary palpus triangular; the antennae each have the third segment short; the tibiae of the front legs are sawlike; and the coxae of the front legs are transverse.*

Uloma impressa Length: 11–12mm. Dark reddish brown, shining. Pronotum wider than long, hind angles obtuse, a deep, transverse

impression at middle of apex, finely sparsely punctured; front of head with a deep, curved impression; last segment of each antenna rounded at tip; elytral striae with deep, coarse punctures (Fig. 409). Under bark.
Eastern part of the United States.

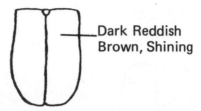

Fig. 409.   Uloma impressa

Uloma imberbis   Length: 8.5–9mm. Dark reddish brown, shining. Pronotum wider than long, sides rounded, finely and sparsely punctured; elytral striae deeply punctured, intervals sparsely punctured; head with a curved impression at apex; last segment of each antenna oblique and pointed.
Eastern part of the United States.

Uloma punctulata   Length: 7–8.5mm. Pale reddish brown. Pronotum with sides parallel behind its middle, rounded toward apex, densely and finely punctured; elytral striae deeply punctured, intervals minutely punctured (Fig. 410).
Beneath bark of pine.
More common in Southern States than elsewhere.

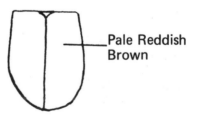

Fig. 410.   Uloma punctulata

Scotobates calcaratus   Length: 14–17mm. Black, shining; elytra bluish black. Pronotum slightly wider than long, front angles obtuse, hind angles rectangular, finely and sparsely punctured; elytral striae coarsely and deeply punctured; last segment of each antenna triangular; tarsi with fine pubescence; coxae of front legs rounded (Fig. 411). Beneath bark, logs, stones, and rubbish.
Eastern half of the United States.

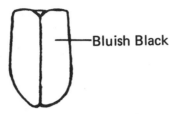

Fig. 411. Scotobates calcaratus

Xylopinus saperdioides Length: 12–16mm. Black, slightly shining; lower surface dark reddish brown. Pronotum squarish, front angles rounded, hind angles acute, finely and densely punctured; elytra narrowed at apices, striae with coarse punctures; last antennal segments triangular; tarsi with silky pubescence.
Beneath bark.
Eastern half of the United States.

Iphthimus opacus Length: 15–20mm. Black. Pronotum squarish, sides rounded, hind angles acutely toothed, coarsely punctured at sides; elytral striae interrupted, coarsely punctured; apical segments of antennae with leaflike plates; tarsi with fine pubescence.
Eastern half of the United States.

Alobates pennsylvanica Length: 20–23mm. Black, slightly shining. Pronotum square shaped, front angles rounded, hind ones acute, finely and sparsely punctured; elytra striae coarsely, deeply punctured; mentum with small lateral lobes and coarsely punctured; outer segments of antennae leaflike, last segment of each antenna rounded at apex; tarsi with fine pubescence (Fig. 412).
Beneath bark and logs.
Throughout the United States.

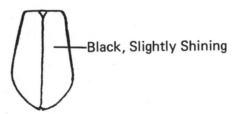

Fig. 412. Alobates pennsylvanica

Upis ceramboides Length: 14–18mm. Black, slightly shining. Pronotum slightly longer than wide, sides rounded, densely punctured; elytra with interlacing elevated ridges, the interspaces with small smooth tubercles; eyes slightly notched; outer segments of antennae leaflike; tarsi with fine pubescence.
Eastern half of the United States.

The following species of the genus Tenebrio *have the third and fourth ventral abdominal segments with horny posterior margins; have the coxae of the front legs rounded; and have the tarsi with spines or setae.*

Tenebrio obscurus　The Dark Mealworm　Length: 14–17mm. Black or dark reddish brown. Pronotum squarish, sides slightly rounded, hind angles acute, coarsely and densely punctured; elytra narrowed to apices, striae indistinct and punctured, intervals granulate.
In flour and meal; in granaries, storehouses, and barns.
Throughout the United States.

Tenebrio molitor　The Yellow Mealworm　Length: 13–16mm. Black or dark reddish brown. Pronotum wider than long, hind angles somewhat acute, finely and densely punctured; elytral striae with fine, indistinct punctures, intervals minutely and densely punctured (Fig. 413).
In same situations as *obscurus*.
Throughout the United States.

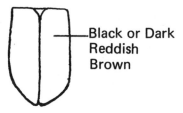

Black or Dark Reddish Brown

Fig. 413.　Tenebrio molitor

Tenebrio picipes　Length: 12–13mm. Black or dark reddish brown. Pronotum wider than long, sides somewhat rounded, an intermingling of coarse and fine punctures; elytral striae with close-set punctures, intervals minutely, densely punctured.
Beneath bark.
Eastern half of the United States.

Anaedus brunneus　Length: 5–5.5mm. Dark reddish brown, with a few long, yellowish hairs; antennae and legs dark reddish yellow. Head coarsely punctured, a rounded elevation above bases of antennae; pronotum wider than long, distinctly narrowed each side in front of hind angles, the latter angles acute, coarsely and sparsely punctured; elytra coarsely, deeply punctured; third and fourth ven-

tral abdominal segments with horny posterior margins; eyes notched; next to last tarsal segment each with two lobes.
Beneath bark, stones, and logs in dry situations.
Eastern half of the United States.

Paratenetus punctatus Length: 3–4mm. Brown, slightly shining, with silvery pubescence. Pronotum slightly wider than long, apex wider than base, sides oblique and finely sawlike, coarsely and deeply punctured; coarsely punctured elytra covered with rows of short setae; third and fourth ventral abdominal segments with horny posterior margins; eyes notched; antennae distinctly clubbed; next to last tarsal segment each with two lobes (Fig. 414).
Eastern half of the United States.

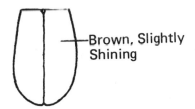

Fig. 414. Paratenetus punctatus

Tarpela micans Length: 10–17mm. Black, bronzed, shining; elytra with blue or greenish and reddish metallic stripes. Pronotum wider than long, notched at apex, coarsely and densely punctured; elytral striae indistinctly punctured; third and fourth ventral abdominal segments with horny posterior margins; front angles of pronotum extending nearly to upper edge of the eyes.
Beneath loose bark of logs; often found in colonies.
Eastern half of the United States.

Helops aereus Length: 7–9mm. Black, bronzed, shining. Pronotum slightly wider than long, densely and finely punctured; elytra with rows of elongate punctures; third and fourth ventral abdominal segments with horny posterior margins; apical segments of antennae broader; eyes slightly notched.
Beneath loose bark; often found in colonies.
Eastern half of the United States.

Meracantha contracta Length: 11–13mm. Black, bronzed. Pronotal sides narrowed to apex, coarsely and rather densely punctured; elytral striae finely punctured, intervals minutely and densely punc-

tured; no inner wings; eyes large, transverse, notched; last segment of maxillary palpus hatchet shaped; coxae of front legs rounded, those of hind legs widely separated; femora of front legs each with an obtuse tooth; sides of front of head obliquely elevated (Fig. 415). Beneath bark and logs.
Throughout the United States.

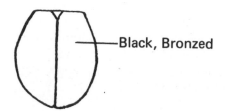

Fig. 415.   Meracantha contracta

Tribolium confusum   *The Confused Flour Beetle*   Length: 4.5–5mm. Reddish brown. Third and fourth ventral abdominal segments horny; eyes somewhat transverse and notched; coxae of front legs somewhat transverse; third segment of each antenna short, last two or three abruptly broadened (Fig. 416).
A common pest of stored food products.
Throughout the United States.

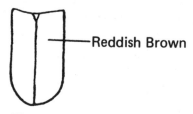

Fig. 416.   Tribolium confusum

The following species from Rhipidandrus flabellicornis *up to and including* Merinus laevis *are generally found throughout the United States. In all of them the third and fourth ventral abdominal segments have horny posterior margins.*

Rhipidandrus flabellicornis   Length: 2–3mm. Black; antennae and legs reddish brown. Eyes large, granulate; antennae comblike beginning at fifth segment of each.

Alphitophagus bifasciatus   Length: 2–2.5mm. Reddish brown to black; antennae and legs paler; elytra marked with dull yellow. Eyes rather rounded; first segment of each tarsus of hind legs longer than second and third combined; last segment of maxillary palpus triangular.

Gnathocerus maxillosus   Length: 3–4mm. Reddish brown. Eyes somewhat transverse and slightly notched; coxae of front legs somewhat transverse; each antenna widening gradually from base to apex; scutellum scarcely wider than long; first segment of each tarsus of hind legs not longer than second and third combined.

Palorus ratzeburgi   The Small-Eyed Flour Beetle   Length: 3–3.5mm. Reddish brown, shining. Pronotum squarish; other structural characters similar to *Gnathocerus maxillosus* except that the eyes are rounded and the scutellum is distinctly wider than long.

Merinus laevis   Length: 18–26mm. Black, slightly shining. Eyes somewhat transverse and notched; coxae of front legs rounded; third segment of each antenna longer than fourth; fourth segment of maxilary palpus triangular; tarsi with a dense coating of silken hairs; femora club shaped.

The following species of darkling beetles from Megasattus erosus up to and including Craniotus pubescens are Western in range. In all of them the ventral abdominal segments are completely horny.

Megasattus erosus   Length: 17–19mm. Black, rather shining. Elytra with elevated smooth areas but no definite ridges; basal segment of each tarsus of front legs long; femora with bristly hairs.

Coniontis viatica   Length: 13–15mm. Black, smooth, shining. Pronotum wider than combined bases of elytra; elytra leaving much of the sides of the body exposed; basal segments of tarsi of front legs short; eyes kidney shaped; tibiae of front legs covered with spines on lower surface. Along the ocean shore of California.

Trichiasida semilaevis   Length: 18–23mm. Dull black. Lower surface with scattered coarse punctures; labrum scarcely visible.

Pelecyphorus aegrotus   Length: 20–23mm. With similar structural characters as *Trichiasida semilaevis* but having the sides of the pronotum wavy and the base notched.

Cnemodinus testaceaous   Length: 7–8mm. Yellowish brown, with scattered yellow hairs. Scutellum triangular, longer than wide; tibiae of front legs each with a terminal spur; mandibles each with a distinct external groove.

Craniotus pubescens   Length: 11–13mm. Black. Tibiae of front legs each with two terminal spurs; coxae of hind legs small and widely separated; legs long and slender; antennae each with eleven segments but appearing as ten because of the very small first segment.

In the remaining species of darkling beetles the third and fourth abdominal segments have the posterior margins horny.

Alaudes singularis   Length: 1.5–2mm. Brownish, somewhat shining; head, pronotum, and legs covered with yellow scales. Eyes somewhat transverse and notched; coxae of front legs rounded; third segment of each antenna longer than fourth; fourth segment of maxillary palpus oval and pointed.
Southwestern United States.

Conibius gagates   Length: 6–7mm. Black, somewhat dull. Head, pronotum, and elytra finely, densely punctured. Eyes somewhat transverse and notched; coxae of front legs rounded; third segment of each antenna longer than fourth; fourth segment of maxillary palpus triangular.
Southwestern United States.

Embaphion muricatum   Length: 15–18mm. Black, sometimes brownish, shining. Structural characters similar to those of *Conibius gagates;* apical segments of antennae broader.
Western half of United States.

Eleodes suturalis   Length: 23–26mm. Black, shining. Structural characters similar to those of *Conibius gagates* but with the tarsi of the front legs spiny.
Midwest.

Eleodes granosa   *The Plains False Wireworm*   Length: 11–14mm. Black, dull, rather grayed by very fine white pubescence. Structural characters similar to those of *Conibius gagates* except that each elytron has five ridges.
California and Nevada.

The Lagriid Bark Beetles

Family Lagriidae
This family includes a number of elongate beetles each with a narrow, somewhat cylindrical prothorax, and having a more or less brassy color. They are closely related to the *Tenebrionidae* but differ in having the next to the last segment of each of the tarsi spongy beneath. They occur under bark and on leaves and the larvae are less retiring than those of the darkling beetles. Most of them occur in the South and Far West.

Arthromacra aenea   Length: 9–14mm. Brilliant green, blue, coppery, or dark brown with metallic sheen above, dark bronze below; antennae reddish brown (Fig. 417).

The most common species in the Eastern United States.

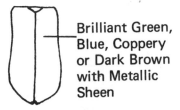

Brilliant Green,
Blue, Coppery
or Dark Brown
with Metallic
Sheen

Fig. 417.   Arthromacra aenea

The Melandryid Bark Beetles

Family Melandryidae

The beetles of this family are of small to moderate size, usually elongate in form, but sometimes oval, convex, or flattened. They are often covered with fine, silky hair.

The adults and larvae are found under bark, in dry wood, in dried fungi, and in other plant matter. A few occur on the foliage of trees and shrubs.

The antennae each have eleven segments, are inserted beneath the very narrow frontal margins, and are threadlike or somewhat thickened toward the apices; the head is usually inserted into the prothorax to the eyes; and the tarsi of the front and middle legs each have five segments, each of those of the hind legs have four, the first segment being very elongated (Fig. 418).

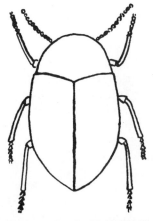

Fig. 418.   Melandryid Bark Beetle

Pisenus humeralis   Length: 3–4mm. Dark reddish brown to black, shining, sparsely covered with short, silky, yellow pubescence; elytra sometimes with a reddish spot at each shoulder. Pronotum almost twice as wide as long, sides tapering towards the base, rounded towards the apex, finely and densely punctured, a distinct pit each side of the middle; elytral apices rounded, coarsely and somewhat less densely punctured than pronotum; coxae of front legs well separated; last three segments of each antenna wider than preceding ones, forming a club; tarsi stout (Fig. 419).
Common on woody fungi.
Central and Eastern United States.

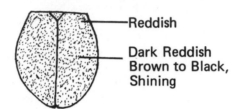

Fig. 419.   Pisenus humeralis

Penthe obliquata   Length: 11.5–14mm. Black, slightly shining; scutellum with long yellow orange hairs. Pronotum wider than long, sides rounded to apex, densely and finely punctured; elytra with rows of deep punctures; third segment of each antenna as long as fourth and fifth combined; eyes large, transverse, slightly notched; coxae of front legs well separated; first segment of each tarsus of hind legs nearly as long as remaining segments combined.
Beneath bark of decaying trees and in dry fungi.
Eastern half of the United States.

Penthe pimelia   Length: 11.5–14mm. Almost identical with *obliquata* except that the scutellum is black.
Eastern half of the United States.

Synchroa punctata   Length: 10–13mm. Dark brown to black, clothed in long, ashy pubescence. Pronotum slightly wider than long, sides narrowing from base to apex, finely and sparsely punctured, deep impression on each side, near base; elytra finely, sparsely punctured; antennae threadlike, slightly sawlike, third segment of each antenna slightly longer than fourth; eyes fairly large, slightly notched; first segment of each tarsus of hind legs as long as remaining segments combined.
Beneath bark.
Eastern half of the United States.

Eustrophinus bicolor   Length: 4.5–6mm. Black, shining, covered with short brownish black pubescence; abdomen and legs reddish brown; last segment of each antenna reddish yellow. Pronotum wider than long, hind angles rectangular, basal margin wavy each side, densely and finely punctured; elytra with rows of coarse punctures, intervals broad, densely and finely punctured; eyes large and notched; tibiae of hind legs as long as femora; coxae of front legs well separated; tibiae of hind legs each with fine teeth or spurs on outer margin.
Beneath bark of decaying logs.
Throughout the United States.

Eustrophus tomentosus   Length: 4–5mm. Reddish brown, slightly shining, covered with short yellowish hairs; lower surface and legs paler brown. Pronotum wider than long, hind angles rounded, basal margin slightly wavy each side, median lobe broad, densely and finely punctured; elytra with rows of fine punctures, intervals densely punctured; tibiae of hind legs as long as femora and each with fine teeth on outer margin; last seven segments of each antenna forming a loose club (Fig. 420).
Beneath bark and in dry fungi.
Eastern half of the United States.

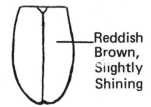

Reddish Brown, Slightly Shining

Fig. 420.   Eustrophus tomentosus

Holostrophus bifasciatus   Length: 4–5.5mm. Reddish brown, shining, covered with short, yellowish hairs; elytra blackish each with two yellowish bands. Pronotum wider than long, hind angles somewhat acute, a prominent lobe at the middle of the base, densely and finely punctured; elytra densely, finely punctured; eyes rather small, widely separated, notched; last six segments of antenna forming a club (Fig. 421).
Eastern half of the United States.

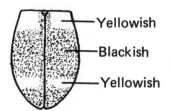

Yellowish

Blackish

Yellowish

Fig. 421.   Holostrophus bifasciatus

Orchesia castanea   Length: 4–5mm. Dark brown, covered with silky, brown hairs; legs somewhat paler. Pronotum wider than long, coarsely and densely punctured toward base, finely punctured toward apex; elytra densely and coarsely punctured, a shallow groove along suture; eyes large, notched; antennae gradually thickened toward apices; tibiae of hind legs shorter than femora, each with a comblike apical spur.
Eastern half of the United States.

Dircaea quadrimaculata   Length: 7–9mm. Dark brown to blackish, shining; elytra each with two irregular yellowish spots. Pronotum wider than long, finely and densely punctured, a feeble impression each side at base; elytra coarsely, sparsely punctured; tibiae of middle and hind legs obliquely cut off at apices; next to last segment of each tarsus notched and more or less lobed beneath (Fig. 422).
Throughout the United States.

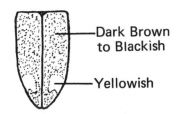

Fig. 422.   Dircaea quadrimaculata

Symphora flavicollis   Length: 3–3.5mm. Blackish, shining; head, pronotum, and legs brownish yellow. Pronotum wider than long, sides rounded, apex cut off, sparsely and coarsely punctured; elytra sparsely and coarsely punctured; eyes oval in outline; last segment of maxillary palpus hatchet shaped; antennae threadlike; tarsi each with next to last segment notched and each more or less with two lobes beneath.
Beneath bark and on foliage.
Eastern half of the United States.

Mystaxus simulator   Length: 5–7mm. Brownish yellow, slightly shining, pubescent; head black; pronotum with black crossband near apex; each elytron with a black spot at base and a black band behind the middle and at apex. Pronotum slightly wider than long, sides rounded, hind angles acute, a long deep impression each side at base, moderately punctured; elytra coarsely and densely punctured; eyes elongate, nearly parallel sided; last segment of maxillary palpus long, curved, and flat; antennae threadlike; third segment of each tarsus of hind legs notched and shorter than second (Fig. 423).
Eastern half of the United States.

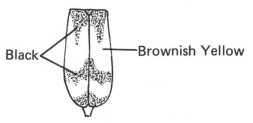

Black— —Brownish Yellow

Fig. 423.   Mystaxus simulator

Melandrya striata   Length: 8–15mm.   Black,   shining.   Pronotum with three broad grooves on basal half, base notched in the middle, finely and sparsely punctured; elytra deeply striate, intervals finely punctured; next to last segment of each tarsus notched and more or less lobed beneath (Fig. 424).
Eastern half of the United States.

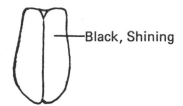

—Black, Shining

Fig. 424.   Melandrya striata

Emmesa labiata   Length: 9–11mm. Black, shining. Pronotum slightly wider than long, sides gradually rounded from base to apex, finely and densely punctured; elytra finely, densely punctured, each with two or three indistinct ridges; antennae stout, apical segments gradually thickened; next to last segment of each tarsus notched and more or less lobed beneath.
On the foliage of various trees and shrubs.
Eastern half of the United States.

Canifa pallipes   Length: 2–2.5mm. Dark brown, covered with fine yellow hairs; legs brownish yellow. Pronotum wider than long, apex and base cut off squarely, finely and densely punctured; elytra finely and somewhat densely punctured; head constricted behind eyes into a short neck; antennae slightly sawlike; tarsi with next to last segment of each notched and more or less lobed beneath; tarsi of hind legs each with first segment nearly twice as long as remaining segments combined.
On the foliage of low trees and shrubs.
Eastern half of the United States.

Osphya varians   Length: 5–8mm. Blackish, with fine, gray hairs; pronotum reddish yellow with two black longitudinal bands that are sometimes fused into one.
Throughout the United States.

Tetratoma truncorum   Length: 4.5–6mm.   Head   and   antennae black; legs and lower surface reddish yellow; elytra steel blue. Pronotum wider than long, sides rounded, hind angles obtuse.
Iowa eastward.

The Spider Beetles

Family Ptinidae
The *spider beetles* are small forms that live, for the most part, in dried animal substances. Some, however, feed on cereal products and dried herbs, others are harmful to articles made from silk, and still others attack insect collections.

The head is small and is retractile into the prothorax; the antennae are inserted upon the front of the head, are rather long, threadlike or slightly sawlike, and are each eleven segmented; the maxillary palpi are short and each is four segmented; the elytra are often swollen and partially enclose the abdomen, thus giving the beetles the hunched appearance of certain spiders; the hind wings are often absent; the tibiae each have two small spurs at the apex; the tarsal claws are spreading or divergent; and the abdomen has five segments (Fig. 425).

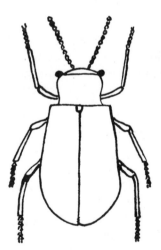

Fig. 425.   Spider Beetle

Gibbium psylloides   The Storehouse Beetle   Length: 2–3.5mm. Dark reddish brown, shining; upper surface smooth; lower surface, antennae, and legs with dense, pale yellowish hairs. Pronotum wider than long, sides straight, tapering toward apex, slightly and finely punctured; elytra polished, swollen, widely overlapping abdomen at sides; hind wings absent; eyes small; legs rather long and slender; antennal segments cylindrical; four abdominal segments visible (Fig. 426).

On grain and vegetable products, woolen material, leather, and even rubber mats in houses, hotels, mills, and granaries.

Throughout the United States.

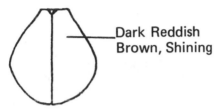

Dark Reddish Brown, Shining

Fig. 426.   Gibbium psylloides

Mezium affine   Length: 3–4mm. Dark reddish brown, shining; whole body except elytra covered with shining, pale yellowish matted pubescence and scales. Pronotum wider than long, sides straight, slightly divergent to apex, each side of middle with a broad, linear elevation, each elevation is parallel to the other, and a shorter, lower, similar elevation laterally; elytra swollen, polished, concealing much of abdomen; hind wings absent; eyes small; abdomen with five visible segments; antennal segments flattened and sawlike (Fig. 427).

Eastern half of the United States.

Dark Reddish Brown, Shining

Fig. 427.   Mezium affine

Ptinus fur   The White-Marked Spider Beetle   Length: 2.5–4.5mm. Dull reddish yellow or pale brown; pronotum with a tuft of yellowish hairs each side of middle; elytra each with an irregular patch of whitish scales behind the shoulder and another forming a crossband near each apex. Pronotum a little narrower than head, nearly as wide as long, constricted toward base, with some tubercles and a distinct median impressed line; elytral striae slightly impressed, coarsely punctured, parallel sided; abdomen with five segments; antennae threadlike, first segment of each stout, second the smallest, and the remaining elongate (Fig. 428).

On a wide variety of animal and vegetable products, including herbarium specimens, stuffed birds, and insect collections.

Throughout the United States.

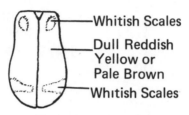

Fig. 428. Ptinus fur

Ptinus hirtellus   The Brown Spider Beetle   Length: 2.7–3.5mm.
Pale brown.
An introduced species.
Widely distributed.

Sphaericus gibboides   Length: 1.8–2.2mm.   Brown   and   clothed with pale brown and yellow scales.
Lives in all kinds of food products.
Throughout the United States.

The Drugstore and Deathwatch Beetles

Family Anobiidae
The beetles of this family are small and generally of a cylindrical form, though some are broadly oval or nearly globular. They live chiefly on dried vegetable matter and in woodwork, furniture, and dead trees. Some are pests in drugstores and groceries where they infest a great variety of substances. The name of *deathwatch beetles* comes from the ticking noise they make by bumping their heads against the walls of the wooden burrows in which they live and, at one time, superstitious people believed the noises foretold a death. Their ticking noise has also given rise to strange tales of haunted houses.

The antennae are inserted on the sides of the head in front of the eyes; they are each nine to eleven segmented and may be threadlike, sawlike, or comblike. The pronotum is usually margined at the sides; there are five abdominal segments; and the coxae of the front and middle legs are cylindrical or somewhat spherical, those of the hind legs are transverse and are usually grooved to receive the femora (Fig. 429).

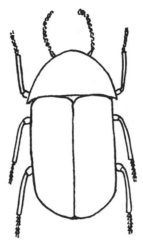

Fig. 429.   Drugstore and Deathwatch Beetle

Xestobium rufovillosum   *The Deathwatch Beetle*   Length: 6–7.5mm.
Dark brown with scattered areas of dull black and yellow hairs.
Pronotum wider than long, sides flattened, front and hind angles
rounded, densely and granularly punctured; elytra also granularly
punctured; antennae each with eleven segments; tarsi broad, densely pubescent beneath (Fig. 430).
Eastern half of the United States.

Dark Brown with
Scattered Areas of
Dull Black and
Yellow Hairs

Fig. 430.   Xestobium rufovillosum

Sitodrepa panicea   *The Drugstore Beetle*   Length: 2.5–3.5mm. Reddish brown, with yellowish pubescence. Pronotum as wide as elytra, narrowed towards the apex, anterior side margins finely sawlike, front and hind angles rounded, sparsely granulate; elytra finely striate, punctured, intervals each with a single row of punctures
each of which bears a hair; last segment of maxillary palpus parallel and obliquely cut off; last segment of labial palpus triangular;
antennae each eleven segmented, first segment of each elongate;
coxae of middle legs separated (Fig. 431).
In drug and grocery stores and in homes where it feeds on drugs
and food products; also injurious to paper items such as books and
manuscripts.
Throughout the United States.

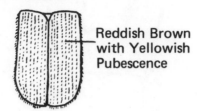

Fig. 431.   Sitodrepa panicea

Hadrobregmus carinatus   Length: 3.5–6.5mm. Reddish brown to blackish. Pronotum almost as wide as elytra, sides rounded, hind angles rounded, finely punctured; elytral striae punctured; antennae each ten segmented, last three elongate; coxae of front and middle legs widely separated.
In logs in wet woods.
Eastern half of the United States.

Trypopitys sericeus   Length: 5–6.2mm. Dark brown, with pale yellowish pubescence. Pronotum about as long as wide, sides parallel, hind angles almost rectangular, with a median impressed line and a transverse impression on each side of the basal third; elytra with regular rows of deep, square punctures, intervals finely and densely punctured; antennae each eleven segmented, more or less sawlike; coxae of middle legs widely separated.
Beneath bark.
Eastern half of the United States.

Lasioderma serricorne   The Cigarette Beetle   Length: 2.2–3mm. Dull reddish yellow or brownish red. Front angles of pronotum acute, hind ones absent, finely and uniformly punctured; elytra without striae; grooves for antennae on head; antennae each eleven segmented, somewhat sawlike (Fig. 432).
On tobacco, cayenne pepper, figs, yeast, and similar substances.
Throughout the United States.

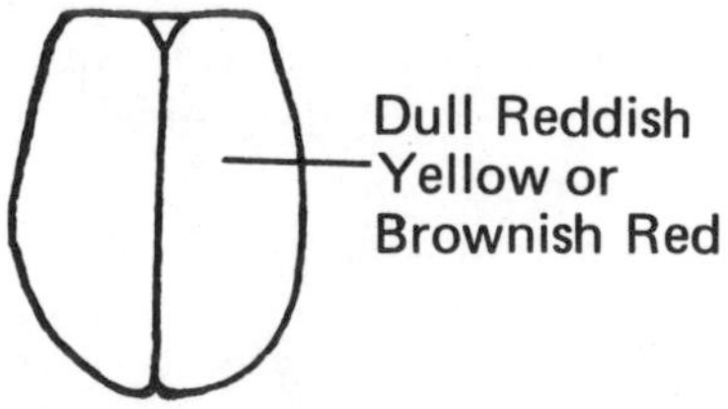

Dull Reddish
Yellow or
Brownish Red

Fig. 432.   Lasioderma serricorne

Ptilinus ruficornis Length: 3–4.5mm. Dull, black; antennae and legs reddish yellow. Pronotum slightly wider than elytra, sides rounded, front angles rectangular, hind ones rounded, a median line ending at base in a tubercle, granulate; elytra finely rough, distinctly punctured; fourth to tenth antennal segments of male fan shaped, fourth to tenth antennal segments of female sawlike; tibiae of front legs each with outer margin prolonged at apex into a horizontal tooth; tarsi as long as tibiae (Fig. 433).
Adults on dead branches of oak and maple, in which the larvae also live.
Eastern United States.

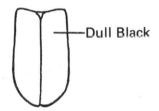

Fig. 433.   Ptilinus ruficornis

The Powder-Post Beetles

Family Bostrichidae

The *powder-post beetles* are rather small insects, elongate or cylindrical in form, and mostly black, dark brown, or reddish brown in color. They live either in living trees or in dry wood, in the latter case often reducing the wood to powder, hence their common name. They often do extensive damage to old dwellings and furniture. Some species are found in woody fungi.

The head is bent downward and is largely concealed from above by the pronotum; the eyes are small; the antennae are each ten segmented and inserted before the eyes; the last three or four segments of each forming a club; the abdomen has five visible segments; the tibiae of the front legs are usually sawlike, each with a single long spur at the apex, each of those of the middle and hind legs has distinct spurs; and the first segment of each tarsus is very short, the fifth segment is long, and each tarsus has simple claws (Fig. 434).

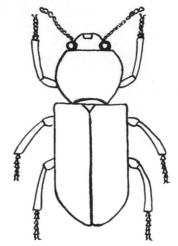

Fig. 434. Powder-post Beetle

Endecatomus rugosus Length: 4–4.5mm. Dark brown to blackish, irregularly covered with tufts of ashy, woolly pubescence. Pronotum widest near base, sides rounded, tapering to apex, densely, rather coarsely granulate; elytra each with a broad, low hump at the base, the disk of each with small granules arranged in a network, and each covered with hairs; head only partially inclined and visible from above; tibiae of front legs each with a large, hooked terminal spur; tarsi each with last segment elongate; antennae each eleven segmented (Fig. 435).
Beneath bark of trees and on woody fungi.
Eastern United States.

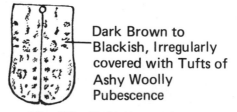

Dark Brown to Blackish, Irregularly covered with Tufts of Ashy Woolly Pubescence

Fig. 435. Endecatomus rugosus

Xylobiops basilare Length: 4–7mm. Blackish to dark reddish brown; elytra each dull reddish yellow on shoulder or basal third; antennae, palpi, and tarsi brownish yellow. Pronotal sides narrowing toward apex, all angles rounded, densely punctured with numerous small tubercles anteriorly; elytra coarsely, densely punctured, each with three smooth, prominent ridges; elytral apical fourth of each sloping, coarsely punctured, and margined with three tubercles; first and second segments of each antenna longer than the middle ones (Fig. 436).

Throughout the United States.

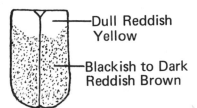

Fig. 436.   Xylobiops basilare

Amphicerus hamatus   The Apple Twig Borer   Length: 6–11.5mm. Brownish black to reddish brown; antennae and legs somewhat paler. Pronotum somewhat spherical, sides rounded, each apical angle produced into a short, clawlike horn, densely and coarsely punctured on basal half, coarsely tuberculate on apical half; elytra coarsely punctured, at extreme apices abruptly sloping, a single spine or tubercle present, which curves inward above each slope; first and second antennal segments shorter than middle ones (Fig. 437).

Adults bore into living twigs of ash, hickory, apple, pear, cherry, peach, plum, and grape; larvae in diseased or dying wood of various kinds.

East of the Rockies.

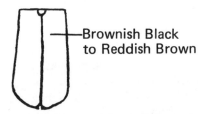

Fig. 437.   Amphicerus hamatus

Lichenophanes bicornis   Length: 7–12mm. Dark brown or brownish black with irregular patches of short pale yellow pubescence. Pronotum spherical, apical margin with two hooklike processes and cut off squarely between them, a median impressed line; elytra coarsely punctured, each with two slight ridges, apical slopes in female with

a low, rounded hump, which in the male is prolonged into a long, curved spine; first and second antennal segments combined shorter than middle ones.
Beneath bark and in old fungi.
Iowa to Florida and east to Atlantic coast.

Polycaon stoutii Length: 11–21mm. Wholly black; head and thorax coarsely punctured; elytra finely punctured.
In dead wood.
Western United States.

Psoa maculata *The Spotted Limb Borer* Length: 7–15mm. Bronze, colored with a covering of gray hairs; elytra blackish or bluish green, with several reddish, yellow, or white spots.
In dead wood.
Western United States.

Scobicia declivis *The Lead Cable Borer* Length: 5–6mm. Black or dark brown.
Feeds on dry wood but often bores into the lead sheathing of telephone cable and hence is also known as the *short circuit beetle.*
Western United States.

The Lyctid Powder-Post Beetles

Family Lyctidae

This family is composed of a small number of beetles that resemble the powder-post beetles in habits. A number of species are serious pests, the larvae living in the sapwood of various trees. They also attack seasoned timber, the pith of vines, and the dried roots of herbaceous plants, and frequently do considerable damage to old buildings.

The head is extended horizontally outward and is not covered by the prothorax; the antennae are each eleven segmented and each has a two-segmented club; the coxae of the hind legs are widely separated; each tarsus has the first segment very short, the fifth elongate; and the abdomen has five ventral segments, the first being the longest (Fig. 438).

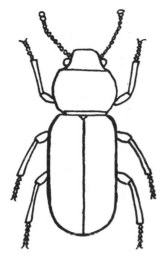

Fig. 438. Lyctid Powder-post Beetle

Lyctus opaculus   The Opaque Powder-Post Beetle   Length: 3.5–5mm. Reddish brown to blackish, with scattered yellow hairs; head, pronotum, and antennae usually darker than rest of body. Pronotum longer than wide, sides gradually widened toward the apex and rounded into apical margin, densely and finely punctured; each elytron with six slightly elevated, broad, longitudinal lines, with two irregular rows of coarse punctures between each set of longitudinal lines (Fig. 439).
On the dead branches of various hardwoods.
Eastern half of the United States.

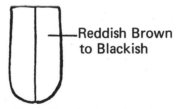

Reddish Brown
to Blackish

Fig. 439. Lyctus opaculus

Lyctus planicollis   The Flat-Necked Powder-Post Beetle   Length: 4–6mm. Black, sparsely covered with short, yellowish white hairs. Pronotum about as long as wide, sides rounded into apical margin, coarsely and densely punctured; each elytron with eleven slightly elevated, longitudinal lines bearing hairs, with two irregular rows

of fine punctures between each set of longitudinal lines (Fig. 440).
In dried timber, lumber, wood products, and in dwellings.
Throughout the United States.

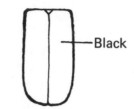

Fig. 440.   Lyctus planicollis

The Minute Tree-Fungus Beetles

Family Cisidae

This family includes very small beetles that live under the bark
of trees and in the dry and woody species of fungi. They are cylindrical or elongate in form, are black or brownish, have the pronotum prolonged over the head, have the abdomen with five ventral
segments (the first being the longest), and have the tarsi each with
four segments (Fig. 441).

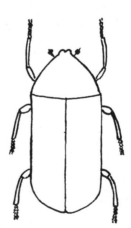

Fig. 441.   Minute Tree-fungus Beetle

Cis cornuta   Length: 2–2.5mm. Dark reddish brown, covered with
erect yellowish hairs; antennae and legs paler. Clypeus with two triangular teeth; antennae each ten segmented (Fig. 442).
Eastern United States.

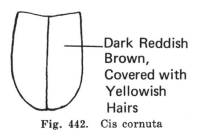

Fig. 442.   Cis cornuta

Cis fuscipes   Length: 2.5–3mm. Black to dark reddish brown; antennae and legs paler. Clypeus without teeth; third segment of each antenna longer than fourth (Fig. 443).
Eastern half of the United States.

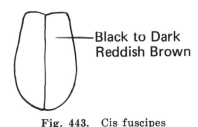

Fig. 443.   Cis fuscipes

Ceracis sallei   Length: 1.3mm. Dull reddish yellow; elytra blackish at bases; antennae each with eight segments.
   Throughout the United States.

The Lamellicorn Beetles

Family Scarabaeidae
   This is a very large family of beetles that vary rather greatly in size, form, color, and feeding habits. Many are dull brown or black, but there are others that are brilliant metallic blue or green or variegated in attractive, contrasting colors. They are mostly short, stout-bodied beetles, but vary from convex to compressed, from broadly oval to elongate-oblong. Quite often the males, and sometimes the females, are ornamented with prominent horns (corns) on the head or pronotum. The most useful character for distinguishing the members of the family from others is the lamellate or leaflike form of each antennal club, the segments composing it being greatly flattened and capable of being brought close together, hence the name *lamellicorn beetles*.
   According to their habits, the beetles of the family can be separated into two well-marked groups: those that feed as both adults and larvae on carrion, dung, excreta, skin, feathers, and similar substances (scavengers), and those that feed as adults on leaves, flowers,

and pollen, and as larvae on roots, plant juices, and decaying wood (leaf chafers).

The antennae each have seven to eleven segments, usually ten however, and each club is of from three to seven leaves, which can be expanded or folded together; the tibiae of the front legs are toothed or scalloped; the tarsi of the middle and hind legs are each five segmented, each of those of the front legs are variable in number; there are six ventral abdominal segments visible; the coxae of the front and middle legs are large and transverse, those of the hind legs are flat and transverse; and the tarsal claws are generally equal (Figs. 444, 445).

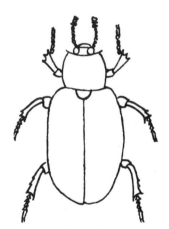

Fig. 444.   Lamellicorn Beetle

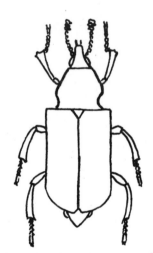

Fig. 445.   Lamellicorn Beetle

Ateuchus histeroides   Length: 6–7mm. Black; bronzed above; chestnut brown, shining beneath. Base of pronotum with a slight groove at the middle, a small pit on each side of the pronotum, disk sparsely punctured; elytral striae finely punctured; coxae of front legs transverse; tibiae of middle and hind legs each dilated at the apex, each of those of hind legs with a single spur.
In cow dung and on dead fish.
Eastern half of the United States.

Pinotus carolinus   Length: 20–28mm. Black, shining. Pronotum finely, rather sparsely punctured; elytra each with four striae, slightly punctured; labial palpi broad, compressed, and each three segmented; coxae of front legs conical (Fig. 446); tibiae of hind legs each with a single spur.
Throughout the United States.

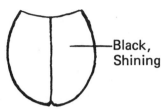

Fig. 446.   Pinotus carolinus

The beetles of the genera Canthon, Copris, *and* Phanaeus *are known as* tumble bugs *because they have the habit of forming round balls of dung, which they roll long distances and then bury in the ground where the females lay their eggs in one side of it. This assures the larvae of having access to food when they emerge from the eggs.*

Canthon laevis   The Common Tumble Bug   Length: 11–19mm. Black with coppery tinge, sometimes dark blue or greenish. Pronotum wider than long, widest at the middle, narrowed to base and apex, basal margin rounded, densely granulate; elytra each with four slightly impressed striae, rather densely granulate. Clypeus with prominent teeth; tibiae of middle and hind legs each curved and slender, each of those of hind legs with a single spur; last three segments of each antennal club with gray, matted hair (Fig. 447). In cow dung.
Throughout the United States.

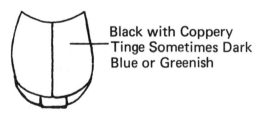

Fig. 447.   Canthon laevis

The species of the genus Copris *unlike those of* Canthon *bury the dung in burrows nearby instead of transporting it to a distance.*

Copris minutus   Length: 8–11mm. Black, slightly shining. Pronotum densely and coarsely punctured, with a broad rounded impression on each side; elytra each with four punctured striae; clypeus notched on anterior margin; labial palpi each broad, compressed, each three segmented; coxae of front legs conical; tibiae of hind legs each with one spur (Fig. 448).
Eastern half of the United States.

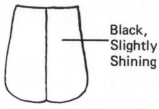

Fig. 448. Copris minutus

Copris tullius Length: 13–18mm. Black, slightly shining. Pronotum densely and coarsely punctured, with three tubercles, median notched, not quite so prominent in female; elytra with broad striae transversely punctured; vertex of head in male with a blunt horn, in female with a tubercle; clypeus notched; tibiae of hind legs each with one spur.
Eastern half of the United States.

The beetles of the genus Phanaeus *excavate tubular burrows near or under dung.*

Phanaeus vindex Length: 14–22mm. Head bronzed; pronotum bright coppery red; elytra metallic green, sometimes tinged with bluish. Pronotum strongly wrinkled; elytra striate, intervals wrinkled and punctured; first segment of each antennal club hollowed to receive the others; clypeus in male usually with a long horn; tarsi absent on front legs of male, slender in female; tarsal claws absent on all legs; tibiae of hind legs each with a single spur (Fig. 449).
From Rockies eastward.

Fig. 449. Phanaeus vindex

The species of the genus Onthophagus *have two-segmented labial palpi; the tibiae of the hind legs each have a single spur; the coxae of the front legs are large and conical; and the tarsal claws each have a long process, bearing setae.*

Onthophagus hecate Length: 6.5–9mm. Black, with purplish tinge, with sparse, short, grayish hairs. Pronotum rather densely granulate, in male with a process notched apically, in female with a transverse protuberance; elytra finely striate, intervals each with two or three rows of fine granules; clypeus and vertex slightly ridged.

In fresh cow dung and in carrion.

Throughout the United States.

Onthophagus orpheus   Length: 5–7mm. Brilliant bronze or metallic green, polished; elytra sometimes bluish. Pronotum sparsely punctured, in male with a long process, notched or forked apically, in female with a transverse, low, distinct protuberance; elytra finely striate, intervals with two series of fine punctures (Fig. 450); in male, clypeus with an indistinct ridge, in female with a distinct one.

In fungi and carrion.

Eastern half of the United States.

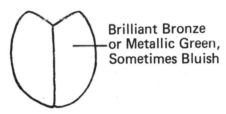

Brilliant Bronze or Metallic Green, Sometimes Bluish

Fig. 450.   Onthophagus orpheus

Onthophagus janus   Length: 4–8mm. Blackish to bronze or greenish, slightly shining and slightly pubescent. Pronotum with sparse, coarse punctures, protuberance in male not as prominent as in *hecate;* elytra finely striate, intervals each with two or three series of fine granules; head in male usually with a slight ridge, which ends on each side in a slender horn.

In decaying fungi.

Eastern half of the United States.

The species of the genus Aphodius *have nine or ten-segmented antennae; the tibiae of the hind legs each have two apical spurs; the tibiae of the middle and hind legs have transverse ridges; and the tibiae of the front legs each expand toward the tip, and the outer margin of each is toothed.*

Aphodius fimetarius   Length: 6–8mm. Black, shining; elytra red; front angles of pronotum reddish yellow. Pronotum coarsely, irregularly punctured, intermingled with finer punctures; elytral striae with scalloped punctures, intervals sparsely punctured; head sparsely and finely punctured; clypeus slightly notched (Fig. 451).

In or beneath cow dung.

Throughout the United States.

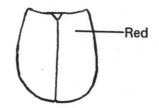

Fig. 451. Aphodius fimetarius

Aphodius granarius Length: 4–6mm. Black, shining; legs reddish brown; antennae paler. Pronotum smooth in male, with coarse and fine punctures intermingled in female; elytral striae with fine sawlike punctures, intervals finely punctured; head with three tubercles; clypeus slightly notched.
In dung and in fungi.
Throughout the United States.

Aphodius distinctus Length: 4.5–6mm. Black, shining; elytra grayish yellow with black spots. Pronotum sparsely punctured in male, more densely so in female; elytral striae with scalloped punctures, intervals finely punctured; clypeus notched; first segment of each tarsus of hind legs longer than next two (Fig. 452).
Throughout the United States.

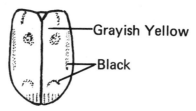

Fig. 452. Aphodius distinctus

Aphodius femoralis Length: 4.5–7mm. Black, shining; pronotal sides dull yellow; elytra light yellowish brown, more yellowish toward the bases, pubescent; antennae and legs reddish brown. Pronotum wider than long, finely punctured in male, more densely in female; elytral striae deep and finely punctured, intervals with a row of punctures on each side near striae; head with three tubercles on vertex; clypeus notched.
Throughout the United States.

Aphodius bicolor Length: 4.5–6mm. Black; elytra black, alternate intervals dotted with reddish; undersurface and legs pale yellow

(which distinguishes this species from the others). Pronotum wider than long, densely punctured, hind angles rounded; elytra deeply striate, striae with fine scalloped punctures; head densely and coarsely punctured; clypeus notched.
Eastern half of the United States.

The species of the genus Ataenius *resemble those of* Aphodius, *though they are somewhat smaller and more slender; the head is without tubercles; the eyes are concealed; the tibiae do not have the transverse ridges; and the outer apical angles of the tibiae of the hind legs each have a spine.*

Ataenius abditus Length: 3.5–4.5mm. Black, slightly shining; legs pale reddish brown; antennae and labial and maxillary palpi paler. Pronotum almost twice as wide as long, densely and somewhat coarsely punctured, hind angles rounded; elytra finely punctured, striae deep and punctured, intervals with sides scalloped; clypeus slightly notched.
Eastern half of the United States.

Ataenius gracilis Length: 3–4mm. Black, shining; legs brownish; antennae, labial and maxillary palpi, tarsi, and narrow margin of pronotum paler. Pronotum wider than long, hind angles rounded, coarsely and densely punctured; deeply and broadly striate, striae indistinctly punctured, each interval with a row of elevations on the sides; clypeus notched; tibiae of hind legs each without the spine.
Eastern half of the United States.

Ataenius spretulus Length: 4.5–5mm. Black, shining; legs, clypeus at sides, and narrow apical margin of pronotum reddish brown. Pronotum wider than long, sides slightly rounded, hind angles rounded, coarsely and finely punctured, the punctures intermingled; elytral striae punctured, intervals scalloped on inner side, shoulders toothed; clypeus with numerous fine wrinkles, slightly notched.
In and beneath cow dung and in fungi.
Eastern half of the United States.

The species of the genus Geotrupes *have eleven-segmented antennae, antennal clubs each of three segments, and plates all of equal width; the tibiae of the hind legs each have two apical spurs; and the clypeus is rounded anteriorly.*

Geotrupes splendidus Length: 12–18mm. Brilliant metallic green, purple, or bronze. Pronotum wider than long, sparsely and finely punctured, more so at sides; elytral striae deep and punctured; head with a median tubercle; first tarsal segment of each of hind legs

shorter than the next three combined (Fig. 453).
Under manure but sometimes on carrion.
Eastern half of the United States.

Brilliant Metallic Green, Purple, or Bronze

Fig. 453. Geotrupes splendidus

Geotrupes blackburnii Length: 14–20mm. Purple or black, sometimes bronzed with green or purple. Pronotum wider than long, sides coarsely but sparsely punctured, the remainder of pronotum relatively free of punctures; elytral striae without punctures or nearly so; head with a median tubercle; first tarsal segment of each of hind legs equal to next three combined.
In or under manure.
Eastern half of the United States.

Geotrupes semiopacus Length: 14–20mm. Purple or black, sometimes bronzed with green or purple. Pronotum wider than long and punctured like *blackburnii;* elytral striae without punctures or nearly so except at sides; head without tubercles; clypeus with tubercle.
In and under manure.
Eastern half of the United States.

The species of the genus Serica *resemble small May beetles in habit and in general appearance. The tibiae of the middle and hind legs each have two spurs; the tarsal claws are equal; and each antennal club is smooth and polished.*

Serica sericea Length: 8–10mm. Purplish brown, slightly shining, iridescent. Pronotum wider than long, finely and shallowly punctured; elytral striae finely, irregularly punctured, intervals sparsely punctured; clypeus slightly notched.
Beneath debris.
Eastern half of the United States.

Serica intermixa Length: 7.5–9.5mm. Dull brownish yellow, sometimes brown or black. Pronotum finely, sparsely punctured; elytral striae with two or three irregular rows of rounded punctures, intervals sparsely punctured; clypeus with a small notch (Fig. 454).
Beneath bark of decayed logs.
Eastern half of the United States.

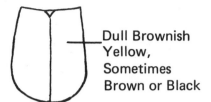

Dull Brownish Yellow, Sometimes Brown or Black

Fig. 454.   Serica intermixa

Serica iricolor   Length: 6–7.5mm. Black, slightly shining, iridescent; pronotum pubescent. Pronotum wider than long, sides curved to apex, roughly punctured; elytral striae punctured, intervals thinly covered with rather long, erect hairs; clypeus notched.
Beneath logs and stones.
Eastern half of the United States.

In the species of the genus Diplotaxis *each antennal club is smooth and polished; the tibiae of the middle and hind legs each have two spurs; the tarsal claws are equal, with a retractile process; the abdomen has five segments; and the coxae of the front legs are conical.*

Diplotaxis sordida   Length: 10–12mm. Reddish brown to blackish, slightly shining; pronotum and elytra with yellowish pubescence. Pronotum finely, densely punctured, margins scalloped; elytra without striae but finely, transversely wrinkled between punctures, clypeus notched.
Beneath stones, logs, and bark.
Eastern half of the United States.

Diplotaxis frondicola   Length: 7–8mm. Pale to dark chestnut brown, slightly shining. Pronotum wider than long, sides rounded, finely and densely punctured; each elytron with three slightly elevated ridges, each ridge with a single row of punctures and a row on each side, intervals coarsely and densely punctured (Fig. 455).
Beneath stones and logs.
Eastern half of the United States.

Pale to Dark Chestnut Brown

Fig. 455.   Diplotaxis frondicola

Diplotaxis atlantis   Length: 11–12.5mm. Chestnut brown or black, shining. Pronotum wider than long, densely and coarsely punctured, base with a smooth space at its middle; elytra with several rows of coarse punctures arranged in pairs and, within each pair, a row of fine punctures, intervals coarsely and densely punctured.
Beneath stones and logs.
Eastern half of the United States.

The species of the genus Phyllophaga *are the well known* may beetles *or* june bugs. *The larvae, known as* white grubs, *feed underground on the roots of grass and various crops such as corn. The adults are nocturnal in habits, appearing at dusk to feed on the leaves of trees and shrubs. There are over a hundred different species and, as they resemble each other closely, they are difficult to identify. Each antennal club is smooth and polished and has three segments; the tibiae of the middle and hind legs each have two spurs; the tarsal claws each have a single tooth; and the coxae of the front legs are transverse.*

Phyllophaga fusca   Length: 17–24mm. Dark reddish brown or blackish, shining. Pronotum widest at base, sides curved and narrowed to apex, variably punctured but never very coarse or very dense; elytra more densely punctured than pronotum; antennae each ten segmented; clypeus slightly notched.
Common about lights.
Throughout the United States.

Phyllophaga fervida   Length: 19.5mm. Dark reddish brown to blackish, shining. Pronotum wider at middle than at base, covered with moderate-sized punctures; elytra slightly punctured, becoming wrinkled toward the bases, a distinct ridge along the suture; clypeus notched; antennae each ten segmented (Fig. 456).
One of the more abundant of the may beetles.
Throughout the United States.

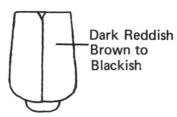

Fig. 456.   Phyllophaga fervida

The species of the genus Dichelonyx *have smooth, polished antennal clubs; the tibiae of the middle and hind legs each have two spurs; the tarsal claws are retractile; the eyes are large and prominent; and the tarsal claws are cleft at the apices.*

Dichelonyx elongata Length: 8–10mm. Head and pronotum brown or reddish brown or blackish; elytra brownish yellow often with greenish, bronze, or purplish sheen. Pronotum extended laterally at middle, densely punctured, slightly pubescent in male, densely so in female; elytra rather coarsely punctured, sparsely pubescent; abdominal segments with dense, white, prostrate hairs (Fig. 457).
Adults on various flowers such as wild rose and wild plum and on the leaves of oak and willow, though they are essentially nocturnal in habits.
Eastern half of the United States.

Brownish Yellow, Often with Greenish, Bronze, or Purplish Sheen

Fig. 457.   Dichelonyx elongata

Dichelonyx subvittata Length: 10–11.5mm. Brownish yellow to orange brown, shining; above with green or bronze sheen; elytra each with a brownish black or dark green stripe, which is often inconspicuous except at shoulder and apex. Pronotum extended laterally at middle, rather coarsely but not densely punctured; elytra wrinkled, rather coarsely punctured, slightly pubescent; abdominal segments with white pubescence laterally.
On leaves of oak and witch hazel.
Eastern half of the United States.

Macrodactylus subspinosus   The Rose Chafer Length: 8–10mm. Dull brownish yellow or reddish brown, densely covered with dull yellow scales or hairs; head, pronotum, and body beneath often darker; tarsi black. Pronotum slightly longer than wide, distinctly narrowed at base and apex; elytra indistinctly striate; tarsi about as long as femora and tibiae combined (Fig. 458).
This beetle appears in early summer and often severely injures ro-

ses and other flowers. It also occurs in large numbers on fruit trees and shrubs, especially grapevines.

Throughout the United States.

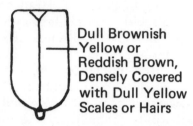

Fig. 458. Macrodactylus subspinosus

Macrodactylus uniformis The Western Rose Chafer Length: 10mm. Yellowish brown; resembles *subspinosus* in structural characters and habits.

Western United States.

The species of the genus Hoplia *have three-segmented, smooth, and polished antennal clubs; the claws of the tarsi of the front and middle legs are unequal in size, each external one being larger, the apices each have two lobes; and the tarsi of the hind legs each have only one claw.*

Hoplia trivialis Length: 6–8mm. Dark brown to blackish, sparsely covered with hairlike scales. Pronotum with oblique sides, slightly rounded.

Beneath boards, stones, and debris in sandy situations near water. Eastern and Central States.

Hoplia trifasciata   Length: 6.5–9mm. Male dull black, pronotum and elytra densely covered with flattened, yellowish gray hairs; female with head black, pronotum and elytra orange- or red brown, covered with pale yellowish scales; lower surface of body with silvery scales. Pronotum narrowed toward the apex, sides angular and rounded (Fig. 459).

On flowers of haw and leaves of oak.

Eastern half of the United States.

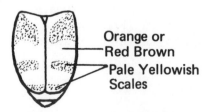

Fig. 459. Hoplia trifasciata

Hoplia callipyge   The Grapevine Hoplia   Length: 7mm. Mottled brown.

Injurious to grapevines and to a number of other plants.

Western United States.

The species of the genus Anomala *have nine segmented antennae, each with a smooth, polished club, and have the tibiae of the hind legs each with two apical spurs.*

Anomala binotata   Length: 9–12mm. Blackish, greenish bronzed, shining; elytra dull yellow, reddish, or dark brown with markings of dark brown. Pronotum wider than long, sides curved, finely and sparsely punctured; elytra with rows of coarse punctures, each with three slightly elevated ridges, and with a membranous border. (Fig. 460).

On the foliage and flowers of shrubs.

Eastern half of the United States.

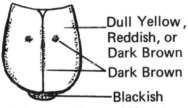

Fig. 460.   Anomala binotata

Anomala undulata   Length: 8–9.5mm. Brownish yellow, shining; pronotum blackish, with greenish bronze; elytra usually with a curved transverse row of dark brown, oval dots near middle and another row at apices, but these dots are sometimes absent or reduced in number. Pronotum wider than long, sides rounded, finely and sparsely punctured; elytra with rows of coarse punctures and with membranous borders (Fig. 461).

On the foliage and flowers of shrubs.

Eastern half of the United States.

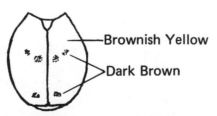

Fig. 461.   Anomala undulata

Anomala innuba Length: 6–7.5mm. Variable in color, often dull yellow, with pronotum and one to three transverse rows of dots on elytra dark brown, sometimes blackish. Pronotum wider than long, sides rounded, coarsely punctured; elytra with rows of coarse, deep punctures and with membranous borders.
On wild flowers.
Eastern half of the United States.

Pachystethus lucicola Length: 8.5–10mm. Color varying from completely brownish yellow to wholly black. Pronotum wider than long, sides rounded, coarsely punctured; elytra with double rows of coarse punctures, intervals finely punctured; antennae each nine segmented, and each with a smooth and polished club; tibiae of hind legs each with two apical spurs; elytra with membranous borders.
On the foliage of shrubs and vines.
Eastern half of the United States.

Strigoderma arboricola Length: 10–12mm. Blackish green, shining; pronotum paler in part or completely so; elytra light yellowish brown, sometimes dark brown in part or completely so; lower surface blackish with a few long, grayish hairs. Pronotum wider than long, sides rounded, hind angles rounded, anterior angles acute, sparsely punctured, rather hairy; elytra deeply striate; antennae each nine segmented, and each with a smooth and polished club; tibiae of hind legs each with two apical spurs; elytra with membranous borders; larger claws of tarsi of front and middle legs cleft.
On the flowers of such shrubs as the wild rose and blackberry.
Eastern half of the United States.

Popillia japonica *The Japanese Beetle* Length: 8–12mm. Deep green, shining; elytra brownish or brownish orange with green margins; abdomen metallic green with white spots along sides. Pronotum wider than long, sides rounded, densely and coarsely punctured; elytra with punctured striae, intervals slightly punctured, with membranous borders; antennae each nine segmented, and each with a smooth and polished club; tibiae of hind legs each with two apical spurs; larger claws of tarsi of front and middle legs cleft (Fig. 462). This beetle, introduced into our country in 1916, has become a pest and is injurious to almost every kind of plant in the eastern half of the United States.

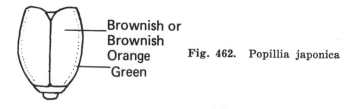

Brownish or Brownish Orange

Green

Fig. 462. Popillia japonica

Pelidnota punctata   The Grapevine Beetle   Length: 17–25mm. Brownish yellow to light brown, shining; head sometimes with black occiput; pronotum with a round black spot on each side laterally; each elytron with three, more or less distinct, rounded, black spots along sides; lower surface, legs, and scutellum green or blackish. Complete upper surface finely and sparsely punctured; antennae each ten segmented, and each with a smooth and polished club; tibiae of hind legs each with two apical spurs; mandibles each with two teeth (Fig. 463).
Adults on grape leaves; larvae on roots of various trees.
Throughout the United States.

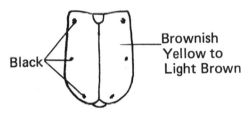

Fig. 463.   Pelidnota punctata

Ligyrus relictus   Length: 18–23mm. Brownish black, shining. Pronotum wider than long, hind angles rounded, finely and sparsely punctured; elytral punctures fine; antennal clubs smooth and polished; mandibles leaflike; tarsi each with a triangular basal segment; head with a transverse ridge interrupted at middle; clypeus with two teeth; tibae of hind legs with hairs at apices.
Beneath rubbish; often attracted to lights.
Eastern half of the United States.

Ligyrus gibbosus   The Carrot Beetle   Length: 11–16mm. Dark brown to black, shining; lower surface reddish brown with long soft hairs. Pronotum wider than long, apex slightly notched, slightly punctured; elytra with coarser punctures than pronotum; antennal clubs smooth and polished; mandibles leaflike; tarsi each with a triangular basal segment; head with a raised line between antennae; clypeus with two teeth; tibiae of hind legs with hairs at apices (Fig. 464).
On the roots of carrots, beets, and other plants; often very abundant and often attracted to lights.
Throughout the United States.

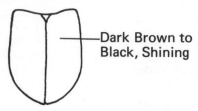

Fig. 464. Ligyrus gibbosus

Cotalpa lanigera The Goldsmith Beetle Length: 20–26mm. Head, pronotum, and scutellum greenish or yellow with a strong metallic sheen; elytra yellowish, less metallic; underparts dark, densely covered with long woolly hairs. Antennal clubs smooth and polished; tibiae of hind legs each with two apical spurs (Fig. 465).
On willow and poplar, occasionally on oak, and attracted to lights. Eastern half of the United States.

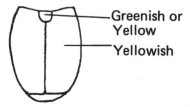

Fig. 465. Cotalpa lanigera

Strategus antaeus Length: 28–31mm. Dark reddish brown, shining; slightly paler beneath, with rather sparse, long hairs. Pronotum wider than long, in male with three erect horns (hence known as the *ox beetle*) and finely punctured, in female with a slight horn, more densely punctured on basal half becoming wrinkled anteriorly; elytra minutely, sparsely punctured; antennal clubs smooth and polished; mandibles leaflike; tarsi each with a triangular basal segment; head with a slight transverse ridge; clypeus with a single tooth (Fig. 466). Eastern half of the United States.

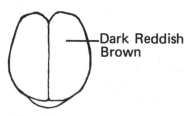

Fig. 466. Strategus antaeus

Xyloryctes jamaicensis *The Rhinoceros Beetle* Length: 25–28mm. Dark reddish brown to brownish black, slightly shining; undersurface rather thickly covered with light reddish brown hairs. Anterior half of pronotum of male almost perpendicular; sides of pronotum rounded and fringed with long, brown hairs, finely and sparsely punctured; elytra striate with rows of rather fine, impressed punctures, the striae deeper and punctures larger in female; antennal clubs smooth and polished; mandibles leaflike; tarsi each with a triangular basal segment; male with a long, curved horn extending from middle of head; clypeus with two lobes; tibiae of hind legs with blunt, rounded teeth at apices (Fig. 467).
Throughout the United States.

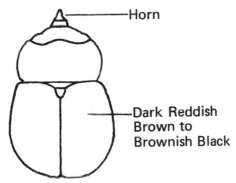

Fig. 467.   Xyloryctes jamaicensis

The genus Dynastes *includes some of the largest known beetles. For instance, the males of* D. hercules *may measure six inches or more;* D. hercules *occurs only in the West Indies and northern South America.*

Dynastes tityus Length: 40–45mm. Yellowish gray; elytra marked with brown to black spots; rarely completely dark reddish brown. Upper surface of male almost completely smooth; female with pronotum sparsely and finely punctured; elytra each with coarse and very fine punctures intermingled on basal half; male with three pronotal horns, side ones short and curved, the middle one with two lobes at tip and curving forward to meet the long curved horn extending from the head; female with a slight tubercle on middle of head; antennal clubs smooth and polished; mandibles leaflike; tibiae each with three teeth (Fig. 468).
Central, South, and Southeastern United States.

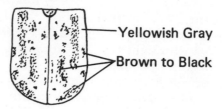

Fig. 468.   Dynastes tityus

Cotinis nitida   The Green June Beetle   Length: 20–23mm. Dull, velvety green above, with sides of pronotum and elytra brownish yellow; head and tibiae shining metallic green; femora and usually abdomen orange yellow. Antennal clubs smooth and polished; clypeus notched and with a hornlike process (Fig. 469) .
On flowers and ripening fruit; also flies at night in great numbers, generally in sandy areas.
Eastern and Southern States.

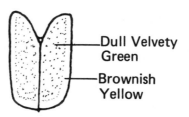

Fig. 469.   Cotinis nitida

Euphoria inda   The Bumblebee Flower Beetle   Length: 13–16mm. Brownish yellow; head and pronotum blackish, slightly bronzed, sometimes with brownish yellow spots, covered with dense yellow pubescence; elytra mottled, each with black spots that sometimes form crossbands; femora and sides of abdomen generally covered with light yellow hairs (Fig. 470) . This beetle gets its name because of the buzzing noise it makes as it flies near the ground.
The adults feed on fruit, the larvae live in decaying wood.
Throughout the United States.

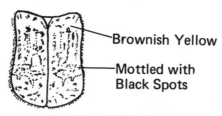

Fig. 470.   Euphoria inda

Euphoria fulgida   Length: 13–18mm. Head and pronotum bright green, pronotum margined at sides with brownish orange, sometimes with minute whitish spots; abdomen green, with white spots on the sides; legs orange brown, tinged with green. Complete upper surface sparsely and finely punctured; antennal clubs smooth and polished; clypeus notched.
On flowers.
Eastern half of the United States.

The species of the genus Osmoderma *are known as the odor-of-leather beetles because when captured, they give off a strong odor of leather.*

Osmoderma eremicola   The Hermit Flower Beetle   Length: 25–29mm. Dark reddish brown or mahogany brown, shining. Pronotum narrower than elytra, deeply impressed median groove on basal half in front of which there is a deep excavation, finely and sparsely punctured; elytra finely and sparsely punctured; antennal clubs smooth and polished; clypeus notched; coxae of hind legs touching; scutellum triangular (Fig. 471).
Adults about edges of open woods and at lights; larvae in hollows of various trees.
Eastern half of the United States.

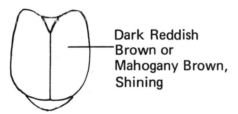

Dark Reddish Brown or Mahogany Brown, Shining

Fig. 471.   Osmoderma eremicola

Osmoderma scabra   The Rough Flower Beetle   Length: 18–25mm. Purplish black, slightly bronzed. Pronotum rather coarsely punctured; elytra wrinkled and irregularly punctured; other characters similar to *eremicola*.
Adults in orchards and open woods. Larvae in the hollows of various trees.
Eastern half of the United States.

Trichiotinus piger   Length: 9–11mm. Head and pronotum blackish, slightly bronzed with green, covered with dense, yellow, erect pubescence; elytra orange brown to blackish, sparsely pubescent, each with two short, white crossbars, sides with a black or slightly reddish, velvety spot; body underneath and femora blackish and somewhat

bronzed, with long, silky, pale yellow hairs; abdomen, tibiae, and tarsi reddish brown. Scutellum rounded, other characters similar to *Osmoderma eremicola* (Fig. 472).
Common on flowers of various wild plants.
Eastern half of the United States.

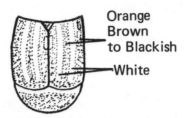

Orange
Brown
to Blackish

White

Fig. 472.   Trichiotinus piger

Trichiotinus affinis   Length: 9–10mm. Usually found with *T. piger*, which it closely resembles. It is, however, smaller and more shining with a pronotum that is more sparsely punctured.
Common on flowers of various wild plants.
Eastern half of the United States.

Valgus seticollis   Length: 6.5–7.5mm. Blackish brown; lower surface sparsely covered with pale yellow scales. Pronotum coarsely punctured, margin with small teeth, a deep groove at its middle; elytra densely granulate and short; antennal clubs smooth and polished; clypeus notched; coxae of hind legs widely separated (Fig. 473).
On various flowers. Adults hibernate in colonies on the ground beneath some shelter, like a log.
Eastern half of the United States.

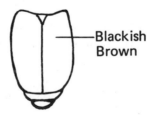

Blackish
Brown

Fig. 473.   Valgus seticollis

Valgus canaliculatus   Length: 5–6mm. Somewhat similar to *seticollis* except that it is smaller, dark reddish brown, and more densely covered with pale yellow scales on the lower surface.
On various flowers.
Eastern United States.

The Skin Beetles

Family Trogidae

This is a small family, formerly included in the *Scarabaeidae,* having less than thirty species in the United States. The members are oblong, convex species in which the surface of the body and the wing covers are usually very rough and covered with a hard incrustation that is difficult to remove. They are small or of medium size and dull grayish brown or dull blackish gray in color. When disturbed, they usually draw the legs against the body and remain motionless, at which time they look much like a small lump of dirt or excrement. They feed upon skin, dried and decomposing animal matter, carrion, hide, fur, feathers, and the like, and are found in the nests of birds and small animals that contain animal remains or debris. Adults stridulate by rubbing the abdomen against the elytra, but what they accomplish by so doing is not known. The beetles are beneficial as scavengers.

The antennae are each ten segmented and each has a club of three segments, which are leaflike or platelike and capable of being folded close together; the scutellum is very small; the elytra cover the abdomen completely on the upper surface; the legs are slender; the coxae touch; the femora of the front legs are enlarged; and five abdominal segments are visible (Fig. 474).

Except for a few species found in the Far West, all of the other species belong to the genus *Trox.*

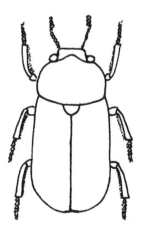

Fig. 474. Skin Beetle

Trox monachus Length: 12–16mm. Dark brownish; antennal clubs light yellowish brown. Pronotum wider than long, with tubercles and fine, matted hairs, sides notched in front of hind angles; elytra with rows of distinct, rounded, widely separated tubercles on alternate intervals, tubercles covered with fine hairs; scutellum spear shaped; head with two tubercles (Fig. 475).

On carrion and feathers.
Throughout the United States.

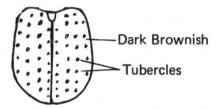

Fig. 475. Trox monachus

Trox suberosus Length: 9–17mm. Dull grayish brown; antennal clubs light yellowish brown. Pronotum wider than long, with fine, matted hair, lateral margins notched in front of hind angles, margins with long, fine hairs; elytra with small tubercles and with tiny tufts of hairs between them; scutellum spear shaped; head with two tubercles (Fig. 476).
On carrion, cow dung, and feathers.
Throughout the United States.

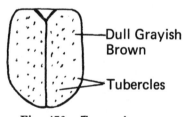

Fig. 476. Trox suberosus

Trox foveicollis Length: 5–6.5mm. Blackish brown; antennal clubs light yellowish brown. Pronotum wider than long, with dense, fine, matted hair and four, large, rounded pits, sides wavy before hind angles; elytra with surface of tubercles bearing short, erect, brownish setae; tibiae of hind legs slightly toothed; head with four tubercles; scutellum oval.
On carrion, feathers, dung, and in bird nests.
Eastern half of the United States.

Trox unistriatus Length: 9–12mm. Dull brownish black; antennal clubs light yellowish brown. Pronotum wider than long, with dense, fine, matted hair, and median ridges, tubercles, and anterior margin with sparse, erect, yellow setae; elytra with large square, strial punctures in regular rows and long lines of fine yellow setae in double rows on odd intervals; scutellum oval; head with two or four tubercles.

On carrion.

Eastern half of the United States.

The Stag Beetles

Family Lucanidae

The beetles of this family are known as the *stag beetles* because of their large mandibles, which in the males of some species are branched like the antlers of a stag. They are mostly moderate in size and mahogany or black in color. The adult beetles live by day in or beneath dead or decaying logs and stumps, though some are said to feed on the exudations of leaves and bark of trees. Many of them are attracted to lights at night. The females lay their eggs in the crevices of the bark of trees and the larvae, which resemble those of the may beetles, live in damp decaying wood.

The antennal clubs each consist of three or four flattened plates that do not fit compactly together as in the *lamellicorn beetles*. The antennae are each ten segmented; the elytra are rounded at the apices; the abdomen has five visible ventral segments; the legs are adapted for digging; the coxae of the front legs are transverse; the tibiae of the front legs are more or less toothed, those of the middle and hind legs each have two teeth; the tarsi are each five segmented; and the claws of the tarsi each have a short, bristle-bearing pad between them (Fig. 477).

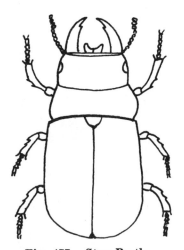

Fig. 477.   Stag Beetle

Pseudolucanus capreolus Length: 22–35mm. Dark reddish brown, smooth, shining; femora light brown. Antennae elbowed or bent at an angle; elytra smooth; mandibles in male as long as pronotum, in female shorter than head; labrum transversely triangular in female, notched in male; mandibles each with one tooth in male and twice as long as those of female (Fig. 478).
In and around decaying logs and stumps; often attracted to lights. Eastern half of the United States.

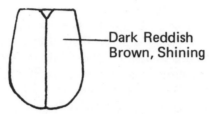

Fig. 478. Pseudolucanus capreolus

Pseudolucanus placidus Length 19–32mm. Complete upper surface distinctly punctured and the mandibles with several teeth; similar to *capreolus*.

Lucanus elaphus *The Giant Stag Beetle* Length: 31–40mm. Dark chestnut brown, shining; antennae and legs black or nearly so. Head of male much wider than pronotum, with a crest above the eyes, narrower in female; mandibles in male as long as elytra, inner edge of each with many small teeth, in female shorter than head; antennae elbowed; labrum elongate, triangular (Fig. 479).
About oak stumps and at lights.
Southeastern United States.

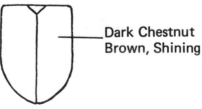

Fig. 479. Lucanus elaphus

Stag Beetle; Lucanus elaphus
(Courtesy of Carolina Biological Supply Company)

Dorcus parallelus   The Antelope Beetle   Length: 15–26mm. Dark brown, nearly black; head and pronotum shining and sparsely punctured. Antennae elbowed; elytra deeply striate, both striae and intervals finely and densely punctured; eyes notched; mandibles each with a large median tooth; tibiae of front legs with many teeth (Fig. 480). About roots of stumps of decayed trees such as oak, linden, and maple; common about lights.
Eastern half of the United States.

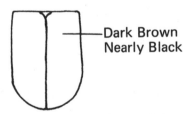

Dark Brown
Nearly Black

Fig. 480.   Dorcus parallelus

Platycerus virescens   Length: 10–12mm. Black or dark reddish brown, sometimes with a brassy or greenish tinge, shining. Antennae elbowed; mandibles of male larger than those of female each with

about six teeth near apex; pronotum wider than long, sides rounded, hind angles obtuse, sparsely punctured in male, more so in female; elytra with three or four, more or less distinct striae, sparsely punctured; tibiae of front legs sawlike (Fig. 481).
Beneath bark and in decaying logs of oak; sometimes on flowers. Northeastern half of the United States.

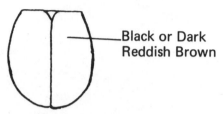

Fig. 481.   Platycerus virescens

Ceruchus piceus   Length: 10–15mm. Blackish or dark reddish brown, shining. Pronotum coarsely and densely punctured; elytra coarsely and densely punctured; slightly striate; coxae touching; mandibles in male as long as head and each with a very large tooth at middle of inner edge, in female one-half as long as head and each with three or four rounded teeth on inner edge.
In decaying logs of various trees.
Eastern half of the United States.

Nicagus obscurus   Length: 7–9.5mm. Blackish or dark brown with sparse, short, indistinct, pale hairs. Complete upper surface coarsely and rather densely punctured; pronotum wider than long, apex narrower than base, margins slightly scalloped, hind angles obtuse; elytra not striate.
About debris in sandy situations.
Eastern half of the United States.

The Horn Beetles

Family Passalidae
   This is a tropical family of beetles and we have only one species. They live in half-decayed logs and stumps and are of especial interest because the adults and larvae live in colonies and communicate with one another by stridulating. The adults tend the larvae in brood galleries.

Popilius disjunctus   *The Horned Passalus*   Length: 32–36mm. Black, shining. Pronotum square shaped, with a deep median impressed line,

hind angles rounded; elytra deeply striate, striae finely punctured; head with a short curved hook or horn; antennae not elbowed, but when at rest appears to be (Fig. 482).
Eastern half of the United States.

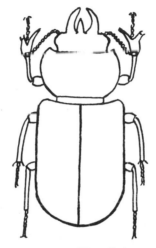

Fig. 482.   Popilius disjunctus

Horned Passalus; Popilus disjunctus

The Longhorn Beetles

Family Cerambycidae
The beetles of this family are well named and can readily be rec-

ognized by their long-to-very-long antennae, often longer than the body. The family is a large one of some 20,000 species, of which more than eleven hundred have been described from North America.

The beetles are moderate or large in size, some measuring over three inches in length, elongate or cylindrical in form sometimes flattened, and vary in color, many being strikingly colored and beautiful in appearance. They are very active fliers and can run swiftly over the ground. Many of them have the habit of remaining motionless on the branches of trees when disturbed and when picked up many make a squeaking or rasping sound. The adults are found on tree trunks and limbs, beneath bark, and on flowers and foliage; some are attracted to light and to sugar.

The larvae, which are known as the *round-headed wood borers* and may take two or three years to mature, live within the solid parts of trees and shrubs or beneath the bark, though a few live in the stems and about the roots of herbaceous plants. Some species are quite destructive to orchard and forest trees in their immature stages, but most of them live primarily in decaying wood.

The antennae are each eleven segmented, and are usually sawlike or with the segments cylindrical, though sometimes beadlike. The tarsi are each five segmented, but each of the fourth segments is always small and appears as a node at the base of the fifth segment; the third segment on each tarsus is lobed. The length of the antennae and the form of the tarsi are distinguishing features that serve to identify the members of this family (Fig. 483).

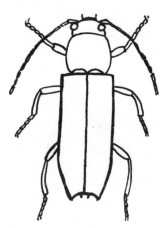

Fig. 483.   Longhorn Beetle

The following six species have a margined pronotum and a labrum attached at the sides.

There are only a few species of the genus Parandra. *They are known as the* aberrant longhorns *and were once a separate family because the fourth tarsal segment is distinct and the antennae are much shorter than other cerambycids.*

Parandra brunnea The Pole Borer Length: 9–18mm. Yellowish brown to deep reddish brown, shining. Pronotum somewhat square shaped; elytra with parallel sides, rounded at apices; antennae of similar segments not extending beyond the base of the pronotum; eyes transverse and slightly notched (Fig. 484).
One of the most destructive borers, injuring poles, crossties, any structural wood in contact with moist ground, and various trees. Throughout the United States.

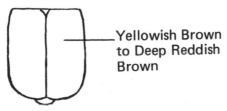

Yellowish Brown
to Deep Reddish
Brown

Fig. 484. Paranda brunnea

Stenodontes dasystomus The Hardwood-Stump Borer Length: 30–46mm. Dark reddish brown to blackish. Pronotum wider than long, with many teeth; elytra finely, sparsely punctured, sutural angle with a small tooth.
Adults attracted to lights; larvae in heartwood of living trees.
Eastern half of the United States.

Orthosoma brunneum Length: 22–45mm. Orange brown or reddish brown, shining. Pronotum wider than long, with three teeth on each side; each elytron with three raised lines, finely and densely punctured (Fig. 485).
In structural timbers in contact with the ground, also in stumps and logs; adults attracted to lights.
Throughout the United States.

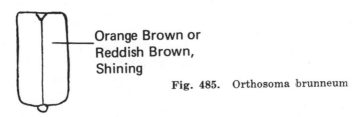

Orange Brown or
Reddish Brown,
Shining

Fig. 485. Orthosoma brunneum

Prionus laticollis   The Broad-Necked Prionus   Length: 22–47mm. Blackish, shining. Pronotum laterally curved, with three teeth or spines on each side, sparsely punctured; elytra roughly and irregularly punctured with three, longitudinal, indistinct, elevated ridges; antennae each with twelve segments that are conical and overlapping in male, more slender and somewhat sawlike in female, fourth and following segments with elevated lines which bear special sense organs (Fig. 486).

Adults in smaller trees, fruit trees, and shrubs; larvae in roots of fruit trees, other trees, shrubs, and grapevines.
Eastern half of the United States.

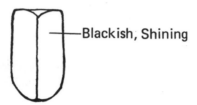

Fig. 486.   Prionus laticollis

Prionus pocularis   The Pine Stump Prionus   Length: 25–45mm. Light reddish brown, shining. Pronotum laterally curved, with three teeth on each side, finely punctured; elytra rather densely punctured, each with three indistinct elevated ridges; antennae more slender than in *laticollis* but otherwise similar.
In living trees as well as dead coniferous logs and stumps.
Middle and Southern States.

Prionus imbricornis   The Tile-Horned Prionus   Length: 22–47mm. Dark reddish brown; similar to *pocularis* except for the antennae, which in the male are composed of 18 to 20 conical, overlapping segments, like the tiles of a roof, hence the name of the species, and which in the female are composed of 16 to 18 sawlike segments.
In various hardwoods such as oak and chestnut; also in the roots of herbaceous plants.
Eastern half of the United States.

Smodicum cucjiforme   The Flat Oak Borer   Length: 7–10mm. Pale, dull yellow, shining. Pronotum slightly longer than wide, sparsely and irregularly punctured; elytra with sides parallel and finely and sparsely punctured; eyes notched; body flattened; antennae each with second segment more than one-third as long as third, segments shining (Fig. 487).
In oak and hickory; also in stored wood.
Eastern half of the United States.

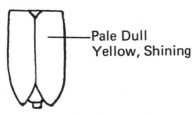

Pale Dull
Yellow, Shining

Fig. 487. Smodicum cucjiforme

Asemum striatum   The Pine Stump Borer   Length: 8.5–12mm. Dull reddish brown to blackish; base of head black; pronotum margined with black; elytra sometimes with dull yellowish pubescence. Pronotum wider than long, sides rounded, with a broad, longitudinal impression; elytra with parallel sides, rounded apices, and several longitudinal, shallow striae; antennae each with second segment more than one-third as long as third, and finely pubescent; eyes hairy and notched. In recently cut or dying trees and stumps.
Eastern half of the United States.

The following species up to and including Batyleoma suturale *have the bases of the antennae partly enveloped by the eyes.* (This taxonomic fact refers to those beetles marked with an *.)

**Oeme rigida   The Cypress and Cedar Borer*   Length: 7–9mm. Pale reddish yellow. Pronotum somewhat spherical, sides rounded to apex, base constricted with a longitudinal groove in the middle; elytra with sides tapering to apices and each with two longitudinal ridges; second segment of each antenna minute (Fig. 488); eyes coarsely granulate; bases of antennae partly enveloped by eyes.
In juniper and cypress.
Eastern States.

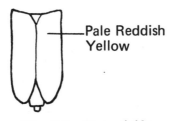

Pale Reddish
Yellow

Fig. 488.   Oeme rigida

**Tylonotus bimaculatus   The Ash and Privet Borer*   Length: 12–16mm. Dark brown or blackish; each elytron with two large, rounded yellow spots. Pronotum somewhat cylindrical with two small, smooth elevations and densely punctured; elytra sparsely and coarsely punctured; eyes coarsely granulate; antennal segments with two grooves; femora strongly clubbed (Fig. 489).

In living or dying ash, hickory, and birch trees, and in privet. Eastern half of the United States.

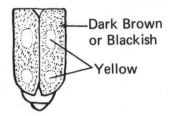

Fig. 489.   Tylonotus bimaculatus

*Cerasphorus cinctus   The Banded Hickory Borer   Length: 16–35mm. Yellowish brown, covered with gray pubescence; elytra usually obliquely marked with yellow. Pronotum cylindrical with a short, acute spine on each side; elytra densely and finely punctured, each apex with two short spines; antennae grooved; scutellum acute, triangular; coxae of front legs rounded; femora each with two short spines at apex (Fig. 490) ; eyes coarsely granulate.
In hickory, oak, and plum; adults attracted to lights.
Throughout the United States.

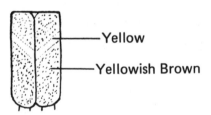

Fig. 490.   Cerasphorus cinctus

*Eburia quadrigeminata   The Ivory-Marked Beetle   Length: 14–24mm. Pale brownish yellow; each elytron with two pairs of ivory white spots. Pronotum cylindrical, with a short, sharp spine on each side, and with two small, blackish tubercles near middle; elytra rather densely and finely punctured, each apex with two spines; antennae each slightly grooved from third segment; eyes coarsely granulate; scutellum rounded behind; coxae of front legs rounded; femora with two spines at apex (Fig. 491).
In oak, hickory, ash, chestnut, maple, cypress, and in lumber.
Eastern half of the United States.

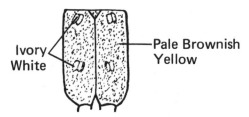

Fig. 491. Eburia quadrigeminata

Romaleum atomarium Length: 19–28mm. Very dark brown, variegated above, with short, yellowish gray pubescence. Pronotum with rounded sides, coarsely punctured, a short, longitudinal tubercle medially at base and a smaller one on each side; elytra rather coarsely and densely punctured, each apex with two spines; eyes coarsely granulate; antennae with spines.
Beneath bark of dead trees and stumps.
Eastern half of the United States.

Romaleum rufulum *The Red Oak Borer* Length: 22–28mm. Reddish brown, covered above with short, dense, tawny pubescence. Pronotum with rounded sides, usually with a small tubercle each side of median line, finely and densely punctured in male, coarsely in female; elytra densely and finely punctured, each apex with two spines; eyes coarsely granulate; antennae with spines (Fig. 492).
Beneath the bark and in the heartwood of oak trees.
Central and Eastern States.

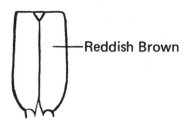

Fig. 492. Romaleum rufulum

Elaphidion mucronatum *The Spined Bark Borer* Length: 15–20mm. Dull reddish brown, irregularly covered with grayish yellow pubescence. Pronotum cylindrical, with a median line and two small, round tubercles each side, finely punctured laterally; elytra coarsely punctured, each apex with two spines; eyes coarsely granulate; antennae with spines (Fig. 493).
Beneath the bark of various hardwoods.
Eastern half of the United States.

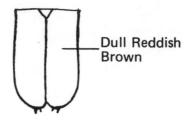

Fig. 493.   Elaphidion mucronatum

Elaphidion incertum   The Mulberry Bark Borer   Length: 11–20mm. Similar to *mucronatum,* except that the pronotum is somewhat spherical with five large flattened elevations.
In hickory and mulberry.
Eastern States.

Psyrassa unicolor   Length: 8–12mm. Light reddish brown, sparsely pubescent. Pronotum cylindrical, longer than wide, sides curved, a transverse groove near base, sparsely and coarsely punctured; elytra densely and coarsely punctured, apices with short spines; eyes coarsely granulate; antennae with small spines, not visible beyond the fourth segment of each antenna; tibiae each with a longitudinal ridge (Fig. 494).
On redbud, oak, hickory, beech, and walnut.
Eastern half of the United States.

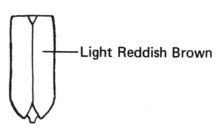

Fig. 494.   Psyrassa unicolor

Stenosphenus notatus   Length: 9–12mm. Black, shining; pronotum reddish, with an oval black spot in the middle; lower surface of head and thorax reddish. Pronotum wider than long, sparsely and coarsely punctured, each puncture with a gray hair; elytra sparsely and finely punctured, each with a notched apex having two spines; eyes finely granulate and notched; second antennal segment of each antenna small, third to seventh with short spines; tibiae ridged.
In dead hickory.
Eastern half of the United States.

Heterachthes ebenus   Length: 7–11mm. Dark brown. Pronotum longer than wide, cylindrical, densely, coarsely, and roughly punctured; elytra elongate, with large punctures widely spaced, apices rounded; eyes large and coarsely granulate; femora club shaped; a very long species.
In branches of dead pines.
Eastern half of the United States.

Heterachthes quadrimaculatus   *The Hickory Borer*   Length: 8–11mm. Yellowish brown to dark brown, shining; each elytron with two circular yellow spots. Pronotum longer than wide, with a wide, shallow median groove and sparsely, coarsely punctured; elytra sparsely, coarsely punctured; eyes large and coarsely granulate; femora club shaped; a very long species (Fig. 495)
In dead branches of poplar, hickory, and tulip.
Eastern half of the United States.

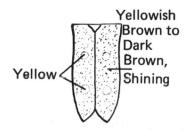

Fig. 495.   Heterachthes quadrimaculatus

Obrium rufulum   Length: 5.5–6.5mm. Pale reddish yellow, shining. Pronotum constricted at base and apex, a tubercle at each side; elytra coarsely punctured, each puncture with a yellowish hair, apices rounded; eyes large, coarsely granulate; femora club shaped (Fig. 496).
In dead branches of oak.
Eastern half of the United States.

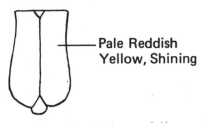

Fig. 496.   Obrium rufulum

Molorchus bimaculatus Length: 5–7mm. Brownish black, slightly shining, with scattered grayish hairs; elytra yellowish, apices and margin black; antennae and legs reddish brown. Pronotum longer than wide, somewhat cylindrical, sides rounded, constricted at base, coarsely and densely punctured; elytra short, coarsely punctured, apices rounded; eyes finely granulate; femora club shaped (Fig. 497).
Larvae in various hardwoods and in grapevines; adults on the flowers of sumac, wild cherry, and hawthorn.
Eastern half of the United States.

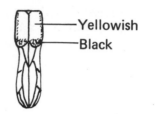

Fig. 497.   Molorchus bimaculatus

Physocnemum brevilineum The Elm Bark Borer Length: 12–16mm. Black; elytra bluish black, with a bronze tinge and each with three short, white or ivory lines. Pronotum wider than long, constricted at base, somewhat spherical, with a rounded tubercle at the sides, covered with a dense, velvety pubescence; elytra granulate, punctured; eyes finely granulate; bases of antennae not enveloped by eyes (an exception to note on page 349); femora club shaped (Fig. 498).
In the bark of elm trees; on sunny days the adults may be found on the trunks.
Eastern half of the United States.

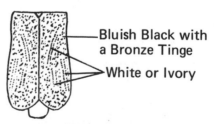

Fig. 498.   Physocnemum brevilineum

Callidium antennatum The Black-Horned Pine Borer Length: 13–14mm. Deep blue black or purplish, shining above, purplish brown beneath. Pronotum wider than long, constricted at base, sides round-

ed, punctured laterally; elytra finely punctured between indistinct elevated ridges; eyes finely granulate; bases of antennae not enveloped by eyes (an exception to note on page 349) ; femora club shaped. Beneath bark and in sapwood of pine, spruce, hemlock, juniper, and cedar.
Throughout the United States.

Callidium violaceum   Length: 10–13mm. Somewhat similar to *antennatum* except for its blue elytra and deeper punctures on the pronotum.
Breeds in conifers.
Throughout the United States.

Phymatodes varius   Length: 6–9mm. Dark brown to black, covered with prostrate pubescence, pronotum partly or wholly reddish brown; each elytron with two narrow light reddish brown crossbars. Pronotum wider than long with rounded sides, constricted at base, rather coarsely punctured; elytra punctured with rounded apices; eyes finely granulate; bases of antennae not enveloped by eyes (an exception to note of page 349) ; femora club shaped (Fig. 499).
Beneath bark of diseased and dead hickory and oak.
Throughout the United States.

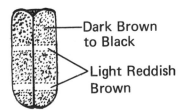

Fig. 499.   Phymatodes varius

Phymatodes amoenus   Length: 5–8mm. Reddish yellow, shining; elytra blue; antennae, tibiae, and tarsi dark brown to black. Pronotum wider than long, somewhat cylindrical, sides rounded, with flattened elevations and finely punctured; elytra rather densely, finely punctured, each puncture with a short hair; other characters like those of *varius*.
In dead grapevines; adults on flowers.
Eastern half of the United States.

Phymatodes dimidiatus   Length: 9–13mm. Dark brown to blackish, shining; elytra with a lighter space at the bases; underneath orange brown. Pronotum wider than long, with rounded sides, constricted

at base, flattened elevations, densely and minutely punctured; elytral apices rounded, densely covered with recumbent pubescence; other characters like those of *varius* (Fig. 500).
In spruce, hemlock, and larch.
Throughout the United States.

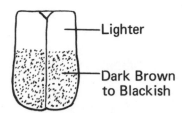

Fig. 500. Phymatodes dimidiatus

Phymatodes testaceus The Tan Bark Borer Length: 8–13mm. Head blackish; pronotum reddish; elytra yellow or blue with yellow at the sides. Pronotum wider than long, sides rounded, sparsely, rather coarsely punctured; elytra densely, finely punctured, apices rounded; other characters like those of *varius*.
Beneath the bark of dead oak (tan bark) and in stored hemlock. Eastern and Central States.

Megacyllene robiniae The Locust Borer Length: 12–18mm. Black, pubescent; head, pronotum, and elytra each with narrow, yellow crossbars, the third one on each elytron shaped like a W; legs reddish brown. Pronotum wider than long, sides rounded, constricted at base; elytra with sides parallel, tapering to apices, apices obliquely cut off; eyes finely granulate; second segments of tarsi of hind legs densely pubescent (Fig. 501).
Larvae in bark and wood of living black locust; adults common on the flowers of goldenrod in the fall.
Throughout the United States.

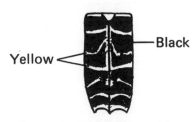

Fig. 501. Megacyllene robinae

Locust Borer; Megacyllene robiniae

Megacyllene caryae The Painted Hickory Borer Length: 12–20mm.
Velvety black; head, pronotum, and elytra each with narrow, yellow
crossbands; the third one on each elytron shaped like a W; legs reddish brown. Pronotum wider than long, sides rounded, constricted at
base; elytra tapering to apices, apices obliquely cut off; eyes finely
granulate; second segment of each of the tarsi of hind legs without
hairs at the middle (Fig. 502).
Beneath the bark and in the sapwood of hickory, ash, hackberry, and
Osage orange.
Eastern and Central States.

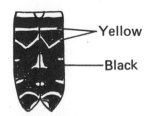

Fig. 502. Megacyllene caryae

Glycobius speciosus   *The Sugar-Maple Borer*   Length: 23–27mm. Black; head with dense, yellow pubescence; pronotum with two short, oblique bands of yellow pubescence on each side; elytra each with five bands of yellow hairs, the second band W shaped, the last band broad on each elytron includes a dark spot. Pronotum wider than long, sides rounded, constricted at base, with fine punctures in male, larger in female; elytral apices cut off; eyes finely granulate; antennae compressed and somewhat sawlike (Fig. 503).
Beneath the bark of living hard maples.
Northeastern States, south through the Appalachians.

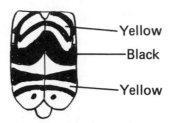

Fig. 503.   Glycobius speciosus

Calloides nobilis   Length: 20–24mm. Brownish black, with dense, velvety pubescence; each elytron with a rounded, yellow spot at the base, a small one near it and the margin, a larger one before the middle, and two narrow, transverse, wavy bands on apical half. Pronotum spherical, sides rounded, finely punctured; elytra minutely punctured, apices rounded; eyes finely granulate; antennae threadlike (Fig. 504). In the bases of dead ash and oak.
Eastern half of the United States.

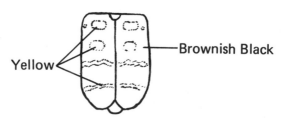

Fig. 504.   Calloides nobilis

Sarosesthes fulminans   Length: 12–20mm. Black; head and pronotum with grayish pubescence, the pronotum with a large black spot in the center and a small, round one on each side; elytra with obscure, zigzag bands of grayish pubescence. Pronotum wider than long, cylindrical, finely punctured; elytral sides slightly curved; eyes finely granulate; antennae threadlike.

Beneath the bark of dead butternut, chestnut, and oak.

Eastern half of the United States.

Xylotrechus undulatus Length: 11–21mm. Black or brown; each elytron with a narrow stripe of yellow pubescence extending from scutellum to about the middle and then curving to the outer margin, a short line of yellow in front of it and two behind it. Pronotum wider than long, sides rounded, constricted at base, wrinkled; elytra finely wrinkled; head with a V-shaped ridge on front; eyes finely granulate (Fig. 505).

Beneath the bark of almost any dead hardwood or conifer.

Throughout the United States.

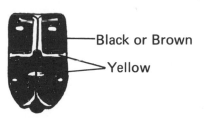

Black or Brown

Yellow

Fig. 505.   Xylotrechus undulatus

Xylotrechus colonus *The Rustic Borer* Length: 8–17mm. Black or dark brown; pronotum with four to six small white or yellowish spots; elytra each with three white or yellowish bands and an apical spot. Pronotum slightly longer than wide, cylindrical, sides rounded, finely granulate on the sides; elytra finely wrinkled, apices obliquely cut off; head with a V-shaped ridge on front; eyes finely granulate. In conifers, particularly pine.

Eastern half of the United States.

Xylotrechus quadrimaculatus *The Beech and Birch Girdler* Length: 12–15mm. Black; pronotum with four spots of yellow pubescence; elytra pale brown with sutural line and three oblique extensions from it dull yellow.

In branches of beech and birch, sometimes maple.

Eastern States.

Neoclytus acuminatus *The Red-Headed Ash Borer* Length: 6–18mm. Reddish brown; elytra each with four straight narrow bands of yellow and an area of dark brown between the third and fourth crossbands. Pronotum slightly tapering toward apex, base constricted with a transverse ridge, a tubercle at middle near apex; elytra with parallel sides, separated toward the apices, apices toothed; first segment of the tarsi of hind legs longer than the following (Fig. 506).

In ash, oak, elm, hickory, persimmon, and hackberry, but also in other hardwoods.

Eastern and Central States.

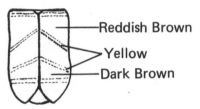

Fig. 506. Neoclytus acuminatus

Neoclytus scutellaris Length: 8–15mm. Black or dark brown, covered with fine, dark brownish pubescence; head with two vertical stripes of yellow on front; pronotum with three yellow transverse bands; each elytron with a base of reddish brown, with three narrow yellow bands, the first curving from scutellum, the second from suture, and the third oblique on apical fourth. Pronotum wider than long, with a transverse ridge, sides rounded, moderately wrinkled; elytra with sides tapering to apices, finely wrinkled, apices obliquely cut off and each with a spine; first segment of each of the tarsi of hind legs longer than the following.

In hickory, elm, white oak, and grapevines.

Eastern half of the United States.

Neoclytus caprea The Banded Ash Borer Length: 15–18mm. Black, whitish pubescence on thorax; pronotum with a narrow, light colored, front margin; each elytron with a white or yellow marking which nearly forms a circle near the base, a jagged one just behind the middle, and an oblique one near the apex.

In ash, elm, and hickory.

Eastern and Central States.

Clytus ruricola Length: 8–14mm. Dark brown to black; pronotum margined with yellow at apex and base; scutellum bright yellow; each elytron with an oval, oblique spot on basal third, a strongly angulated band extending from suture, and an oblique bar back of the middle, all yellow; antennae and legs reddish brown; femoral clubs blackish. Pronotum wider than long, somewhat spherical, finely granulate; elytral apices obliquely cut off (Fig. 507).

In various hardwoods such as hickory, elm, and oak; adults often found on flowers.
Eastern half of the United States.

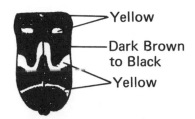

Fig. 508. Clytopeptus albofasciatus

Clytopeptus albofasciatus Length: 8–10mm. Black or light to deep brown; basal half of each elytron reddish or light brown, each elytron with a white apex and two transverse fine white lines. Pronotum longer than wide, sides rounded, base constricted, finely wrinkled; elytra finely and sparsely punctured, apices broadly cut off (Fig. 508).
In hickory, oak, and grapevines.
Eastern half of the United States.

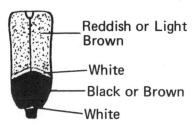

Fig. 507. Clytus ruricola

Cyrtophorus verrucosus Length: 6–10mm. Black; each elytron from base to beyond middle reddish brown and with three narrow, oblique, white lines and a fourth similar line at end of brown portion; femora reddish brown. Pronotum longer than wide, sides rounded, constricted at base, a prominent crest at middle, finely wrinkled; raised areas on basal part of each elytron with long pubescence, apices squarely cut off; eyes notched, second segment of each antenna distinctly shorter than the fourth, third with a spine.
Larvae beneath bark of peach, linden, walnut, and other trees; adults on flowers of trees and shrubs.
Eastern half of the United States.

Euderces picipes Length: 5–8mm. Black or dark reddish brown, shining, covered with sparse, grayish pubescence; each elytron with an oblique, ivory or white band at middle and usually a broad, pale reddish brown area basally. Pronotum longer than wide, cylindrical, constricted at base, with fine, closely set lines; elytra sparsely punctured on basal two-thirds, apices rounded; eyes oval, slightly notched, finely granulate; scutellum rounded (Fig. 509). This species looks like an ant.

Larvae in the dead branches of various hardwoods; adults common on flowers.

Eastern half of the United States.

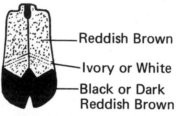

Fig. 509.   Euderces picipes

Tragidion coquus Length: 16–25mm. Black, densely pubescent; each elytron with a large, round, yellowish brown spot near the base. Pronotum somewhat square shaped, sides rounded, constricted at base, an acute spine near middle, with a median and two flattened elevations on each side; elytra minutely punctured, each with three elevated ridges, apices rounded; eyes finely granulate; scutellum triangular; antennae threadlike, segments five to eleven of each ridged (Fig. 510).

Eastern half of the United States.

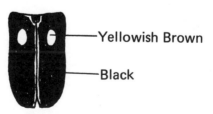

Fig. 510.   Tragidion coquus

Purpuricenus humeralis Length: 14–18mm. Black; each elytron with a large, triangular reddish spot on the shoulder. Pronotum wider than long, coarsely punctured, constricted at base, with a spine on each side, and with a median and two lateral tubercles; elytra deeply and rather coarsely punctured at the bases, more finely so at the apices, apices notched; scutellum triangular (Fig. 511).

In the dead branches of hickory, birch, oak, and black locust; adults on roadside flowers in summer.

Central and Eastern States.

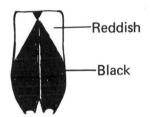

Fig. 511. Purpuricenus humeralis

Batyleoma suturale Length: 6–8.5mm. Dark red, shining; antennae, legs, and often the suture of the elytra varying from dusky red to black. Pronotum wider than long, sides rounded, constricted at base, minutely, sparsely punctured; elytra coarsely, sparsely punctured, apices rounded; scutellum acutely triangular (Fig. 512).

Larvae in the dead branches of hickory, chestnut, and oak; adults common on the flowers of new jersey tea, dogwood, and wild carrot. Throughout the United States.

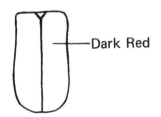

Fig. 512. Batyleoma suturale

The following species up to and including Desmocerus palliatus *have the head constricted behind the eyes and the coxae of the front legs conical. (This taxonomic fact refers only to those beetles marked with **.)*

**Pidonia aurata* Length: 8–10mm. Reddish yellow to reddish brown; elytra with sides and suture margined with black. Pronotum longer than wide, constricted at base and apex, sides wavy, densely

and minutely punctured; elytra coarsely and densely punctured, apices rounded; eyes notched; first three segments of each of the tarsi of hind legs each with a pubescent patch (Fig. 513).
Adults on various flowers.
Eastern half of the United States.

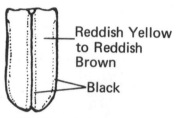

Fig. 513.   Pidonia aurata

**Grammoptera exigua   Length: 4–7mm. Black, shining; pronotum sometimes with a red margin, covered with golden pubescence; legs reddish or black. Pronotum wider than long, bell shaped, constricted at apex, sides wavy, finely and densely punctured; elytra densely and coarsely punctured, sides nearly parallel, apices rounded; first segment of each of the tarsi of hind legs with a pubescent patch.
Larvae in dead poplar and linden; adults on flowers.
Eastern half of the United States.

**Leptura emarginata   Length: 27–31mm. Black, with silky pubescence; elytra reddish brown, except apices which are black. Pronotum wider than long, somewhat bell shaped, hind angles prolonged and acute, finely and sparsely punctured; elytra wedge shaped, finely and densely punctured, apices notched (Fig. 514).
In decaying logs of various hardwoods.
Eastern half of the United States.

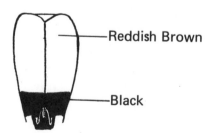

Fig. 514.   Leptura emarginata

**Leptura lineola Length: 8–11mm. Black; elytra and legs a dull yellow brown, the elytra with longitudinal black stripes, those along the sides often broken into spots. Pronotum wider than long, somewhat bell shaped, hind angles prolonged and acute, densely and finely punctured; elytra coarsely punctured, apices transversely cut off and slightly notched.
In various hardwoods; adults on various flowers, especially new jersey tea and wild rose.
Eastern half of the United States.

The species of the genus Typocerus *have the pronotum trapezoidal and the antennae with impressed pore-bearing spaces on the sixth or seventh and the following segments.*

**Typocerus zebratus Length: 8–14mm. Black, densely covered with pale pubescence; pronotum with yellow pubescence at the base and apex; elytra each with four transverse yellow bands, which may sometimes be reduced to spots or be completely absent. Pronotum wider than long, constricted at apex, closely punctured, hind angles produced over shoulders; elytra wedge shaped, finely, densely punctured, apices pointed (Fig. 515).
In decayed pine stumps; adults on various flowers, especially sumac.
Eastern United States.

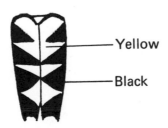

Fig. 515. Typocerus zebratus

**Typocerus lugubris Length:9–11mm. Black, with prostrate black hairs; shoulders each sometimes with a reddish spot; lower surface black, with yellow hairs. Structural characters similar to *zebratus.*
Larvae in pine stumps; adults on various flowers.
Eastern half of the United States.

**Typocerus velutinus Length: 8–14mm. Head, pronotum, antennae, and lower surface black; pronotum with yellow pubescence; elytra reddish brown, each with narrow, transverse yellow bands. Pronotum with small, granulate punctures; elytra with small, close-set punc-

tures; other characters similar to *zebratus*.
Larvae in decaying hardwoods and conifers; adults on various flowers. One of the most common of the longhorn beetles.
Eastern half of the United States.

**Anoplodera rubrica*   Length: 10–16mm. Black; elytra reddish; abdomen of male red, of female black. Pronotum somewhat square shaped, narrowed toward the apex; elytra tapering toward apices, coarsely and rather densely punctured, sides wavy.
Larvae in decayed hardwoods and conifers; adults on various flowers.
Eastern half of the United States.

**Anoplodera nitens*   The Chestnut Bark Borer   Length: 10–15mm. Dark brown to black; pronotum with yellow margins; elytra each with four yellow crossbands; antennae, legs, and abdomen partially light brown. Pronotum wider than long, constricted at apex, with a transverse groove at apex and base, densely and finely punctured; elytra finely punctured, apices obliquely cut off (Fig. 516).
Larvae in living chestnut and oak trees; adults on various flowers.
Eastern States.

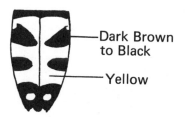

Fig. 516.   Anoplodera nitens

**Anoplodera proxima*   Length: 14–17mm. Black; elytra light orange brown, apices marked with black; complete surface covered with sparse, short yellowish hairs. Pronotum narrowed toward the apex, sides forming an angle at middle, a transverse groove at base, hind angles rounded; elytra slightly lobed at bases, apices separated, notched (Fig. 517).
In decayed gum trees.
Eastern half of the United States.

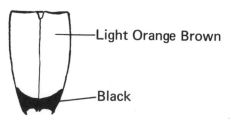

Fig. 517.   Anoplodera proxima

**Anoplodera canadensis* Length: 10–20mm. Black; elytral bases usually reddish. Pronotum somewhat square shaped, narrowed toward the apex, coarsely punctured, more sparsely toward the sides, with irregular, smooth spaces, covered with dark grayish pubescence; elytra coarsely, sparsely punctured, sides slightly rounded, apices notched, angles acute.
In dead pine, spruce, and hemlock.
Eastern half of the United States.

**Anoplodera vittata* Length: 10–13mm. Black to light brown; head and pronotum darker; elytra each with a reddish, median longitudinal stripe. Pronotum narrowed at apex, finely and sparsely punctured; elytra narrow and elongate, with a transverse impression near scutellum, finely and sparsely punctured, apices squarely cut off.
Larvae in conifers and some hardwoods; adults abundant on flowers.
Eastern half of the United States.

**Encyclops coerulae* The Oak Bark Scaler Length: 7–9.5mm. Metallic bluish black or greenish black, slightly shining; head and pronotum reddish brown, the pronotum with a narrow, elongate, black median stripe; elytral shoulders reddish brown. Pronotum longer than wide, sides rounded, densely and coarsely punctured; elytra densely and coarsely punctured, apices rounded; front of head vertical; second segment of each tarsus of hind legs longer than third, the first pubescent (Fig. 518).
Adults on various flowers; larvae in white oak and other hardwoods.
Eastern half of the United States.

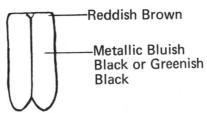

Fig. 518.   Encyclops coerulae

**Toxotus vittiger* Length: 11–21mm. Black, rather shining; elytra reddish, each with two longitudinal whitish stripes. Pronotum wider than long, constricted at apex and base, with spines or tubercles at the sides, finely punctured; elytra finely and densely punctured, sides narrowed to middle, shoulders prominent, apices obliquely cut off; front of head oblique; tibiae of hind legs each with spurs inserted in a deep excavation (Fig. 519).
On flowers of viburnum.
Eastern half of the United States.

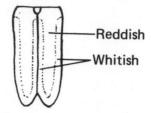

Fig. 519.   Toxotus vittiger

Stenocorus inquisitor Length: 11–18mm. Black, variegated with brown and grayish pubescence; elytra with reddish brown spots. Pronotum wider than long, with a sharp spine at each side; elytra slightly narrowed to apices, each elytron with four smooth distinct raised ridges, intervals coarsely punctured, apices rounded; antennae short, barely reaching bases of elytra; eyes small, slightly notched; front of head oblique; tibiae each with a spur at the tip.
In various conifers.
Throughout the United States.

Evodinus monticola Length: 8–12mm. Dark brown to black; elytra yellow, with three rather large spots or blotches along side margins (which are sometimes connected) and apices black. Pronotum longer than wide, sides with an obtuse tubercle; elytra minutely punctured, with prominent shoulders, apices separated and obliquely cut off; front of head oblique; eyes notched; tibiae each with a spur at the tip (Fig. 520).
Larvae beneath bark of dead hemlock; adults on various flowers.
Eastern half of the United States.

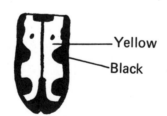

Fig. 520.   Evodinus monticola

Gaurotes cyanipennis Length: 9–12.5mm. Head, pronotum, and undersurface black; elytra bluish green, shining; antennae and legs brownish yellow. Pronotum wider than long, constricted before apex, sides wavy, minutely and sparsely punctured; elytra much wider at both bases together than pronotum, sparsely and finely punctured, shoulders prominent, apices squarely cut off; front of head oblique; tibiae each with a spur at the tip.

In butternut and other hardwoods.
Eastern United States.

**Acmaeops directus* Length: 6–8mm. Light brown; elytra dull yellow, each with a sutural and median stripe and side margins black. Pronotum somewhat square shaped, narrowed at apex, sides rounded, with an apical and basal transverse depression, finely and densely punctured, pubescent; elytra coarsely and densely punctured, apices rounded; front of head oblique; eyes small; tibiae each with a spur at tip (Fig. 521).
A rather common species, adults on various flowers.
Eastern half of the United States.

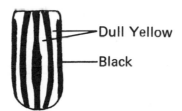

Fig. 521. Acmaeops directus

**Acmaeops bivittatus* Length: 6–10mm. Usually dull brownish yellow; pronotum with two black spots on disk; each elytron with two longitudinal black stripes; very variable in color and markings may sometimes be absent. Pronotum widest at base, sides with a small tubercle, densely punctured, pubescent; elytra much wider than pronotum, sides rounded, moderately coarsely punctured, apices rounded; front of head oblique; eyes small; tibiae each with a spur at tip.
Adults on various flowers.
Eastern half of the United States.

The following species of the genus Strangalina *have the terminal segment of the labial palpus slender, its length much more than twice the width, and the antennal segments six to eleven with small, oval, deep punctures near the apices.*

**Strangalina acuminata* Length: 7–11.5mm. Black; elytra dull yellow, with suture and lateral margins black; sparsely covered with yellowish, prostrate pubescence above, more densely beneath. Pronotum about as wide as long, constricted at base, finely and densely punctured; elytra finely and densely punctured, apices obliquely cut off.
Larvae in dead ironwood and alder; adults on various flowers such as viburnum.
Eastern half of the United States.

**Strangalina famelica* Length: 12–14mm. Dull brownish yellow, with bright yellow pubescence; pronotum with two broad, black, longitudinal stripes; elytra with some lateral black spots and a black band near apices; antennae and undersurface blackish. Pronotum wider than long, constricted at apex, finely and sparsely punctured; elytra slender, narrowed to apices which are pointed, finely and sparsely punctured.
Larvae in decayed yellow birch and oak; adults on various flowers. Eastern half of the United States.

**Strangalina luteicornis* Length: 9–14mm. Yellowish brown; pronotum with two black, longitudinal stripes; elytra each with three black crossbands. Pronotum widest at base, constricted at apex, densely and finely punctured; elytra tapered, finely and somewhat sparsely punctured, apices obliquely notched with an acute outer angle (Fig. 522).
Larvae in decaying beech, elm, and grapevines; adults on various flowers, especially sumac.
Eastern half of the United States.

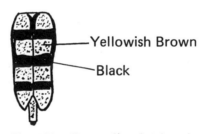

Fig. 522. Strangalina luteicornis

**Strangalina bicolor* Length: 10–14mm. Pale reddish yellow; elytra black. Pronotum wider than long, constricted at apex, hind angles acute, finely and densely punctured; elytra tapering to apices, densely and finely punctured, apices obliquely notched, with acute outer angles.
Larvae in dead maple and oak; adults on various flowers.
Eastern half of the United States.

**Desmocerus palliatus* The Elder Borer Length: 17–24mm. Dark metallic blue; elytra each with basal one-third reddish yellow or yellow. Pronotum wider than long, constricted at apex, transversely wrinkled, hind angles acute; elytra densely and rather coarsely punctured, each with three fine elevated ridges, apices obliquely rounded; antennal segments three to five widened at tips; eyes deeply notched (Fig. 523).
Larvae in elder; adults on the flowers of the same plant.
Eastern United States.

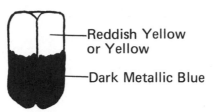

Reddish Yellow
or Yellow

Dark Metallic Blue

Fig. 523.   Desmocerus palliatus

The remaining species of this family have the tibiae of the front legs grooved and the last segment of each palpus cylindrical and pointed. (This taxonomic fact refers only to those beetles marked with ***.)

The species of the genera Monochamus, Goes, *and* Plectrodera *have a scar at the tip of the first segment of each antenna.*

Monochamus titillator   *The Southern Pine Sawyer*   Length: 20–30mm. Brownish; elytra mottled irregularly with gray and white pubescence. Pronotum slightly longer than wide, cylindrical, sides spined, sparsely to densely punctured; elytra sparsely and rather coarsely punctured, shoulders prominent, apices rounded each with a long tooth or spine; antennae greatly elongated, longer than body in female, at least one and one-half times as long as body in male; legs long, the front pair even longer in male (Fig. 524).
Beneath the bark of recently killed or felled pine, spruce, and balsam fir trees.
Eastern and Southern States.

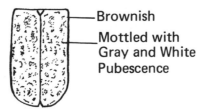

Brownish

Mottled with
Gray and White
Pubescence

Fig. 524.   Monochamus titillator

Monochamus carolinensis   *The Pine Sawyer*   Length: 13–18mm. Grayish or reddish brown, variegated with dark brown; elytra paler. Pronotum coarsely, roughly punctured in middle, transversely wrinkled near base and apex; elytra coarsely punctured on each basal half, finely so toward apices; other structural characters like those of *titillator*.
In pine.
Eastern half of the United States.

Monochamus notatus   *The Northeastern Sawyer*   Length: 18–

32mm. Dark yellow brown, mottled with light gray and white; pronotum with four small, whitish, irregular patches; elytra with numerous scattered patches of gray and brown. Pronotum slightly constricted at base and apex, with a broad tubercle at sides; elytra elongate, slightly tapering toward apices which are rounded; antennae and legs as in *titillator*.
In the inner bark and sapwood of dead and dying spruces and balsam firs.
Northeastern States.

***Monochamus scutellatus* The White-Spotted Sawyer* Length: 15–28mm. Black, distinctly bronzed; elytra with small or no patches of gray and brown pubescence; scutellum with white pubescence. Pronotum transversely wrinkled; elytra coarsely and roughly punctured; antennae and legs as in *titillator*.
In pine.
Throughout the United States except the South.

The antennae in the species of the genera Goes *are only as long as the body or a little longer in the male, and are shorter in the female; the tibiae of the front legs each have two small, terminal spurs. (See note before* Monochamus).

***Goes debilis* The Oak-Branch Borer* Length: 11–16mm. Brown or reddish brown; head, pronotum, and last third of each elytron with reddish yellow pubescence, basal half of each elytron mottled with grayish pubescence. Pronotum wider than long, sides with tubercles that terminate in a blunt spine, coarsely and sparsely punctured; elytra with a few tubercles at each base, then coarsely punctured but more finely so toward each apex, apices rounded.
In the small branches of living hickory and oak.
Eastern States.

***Goes tigrinus* The White-Oak Borer* Length: 25–30mm. Dark brown, covered with rather dense, white pubescence; elytra each with two dark brown transverse bands. Pronotum wider than long with three small, obtuse tubercles and laterally with a stout tubercle; elytra with small, black tubercles at each base, then finely and sparsely punctured, apices rounded.
In white oak.
Eastern United States.

***Goes pulcher* The Living Hickory Borer* Length: 18–25mm. Dark brown, covered with yellowish pubescence; elytra clay yellow with a conspicuous darker band across each base and another about each middle. Pronotum wider than long, with tubercles at the sides and grooved at basal and apical margins; elytra coarsely punctured, punctures finer toward the apices, bases with slight tubercles, apices slightly square (Fig. 525).

In hickory and oak.

Eastern half of the United States.

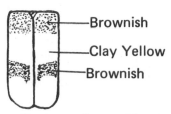

Fig. 525.   Goes pulcher

***Goes pulverulentus   The Living Beech Borer   Length: 12.5–25.5mm. Brown, clothed with short whitish hairs; each elytron with an indistinct band at base, and another behind middle, of darker brown pubescence; scutellum sometimes clay yellow. Pronotum wider than long, sides with a small tubercle, coarsely punctured; elytra with small tubercles at each base, then coarsely punctured but more finely so toward each apex.

In the small branches and trunks of oak, beech, ironwood, elm, and sycamore.

Eastern States.

***Plectrodera scalator   The Cottonwood Borer   Length: 22–40mm. Black, shining; pronotum with four broad, dense, white, longitudinal stripes, one on either side of middle and one below each lateral tubercle; elytra with dense, white pubescence in irregular, transverse bands; antennae and legs with thin grayish white pubescence. Pronotum wider than long, with three flattened elevations and a transverse impression at the base and apex; elytra finely punctured, apices rounded; pronotum with strong lateral spines. (See note before Monochamus.)

In living cottonwood and willow trees.

In the Central and Southern States.

The species of the genus Dorcaschema have the tibiae of the middle legs grooved, the antennae twice as long as the body in the male and one and one-fourth times as long as the body in the female, and the elytra rounded at the apices.

***Dorcaschema wildii   Length: 15–22mm. Brown; pronotum and elytra densely covered with yellow gray pubescence, with light gray

pubescence toward the sides; elytra each with many small, rounded, bare spots and a large irregular spot behind each middle, often with a lateral stripe of yellowish pubescence extending from middle to apex on each elytron. Pronotum longer than wide, transversely wrinkled, indistinctly punctured (Fig. 526).
In mulberry and Osage orange.
Eastern half of the United States.

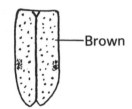

Fig. 526. Dorcaschema wildii

Dorcaschema alternatum Length: 8–13mm. Brown, covered with sparse, recumbent gray and light brown pubescence; pronotum with four fine stripes of yellow pubescence; each elytron with three rows of irregular spots of yellow pubescence. Pronotum longer than wide, distinctly punctured and with an elongate, smooth space at the middle; elytra sparsely and coarsely punctured.
In mulberry and Osage orange.
Eastern half of the United States.

Dorcaschema nigrum Length: 8–10mm. Black. Head with a narrow raised line; pronotum coarsely and roughly punctured; elytra minutely granulate, sparsely and finely punctured.
In hickory.
Eastern United States.

Hetoemis cinera Length: 8–12mm. Black, covered with dense, short, recumbent gray pubescence. Pronotum wider than long, with a smooth median line and fine, transverse striae; elytra densely and finely punctured, punctures hidden by dense pubescence; tibiae of middle legs grooved; elytra with pointed apices.
In walnut, mulberry, hickory, hackberry, linden, and Osage orange.
Eastern half of the United States.

Psenocerus supernotatus *The Currant-Tip Borer* Length: 3–6mm. Dark reddish brown or blackish; elytra each with a narrow, oblique band near middle, and a curved band on apical third of white pubescence; scutellum with white pubescence. Pronotum wider than long, constricted at base, sides rounded; elytra each with a distinct protuberance at each base, apices rounded; third and fourth antennal segments equal and longer than other segments; tarsal claws divergent.

In stems of currant, gooseberry, grapevines, and sometimes in apple twigs.

Throughout the United States.

Eupogonius tomentosus Length: 5.5–8mm. Reddish brown to orange brown, sparsely covered with long erect hairs; elytra with irregular, transverse, fine, whitish streaks and dots. Pronotum wider than long, with an acute tubercle at the sides, coarsely and densely punctured; elytra coarsely punctured, punctures finer toward apices, apices rounded; antennae not longer than body and covered with long, waving hairs, first segment of each shorter than third; eyes coarsely granulate.

Larvae in dead pine, spruce, and cedar. Adults on fresh pine slash.

Eastern half of the United States.

Eupogonius vestitus Length: 6–9mm. Light to blackish brown, covered with sparse, erect hairs; elytra mottled with small patches of dense, yellowish brown hairs. Pronotum wider than long, with an acute tubercle at each side, densely and rather coarsely punctured; elytra coarsely and densely punctured, punctures finer apically, apices rounded; antennae and eyes like *tomentosus*.

Larvae in dogwood, hickory, walnut, pine, and perhaps other trees; adults on fresh slash.

Eastern half of the United States.

Ecyrus dasycerus Length: 6–9mm. Dark brown, with brown, gray, white, and black pubescence; elytra each with a narrow, curved black band on basal third. Pronotum somewhat square shaped, cylindrical, constricted at base, densely, finely punctured; elytra coarsely, densely punctured; antennae hairy; tibiae of front legs each expanded at tip.

Larvae in redbud, hickory, and other hardwoods; adults on leaves of elm and wild grapevines.

Eastern half of the United States.

Oncideres cingulatus *The Hickory Twig Girdler* Length: 9–17mm. Blackish or reddish brown to clay yellow; pronotum with three small, black spots; elytra each with a broad, light band. Pronotum wider than long, constricted at base, sides wavy, wrinkled with large scattered punctures; elytra granulate, each punctured at the base, then wrinkled, punctured to near the apex, apical one-fourth coarsely punctured, apices rounded; front of face large and flat; antennae fringed beneath, third segment of each longest (Fig.

527). The female lays her eggs on twigs of hickory, elm, poplar, gum, basswood, and other trees; then girdles the twig below the eggs. The twig dies, and, broken off by the wind, falls to the ground where the larvae mature.

Adults rather abundant in August and September.

Eastern States.

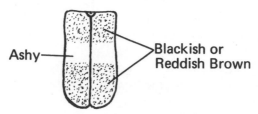

Fig. 527. Oncideres cingulatus

***Hippopsis lemniscata* Length: 10–13mm. Dark reddish brown; pronotum with two whitish lines on each side; each elytron with three whitish lines; antennae pale brown. Pronotum longer than wide, coarsely and densely punctured; elytra very long, sides gradually convergent toward apices, coarsely and deeply punctured, apices acute; antennae very long, about three times the length of the body in male, bristle shaped, fringed beneath; last segment of labial and maxillary palpus conical and pointed; coxae of front legs bent at an angle; tibiae of middle legs grooved (Fig. 528).

Larvae in stems of ragweed and other herbaceous plants; adults on various plants such as ragweed, tickweed, etc.

Eastern half of the United States.

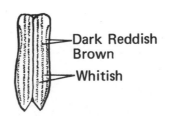

Fig. 528. Hippopsis lemniscata

***Aegoschema modesta* Length: 10–13mm. Dark brown, covered with dense, short, prostrate, yellowish and gray pubescence—the gray pubescence forming three obscure, oblique bands on each elytron. Pronotum almost as long as wide, with tubercles at the sides, middle of base with an oblong, obtuse tubercle, finely but deeply punctured; each elytron with an oblong, obtuse raised space at middle, apices rounded; first segment of each antenna large and club-shaped; coxae of front legs spherical; femora club shaped; tibiae of middle legs grooved.

In various dead hardwoods.

Throughout the United States.

Amniscus maculus Length: 4–9mm. Dark reddish brown, sparsely pubescent; pronotum with white pubescence at sides and with a broad, brown streak on either side of the middle and which is bounded on each side by a line of two or three bare tubercles; elytra each with a broad, whitish band behind each middle and each with a series of six longitudinal brownish black spots. Pronotum wider than long, constricted at apex, coarsely punctured, with five obtuse tubercles in the middle and broad tubercles on the sides; elytra with raised or rounded areas at each base, sparsely and coarsely punctured, apices obliquely cut off; coxae of front legs spherical; first segment of each antenna nearly cylindrical.

In walnut, butternut, hickory, oak, beech, and dogwood.

Eastern half of the United States.

Amniscus sexguttatus Length: 6–10mm. Reddish brown or dull yellow, mottled with grayish pubescence; each elytron with three dark spots; otherwise similar to *maculus*.

In dead pine, spruce, and larch.

Eastern half of the United States.

Astyleiopus variegatus Length: 6–12mm. Reddish or yellowish brown, mottled with black; pronotum with a dark M-shaped mark; elytra with three common blackish bands and each with a black, chevron-shaped spot at apex, suture and four elevated lines whitish. Pronotum wider than long, tubercles at sides small and ending in a short tooth, sparsely and finely punctured; elytra with raised areas at each base which vary in size, each with four elevated ridges and with deep moderate-sized punctures, apices rounded; antennae slightly fringed on basal segment of each, which is cylindrical.

In elm, walnut, honey locust, and virginia creeper.

Eastern half of the United States.

Graphisurus fasciatus Length: 8–14mm. Dark reddish brown, with dense ashy or light yellowish brown pubescence; pronotum with two black dots on disk; elytra sprinkled with small dark dots and blotches. Pronotum wider than long, tubercles at each side obtuse with a short spine; punctures fine and scattered; elytra each with elevated areas at each base, coarsely and sparsely punctured, apices notched;

antennal segments third and fourth densely fringed beneath with short hairs.
In various hardwoods.
Eastern half of the United States.

Sternidius alpha Length: 4–7mm. Dark reddish brown, with sparse, grayish pubescence; pronotum with three small, brownish black spots; elytra each with four rows of small, black dots and an acute, angular, brownish black band behind each middle. Pronotum wider than long, tubercles at sides small, finely and densely punctured; elytra with prominent basal raised areas, finely punctured, each elytron with four indistinct elevated ridges with small, tufted tubercles; femora club shaped; first segment of each of the tarsi of hind legs equal in length to second and third together.
In sumac, sycamore, apple, hickory, and locust.
Throughout the United States.

Urgleptes signatus Length: 4.5–6.5mm. Head and pronotum dark rusty brown; elytra, antennae, and legs paler; pronotum with four indistinct, brownish longitudinal stripes; each elytron with seven irregular, brownish black markings. Pronotum wider than long, narrowed toward the apex, tubercles at each side small with a spine; elytra each with round, elevated area at the base, finely and sparsely punctured, apices narrowly rounded; antennae fringed beneath with widely scattered hairs; first segment of each of the tarsi of hind legs nearly equal to remaining segments combined.
In sumac.
Eastern half of the United States.

Urgleptes querci Length: 4–5mm. Rusty brown to blackish on upper side, pale yellowish to black beneath; sparsely covered with ashy pubescence; pronotum with two indistinct, irregular, brownish black longitudinal stripes; elytra each with six to seven dark brown or brownish black markings.
Eastern half of the United States.

Urgleptes facetus Length: 3.1–4.2mm. Dark reddish brown, sparsely covered with brownish black pubescence; pronotum with a large W-shaped, ashy spot in the middle; each elytron with two large ashy markings.
In oak and hawthorn.
Eastern half of the United States.

Lepturges confluens Length: 6–9mm. Reddish to a dull yellow brown to dark rusty brown; covered with dull, ashy pubescence; pronotum with four ovate spots of yellowish brown pubescence, these sometimes running together to form a longitudinal stripe each side of middle and another laterally; each elytron with a number of yellowish brown markings. Pronotum wider than long, sides narrowing to apex, side tubercles stout, each with a'short tooth, swollen at apex, base coarsely and densely punctured; elytra each with raised areas at base, coarsely and densely punctured; antennae sparsely fringed beneath with short hairs; first segment of each of the tarsi of hind legs longer than rest of segments combined.

In beech and black walnut.

Eastern half of the United States.

Hyperplatys aspersus Length: 4–6.5mm. Reddish brown, covered with dense, grayish pubescence; pronotum with four, small round, blackish spots arranged in a transverse row; each elytron sprinkled with similar dots and usually with a large, black blotch behind middle. Pronotum wider than long, constricted at base, finely and sparsely punctured; elytra each with prominent, raised areas at the base, a distinct ridge on each outer side, coarsely and densely punctured, apices notched; antennae with a few fringed hairs beneath; first segment of each of the tarsi of hind legs as long as following three combined (Fig. 529).

In poplar and shadbush.

Eastern half of the United States.

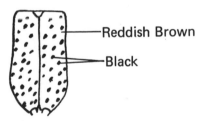

Fig. 529. Hyperplatys aspersus

Hyperplatys maculatus Length: 4–6.5mm. Similar to *aspersus*, except that the each elytron has a distinct, blackish longitudinal stripe along the sides.

In willow.

Eastern half of the United States.

Dectes sayi Length: 6–10.5mm. Dark reddish brown to black, covered with dense, grayish pubescence. Pronotum somewhat square-shaped, slightly longer than wide, side tubercles slight, each with an acute spine, densely and finely punctured; elytra each with slight, raised areas at the base, finely and densely punctured, apices ob-

liquely cut off; first segment of each of the tarsi of hind legs as long as next two combined.
In living stems of ragweed, thoroughwort, and cocklebur.
Eastern half of the United States.

Dectes texanus Length: 6–10mm. Black, but otherwise similar to *sayi*.
Eastern half of the United States.

Cyrtinus pygmaeus Length: 2–3.7mm. Dark brown; elytra each with a transverse blotch of white pubescence basally and an oblique band of white before the middle; antennae ringed with yellow. Pronotum longer than wide, constricted at the base, sparsely and minutely punctured; each elytron with a spine near the scutellum, finely and densely punctured; eyes small, each divided into two lobes; antennae longer than body; femora club shaped.
Larvae in the dead branches of various hardwoods; adults on the branches.
Eastern half of the United States.

The species of the genus Saperda *are rather large, cylindrical beetles, with eyes finely granulate and deeply notched, antennae as long or slightly longer than the body, pronotum cylindrical, elytra wider at bases than pronotum, and the first segment of each of the tarsi of the hind legs very elongated.*

Saperda candida *The Round-Headed Apple Tree Borer* Length: 15–20mm. Light brown above, with two white longitudinal stripes extending from front of head to apices of elytra (Fig. 530).
Larvae very destructive to apple trees as well as to other fruit trees and to such related species as mountain ash, shadbush, and thorn apple.
Eastern part of the United States.

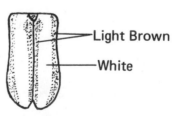

Fig. 530.   Saperda candida

Saperda obliqua *The Alder Borer* Length: 16–20mm. Light reddish brown; pronotum with four dark brown stripes; elytra each with four oblique, parallel bands of dark brown; antennae with colored rings (Fig. 531).
In alder and birch.
Eastern half of the United States.

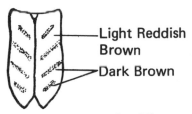

Fig. 531. Saperda obliqua

Saperda calcarata *The Poplar Borer* Length: 25–31mm. Reddish brown, densely covered with gray and yellow pubescence; pronotum with three yellow stripes; front of head and scutellum yellow; elytra each with numerous orange yellow lines and blotches.
In poplar and willow trees.
Throughout the United States.

Saperda tridentata *The Elm Borer* Length: 9–16.5mm. Dark brown or brownish black, densely covered with gray pubescence; pronotum with an orange stripe on each side; elytra each with several rounded, black spots near each base and apex, and with an orange stripe near each margin from which extend three crossbars of the same color—the one near the base nearly transverse, the other two oblique, the middle one reaching the suture.
In elm and maple.
Eastern States.

Saperda cretata *The Spotted Apple Tree Borer* Length: 12–20mm. Cinnamon brown; pronotum with a white stripe on each side; each elytron with an oblong, white spot in the middle and another small, white spot before apex (Fig. 532).
In apple and in various species of hawthorns.
Throughout the United States.

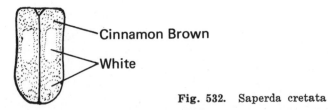

Fig. 532. Saperda cretata

Saperda discoidea *The Hickory Saperda* Length: 10–11mm. Male usually blackish, with gray pubescence that forms an indistinct, longitudinal stripe in the middle and along the sides of pronotum; femora reddish brown, tibiae and tarsi often darker; female reddish brown, with olive or grayish yellow pubescence; each elytron with a yellow crescentic bar and a yellow spot before and behind the bar. In hickory and butternut.
In the Eastern and Central States.

Saperda vestita *The Linden Borer* Length: 12–21mm. Dark reddish brown, clothed with dense olive yellow pubescence; each elytron with three small, black dots (Fig. 533).
In linden trees.
Eastern half of the United States.

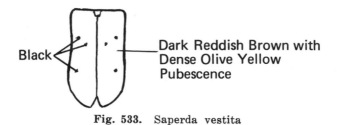

Black — Dark Reddish Brown with Dense Olive Yellow Pubescence

Fig. 533. Saperda vestita

Saperda concolor *The Poplar Gall Saperda* Length: 11–13.8mm. Black, completely covered by a dense, gray or yellowish gray pubescence; pronotum with a deeper gray stripe along the sides; antennae black, ringed with gray.
In poplar and willow.
Eastern and Central Western States.

Saperda fayi *The Thorn-Limb Borer* Length: 10–12mm. Reddish brown, lower surface gray; pronotum with two white stripes; each elytron with two large, white spots and another between them. Larvae make gall like swellings in the stems of species of hawthorns.
Northeastern and Central States.

Mecas inornata Length: 8–15mm. Black, thickly covered with gray pubescence; pronotum with a naked area each side of middle. Pronotum wider than long, sides rounded; elytra finely but sparsely punctured, apices rounded; eyes notched; tarsal claws cleft. Resembles *Saperda concolor* in size, shape, and color.

In the stems of herbs, unlike the genus *Saperda*, which live in wood. Central and Western States.

The species of the genus Obera *are slender, elongate, and cylindrical, and have notched eyes, antennae not longer than the body, and the tarsal claws broadly toothed.*

***Obera schaumii* *The Poplar Twig Borer* Length: 10–14mm. Color variable but usually pale yellow or brownish yellow; elytra, antennae, and tarsi often black. Pronotum with four round, black, smooth callosities arranged in a curved line, coarsely punctured; elytra with indistinct ridges, coarsely punctured.
In twigs of poplar.
Central States.

***Obera tripunctata* *The Dogwood Twig Borer* Length: 8–16mm. Color variable, head dark brown; pronotum yellow with three black spots; elytra black, each with a wide yellowish stripe; body beneath usually yellow for the most part, but sometimes completely black. Pronotum with two callosities, sparsely punctured; elytra with rows of coarse, deep punctures, apices squarely cut off (Fig. 534).
In elm, dogwood, viburnum, and many fruit trees.
Eastern and Central States.

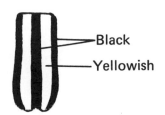

Fig. 534. Obera tripunctata

***Obera bimaculata* *The Raspberry Cane Borer* Length: 8–13mm. Black, shining; pronotum yellow with two round, black spots and sometimes a third one. Pronotum with two callosities, deeply and coarsely punctured; elytra with rows of coarse punctures, apices squarely cut off.
In raspberry and blackberry plants.
Eastern half of the United States.

***Obera ocellata* *The Sumac-Stem Borer* Length: 13–14mm. Head, pronotum, femora, and lower surface reddish; antennae, tibiae, and tarsi dark brown or black; elytra black, with gray pubescence; prono-

tum with two small, black, rounded dots on disk. Pronotum wider than long, sides wavy, with a small, flattened callosity each side of middle, sparsely and coarsely punctured; elytra with rows of coarse punctures, apices rounded.
In sumac.
Eastern and Central States.

***Obera ruficollis   The Sassafras-Stem Borer   Length: 15–18mm.
Pale reddish yellow or orange; antennae, elytra, tibiae, and tarsi black; elytra with gray pubescence. Pronotum somewhat square shaped, coarsely punctured; elytra with irregular rows of rather fine, oblong punctures, apices more or less squarely cut off.
In sassafras.
Eastern half of the United States.

***Obera ferruginea   The Willow-Branch Borer   Length: 10–11mm.
Uniformly pale reddish; pronotum with four black spots arranged in a semicircle; each elytron with a dark spot at the shoulder.
In willow.
Throughout the United States.

***Obera myops   The Rhododendron-Stem Borer   Length: 12–16mm.
Pale yellow; pronotum with two black spots; elytral margins darker.
In rhododendron, laurel, azalea, and related plants.
Northeastern States.

The species of the genus Tetraopes are known as the milkweed beetles, for the larvae feed on the roots of milkweed. They are elongate, cylindrical insects with the eyes divided so that there appear to be four eyes; the antennae are shorter than the body, the femora are cylindrical, and the tarsi have cleft claws.

***Tetraopes melanurus   Length: 8–12mm. Red; pronotum with four round, black spots; each elytron with black from before middle to apex, this spot almost divided near its middle, also a small, black spot at shoulder. Pronotum wider than long, almost smooth; elytra rather coarsely and densely punctured, apices rounded (Fig. 535).
Eastern half of the United States but more common in the South.

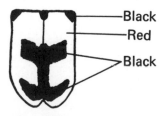

Fig. 535.   Tetraopes melanurus

***Tetraopes tetrophthalmus* The Red Milkweed Beetle* Length: 9–14mm. Red; pronotum with four black spots; elytra each with three black spots and also one at each shoulder; scutellum and body beneath black. Pronotum wider than long, with a smooth median tubercle (Fig. 536).
Eastern half of the United States.

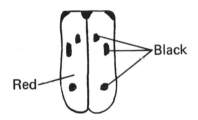

Fig. 536. Tetraopes tetrophthalmus

***Tetraopes femoratus* Length: 12–17mm. Pronotum, elytra, and femora red; lower surface, tibiae, tarsi, four rounded dots on pronotum, scutellum, shoulders, and three rounded spots on each elytron black; antennae black, ringed with gray.
Eastern half of the United States.

The Leaf Beetles

Family Chrysomelidae
From their name it is to be suspected that the beetles of this family feed on the leaves of various plants, as indeed they do, both as adults and larvae. The family is a large one, about one-tenth of the known beetles belonging to it; there are about a thousand species from North America.

They are small or moderate in size—though some are so tiny as to be almost microscopic—are usually oval in outline, and are in attractively variegated colors. Many of them are spotted or striped in brightly contrasting colors, while others have metallic hues, and still others are simply dull brown or black. The antennae are usually of moderate length, are each eleven segmented, and may be threadlike, sawtoothed, or clubbed; the head may be prominent and more or less constricted, or may be hidden beneath a shieldlike pronotum; the eyes are either entire or slightly notched, and finely granulate; the labial palpi are each three segmented, the maxillary palpi are each four segmented; the elytra usually cover the abdomen, though sometimes the last dorsal abdominal segment is exposed; the legs are usually short, the tibiae of the hind legs are often enlarged for jumping; and the tarsi each have five segments (Figs. 537, 538).

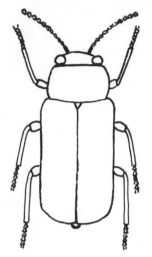

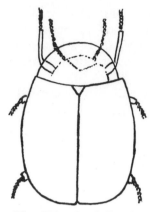

Fig. 538. Leaf Beetle

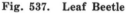

Fig. 537. Leaf Beetle

The eggs are laid on the leaves or stems of the plants upon which the larvae feed. The larvae are, for the most part, soft bodied and more or less brightly colored. Some are flattened and armed with spines; others are partially covered with their excrement. Most of them are free living, but some are leaf miners, casebearers, or root feeders. When about to pupate, many of the free-living species fasten themselves by the tip of the abdomen to a leaf and enter their resting period in the manner of the butterflies; others pupate in the ground, while the casebearers transform to adults within their larval cases.

The species of the genus Donacia *in appearance are likely to be mistaken for cerambycids and hence are known as the* long-horned leaf beetles. *They are elongate in form with slender antennae; the pronotum is narrower than the elytra; the tarsi are dilated and spongy beneath and the third segment of each has two lobes; and the tarsal claws have a slight appendage at each base.*

Donacia proxima Length: 8–11mm. Purplish black, often with a green sheen; head and pronotum darker; covered beneath with dense, gray pubescence; antennae and legs black. Pronotum square shaped, with a median impressed line, punctured at base and apex; elytra with coarse punctures in rows; femora of hind legs each with one to three teeth.
On water plants.
Eastern half of the United States.

Donacia cincticornis Length: 7–11mm. Dark brownish yellow, shining, sometimes tinged with green; head and pronotum darker; antennae and legs reddish brown to blackish; covered beneath with dense, dark gray pubescence. Pronotum wider than long, median line distinct, sides wrinkled; elytra with two slight transverse impressions, punctures in rows; femora of hind legs each with one to three teeth (Fig. 539).
On yellow water lily and pondweed.
Eastern half of the United States.

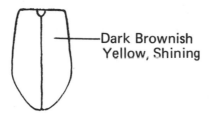

Fig. 539.   Donacia cincticornis

Donacia piscatrix Length: 6.5–9mm. Color variable, bronze, green, or brownish yellow, shining, covered with gray pubescence underneath; antennae and legs reddish yellow. Pronotum square shaped, each side with two rounded tubercles, median line slightly elevated, sparsely and finely punctured; elytra with coarse punctures in rows, intervals finely wrinkled.
On yellow water lily.
Throughout the United States.

Donacia emarginata Length: 6–8mm. Bright metallic blue; antennae black. Pronotum longer than wide, sides with rounded tubercle near apex, median line distinct, finely and densely punctured; elytra with a slight impression in front of middle, intervals transversely wrinkled, apices rounded (Fig. 540).
On sedges.
Throughout the United States.

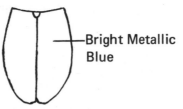

Fig. 540.   Donacia emarginata

Donacia metallica   Length: 5.5–7mm. Color variable, usually green-ish or bronzed, sometimes blackish, shining; legs darker. Pronotum longer than wide, slight tubercles on sides, median line distinct but fine, finely and densely punctured; elytral punctures coarse, intervals nearly smooth, apices rounded.
On skunk cabbage.
Eastern half of the United States.

Donacia subtilis   Length: 7–10mm. Dark bronze to green or pur-plish black, shining; antennae and legs reddish brown to blackish. Pronotum longer than wide, transversely wrinkled with punctures between wrinkles; each elytron with two shallow impressions near middle, punctures in irregular rows, intervals wrinkled, each apex squarely cut off.
On sedges and arrow arum.
Eastern half of the United States.

Orsodacne atra   Length: 4–8mm. Color variable, ranging from brown-ish yellow to black or a combination of the two colors; pronotum sometimes with a large, dark spot; elytra sometimes striped. Prono-tum bell shaped, narrowed at base, roughly and sparsely punctured; elytra irregularly and coarsely punctured; antennae less than half as long as body.
Found most frequently in spring on the blossoms of willow and other plants where beetles of several different color varieties may be found on the same tree.
Throughout the United States.

Syneta ferruginea   Length: 6–8mm. Head, pronotum, and antennae brownish yellow; elytra, legs, and lower surface paler. Pronotum longer than wide, with three teeth at each side, densely and coarse-ly punctured; each elytron with four slightly elevated ridges, each interval with from three to five irregular rows of coarse punctures; antennae less than half as long as body (Fig. 541).
On oak and hazel.
Eastern half of the United States.

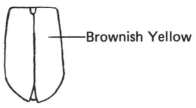

Fig. 541.   *Syneta ferruginea*

Crioceris asparagi   The Asparagus Beetle   Length: 6–7mm. Head dark metallic blue; pronotum red, with two bluish spots; elytra dark blue, each with three or four large, yellow spots on each side, which merge into a reddish yellow margin. Pronotum longer than wide, sides rounded, cylindrical, finely and sparsely punctured; elytra with many rows of coarse punctures, apices rounded; head constricted behind eyes into a neck (Fig. 542).

On asparagus; does considerable damage to asparagus plants.

An introduced species found throughout the United States.

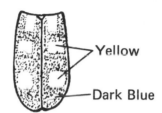

Fig. 542.   Crioceris aspargi

Crioceris duodecimpunctata   The Twelve-Spotted Asparagus Beetle Length: 6–7mm. Dull orange red, shining; head and pronotum reddish brown; each elytron with six small black spots. Pronotum square shaped, minutely punctured and wrinkled, sides rounded, cylindrical; elytra with many rows of coarse punctures, apices rounded; head constricted behind eyes into a neck (Fig. 543).

On asparagus; does considerable damage to asparagus plants.

An introduced species found throughout the United States.

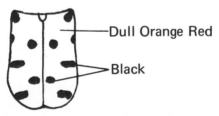

Fig. 543.   Crioceris duodecimpunctata

Lema collaris   Length: 4–5mm. Head black, sometimes red; pronotum red; elytra shining green or blue. Head with a median groove; pronotum constricted at middle, finely and sparsely punctured; elytra much wider than pronotum, with irregular rows of coarse, oblong punctures; antennae a little longer than one-third of the body length (Fig. 544).

Adults on the foliage of low-growing herbaceous plants in moist, sandy situations.

Eastern half of the United States.

Green or Blue Shining

Fig. 544.   Lema collaris

Lema trilineata   The Three-Lined Potato Beetle   Length: 6–7.5mm. Reddish yellow; pronotum usually with two small, black spots on disk; elytra slightly paler, with both sutural margins and a rather wide lateral stripe black. Pronotum constricted at middle, a few coarse punctures on sides near apex; elytra with rows of punctures and much wider than pronotum; antennae a little longer than one-third of the body length (Fig. 545).

This beetle, also known as the *old-fashioned potato beetle,* is found on the foliage of potato and other members of the nightshade family.

Throughout the United States.

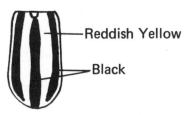

Reddish Yellow

Black

Fig. 545.   Lema trilineata

Anomoea laticlavia   Length: 6–8mm. Head, pronotum, and femora reddish yellow; elytra paler, suture and side edges margined with black; antennae, tibiae, and tarsi black; lower surface covered with dense, gray pubescence. Pronotum wider than long, sides rounded, hind margin wavy; elytra finely and indistinctly punctured; antennae sawlike; coxae of front legs touching (Fig. 546).

Adults on low-growing herbaceous plants and on such trees as willow and honey locust.
Eastern half of the United States.

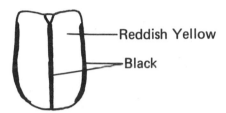

Fig. 546.   Anomoea laticlavia

Babia quadriguttata   Length: 3–5.3mm. Black, shining; each elytron with a large shoulder spot of reddish orange and a smaller apical one of the same color. Pronotum slightly narrower than elytra, finely and densely punctured; elytra with irregular rows of punctures, intervals with scattered punctures; antennae sawlike; coxae of front legs touching (Fig. 547).
Adults on milkweed and other plants.
Throughout the United States.

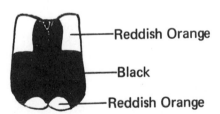

Fig. 547.   Babia quadriguttata

Chlamisus gibbosa   Length: 2.6–4.5mm. Brown, slightly bronzed; elytra and legs sometimes black. Pronotum with a large tubercle in the middle, finely and densely wrinkled, with antennal grooves on the lower surface; each elytron with twelve to fifteen tubercles, the four largest being arranged in an oblique row extending from shoulder to suture, intervals between tubercles sparsely and coarsely punctured; antennae each sawlike beyond the fourth or fifth segment. When disturbed they retract their legs, draw in their antennae, and roll off the leaves. They then resemble the excrement of certain caterpillars so closely that they are difficult to find.
Adults on the foliage of various plants.
Eastern half of the United States.

Exema pennsylvanicus   Length: 3–3.6mm. Black; pronotum with yellow markings; elytra usually with a few yellow spots; antennae and legs yellow, femora and tibiae sometimes partly blackish. Pronotum wider than long, sides narrowed toward the apex, punctures dense, circular, and moderately coarse; elytra coarsely, densely punctured, each with about eleven coarse tubercles; pronotum with antennal grooves on lower surface; antennae each sawlike beyond sixth segment.
Eastern half of the United States.

The species of the genus Pachybrachis *have the pronotum as wide as the elytra and margined at base, and the femora of the front legs distinctly stouter than those of the hind legs.*

Pachybrachis pubescens   Length: 3.4–4.8mm. Black, slightly shining, covered with short sparse pubescence; antennae and legs reddish brown. Both pronotum and elytra with coarse punctures; a prominent, elevated knob at each shoulder angle of elytra.
Eastern half of the United States.

Pachybrachis tridens   Length: 2–3mm. Head light yellow, vertex black and sometimes a spot of the same color on the frontal region; pronotum light yellow with either a black, Y-shaped spot or an oblong, median spot plus a smaller, black round spot on each side; elytra light yellow with a black common crosslike spot on both and each elytron also with a narrow marginal line and a small shoulder spot black; antennae and legs yellow; femora of hind legs often each with a black spot. Pronotum sparsely, coarsely punctured; elytra with irregular rows of coarse punctures.
Adults on the foliage of hickory, elm, and willow, and on various roadside plants.
Eastern half of the United States.

Pachybrachis othonus   Length: 3.5–4mm. Black; labrum and three spots on front of head yellow; margins and median line of pronotum yellow; elytra each with two yellow stripes; antennae blackish; legs yellow. Pronotum wider than long, densely punctured with wrinkles; elytra with a few rows of coarse, closely set punctures (Fig. 548).
Adults on the foliage of various plants, especially along the roadside.
Eastern half of the United States.

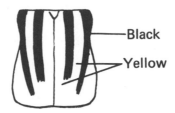

Fig. 548.   Pachybrachis othonus

Pachybrachis trinotatus   Length: 4–5mm. Black; head with two red spots; apical and lateral margins, two basal spots, and a small median line on pronotum reddish. Pronotum deeply and coarsely punctured; elytra coarsely and irregularly punctured; a prominent, elevated knob at each shoulder angle of elytra.
On new jersey tea and wild indigo.
Eastern part of the United States.

The species of the genus Cryptocephalus *have the head retracted within the thorax when at rest, have the pronotal sides with small scallops, and have the base of the pronotum as wide as the elytra.*

Cryptocephalus venustus   Length: 4.5–6mm. Head and pronotum reddish brown; pronotum with sides and two oblique, basal spots yellow; elytra yellow, each with two broad, oblique, black or brown stripes; legs and undersurface reddish brown. Pronotum finely punctured; elytra with rows of fine punctures. The pattern and coloration of this beetle is quite variable, the pronotum often being completely reddish or the elytra often black, with the sides, a narrow line at the suture, and a common basal spot yellow.
On potato and other garden plants as well as those growing in the wild.
Eastern half of the United States.

Cryptocephalus notatus   Length: 4–5.5mm. Black, shining; elytra each with a reddish, oblong shoulder spot extending across each base and along the sides, with another rounded spot at each apex. Pronotum finely and sparsely punctured; elytra each with five regular rows of coarse punctures (Fig. 549).
On the foliage of low-growing plants.
Eastern half of the United States.

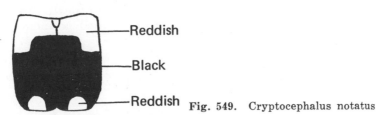

Fig. 549.   Cryptocephalus notatus

Cryptocephalus quadruplex   Length: 4–5.5mm. Black; each elytron with a red, oblong spot at the shoulder and a rounded red spot at the apex.
On the foliage of low-growing plants.
Eastern half of the United States.

Cryptocephalus mutabilis   Length: 4–6.5mm. Reddish brown, shining; pronotum with yellow apical and side margins; elytra pale yellow, with a large common brown spot, which extends backward along suture, each elytron also with six or seven small, brown spots (which may be more or less confluent or absent). Pronotum finely, sparsely punctured; elytra with rows of distant punctures, the sixth and seventh rows of each somewhat confused.
Eastern half of the United States.

Diachus auratus   Length: 1.4–2mm. Head and pronotum dark reddish brown, somewhat bronzed; elytra either metallic green or brown; antennae, legs, and lower surface brownish yellow; abdomen black. Pronotum finely wrinkled; elytra with rows of fine punctures; eyes slightly notched; antennae not more than half as long as body; pronotal sides with small scallops.
On various plants.
Eastern half of the United States.

   The following species up to and including Chrysochus auratus *have the third segment of each tarsus deeply cleft, nearly dividing the segment.* (This taxonomic fact refers to those beetles marked with an *.)

Chrysodina globosa   Length: 2.5–3.5mm. Dark blue or black, with a bronze or greenish sheen, shining; legs brownish yellow. Pronotum wider than long, sides rounded, apex only half as wide as base, minutely punctured; elytra finely and densely punctured; third segment of each antenna longer than second.
Eastern half of the United States.

Nodonota puncticollis   Length: 3.5–4.5mm. Bluish, greenish, or bronzed, shining; basal segments of antennae and legs reddish yellow. Head and pronotum with minute cracks or wrinkles; pronotum with dense, elongate punctures, sides slightly rounded, front angles acute; elytra coarsely, irregularly punctured; third segment of each antenna longer than the second; tarsal claws each with an appendage.
On flowers and foliage of various plants.
Throughout the United States.

Colaspis brunnea Length: 4–6mm. Dull brownish yellow or reddish yellow; legs pale yellowish. Pronotum wider than long, sides rounded, angles prominent, sparsely, evenly punctured; elytra with faint ridges, with two or three rows of deep punctures between the ridges; tarsal claws each with an appendage (Fig. 550).
On various wild and cultivated plants.
Throughout the United States.

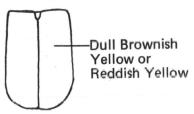

Fig. 550.   Colaspis brunnea

Rhabdopterus picipes Length: 4–6mm. Dark brown to black, shining; elytral margins sometimes greenish bronze; antennae, tibiae, and tarsi reddish yellow; femora and apices of antennae sometimes dark brown; lower surface of body greenish; abdomen black. Pronotum wider than long, sides rounded, finely and sparsely punctured; hind angles prominent; elytra coarsely and irregularly punctured; tarsal claws each with an appendage.
Eastern half of the United States.

Graphops pubescens Length: 3.5–4mm. Black, coppery bronzed, sparsely covered with ash gray pubescence. Pronotum slightly wider than long, finely and sparsely punctured in the middle, with fine cracks or wrinkles on sides and basal half; elytra with rows of fine punctures which disappear or become inconspicuous apically; head with a groove above the eyes.
On various plants, especially evening primrose.
Eastern half of the United States.

Graphops nebulosus Length: 3.3–4mm. Black, slightly bronzed, shining, at times greenish, covered with a thin, gray pubescence. Pronotum wider than long and finely, densely, irregularly punctured; elytra rather coarsely, irregularly punctured; head with a groove above the eyes.
Larvae live in the roots of strawberries; adults on vegetation.
Eastern half of the United States.

Xanthonia decemnotata Length: 2.5–4mm. Dull reddish brown, clay

yellow or completely reddish yellow, covered with very sparse brownish pubescence; each elytron usually with eight or ten blackish spots; antennae and legs pale reddish yellow. Head and pronotum finely, densely punctured; elytra with large, close punctures; femora of front legs of male each with a small tooth.
On oak, beech, and elm.
Eastern half of the United States.

Fidia viticida The Grape Rootworm Length: 5.5–7mm. Dark reddish brown, covered with grayish yellow pubescence; antennae and legs paler. Pronotum wider than long in female, sometimes longer than wide in male, cylindrical, finely and densely punctured; elytra with irregular rows of coarse punctures, shoulders prominent; third segment of each antenna longer than second (Fig. 551).
On grapevines and virginia creeper.
Eastern half of the United States.

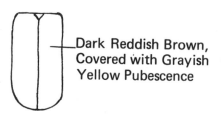
Dark Reddish Brown, Covered with Grayish Yellow Pubescence

Fig. 551. Fidia viticida

Adoxus obscurus The Western Grape Rootworm Length: 4–6mm. Head, pronotum, lower surface, and femora dark brown or blackish; elytra, tibiae, and basal half of each antenna brown, with prostrate yellowish hairs. Pronotum somewhat spherical, much narrower than elytra, finely and densely punctured; elytra with irregular rows of fine punctures.
Adults eat characteristic holes in the leaves of grapevines; the larvae feed on the roots.
Throughout the United States.

Glyptoscelis pubescens Length: 7–10mm. Dark brown, with a metallic sheen, shining; irregularly covered with thin, short, white pubescence. Pronotum wider than long, narrowed suddenly to apex, with a distinct, lateral margin, finely and densely punctured; elytra parallel sided, finely and densely punctured, apices rounded.
On pine, hickory, and wild grapevines.
Eastern half of the United States.

Paria canella Length: 3–4mm. Reddish yellow, shining; pronotum black or yellow; elytra wholly black, wholly yellowish, or yellowish with black spots. Pronotum margined, variably punctured; elytra with rows of fine punctures; tibiae of middle and hind legs each notched on outer edge near apex. This species is very variable in color and markings.

Common on a variety of plants and sometimes injurious to strawberries, raspberries, etc.

Throughout the United States.

Chrysochus auratus *The Goldsmith Beetle* Length: 8–11mm. Green, shining; elytra often with a brassy, and sometimes bluish tinge; antennae, legs, and undersurface bluish green. Head and pronotum with a few coarse, deep punctures, mixed with fine ones; elytra finely, irregularly, and sparsely punctured; pronotum with lateral margins (Fig. 552).

On dogbane and milkweed.

Eastern half of the United States.

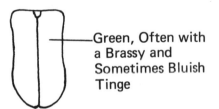

Green, Often with a Brassy and Sometimes Bluish Tinge

Fig. 552.   Chrysochus auratus

In the following species up to and including Psylliodes punctulata *the pronotum has a lateral margin.* (This taxonomic fact refers only to those beetles marked **.)

**Hydrothassa vittata* Length: 3.5–4.5mm. Greenish black, shining; pronotum with side margins of reddish yellow; each elytron with a reddish yellow marginal stripe and a narrow, paler one in the middle; antennae, legs, and undersurface black. Pronotum wider than long, finely and sparsely punctured, apex deeply notched; elytra with sides parallel, rows of somewhat fine and deep punctures, an elevated knob on the shoulder angle with a ridge; last segment of maxillary palpus oval (Fig. 553).

Eastern half of the United States.

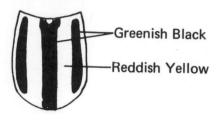

Fig. 553. Hydrothassa vittata

**Labidomera clivicollis* Length: 9–11mm. Dark bluish or greenish black; elytra orange yellow, with variable, broad, curved, black markings. Pronotum wider than long, finely and sparsely punctured; elytra with rather sparse, fine punctures in irregular double rows; last segment of maxillary palpus shorter than preceding one; femora of front legs of male strongly toothed (Fig. 554).
On milkweed.
Throughout the United States.

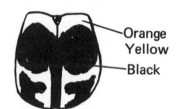

Fig. 554. Labidomera clivicollis

**Leptinotarsa decimlineata* *The Colorado Potato Beetle* Length: 5.5–11mm. Dull yellow; pronotum with a narrow V-shaped spot in the middle and six small spots on each side, all black; elytra with black stripes, the second and third of each united near apex; undersurface reddish yellow, legs darker, apices of femora and tarsi blackish. Elytra with an undulating row of punctures on the two sides of the black stripes; last segment of maxillary palpus shorter than preceding one (Fig. 555).
On potatoes as well as other members of the nightshade family.
Throughout the United States.

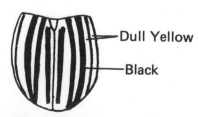

Fig. 555. Leptinotarsa decimlineata

**Zygogramma suturalis Length: 5–7mm. Brown with a slight bronze or greenish sheen; elytra dull yellow with dark brown stripes. Pronotum wider than long, sparsely and coarsely punctured; elytra coarsely punctured; last segment of each tarsus toothed beneath; tarsal claws parallel and united at bases (Fig. 556).
On ragweed in spring, on goldenrod in the fall.
Colorado eastward.

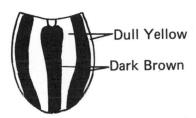

Fig. 556. Zygogramma suturalis

**Calligrapha lunata Length: 7–8mm. Light red brown to brown, shining; elytra yellow, each with the suture and three stripes red brown or brown, the three stripes often united into a broad stripe on each. Pronotum wider than long, sides curved near apex, finely and sparsely punctured; elytra coarsely and irregularly punctured.
On roses.
Eastern half of the United States.

**Calligrapha philadelphica Length: 8–9mm. Dark metallic olive green; elytra yellowish white, each with numerous small dark spots; the suture paler with a black line on each side on elytra. Pronotum with coarse, sparse, and irregular punctures; elytra with sparse, shallow punctures.
On the foliage of dogwood, linden, and elm.
Eastern half of the United States.

**Calligrapha multipunctata Length: 6.5–8.5mm. Dark reddish brown or dark olive green, slightly bronzed; pronotum pale yellowish, with a large, dark reddish brown spot; elytra pale yellow with dark stripes and many black or greenish spots. Pronotum and elytra finely and sparsely punctured (Fig. 557).
On red haw.
Throughout the United States.

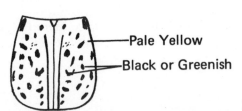

Fig. 557. Calligrapha multipunctata

Calligrapha rhoda   Length: 7–8mm. Dark olive green, slightly metallic; elytra yellowish white, each often with apical two-thirds dull reddish yellow, and each with a large, curved, shoulder, crescent-shaped mark enclosing two small spots that often run together, and also with about eleven small spots behind shoulder mark, all of which are dull green; a common sutural stripe with three short spurs on each side on elytra. Head and pronotum finely wrinkled, coarsely and sparsely punctured; elytra coarsely punctured.
On hazel.
Eastern half of the United States.

Phaedon viridis   Length: 2–3mm. Black with brassy or greenish sheen, shining. Pronotum wider than long, with cracks or wrinkles; elytra with rows of punctures; last segment of maxillary palpus oval; third segment of each tarsus notched and with two lobes.
Eastern half of the United States.

Gastrophysa polygoni   Length: 4–5mm. Head, elytra, and undersurface metallic green or blue; pronotum, base of antennae, legs, and tip of abdomen reddish; tarsi and apical two-thirds of antennae black. Pronotum wider than long, sides rounded, coarsely and sparsely punctured; last segment of maxillary palpus oval (Fig. 558).
On knotgrass.
Throughout the United States.

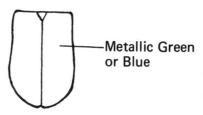

Fig. 558.   Gastrophysa polygoni

Gastrophysa cyanea   *The Green Dock Beetle*   Length: 4–5.5mm. Metallic green or blue, shining; antennae, legs, and undersurface black. Head and pronotum finely, sparsely punctured; elytra densely, roughly punctured; last segment of maxillary palpus oval; third segment of each tarsus notched and with two lobes.
On dock and rhubarb.
Throughout the United States.

Lina interrupta   Length: 6.5–9mm. Black or dark metallic green; pronotum with yellow sides; elytra red or dull yellow, each with seven small, black spots which are sometimes merged into transverse bands; bases of antennae and tibiae reddish. Pronotum finely punctured in dark area, coarsely punctured on sides; elytra coarsely and irregularly punctured; last segment of maxillary palpus oval; tibiae grooved.

On willow, poplar, aspen, and alder.

Throughout the United States.

Lina scripta Length: 6.5–9mm. Dull reddish or greenish yellow; pronotum black, sides yellow; elytra yellow, each with suture black and two small basal spots, three short, median lines, one small spot near suture, and a curved, lateral line near apex on each elytron all black. Pronotum finely, sparsely punctured in dark area, coarsely and sparsely punctured on sides; elytra coarsely and densely punctured; last segment of maxillary palpus oval; tibiae grooved (Fig. 559).

On willow and poplar.

Throughout the United States.

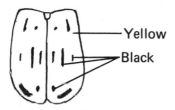

Fig. 559.   Lina scripta

Lina tremulae Length: 7–9mm. Head and pronotum green; elytra yellowish brown.

On willow and poplar. An introduced European species.

Eastern United States.

The species of the genus Diabrotica *have slender antennae, the second segment of each nearly equal to the third; the pronotum is wider than long with two pits on disk and has a lateral margin; the coxae of the front legs are touching; the tibiae of the middle and hind legs each have terminal spurs; the tarsi of the hind legs each have the first segment longer than the next two combined; and the tarsal claws each have two equal lobes.*

Diabrotica undecimpunctata *The Spotted Cucumber Beetle* Length: 6–7mm. Greenish yellow, shining; head black; each elytron with three pairs of black spots arranged transversely; antennae dark brown, the three basal segments yellowish (Fig. 560).

Adults on cucumber, melon, and goldenrod where they feed on the flowers and leaves; larvae in the roots of corn and sometimes quite injurious in the South, hence the insect is also known as the *southern corn rootworm*.

Throughout the United States.

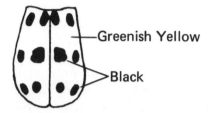

Fig. 560. Diabrotica undecimpunctata

Southern Corn Rootworm; Diabrotica duodecimpunctata

**Diabrotica vittata   The Striped Cucumber Beetle Length: 4.5–6mm. Orange yellow; head black; elytra with a common sutural stripe and each singly with a lateral stripe all black (Fig. 561).

Adults on members of the melon family; sometimes on the foliage of beans, peas, and corn; larvae in the roots. Very injurious to cucumber and melon vines.

East of the Rockies.

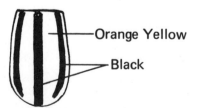

Fig. 561. Diabrotica vittata

**Diabrotica longicornis*   *The Western Corn Rootworm*   Length: 5–6mm. Pale green or greenish yellow.
Adults on corn silk and on the flowers of goldenrod and sunflower; larvae in the roots of corn.
From Nova Scotia southward to Alabama, westward to New Mexico, and north to North Dakota.

The species of the genus Galerucella *have the head exposed and usually with a distinct median impressed line; the antennae are one-half or more the length of the body, the third segment of each longer than the fourth; the pronotum has a median and two lateral impressions; the tibiae are ridged on the outer sides; and the tarsal claws each have two equal lobes.*

**Galerucella americana*   Length: 4–6mm. Brown yellow to gray brown, slightly shining; head and pronotum with a median black spot; each elytron with three narrow, black stripes. Pronotum wider than long, sides rounded, coarsely and densely punctured, in female less so; elytra coarsely and rather densely punctured, shoulders rounded.
On goldenrod.
Eastern half of the United States.

**Galerucella cavicollis*   *The Cherry Leaf Beetle*   Length: 4.3–6mm. Orange or reddish brown, rather shining; antennae black, tibiae and tarsi sometimes black; finely, sparsely pubescent. Pronotum wider than long, sides rounded, coarsely and rather densely punctured; elytra coarsely punctured (Fig. 562).
On peach, plum, and cherry.
Eastern United States.

Orange or Reddish Brown, Shining

Fig. 562.   Galerucella cavicollis

**Galerucella nymphaeae*   *The Water Lily Leaf Beetle*   Length: 4.5–6mm. Dull brownish yellow with fine pubescence; head above almost totally black; antennae ringed, apices of segments blackish; pronotum with three black spots; elytra blackish, side margins and

apices yellowish. Pronotum wider than long, sides angled, middle coarsely punctured, rest of pronotum without punctures or nearly so; elytra coarsely, densely punctured.
On water lilies.
Throughout the United States.

**Galerucella decora* Length: 4.5–5.5mm. Brownish red or yellow, covered with fine, silky pubescence; elytra usually darker; antennae blackish or with basal segments dull yellow. Pronotum wider than long, sides rounded; elytra coarsely, densely punctured.
On willow.
Throughout the United States.

**Galerucella xanthomelaena* The Elm Leaf Beetle Length: 5–7mm. Olive brown or yellowish brown, pubescent; head spotted with black on vertex and behind the eyes; pronotum with three black spots; elytra each with a broad, lateral black stripe and a shorter one in the middle. Pronotum wider than long, sides slightly angled, sparsely punctured; elytra finely punctured (Fig. 563). This beetle is an immigrant from Europe, arriving here about 1834, and has become a serious pest of elm trees.
Both the adults and larvae feed on elm leaves.
Eastern United States.

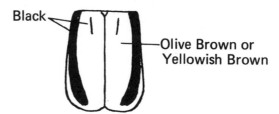

Fig. 563.   Galerucella xanthomelaena

Elm Leaf Beetle; Galerucella xanthomelaena
(Courtesy of C. A. Thomas, Clemson University)

In the species of the genus Trirhabda *the head has a black spot on the occiput; the fourth segment of each antenna is longer than the third; the pronotum is wider than long; the tibiae each have a ridge on the outer edge; and the first segment of each tarsus is longer than the following.*

**Trirhabda canadensis* *The Goldenrod Beetle* Length: 7–10mm. Pale yellow, slightly shining; antennae, tarsi, and sides of abdomen blackish; elytra with a narrow, black lateral and sutural stripe joined at apices; scutellum completely black. Pronotum sparsely, coarsely punctured; elytra finely and densely punctured, covered with dense, pale pubescence (Fig. 564).
On goldenrod.
Throughout the United States.

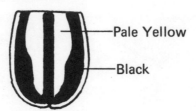

Fig. 564. Trirhabda canadensis

**_Trirhabda bacharidis_ Length: 7.5–12mm. Pale yellow, slightly shining; each elytron with a black lateral stripe which widens and connects with a black sutural stripe; scutellum black. Pronotum sparsely, coarsely punctured; elytra densely and shallowly punctured, covered with dense, pale yellowish pubescence.
On groundsel tree.
Eastern half of the United States.

**_Trirhabda virgata_ Length: 6–9mm. Yellowish; antennae dark; pronotum with three black spots; each elytron with a black lateral and sutural stripe. Pronotum sparsely, coarsely punctured; elytra coarsely and densely punctured, sparsely pubescent.
On goldenrod.
Eastern half of the United States.

**_Monoxia puncticollis_ Length: 7–9mm. Pale yellow to dark brown; elytral margins and suture sometimes marked with black. Antennae do not reach the middle of the body; third segment of each antenna longer than fourth.
Throughout the United States.

**_Luperodes meraca_ Length: 4–5mm. Deep metallic blue, shining; antennae, tibiae, and tarsi brown yellow, femora darker. Pronotum somewhat square shaped, sparsely and finely punctured; elytra transversely wrinkled with a few fine punctures intermingled; head transversely grooved between eyes, ridged between antennae; antennae slender, more than half as long as body; tibiae each with a terminal spur; first segment of each tarsus longer than second and third together; tarsal claws each with an appendage.
Eastern half of the United States.

**_Cerotoma trifurcata_ The Bean Leaf Beetle Length: 4–8.5mm. Yellow or red, shining; head and scutellum black or deep blue; underside black; elytra each with a lateral stripe almost reaching apex, and each with three rounded spots in a line close to suture. Pronotum wider than long, finely and densely punctured; elytra with irregular rows of fine, sparse punctures; first segment of each antenna longer than fourth; first segment of each tarsus of hind legs as long as the rest combined; tarsal claws each with a tooth or lobe (Fig. 565).

On various legumes and often quite destructive.

Eastern half of the United States.

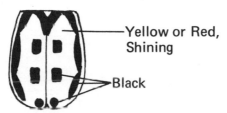

Fig. 565.   Cerotoma trifurcata

**Blepharida rhois   The Sumac Flea Beetle   Length: 5–6.5mm. Reddish brown; elytra irregularly marked with pale yellow; antennae blackish; legs and undersurface reddish brown. Pronotum wider than long, sides rounded, hind angles obtuse, finely and sparsely punctured, and with a row of coarse punctures at margin; each elytron with nine rows of coarse, deep punctures; antennae each with eleven segments, the last one with a small, conical, terminal appendage; tibiae of middle and hind legs notched, the notch containing a comblike brush of bristles; first segment of each tarsus broadly triangular; tarsal claws cleft (Fig. 566) .

On sumac.

Throughout the United States.

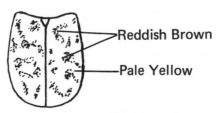

Fig. 566.   Blepharida rhois

In the species of the genus Oedionychus the tibiae of the hind legs each are notched and bordered by a sharp angle or small tooth, the last segment of each of the tarsi of the hind legs is spherically swollen.

**Oedionychus vians* Length: 4–7mm. Dull black, sometimes with a slight greenish or purplish tinge; pronotum brownish yellow, with an inverted W-shaped black spot or with a large transverse spot, margins paler; tip of abdomen brownish yellow. Pronotum wider than long, coarsely and sparsely punctured; elytra with minute cracks or wrinkles and finely, sparsely punctured; third segment of each antenna longer than fourth.
On oak.
Colorado eastward.

**Oedionychus miniata* Length: 4–7mm. Brownish yellow, somewhat shining; pronotum with a transverse brown spot; each elytron with a black sutural and median stripe; tibiae of front and middle legs and all tarsi blackish; lower surface of body reddish brown. Pronotum wider than long, sides rounded, with minute wrinkles or cracks; elytra finely, sparsely punctured.
On herbaceous plants and low-growing shrubs.
Eastern half of the United States.

**Oedionychus quercata* Length: 3.5–4.5mm. Blackish or dull tan, slightly shining; front of head, pronotum, legs, and narrow margins of elytra pale yellow. Pronotum wider than long, side margins widely flattened, finely and sparsely punctured; elytra finely and closely punctured, elevated knob on shoulders distinct (Fig. 567).
On various kinds of foliage.
Colorado eastward.

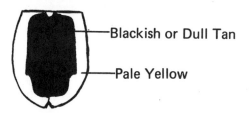

Fig. 567. Oedionychus quercata

In the species of the genus Disonycha *the front of the head is ridged with two tubercles, the first segment of each tarsus is twice the length of the second, the tarsal claws have appendages.*

**Disonycha triangularis* Length: 4.5–7mm. Black or blue black, shining; pronotum yellow with three black dots arranged in a triangle. Pronotum wider than long, sides slightly rounded, margins narrow, finely punctured; elytra finely and somewhat densely punctured (Fig. 568).

On beets, spinach, chickweed, and on low-growing herbaceous plants in damp places.
Throughout the United States.

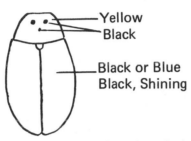

Fig. 568. Disonycha triangularis

Disonycha xanthomelas The Spinach Flea Beetle Length: 4.5–6mm. Similar to *triangularis* except that the pronotum is wholly yellow, the elytra have a greenish tinge, and the abdomen is yellow.
On spinach and a number of wild plants.
Throughout the United States.

Disonycha pennsylvanica Length: 5.5–7.5mm. Black, shining; head blackish; bases of antennae yellow; pronotum yellow and usually with three black spots which sometimes fuse to form a transverse band; elytra yellow each with a black sutural stripe, a narrow black stripe close to each margin, and a black median stripe. Pronotum wider than long, side margins wide, nearly smooth; elytra finely, sparsely punctured.
Eastern half of the United States.

Disonycha caroliniana Length: 5.5–6.5mm. Yellow, shining; antennae, tibiae, and tarsi black; pronotum with two black spots; elytra each with a narrow black stripe along suture, another black stripe near each side margin, and a black median stripe. Pronotum wider than long, sides slightly rounded, smooth or slightly punctured; elytra finely, sparsely punctured.
Eastern half of the United States.

In the species of the genus Altica *the pronotum has a transverse impressed line across its base; the tibiae of the hind legs each have a short spur at the apex; and the tarsal claws are each widened at the base.*

Altica chalybea The Grapevine Flea Beetle Length: 4–5.2mm.

Dark metallic blue, shining, sometimes metallic green or coppery; undersurface and legs blue black. Pronotum wider than long, almost smooth, with minute and scattered punctures; elytra finely, sparsely punctured (Fig. 569).

On wild grapevines, poison ivy, and virginia creeper.

Throughout the United States.

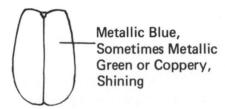

Metallic Blue,
Sometimes Metallic
Green or Coppery,
Shining

Fig. 569.   Altica chalybea

Altica ignita   The Strawberry Flea Beetle   Length: 3–4mm. Bronze, green, or brassy green, shining, sometimes purplish; underside and legs blue black. Pronotum wider than long, minutely and sparsely punctured; elytra sparsely punctured.

On strawberries, roses, and a number of wild plants.

Throughout the United States.

Altica ambiens   Length: 5–6mm. Cobalt blue to greenish blue; undersurface and legs blue black. Pronotum wider than long; elytra finely, distinctly punctured.

On alders.

Maine to Minnesota and New Mexico.

In the species of the genus Epithrix *the body above has patches, or series, of hairs; the front of the head has a V-shaped ridge; and the pronotum has a curved basal impression.*

Epithrix cucumeris   The Potato Flea Beetle   Length: 1.5–2.5mm. Black, shining; antennae and legs brownish orange or reddish yellow except the femora of the hind legs which are blackish. Pronotum wider than long, finely, rather densely punctured; elytral punctures coarse, arranged in series (Fig. 570).

On all members of the nightshade family; it is a rather serious pest.

Throughout the United States.

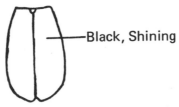

Fig. 570.   Epithrix cucumeris

**Epithrix parvula*   *The Tobacco Flea Beetle*   Length: 1.5–2mm.
Dull reddish yellow; antennae and legs pale reddish yellow; undersurface brown; elytra each sometimes with a dark transverse band.
On tobacco, potato, tomato, eggplant, and a variety of other plants;
especially destructive to tobacco where the adults eat holes in the
leaves.
Throughout the United States.

**Orthaltica copalina*   Length: 2–3mm. Brown or blackish, shining;
legs reddish yellow. Pronotum wider than long, coarsely and rather
sparsely punctured, basal impression deep and ends curved toward
base; elytra each with nine rows of coarse, dense punctures; tibiae
of hind legs each with a short spur.
On sumac and poison ivy.
Eastern half of the United States.

**Derocrepis erythropus*   Length: 2.5–3.5mm. Head, pronotum, and
legs reddish yellow or brown orange, shining; elytra metallic blue
black or blue green. Pronotum wider than long, sides slightly rounded, smooth except for a basal groove which ends in a short, longitudinal impression on each side; elytra with regular rows of punctures; front of head grooved; antennae half as long as body.
On black locust as well as on other trees, such as peach and apple.
Throughout the United States.

**Chalcoides nana*   Length: 2.3–3.5mm. Color variable, bronze or
metallic blue or green, shining; antennae and legs reddish yellow;
undersurface blackish. Pronotum wider than long, sides slightly
rounded, coarsely and sparsely punctured, basal groove ending in a
short, longitudinal impression on each side; elytra coarsely punctured at bases, more finely at apices; front of head with a curved
groove; antennae half as long as body.
On willow and poplar.
Eastern half of the United States.

In the species of the genus Chaetocnema *the tibiae of the hind
legs are each wavy near the apex and each has a distinct tooth on
the outer margin.*

Chaetocnema denticulata   The Toothed Flea Beetle   Length: 2.3–2.5mm. Blackish, with a brassy bronze luster; fifth or sixth antennal segments orange, remaining blackish; femora of front and middle legs brown, of hind legs bronzed, remainder of legs orange or reddish yellow. Pronotum wider than long, sides rounded, coarsely and regularly punctured; elytra coarsely, deeply punctured.
On grasses in meadows; also on corn, beets, and sorghum.
Throughout the United States.

Chaetocnema pulicaria   The Corn Flea Beetle   Length: 1.5–2.5mm. Black, slightly bronzed with blue or green, shining; basal three or four antennal segments orange, remaining blackish; femora blackish, tibiae and tarsi brownish yellow. Pronotum wider than long, narrowed toward the apex, sides rounded, basal marginal line punctured to middle; elytra with rows of coarse, close-set punctures.
On corn, sometimes a serious pest.
Throughout the United States.

Chaetocnema confinis   The Sweet Potato Flea Beetle   Length: 1.5–1.8mm. Black, with tinge of bronze, slightly shining; legs reddish yellow; femora of hind legs black. Pronotum wider than long, narrowed toward the apex, apical angle obliquely cut off, coarsely punctured; elytra with rows of coarse, deep punctures, intervals finely punctured.
A common pest of sweet potatoes; also feeds on corn, wheat, and other plants.
Throughout the United States.

In the species of the genus Systena *the tibiae of the hind legs are grooved and ridged on the outer edges and the tarsal claws have appendages.*

Systena hudsonias   Length: 3.5–4.7mm. Black, shining; antennal segments three to seven brown or yellow. Pronotum wider than long, with fine cracks or wrinkles; elytra coarsely, densely punctured.
On greater ragweed, elder, and other plants.
Throughout the United States.

Systena frontalis   The Red-Headed Flea Beetle   Length: 3.5–4.8mm. Black, slightly shining; head reddish or yellowish. Pronotum wider than long, distinctly punctured; elytra densely punctured.
On such cultivated plants as cabbage, beans, beets, potatoes, and corn, and on various wild plants including smartweed, pigweed, ragweed, and others.
East of the Rocky Mountains.

**Systena taeniata*   *The Pale-Striped Flea Beetle*   Length: 3–4.5mm.
Head and pronotum reddish or brownish yellow, shining; elytra black,
each with a broad yellow stripe down the middle. Pronotum wider
than long, finely, sparsely punctured; elytra finely, densely punctured.
This species is highly variable in shades and marking.
On such cultivated plants as cabbage, sugar beets, beans, tomatoes,
and corn, and on various wild plants including ragweed, pigweed,
lamb's quarters, cocklebur, and others.
Throughout the United States.

**Longitarsus melanurus*   Length: 2–2.5mm. Dark reddish yellow or
reddish brown to black; shining. Pronotum wider than long, sides
slightly rounded, sparsely and rather coarsely punctured; elytra
coarsely and rather densely punctured; first segment of each of the
tibiae of hind legs as long as remaining segments together; tibiae of
hind legs grooved and each with a long spine at apex.
Rather common on various plants.
Eastern half of the United States.

In the species of the genus Phyllotreta *the tibiae of the hind legs
are each slightly excavated near the tip and each has a spur in the
middle beneath.*

**Phyllotreta armoraciae*   *The Horseradish Flea Beetle*   Length:
2.6–4mm. Black, shining; elytra dull yellow, with a common sutural
stripe and each with side and apical margins black. Pronotum wider
than long, finely and sparsely punctured; elytra more coarsely and
densely punctured (Fig. 571).
An imported species and a serious pest of horseradish.
Eastern half of the United States.

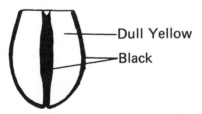

—Dull Yellow
—Black

Fig. 571.   Phyllotreta armoraciae

**Phyllotreta striola*   *The Striped Cabbage Flea Beetle*   Length: 2.5–
3mm. Black, shining; each elytron with a longitudinal, wavy, yellowish stripe narrowed in the middle and curved inward at each end.
Pronotum wider than long, coarsely and rather sparsely punctured;

elytra more coarsely and densely punctured (Fig. 572).
On members of the mustard family, as on cabbage.
East of the Rockies.

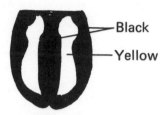

Fig. 572. Phyllotreta striola

Phyllotreta bipustulata Length: 1.6–2.5mm. Black, shining; each
elytron with two yellowish or orange spots. Pronotum wider than
long, finely and sparsely punctured; elytra coarsely and rather densely punctured.
On various plants.
Eastern half of the United States.

Phyllotreta pusilla *The Western Flea Beetle* Length: 1.5–2mm.
Black or dark olive green.
Does considerable damage to mustard crops.
Found in the western half of the United States.

Dibolia borealis Length: 2.5–3.5mm. Black, coppery bronzed, or
bluish, at times green; antennae and legs reddish yellow; undersurface and femora of hind legs blackish. Pronotum wider than long,
sides curved, fine and coarse punctures intermingled; elytra with
rows of fine, close-set punctures, second, fourth, and sixth intervals
with coarser punctures than others; front of head ridged and with
tubercles; tibial spurs of hind legs large and broad, deeply notched.
Larvae mine in leaves of plantain; adults on vegetation.
Eastern half of the United States.

Psylliodes punctulata *The Hop Flea Beetle* Length: 2–2.7mm.
Black, bronzed, sometimes brassy or greenish, shining. Pronotum
slightly wider than long, base rounded with a distinct marginal line,
coarsely punctured; elytra with rows of punctures; antennae each
with ten segments; first segment of each tarsus of hind legs more
than half the length of tibiae.
On rhubarb, hops, and other plants.
Eastern half of the United States.

Anoplitis inaequalis Length: 3.5–4.5mm. Variable in color from

brownish red to blackish; when brownish red the elytra have a few irregular black marks, when blackish the elytra have a few scattered red streaks; antennae black; legs pale yellowish. Pronotum slightly wider than long, sides slightly rounded, coarsely and deeply punctured; elytra with margins and apices sawlike, and each with three ridges and eight rows of punctures; eyes prominent.
On various legumes.
Eastern half of the United States.

Chalepus scapularis   Length: 5–7.5mm. Black; pronotum red with a dark center; elytra black with red shoulders. Pronotum wider than long, sides slightly angled at middle, deeply and coarsely punctured; elytral shoulders prominent, each elytron with four ridges, the third and fourth separated by four rows of coarse, deep punctures; elytral margins and apices sawlike.
On honey locust.
From Arizona eastward.

Chalepus dorsalis   The Locust Leaf Miner   Length: 6–6.5mm. Head, antennae, legs, lower surface, and a triangular area widening toward apices on elytra black; pronotum and rest of elytra reddish orange or scarlet. Pronotum wider than long, sides slightly rounded, coarsely and deeply punctured; each elytron with four ridges, the first and second separated by four rows of coarse, deep punctures, elytral margins and apices sawlike (Fig. 573).
On locust.
Eastern half of the United States.

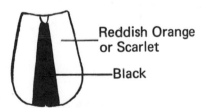

Fig. 573.   Chalepus dorsalis

Baliosus ruber   Length: 4.5–7mm. Reddish yellow to rosy; elytra with indistinct, deep red markings along lateral edges and apical halves; undersurface reddish; legs reddish yellow. Pronotum widened at base, coarsely and deeply punctured; elytral shoulders prominent, margins sawlike; each elytron with four ridges and with four rows of coarse, deep punctures between third and fourth ridges.
On basswood, oak, locust, and maple.
Throughout the United States.

Microrhopala vittata   Length: 5–7mm. Black or bluish black; head, pronotum, and second ridge and marginal line of elytra red. Pronotum wider than long, coarsely and sparsely punctured; elytra each with four rows of oblong punctures arranged in pairs.
On goldenrod.
Eastern half of the United States.

Microrhopala excavata   Length: 4–5.5mm. Bluish black, violet, or greenish. Pronotum wider than long, coarsely and irregularly punctured; elytra each with four rows of coarse, deep punctures, the two inner rows smaller and less deep, margins sawlike.
Eastern half of the United States.

Chelymorpha cassidea   The Milkweed Tortoise Beetle   Length: 8–11.5mm. Brick red or yellow; pronotum with four black dots in a transverse row and two others behind them; elytra each with six dots and a common sutural one black. Pronotum wider than long (tortoiselike), with coarse and fine punctures intermingled, basal margin wavy, apical margin notched leaving the head partly visible; elytra coarsely and rather densely punctured (Fig. 574).
On milkweed, members of the morning glory family, and sometimes on raspberries.
Throughout the United States.

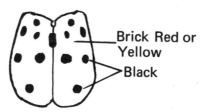

Fig. 574.   Chelymorpha cassidea

Deloyala guttata   The Mottled Tortoise Beetle   Length: 5–6mm. Light yellow; basal part of pronotum sometimes with a black spot enclosing two small, pale ones; elytra black, with irregular yellow spots, margins yellow except at shoulders, suture, and apices; undersurface black with margins yellow; antennae yellow, the last two segments of each dusky. Flattened margins of pronotum and elytra broad (tortoiselike), thin, and almost transparent; elytra with irregular rows of deep, coarse punctures; head covered by rounded front margin of pronotum; prothorax on underside with a groove for receiving antennal segments two, three, and four.
On members of the morning glory family.
Throughout the United States.

Plagiometriona clavata   Length: 7–7.5mm. Brilliant brassy or green-ish gold; when dead a dull reddish yellow; undersurface and last four segments of antennae black. Margins of pronotum and elytra broadly flattened, very thin, and translucent; elytra with many conical tuber-cles and a network of ridges with shallow punctures between ridges; head covered by rounded front margin of pronotum.

On members of the morning glory family and on sycamore, linden, and oak.

Throughout the United States.

Metriona bivittata   Length: 4.5–6mm. Pronotum pale yellow, with a large, triangular, brownish red spot; elytra pale yellow, each with a black or brown sutural stripe and two longitudinal stripes of the same color; undersurface and legs blackish. Pronotum coarsely, shallowly, sparsely punctured; elytra with rows of coarse, deep punc-tures; head covered by rounded front margin of pronotum.

On sweet potato and bindweed.

Throughout the United States.

Metriona bicolor   *The Goldbug or Golden Tortoise Beetle*   Length: 5–6mm. Brilliant brassy or greenish gold when living, dull reddish yellow after death; undersurface and last four segments of antennae black. Pronotum finely, sparsely punctured; each elytron with a small, rounded, depressed space at basal third and a large, oblong one near margin, small and shallow punctures arranged in regular rows; head covered by rounded front margin of pronotum (Fig. 575).

On bindweed and morning glory.

Eastern half of the United States.

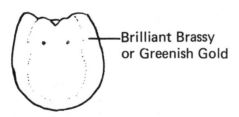

Brilliant Brassy or Greenish Gold

Fig. 575.   Metriona bicolor

The Pea and Bean Weevils

Family Mylabridae

This is a small family with relatively only a few species. The beetles are small and chunky, with the head prolonged into a broad, square-shaped beak, and they differ from most of the *Chrysomelidae* by having short, saw-toothed antennae and the tip of the abdomen exposed. The antennae each have eleven segments and are inserted in front of the eyes, which are large and more or less notched; the pronotum has a basal margin, sometimes apical and lateral ones also; the abdomen has five segments; the coxae of front legs are oval, those of the hind legs are transverse; the femora of the hind legs are dilated and often toothed; the tarsi each have the first segment elongate, the third with lobes; and the tarsal claws are each usually broadly toothed at the base (Fig. 576).

Larvae live in the seeds of legumes; adults are found on foliage and in stored peas, beans, and other seeds.

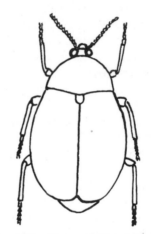

Fig. 576. Pea and Bean Weevil

Mylabris pisorum   The Pea Weevil   Length: 4–5mm. Black, slightly shining, densely covered above with reddish brown and whitish pubescence; pronotum with a more or less triangular whitish area; elytra varied with yellowish, grayish, and whitish pubescence; the apical dorsal segment of the abdomen with gray pubescence and two oval black spots; antennae and legs black, the first three antennal segments and tibia and tarsi of front legs reddish; undersurface black, sparsely covered with gray pubescence. Pronotum wider than long, narrowed toward the apex, the sides notched and toothed, coarsely and deeply punctured; elytra striate, the striae finely punctured; femora of hind legs each with a strong, acute tooth (Fig. 577).

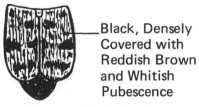

Black, Densely
Covered with
Reddish Brown
and Whitish
Pubescence

Fig. 577. Mylabris pisorum

The eggs are laid on the young pods of peas in the spring and on hatching the larvae bore through the pods where they grow and pupate. The adults hibernate in the field and in stored peas, but do not lay any eggs in the latter.
Throughout the United States.

Althaeus hibisci Length: 2–3mm. Black, slightly shining, rather sparsely covered with grayish yellow pubescence; elytra with many irregular, transverse, smooth areas; antennae reddish brown; legs rusty red, femora of hind legs black. Pronotum wider than long, tapering toward the apex, sides rounded, sparsely punctured; elytra with punctured striae, intervals flattened, sprinkled with punctures; femora of hind legs with an obliquely cut off spine.
Adults on the flowers of redbud, dogwood, and other flowering plants during late spring and early summer; adults and larvae also in seeds, especially those of the rose mallow, throughout the year.
Eastern half of the United States.

Gibbobruchus mimus Length: 2.5–3.5mm. Dull reddish brown, variegated with gray, black, and white pubescence; pronotum with a brownish black ridge; elytra with a common heart-shaped, brownish black area behind scutellum and many small, blackish, oblong spots; antennae and legs brownish; femora and tibiae of hind legs ringed with brownish black. Pronotum somewhat bell shaped; elytra with punctured striae, intervals flat with minute punctures; femora of hind legs each with a strong tooth, followed by four smaller ones.
Adults on various wild flowers in late spring and early summer; larvae in seeds.
Eastern half of the United States.

Acanthoscelides obtectus *The Bean Weevil* Length: 2.5–4mm. Blackish, with dark gray tawny pubescence; elytra with short, transverse bands of brownish pubescence; abdomen dull reddish brown, antennae black, except for the rusty red apical and basal segments; legs reddish brown. Pronotum wider than long, sides rounded, narrowed towards the apex, coarsely and sparsely punctured; elytra with punctured striae, intervals with minute, dense punctures; femora of hind legs each with one strong tooth and two smaller ones (Fig. 578).

A pest of all varieties of dried beans in which it breeds and in which it may be found throughout the year.
Throughout the United States.

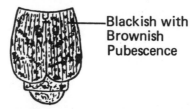

Fig. 578.   Acanthoscelides obtectus

Amblycerus robiniae   Length: 7–7.5mm. Dull reddish brown, covered with grayish pubescence; pronotum sometimes partly black; elytra each with small, black spots arranged in five irregular rows. Pronotum nearly semicircular, sides wavy, sparsely rather coarsely punctured; elytra with punctured striae, intervals with minute and dense punctures, apices rounded; tibiae of hind legs compressed and cylindrical, each with two unequal spurs (Fig. 579).
Adults on bark and foliage of honey locust; larvae in the seeds.
Eastern half of the United States.

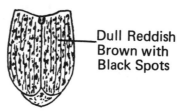

Fig. 579.   Amblycerus robiniae

The Primitive Weevils

Family Brentidae
This is essentially a family of tropical beetles, less than ten species occurring in the United States. They are elongate, slender, of small to moderate size, with the mouthparts usually differing greatly between the sexes. The antennae each have ten or eleven segments; the eyes are small and rounded; the beak is straight and there is no labrum; the abdomen has five ventral segments, the first and second long, the third and fourth short, the fifth longer than fourth

and rounded posteriorly; the femora are club shaped; and the tarsi have spongy pubescence, third segment of each tarsus with two lobes (Fig. 580).

The mandibles of the male are each curved, flattened, pointed, and toothed on the inner edge; those of the female are small and pincer shaped, at the end of a slender beak. The female uses this beak to bore deep holes in the wood beneath the bark of trees, sometimes taking the better part of a day at each hole, in which she lays one egg. The male stands guard and helps the female in extracting the beak, which occasionally gets stuck in the wood.

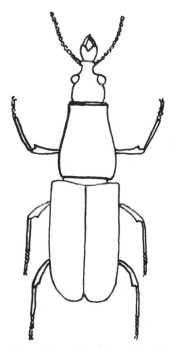

Fig. 580.   Primitive Weevil

Arrhenodes minutus   Length: 7.2–17mm. Dark reddish brown to blackish; elytra each with narrow, elongate, yellowish spots that often unite to form two or three transverse bands. Pronotum longer than wide, constricted at base, sides rounded, converging to apex, minutely and sparsely punctured; elytral striae deep, lateral ones coarsely punctured (Fig. 581).

Adults beneath the bark of oak, poplar, and beech; the larvae bore through the heartwood.

Throughout the United States.

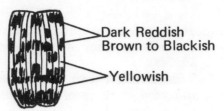

Fig. 581. Arrhenodes minutus

The Fungus Weevils

Family Anthribidae

This is another small family of beetles that are characterized by having the beak broad and flat and often very short. The antennae are each either long and threadlike, or short and with a three segmented club; the labial palpi are each three segmented, the maxillary ones are each four segmented; the pronotum has a transverse raised line; the coxae of the front legs are spherical, those of the hind legs are transverse; and the tarsi are each four segmented, the second segment of each is triangular and partially covers the third so that there appears to be only three segments (Fig. 582).

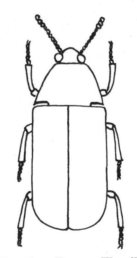

Fig. 582. Fungus Weevil

The larvae of some species infest woody fungi, others breed in the smut of corn and wheat, and still others in dead wood. The adults may be found beneath old bark or on dead twigs.

Eurymycter fasciatus Length: 6.5–9.5mm. Dark brown to brownish black; beak with a large spot of white pubescence; elytra each with a broad, transverse white band. Pronotum roughly sculptured, with a transverse, rounded impression before middle, and a transverse raised line about one-fifth from base; elytra with many short wrinkles and with rows of large punctures (Fig. 583).

On dead twigs and fungi, especially fungi growing on dead beech. Throughout the United States.

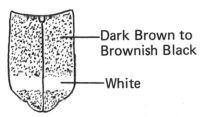

Fig. 583. Eurymycter fasciatus

Euparius marmoreus Length: 3.5–8.5mm. Brownish black; densely covered with pale brown and grayish yellow pubescence covering beak, apical third of pronotum, and forming a large, common sutural spot on elytra; legs ringed with gray and black or dark brown. Pronotum narrowed toward the apex, a broad, shallow, median groove on basal half in which is a low, broad ridge, coarsely and densely punctured; elytra with rows of coarse, deep punctures; eyes oval, prominent; third segment of each antenna twice as long as second (Fig. 584).

In woody fungi and under bark.
Eastern half of the United States.

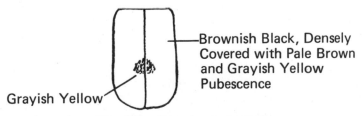

Fig. 584. Euparius marmoreus

Brachytarsus sticticus Length: 2.5–3mm. Brown, densely covered with short, dark brown, and grayish yellow pubescence; elytra with many, small, rounded spots and two larger, dark brown ones; antennae pale reddish brown, the three apical segments brownish black; legs pale reddish, femora brownish black medially. Pronotum with anterior margin rounded, partially concealing the head, finely and densely punctured; elytral striae fine; eyes notched; second segment of each tarsus triangular and notched, third with two lobes; tarsal claws toothed near bases.

Larvae in the smut of corn and wheat; adults on low herbaceous plants and also on the flowers of the buttonbush.

Eastern half of the United States.

Araecerus fasciculatus   The Coffee Bean Weevil   Length: 2.5–4.5mm. Dark brown or blackish mottled with yellow or brown pubescence; antennae and legs reddish brown in part (Fig. 585).

The beetle is a pest in stored coffee; also found in the seeds of cotton, pokeweed, and other plant products.

Throughout the United States.

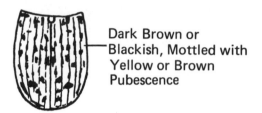

Dark Brown or Blackish, Mottled with Yellow or Brown Pubescence

Fig. 585.   Araecerus fasciculatus

The New York Weevil

Family Belidae

This family is represented in our country by a single species:

Ithycerus noveboracensis   The New York Weevil   Length: 12–18mm. Black, shining, covered with ash gray and pale brown pubescence, the hairs prostrate; the ash gray hairs form a narrow median and two lateral stripes on pronotum and a narrow stripe on each alternate interval of the elytra, each of these bearing three or four small, rounded tufts of black hairs; scutellum grayish white (Fig. 586). Pronotum about as wide as long, apex and base squarely cut off, sides slightly rounded, with dense wrinkles; bases of elytra nearly twice as wide as pronotum, sides converging to apices; elytra indis-

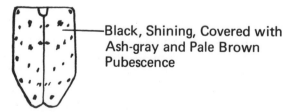

Black, Shining, Covered with Ash-gray and Pale Brown Pubescence

Fig. 586.   Ithycerus noveboracensis

tinctly striate, the striae coarsely punctured; mandibles notched; eyes small, rounded; third segment of each antenna longer than second, antennal clubs small, oval, and pointed; tarsi broad, pubescent beneath, third segment of each with two lobes; tarsal claws with a small, pointed tooth (Fig. 587).

On oak, hickory, and beech; also destructive to apple, peach, plum, pear, and cherry trees. The larvae appear in early spring and at first gnaw the bark of twigs, then later feed on the buds and foliage. The adults may be found in the crevices in the bark of the trees. Throughout the United States.

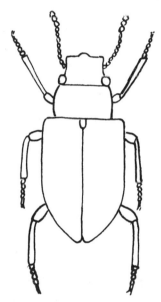

Fig. 587.   New York Weevil

The Snout Beetles

Family Curculionidae

This is a very large family, over 40,000 species being known, of which some eighteen hundred occur in North America north of Mexico. It includes the typical *snout beetles,* the head being prolonged into a well defined beak, which is usually long and curved downward; many of the snout beetles are important economic pests.

The labial and maxillary palpi are short, rigid, and nearly always hidden; the head is spherical; the antennae are sometimes straight, but are usually bent at an angle and each with a three-segmented club; the coxae of the front and middle legs are rounded, those of the hind legs are oval (Fig. 588).

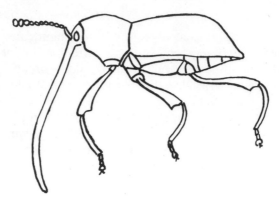

Fig. 588.　Snout Beetle

The snout beetles may be found on various parts of plants; the larvae, which look like maggots, for the most part feed on the internal tissues of stems and fruits though some are external plant feeders. The adults often bask in the sunshine and when disturbed may fold up their antennae and legs and drop to the ground where they "play 'possum."

Eugnamptus collaris　Length: 3.5–4.7mm. Black; elytra bluish black; other parts variable in color. Pronotum somewhat squarish, a shallow, median impression on basal half, coarsely and sparsely punctured; each elytral interval with a fine ridge and a row of setae-bearing punctures; mandibles of male each with one tooth, mandibles of female each with two teeth.
On oak, walnut, hickory, and butternut; also on various herbaceous plants.
Texas eastward.

Rhynchites bicolor　*The Rose Curculio*　Length: 5–6.5mm. Head behind the eyes, pronotum, and elytra bright red; other parts black. Beak as long as head and pronotum, with elongate punctures; pronotum cylindrical, finely and densely punctured; elytra with indistinctly punctured striae, intervals with dense, coarse punctures; mandibles flat, toothed on inner and outer sides; tibiae each with short, terminal spurs (Fig. 589).
Often very common on wild roses, sometimes a pest on cultivated ones; also on blackberries and raspberries. *Curculio* is from the Latin, meaning a grain weevil; hence rose curculio is a weevil found primarily on roses.
Throughout the United States.

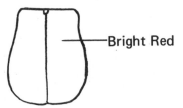

Fig. 589. Rhynchites bicolor

Attelabus analis Length: 5–6mm. Base of head, pronotum, elytra, and abdomen bright red; other parts bluish black. Beak shorter than head, the head with two grooves between eyes; pronotum bell shaped, sparsely and finely punctured; elytra with rows of shallow punctures; coxae of front legs conical, those of middle and hind legs transverse; tibiae each sawlike on inner side with two sturdy hooks at tip (Fig. 590).
On leaves or beneath bark of hickory, oak, and walnut.
Eastern half of the United States.

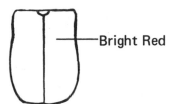

Fig. 590. Attelabus analis

Attelabus nigripes Length: 3.5–4.5mm. Similar in coloration to *analis* except that all of the undersurface of the body is usually dull red. Pronotum narrowed to apex, finely punctured; elytra with rows of coarse, rather deep punctures; femora of front legs stout, each with two teeth in male.
On hickory and sumac.
Eastern half of the United States.

Attelabus bipustulatus Length: 3–4mm. Black, with a bluish tinge; each elytron with a reddish spot on the shoulder. Beak shorter than head, the head with a groove between the eyes; pronotum bell shaped, finely and sparsely punctured; elytra with rows of small punctures; femora of front legs each with a small, acute tooth (Fig. 591).
On hickory, oak, and walnut.
Eastern half of the United States.

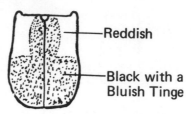

Fig. 591.   Attelabus bipustulatus

Cylas formicarius   The Sweet Potato Weevil   Length: 5–6mm.
Pale reddish brown or salmon; elytra bluish black; head and beak
blackish. Beak twice as long as head; last segment of each antenna
cylindrical and elongate, especially in the male; pronotum longer
than wide, smooth; elytra elongate-oval, shoulders oblique, with
fine, slightly punctured striae, intervals smooth; claws of each tarsus
united at base; body antlike in shape (Fig. 592).
On sweet potato, various members of the morning glory family, and
some composite flowers, such as sunflowers, goldenrod, asters, and
dandelions.
Florida to Texas.

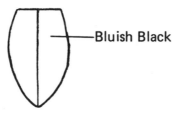

Fig. 592.   Cylas formicarius

Apion patruele   Length: 1.6–2mm. Black, shining, sparsely covered
with whitish pubescence. Beak as long as head and pronotum together in male, longer in female; front of head grooved; pronotum
wider than long, a rounded pit at base, coarsely and rather densely
punctured; elytra with prominent shoulders, stria with large, deep
punctures; last segment of each antennal club longer than either of
two preceding; body pear shaped.
On legumes as well as on witch hazel.
Eastern half of the United States.

Apion griseum   Length: 1.7–2mm. Black, slightly bronzed, rather
densely covered with whitish or yellowish pubescence. Beak as long
as or slightly longer than head and pronotum combined; pronotum
wider than long at base, sides converging to apex, a small pit at base,

densely and rather coarsely punctured; elytral striae coarsely punctured; last segment of each antennal club longer than either of two preceding; body pear shaped (Fig. 593).

On various legumes.

Eastern half of the United States.

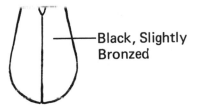

Fig. 593.   Apion griseum

Phyxelis rigidus   Length: 3.5–4.5mm. Dull brown, densely covered with small, gray scales and often with a brown or yellowish waxy crust; tarsi and segments of each antenna between first segment and club reddish brown. Pronotum wider than long, apex and base squarely cut off, sides slightly rounded, with many short hairs arising from small tubercles; elytra with base squarely cut off, slightly striate, striae coarsely punctured; beak longer than head, with grooves for the reception of antennae (Fig. 594); the antennae bent at an angle; scutellum not visible; third segment of each tarsus with two lobes and brushlike.

On various herbaceous plants.

Eastern half of the United States.

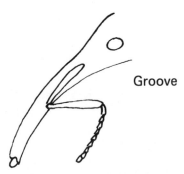

Fig. 594.   Head of a Curculionid Showing Beak and Groove for Reception of Antenna

Anametis granulata   Length: 5–7mm. Dark brown, densely covered with grayish scales; antennae and tarsi reddish brown. Pronotum wider than long, apex and base squarely cut off, sides slightly rounded; elytral striae with small, deep punctures, each interval with two irregular rows of setae; beak longer than head, with grooves for the reception of antennae; the antennae bent at an angle; scutellum small, triangular; third segment of each tarsus with two lobes and brushlike.
Common on the foliage of trees and shrubs.
Eastern half of the United States.

Pandeleteius hilaris   *The Gray-Sided Oak Weevil*   Length: 4–5mm. Brown, densely clothed with silvery gray, brownish black, and pale grayish brown scales; antennae and tarsi reddish brown. Pronotum somewhat cylindrical, sides rounded, coarsely and deeply punctured; elytra squarely cut off at bases, each elytron with ten striae that are coarsely, deeply punctured; beak slightly shorter than head, with grooves for the reception of the antennae; the antennae bent at an angle; scutellum small, triangular; front legs longer, the femora larger than those of the other legs; tibiae of front legs each with a tooth on inner edge (Fig. 595).
On various oaks, also new jersey tea and smartweed.
Florida to Texas and northward.

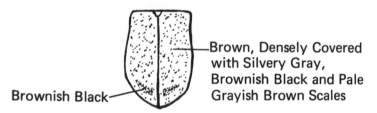

Brown, Densely Covered with Silvery Gray, Brownish Black and Pale Grayish Brown Scales

Brownish Black

Fig. 595.   *Pandeleteius hilaris*

Polydrusus americanus   Length: 4.5–5.5mm. Brown, shining; densely covered with pale gray and orange brown scales, the scales forming three narrow stripes on pronotum, and a large common spot on elytra; antennae and legs reddish brown. Pronotum square shaped, apex obliquely and base squarely cut off, sparsely punctured; elytra with fine punctured striae, each interval with a single row of short hairs, shoulders prominent; beak shorter than head, with grooves for the reception of antennae; the antennae bent at an angle (Fig. 596).
On beech.
Eastern half of the United States.

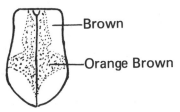

Fig. 596. Polydrusus americanus

Graphognathus leucoloma *The White-Fringed Beetle* Length: 9–12mm. Blackish, densely covered with ashy and gray brown scales, scutellum whitish scaled; elytral sides with white, longitudinal stripes. Pronotum wider than long, sides rounded, finely and sparsely punctured; elytra with sides rounded, tapering to apices, with indistinct rows of coarse punctures, intervals with scattered fine granules; beak half the length of pronotum, with a ridge each side; coxae of front legs large and femora of front legs larger than those of the middle and hind legs (Fig. 597). Males of this species appear to be unknown, only females hatching from unfertilized eggs.
This is an introduced species occurring throughout the southeastern part of the United States where it attacks various kinds of truck crops.

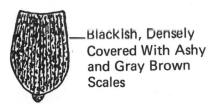

Blackish, Densely Covered With Ashy and Gray Brown Scales

Fig. 597. Graphognathus leucoloma

Barypeithes pallucidus Length: 2.5–3.5mm. Dark reddish brown to blackish, shining, sparsely covered with yellow hairs; antennae and legs pale reddish brown. Pronotum somewhat spherical, about as long as wide, sides rounded, coarsely and sparsely punctured; elytral striae deep, with coarse punctures, each interval with a row of long, yellowish hairs; beak and head shorter than pronotum; antennae inserted near base of beak, segments three to seven beadlike; tarsal claws united.
Eastern half of the United States.

Brachyrhinus ovatus *The Strawberry Crown Girdler* Length: 5–6mm. Black, shining, covered with sparse, yellowish pubescence; an-

tennae and legs reddish brown. Pronotum somewhat spherical, apical and basal margins squarely cut off, with many longitudinal ridges; elytral striae with coarse, deep punctures; beak as long as head, with deep grooves for the reception of the antennae that are long and each with an oval club acute at apex; tarsi dilated, pubescent, third segment of each with deep lobes; tibiae of hind legs each with two short spurs (Fig. 598).
On strawberries and muskmelon.
Eastern half of the United States.

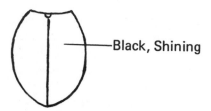

Fig. 598.   Brachyrhinus ovatus

*Epicaerus imbricatus   The Imbricated Snout Beetle   Length: 7.5–11.5mm. Upper surface densely clothed with greenish brown or brownish black imbricated or overlapping scales, which have suggested the popular name; a median, longitudinal stripe of pale scales on pronotum; two irregular, white crossbands on each elytra; undersurface and legs nearly white (Fig. 599).
On raspberries, melons, cabbages, cucumbers, and apple and cherry trees.
Throughout the United States.

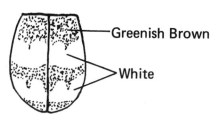

Fig. 599.   Epicaerus imbricatus

In the following species up to and including Cryptorhynchus lapathi, *the antennae are more or less bent at an angle; the beak has grooves for the reception of the antennae; the club of each antenna is usually ringed; the tarsi are each usually dilated at the tip, the third segment of each tarsus has two lobes and is spongy beneath; and the beak is usually elongate.* (This taxonomic fact refers only to those beetles marked with an *.)

**Sitona flavescens   The Yellow Clover Curculio*   Length: 4.5–5.5mm. Black, densely covered above with rusty brown and blackish brown hairlike scales, the darker ones forming two indistinct stripes on head and pronotum; antennae except clubs, tibiae, and tarsi reddish brown; lower surface with grayish hairs. Pronotum square shaped, finely and densely punctured; elytral striae finely, minutely punctured; beak short.
Both adults and larvae are injurious to clover.
Throughout the United States.

**Sitona hispidulus   The Clover Root Curculio*   Length: 3–5mm. Black, shining, densely covered above with small, coppery or grayish scales, the scales forming a narrow median, and two broader, lateral stripes on pronotum; antennae except clubs, tibiae, and tarsi reddish brown. Pronotum somewhat square shaped, coarsely, sparsely, deeply punctured; elytra slightly striate, striae punctured, each interval with one row of stout, grayish setae; head and beak as long as pronotum (Fig. 600).
Adults feed on the leaves of clover and other legumes, the larvae on the roots.
Throughout the United States.

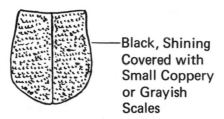
Black, Shining
Covered with
Small Coppery
or Grayish
Scales

Fig. 600.   Sitona hispidulus

**Hypera punctata   The Clover Leaf Weevil*   Length: 5–8.5mm. Black, densely covered with brown, yellow brown, or dark brown scales and with many short bristles. Pronotum slightly wider than long, sides converging to base, finely and densely punctured; elytra rounded at apices, striae finely punctured; beak shorter than pronotum, its lower surface, sides, and apex polished (Fig. 601).
Common in almost any clover field. The green and pinkish larvae climb up the plants at night and feed on the leaves; external feeding by the larvae is rather unusual in this family. An introduced species.
Widely scattered throughout the United States.

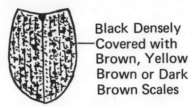

Black Densely Covered with Brown, Yellow Brown or Dark Brown Scales

Fig. 601. Hypera punctata

*Phytonomus nigrirostris The Lesser Clover Leaf Weevil Length: 3.5–4.5mm. Reddish brown or black, thickly covered with light green, sometimes yellowish, scalelike hairs; head black with a median line of whitish hairs; pronotum frequently with a narrow median line of whitish hairs and a wider line of black hairs on each side of median line; antennae and legs reddish brown. Pronotum slightly longer than wide, coarsely and densely punctured; elytral striae punctured, each interval with a row of short, stiff, whitish hairs; beak longer than pronotum, curved and polished, a ridge above; mandibles notched. On clover and alfalfa.
Eastern half of the United States.

*Listronotus caudatus Length: 10–12mm. Black, densely covered with brownish yellow scales; head, beak, sides of pronotum, and a few spots on sides of elytra paler; antennae reddish brown. Pronotum wider than long, finely and densely punctured; elytra notched basally, striae fine and minutely punctured, each interval with a row of small setae; beak longer than pronotum; tibiae strongly spined. On various aquatic plants such as smartweed and arrowhead.
Eastern half of the United States.

*Hyperodes solutus Length: 3–5mm. Black to reddish brown. densely covered above with rounded clay yellow scales; elytra each with an irregular triangular spot of black scales just behind the middle; antennae and legs reddish brown. Pronotum somewhat square shaped, sides slightly rounded, densely and finely punctured; elytral sides parallel, then narrowed to apices, elytral striae fine with distant punctures, each interval with a row of short, whitish setae; beak as long as pronotum, with a fine, median ridge; femora club shaped; tibiae each ending in a somewhat sharp point (Fig. 602).
On various aquatic plants such as arrow arum and arrowhead.
Eastern United States.

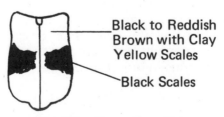

Black to Reddish Brown with Clay Yellow Scales

Black Scales

Fig. 602. Hyperodes solutus

*Pissodes strobi   The White Pine Weevil   Length: 4.5–6mm. Light to dark brown; pronotum usually with three basal spots and one small, round dot on either side of median line, covered with white scales; elytra each near suture marked with sparse, white scales, two spots of white scales on each apical third, and lateral to these a transverse, brownish yellow spot, basal one-third each with a spot of pale or brownish yellow scales; femora ringed with whitish scales. Pronotum wider at base than at apex, densely and finely punctured; elytral sides converging to apices, striae finely punctured, third and fifth intervals elevated; beak slender, cylindrical; antennae inserted on sides of beak, first segment of each antennal club large, sparsely covered with short hairs and long bristles; coxae of front legs slightly separated; tibiae each with ridges and a long, curved, apical claw, which is dilated and fringed with hairs (Fig. 603).
On various pines; a serious pest of white pine in Eastern United States; also on spruce.
Wisconsin eastward.

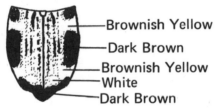

Brownish Yellow
Dark Brown
Brownish Yellow
White
Dark Brown

Fig. 603.   Pissodes strobi

*Hylobius pales   The Pales Weevil   Length: 7–10mm. Dark reddish brown; elytra each with scattered, small tufts of fine, gray or yellowish hairs, those tufts behind the middle forming two oblique crossbars. Pronotum wider than long, sides rounded, coarsely punctured; elytral striae with large, oblong punctures; abdomen beneath sparsely, finely punctured; beak stout, cylindrical, slightly curved; third to sixth antennal segments beadlike; eyes large, granulate; coxae of front legs touching; femora club shaped and toothed (Fig. 604).
On pine. A serious pest on cutover pine lands, the beetle feeding on the tender bark of the twigs of seedlings, usually at night, or beneath the cover of litter in the daytime.
Maine to Florida and west to the Great Lake States.

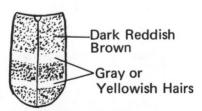

Dark Reddish
Brown

Gray or
Yellowish Hairs

Fig. 604.   Hylobius pales

Notaris puncticollis   Length: 4.5–6.5mm. Black or dark reddish brown, sparsely covered with short, prostrate, yellowish white hairs, the hairs forming a transverse spot on each elytron. Pronotum somewhat spherical, as long as wide, sides slightly rounded, coarsely and densely punctured; elytral sides converging to apices, striae with coarse, square-shaped punctures, shoulders rounded; beak slender, cylindrical, and curved, longer than pronotum; tibiae of hind legs slightly spined.
On various aquatic plants such as arrow arum.
Eastern half of the United States.

Tychius griseus   Length: 2.3–2.5mm. Blackish to reddish brown; upper surface with dense yellowish gray scales; lower surface with grayish white scales; apical third of beak, antennae, and legs reddish brown. Pronotum longer than wide, sides slightly rounded, finely and densely punctured; elytral sides converging from bases to apices, striae fine and punctured, intervals flat, apices rounded; beak as long as pronotum.
Eastern half of the United States.

Magdalis barbita   The Black Elm Bark Weevil   Length: 4–6mm. Black, slightly shining. Pronotum somewhat square shaped, with a short spine and several small teeth near anterior angles, densely and coarsely punctured; elytral striae coarsely punctured, intervals with minute cracks or wrinkles; beak longer than pronotum, cylindrical, and slightly curved; antennal clubs each four segmented; coxae of front legs touching; femora toothed; tibiae each with a strong, curved spine at the apex (Fig. 605). There are a number of other species of *Magdalis* that are fairly common in the Eastern States, including the *red elm bark weevil, Magdalis armicollis,* which, though not a vector of the Dutch elm disease, weakens decadent elm trees and thus paves the way for the disease.
Under the bark of hickory, walnut, elm, and oak.
New England to Texas.

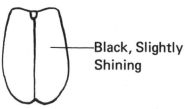

Fig. 605.   Magdalis barbita

The genus Curculio *contains the* nut *and* acorn weevils. *These beetles have a stout body and a very long, slender beak; the beak of the female is used for drilling holes into nuts and acorns through which the eggs are laid. The antennae are bent at an angle, are very long and slender, and have the clubs elongate and oval, pointed and pubescent; the coxae of the front legs are touching; the femora toothed; the tarsi are dilated; and the tarsal claws are toothed.*

Curculio proboscideus   The Large Chestnut Weevil   Length: 8–11mm. Dark brown, densely but irregularly covered with yellowish, scalelike hairs. Second segment of each antenna longer than the third; beak of female often nearly twice as long as the body (Fig. 606).
In chestnuts (see note after lesser chestnut weevil).
Eastern half of the United States.

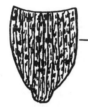

——Dark Brown, Densely
but Irregularly Covered
with Yellowish
Scalelike Hairs

Fig. 606.   Curculio proboscideus

Curculio auriger   The Lesser Chestnut Weevil   Length: 4.5–7mm. Black with brownish scales; pronotum with a paler line near each side; elytra with numerous, pale, yellow spots which sometimes form bands. Second segment of each antenna shorter than the third; beak of female curved and nearly twice as long as the body.
In chestnuts. The virtual elimination of the chestnut tree by the chestnut blight has decreased the importance of both the large and lesser chestnut weevils.
Eastern half of the United States.

Curculio caryae   The Hickory Nut and Pecan Weevil   Length: 7–9mm. Brownish, with sparse, yellowish hairs. Pronotum wider than long and closely punctured; femoral teeth rectangular (Fig. 607).
In hickory and pecan nuts.
Eastern half of the United States.

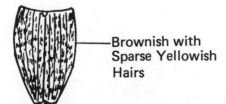

——Brownish with
Sparse Yellowish
Hairs

Fig. 607.   Curculio caryae

Curculio obtusus   The Hazel Nut Weevil   Length: 6–8mm. Blackish brown, clothed above with ash gray to yellowish scalelike hairs; pronotum and elytra marked with paler scales. Beak of female only two-thirds as long as body, that of male somewhat shorter; outer edge of each femoral tooth oblique; appendages of tarsal claws broad, nearly or quite rectangular (Fig. 608).
In hazel nuts; infested nuts fall early.
Eastern half of the United States.

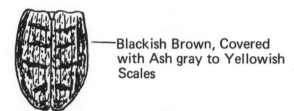

Blackish Brown, Covered with Ash gray to Yellowish Scales

Fig. 608.   Curculio obtusus

Curculio rectus   Length: 8.5–9mm. Brownish, with a covering of pale brown hairlike scales. Beak of female straight and nearly twice as long as the body, that of the male is somewhat shorter than the body; femoral teeth small.
In acorns.
Eastern half of the United States.

Tachypterellus quadrigibbosus   The Apple Curculio   Length: 3–4.5mm. Dark red; beak, antennae, and legs paler; pronotum and basal half of each elytron thinly covered with grayish pubescence; pronotum with three lines of white pubescence; each elytron with two reddish tubercles. Pronotum densely and coarsely punctured, base about twice as wide as apex; elytra transversely impressed behind scutellum. Beak long and slender, slightly curved, with antennal grooves; antennal clubs elongate and pointed; femora of front legs each with two teeth, each of those of the middle and hind legs with one tooth; tibiae each with a small hook at tip; each tarsal claw with a long tooth (Fig. 609).
Adults on the flowers of fruit trees, red haw, and shadbush; larvae attack apples and pears.
Throughout the United States.

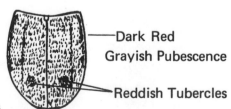

Dark Red
Grayish Pubescence

Reddish Tubercles

Fig. 609.   Tachypterellus quadrigibbosus

Anthonomus grandis   *The Cotton Boll Weevil*   Length: 4–7.5mm.
Reddish brown to blackish, covered with coarse, pale yellowish,
scalelike hairs forming numerous small dots on the elytra. Pronotum
wider than long, sides rounded to apex, densely and coarsely punctured; elytra oblong, narrowing to apices, striae deep with close-set
punctures, apices rounded; head conical, deeply pitted in front;
tibiae of front and middle legs each with a hook, each of those of
the hind legs spined; tarsal claws toothed (Fig. 610).
Larvae in the cotton bolls where they destroy the seeds; the adults
feed on the bolls and leaves.
This beetle, introduced from Mexico in the 1890s, is a serious economic problem in the cotton-growing states.

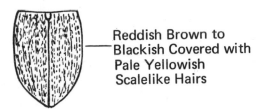

Reddish Brown to
Blackish Covered with
Pale Yellowish
Scalelike Hairs

Fig. 610.   Anthonomus grandis

Anthonomus signatus   *The Strawberry Weevil*   Length: 2–3mm.
Blackish, slightly shining; pronotum with three indistinct stripes of
whitish pubescence; scutellum covered with whitish pubescence; elytra reddish brown, with a naked band behind the middle and a small
naked area around scutellum; antennae and legs reddish brown. Pronotum widest at the base, sides rounded, densely and coarsely punctured; elytral striae deep with large punctures, intervals finely punctured; beak longer than head and pronotum, slender and slightly
curved with a ridge on top; tibiae of front and middle legs each with
a hook, each of those of the hind legs spined; tarsal claws toothed
(Fig. 611); femora of front legs each with one tooth.
On strawberries, raspberries, blackberries, and dewberries. The females are most destructive to the buds in which they lay their eggs
and then cut the stems so that the buds fall to the ground.
Eastern half of the United States.

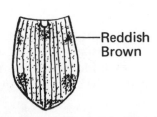

Reddish
Brown

Fig. 611.   Anthonomus signatus

Anthonomus scutellaris The Plum Gouger Length: 5–6mm. Dark reddish brown with a covering of long yellowish and gray hairs that form a mottled pattern on pronotum and elytra (Fig. 612). On both wild and cultivated plums. Massachusetts to Kansas and south to Georgia and Texas.

Dark Reddish Brown with a Covering of Yellowish and Gray Hairs

Fig. 612. Anthonomus scutellaris

Elleschus ephippiatus Length: 1.5–3.4mm. Reddish brown, covered with pale yellowish and light brown pubescence; elytra each with a large dark spot near scutellum and another behind the middle, the spots usually connected along the suture. Pronotum widest at the middle, sides rounded, finely punctured; elytral striae with large, close-set punctures; beak shorter than head and pronotum combined, cylindrical; antennal grooves deep; tibiae curved at apices; tarsal claws each with an appendage. On willow. Eastern half of the United States.

Rhynchaenus ephippiatus Length: 2.5–3.5mm. Dark reddish brown to blackish; head and pronotum sparsely covered with grayish or dull yellow hairs; scutellum with dense, white pubescence; elytra each with some brown pubescence, also with two bands of whitish or yellowish gray pubescence; antennae, beak, tarsi, and femora of middle legs reddish brown. Pronotum slightly wider than long, finely and densely punctured; elytra at middle nearly twice as wide as pronotum, striae coarsely punctured; beak stout, shorter than head and pronotum, cylindrical; eyes large; second to fourth antennal segments elongate; femora of hind legs very thickened; tarsal claws each with a short, broad tooth. On willow. Throughout the United States.

Rhynchaenus pallicornis Length: 2.5–3mm. Black, shining, thinly covered with grayish yellow hairs; antennae and tarsi pale reddish brown. Pronotum as wide at middle as long, sides slightly rounded, densely covered with coarse, shallow punctures; elytra wider than

pronotum, striae slightly impressed with coarse, deep punctures, intervals finely and sparsely punctured; beak stout, almost as long as head and pronotum; eyes large; second to fourth antennal segments elongate; femora of hind legs very thickened; tarsal claws each with a short, broad tooth (Fig. 613).
Adults on willow, alder, and apple; larvae leaf miners in alder, apple, cherry, and elm.
Maine west to Oregon and south to Texas.

Black, Shining, Thinly Covered with Grayish Yellow Hairs

Fig. 613. Rhynchaenus pallicornis

Acalyptus carpini Length: 2.2–2.8mm. Black, covered with short, grayish white pubescence; antennae and legs reddish brown. Pronotum wider than long, sides slightly rounded, finely and densely punctured; elytra indistinctly striate, intervals finely punctured, apices rounded; beak slender, curved, as long as head and pronotum; antennal clubs pubescent; tibiae of hind legs each with a short spine at apex.
On willow.
Eastern half of the United States.

Gymnetron tetrum Length: 2.3–3.8mm. Black, densely covered with dull yellowish pubescence. Pronotum wider than long, sides rounded, finely and densely punctured; elytral sides rounded; striae fine, deep and coarsely punctured; beak nearly straight, as long as pronotum; second segment of each antenna longer than third, and each club short and oval; coxae of front legs touching; femora toothed.
Very common; on mullein.
Throughout the United States.

Lixus concavus The Rhubarb Beetle Length: 10–13.5mm. Black, sparingly covered with fine, grayish pubescence, often covered with orange red pollen; antennae and tarsi reddish brown. Pronotum wider than long, sides slightly rounded, a deep median impression from near apex to base, sparsely and coarsely punctured with fine punctures intermingled; elytra with rows of small, distinct punctures, in-

tervals finely and densely punctured; beak slender, cylindrical; antennae slender; scutellum triangular, minute; tarsi broad, third segment of each with two lobes (Fig. 614).
In stems of rhubarb, dock, sunflower, and thistle.
Throughout the United States.

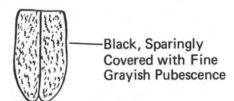

Black, Sparingly Covered with Fine Grayish Pubescence

Fig. 614. Lixus concavus

Lixus scrobicollis Length: 6.5–9mm. Black with scanty gray pubescence, which forms pale stripes on pronotum and elytra.
In ragweed.
Found Texas to the Atlantic coast.

Lixus terminalis Length: 8–12mm. Reddish brown, shining.
Iowa to New England and Florida.

Madarellus undulatus Length: 2.7–4.7mm. Black, very shining; pronotum often red. Pronotum wider than long, minutely and sparsely punctured; elytra narrower at combined bases than pronotum, tapering to apices, striae deep and narrow and finely punctured, intervals finely and slightly punctured; beak slender, long, and somewhat curved; antennal clubs elongate-oval, pubescent; coxae of front legs widely separated; femora minutely toothed; third segment of each with two lobes; body wedge shaped.
On wild grapevines, poison ivy, and virginia creeper.
Eastern half of the United States.

Psedobaris nigrina Length: 2.5–3.7mm. Black, shining. Pronotum wider than long, rounded and converging apically, deeply and densely punctured, median line smooth or almost so; elytral striae deep, finely and sparsely punctured, each interval with a row of large punctures; beak rounded; antennal clubs pubescent; coxae of front legs widely separated; tarsal claws united basally.
Eastern half of the United States.

Trichobaris trinotata The Potato Stalk Borer Length: 3–4mm. Black, densely covered with short, white, prostrate hairs. Pronotum about as wide as long, coarsely and densely punctured; elytra finely striate, striae minutely punctured, each interval with about three rows of scalelike hairs; beak short and stout; antennal clubs small, oval, pubescent; coxae of front legs narrowly separated; tibiae with a claw at apex; tarsi each with the third segment dilated and with two teeth; tarsal claws united basally (Fig. 615).

On potato, eggplant, horse nettle, jimson weed, ground-cherry, and cocklebur.

New England south to Florida and west to Colorado and southern California.

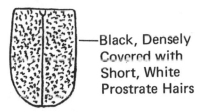

Black, Densely Covered with Short, White Prostrate Hairs

Fig. 615.   Trichobaris trinotata

Craponis inaequalis The Grape Curculio Length: 2.5–3mm. Dark brown with whitish and brown hairs forming spots and lines on elytra. Pronotum with four large tubercles (Fig. 616).

On wild and cultivated grapes. The adults feed on grape leaves until the berries are about a fourth grown, when the female lays her eggs in them. The larvae feed on the pulp and seeds and the infested berries usually drop to the ground.

New England to Florida and the Midwest.

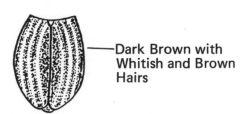

Dark Brown with Whitish and Brown Hairs

Fig. 616.   Craponis inaequalis

Centrinaspis picumnus Length: 2.1–2.7mm. Dark reddish brown to black; upper surface densely covered with long, dull yellow to white scales; undersurface with paler and broader scales; head without scales. Pronotum wider than long, conical, narrowed toward apex,

finely and densely punctured; elytra punctured, narrowed to apices, striae deep, each interval with two or three rows of scales; beak cylindrical, long and slender; mandibles elongate, prominent.
On various flowers, including snakeroot and the flowers of dogwood.
Eastern half of the United States.

Odontocorynus scutellum-album   Length: 3–4.8mm. Male black, antennae and tarsi dark reddish brown; female with more or less reddish tinge; upper surface of both sparsely covered with small, white scales. Pronotum wider than long, sides rounded, deeply and densely punctured; elytra wider at base than pronotum, with coarse, deep punctures, striae deep, intervals punctured, each puncture with a small scale; beak longer than pronotum; basal segment of each antennal club in male with a polished area that bears an erect, pointed projection; each antennal club simple in female.
On various flowers but especially those of mullein.
Eastern half of the United States.

Cylindrocopturus quercus   Length: 2.5–3mm. Black, shining; sides of pronotum, base of beak, and undersurface covered with dense grayish white scales; antennae dark reddish brown. Pronotum slightly wider than long, coarsely and densely punctured; elytra wider than pronotum, sides converging to apices, striae fine and deep and coarsely punctured, each interval with two irregular rows of punctures which are hidden by scales; beak slender, curved; antennal clubs short and stout, basal segment of each shorter than other two combined.
Eastern half of the United States.

Mononychus vulpeculus   Length: 4.5–5mm. Black, slightly shining; sides of pronotum, basal third of elytral suture, and undersurface, except middle of third and fourth abdominal segments, densely covered with yellowish white scales; antennae dull yellow. Pronotum coarsely, densely punctured; elytral striae coarsely punctured, each interval with one or two rows of coarse punctures; beak long, cylindrical; legs slender; tibiae obliquely fringed at apices; tarsi each with one claw.
On the flowers of iris.
Eastern half of the United States.

Ceutorhynchus rapae   The Cabbage Curculio   Length: 2.7–3.2mm. Black, covered above with very small, hairlike, yellowish scales which fade to gray in older specimens; undersurface with large, grayish scales. Pronotum wider at base than long, densely and coarsely punctured; elytra wider at combined bases than pronotum, sides converging to apices, striae fine, punctured; beak slender, cylindrical,

longer than head and pronotum combined; third segment of each
tarsus with two lobes; tarsi each with two claws (Fig. 617).
On both the wild and cultivated members of the mustard family,
including cabbages. An introduced species.
Throughout the United States.

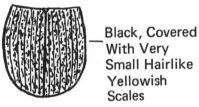

Black, Covered
With Very
Small Hairlike
Yellowish
Scales

Fig. 617.   Ceutorhynchus rapae

Ceutorhynchus punctiger Length: 3–3.2mm. Black, densely covered
with brownish hairs and white scales, the scales arranged in a single
row in each stria and forming an oblong sutural spot behind scutellum; tarsi reddish brown; undersurface densely covered with white
scales. Pronotum wider than long, apical margin raised, lateral margins each with a small tubercle, a deep pit in middle of base, coarse
ly and densely punctured; elytral striae narrow and finely punctured;
beak long and slender; femora of front and hind legs toothed; tarsal claws each with a long tooth that is almost split into two lobes.
On members of the composite family, such as dandelion and lettuce.
Eastern half of the United States.

Rhinoncus pyrrhopus Length: 2.3–2.7mm. Black, densely covered
above with brownish hairs and whitish scales, the scales forming a
conspicuous scutellar spot; pronotum and elytra with numerous spots
of white scales; undersurface densely covered with white scales; antennae and legs pale reddish brown. Pronotum wider than long,
coarsely and densely punctured, lateral tubercles small; elytra with
combined bases wider than pronotum, sides rounded, striae punctured, each interval with a row of small tubercles; beak short, stout,
slightly pubescent; eyes large; coxae widely separated; third segment
of each tarsus with two lobes.
On dock and smartweed.
Eastern half of the United States.

Conotrachelus nenuphar The Plum Curculio Length: 4.5–6.5mm.
Dark brown, with brownish yellow pubescence; each side of pronotum with a forked line of pubescence; elytra each with a band of
yellow and white hairs back of the middle. Pronotum as wide at

base as long, coarsely and roughly punctured, a ridge in front of middle; elytra with an interrupted longitudinal ridge; beak stout, rounded, slightly longer than head and pronotum; coxae of front legs touching; tibiae each with a hook (Fig. 618).

On plum, cherry, apple, peach, and other fruit trees.

Generally east of the Rockies.

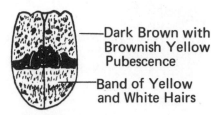

Fig. 618. Conotrachelus nenuphar

Conotrachelus juglandis The Walnut Curculio Length: 5–7mm. Dark brown, with brownish yellow pubescence which forms a forked line on each side of the pronotum, a broad band just behind middle of each elytron, and two rings on each femur. Pronotum wider than long, sides rounded, a ridge in front of the middle, four small tubercles, coarsely punctured; elytra with rows of large, square-shaped punctures; beak cylindrical, pubescent, longer than head and pronotum combined; coxae of front legs touching; tibiae each with a hook (Fig. 619).

On walnut, butternut, and hickory; the larvae live in the undeveloped nuts causing them to fall.

Eastern half of the United States.

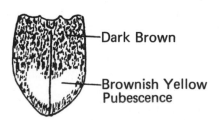

Fig. 619. Conotrachelus juglandis

Conotrachelus crataegi The Quince Curculio Length: 4–6mm. Brownish black, densely covered with yellowish and ashy gray scales; undersurface thinly covered with grayish yellow scales. Pronotum, coarsely punctured, as broad as long, a ridge at the middle; each elytron with four prominent ridges, with two conspicous rows of punctures in the intervals between, shoulders each with a small blunt tooth; beak longer than head and pronotum, striate and punctured; femora each with a large tooth; coxae of front legs touching; tibiae each with a hook.

On quince and hawthorn.

New England to Iowa and southward.

*Conotrachelus anaglypticus   The Cambium Curculio   Length: 3.5–4.7mm. Dark reddish brown to black with scant covering of yellowish, scalelike hairs that form two narrow lines on sides of pronotum, a broad, oblique spot or stripe on each shoulder of elytra, and a broad band on the apical half of each femur; elytra each with an indistinct white band just behind the middle. Pronotum slightly longer than wide, with a broad shallow groove, and two low crests in front, finely netted, punctured; bases of elytra much wider than pronotum, striae with large, square-shaped punctures, alternate intervals with a ridge; beak almost as long as head and pronotum combined, striate; coxae of front legs touching; tibiae each with a hook (Fig. 620).

On a variety of fruit, shade, and forest trees, including hickory, birch, beech, maple, chestnut, and oak.

New England south to Florida and west to Iowa.

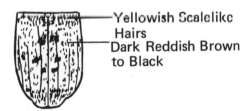

Fig. 620.   Conotrachelus anaglypticus

*Tyloderma fragariae   The Strawberry Crown Borer   Length: 3.5–4.2mm. Black; elytra and legs reddish brown, each elytron marked by three black bars. Pronotum slightly wider than long, sides rounded, converging to apex; elytra with sides oval, converging to apices, smooth; beak short, stout; third segment of each tarsus dilated (Fig. 621).

A destructive pest on strawberries.

Eastern half of the United States.

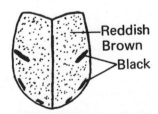

Fig. 621.   Tyloderma fragariae

Cryptorhynchus lapathi   The Poplar and Willow Borer   Length: 7.5–10mm. Black, densely covered with dull black and whitish scales, with scattered tufts of erect, black bristles; apical third of each elytron and an oblique band on basal third of pronotum with dense, white scales; antennae and legs reddish brown. Pronotum wider than long, constricted at apex, coarsely and densely punctured, with a median ridge; elytral striae punctured, alternate intervals with tufts of hair; beak as long as head and pronotum, densely punctured; eyes widely separated; femora grooved beneath (Fig. 622).
On willow, poplar, alder, and birch. An introduced species.
Eastern half of the United States.

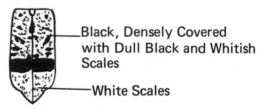

Black, Densely Covered with Dull Black and Whitish Scales

White Scales

Fig. 622.   Cryptorhynchus lapathi

Dryophthorus americanus   Length: 2–3mm. Brownish or blackish, covered with grayish yellow scales; antennae and legs paler. Pronotum longer than wide, constricted near apex, coarsely and densely punctured; elytral striae broad, coarsely punctured; beak slightly more than half the length of the pronotum; eyes oval, granulate; antennal clubs elongate-oval; tarsi each five segmented.
On old logs and beneath the bark of pine.
Eastern half of the United States.

Cossonus platalea   Length: 5.5–6.5mm. Black, shining; antennae and tarsi reddish brown. Pronotum as wide as long, narrowed abruptly at apex, sides rounded, sparsely punctured; elytral striae with coarse, square-shaped punctures; beak not as long as pronotum, dilated at tip; antennae inserted near tip of beak.
Beneath bark of walnut, butternut, poplar, elm, and pine.
Eastern half of the United States.

Stenoscelis brevis   Length: 2.8–3.2mm. Black, slightly shining; elytra and legs brownish; antennae and tarsi reddish brown. Pronotum wider than long, constricted near apex, sides slightly rounded, hind angles rounded, coarsely and densely punctured; elytral sides parallel, obtusely rounded at apices, striae with coarse, square-shaped punctures, intervals with a row of minute punctures; beak shorter than head; antennal clubs rounded.
Beneath bark and in dead and decayed wood.
Eastern half of the United States.

The Billbugs

Family Rhynchophoridae
The members of this family, known as the *billbugs* and *grain weevils,* are small or moderately sized beetles. The larvae of the larger species feed upon the roots and bore in the stems of plants, especially grass and corn, while those of the smaller species infest seeds and grain.

The beak is long, slender, and curved; the antennae are elbowed and are inserted near the base of the beak; the elytra are short exposing the apical dorsal segment of the abdomen; the coxae are separated; and the tibiae are short and each with a hook at the tip (Fig. 623).

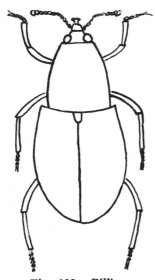

Fig. 623. Billbug

Rhodobaenus tredecimpunctatus The Cocklebur Billbug Length: 7–10mm. Red, with black spots, five on pronotum and four on each elytra; undersurface and beak black. Pronotum longer than wide, somewhat constricted near apex, sides curved near apex, finely and sparsely punctured; elytral striae fine, sparsely punctured, intervals flat and smooth; beak two-thirds as long as pronotum; antennal clubs broadly oval; third segment of each tarsus broad and spongy beneath (Fig. 624).
On ironweed, cocklebur, ragweed, joe-pye weed, and other members of the composite family.
Throughout the United States.

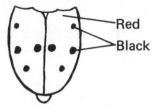

Fig. 624. Rhodobaenus tredecimpunctatus

In the species of the genus Calendra *the antennal clubs are broadly oval; the beak is shorter than the pronotum, slender and swollen at its base; the antennal grooves are pitlike and near the eyes; the pronotum is longer than wide; and the elytra are wider than the pronotum and the elytral apices are rounded.*

Calendra cariosa Length: 7.5–11mm. Black, with a grayish crust; elevated parts above and undersurface shining. Pronotum longer than wide, with three longitudinal raised lines, the outer ones irregular and entire, the middle one widening to a rhomboid figure midway of the pronotum, then ending abruptly or sometimes continuing as a fine line, lines sparsely and minutely punctured, the intervals and sides of pronotum coarsely punctured; elytral striae fine, with coarse, deep punctures, each interval with a single row of minute punctures, third interval each strongly elevated on basal half.
On rushes and sedges but also attacks corn.
East of the Mississippi River.

Calendra parvula The Bluegrass Billbug Length: 5–8mm. Black, with a gray crust; antennae and tarsi reddish brown. Pronotum longer than wide, sides rounded, finely punctured; elytra finely striate, with coarse punctures, alternate intervals slightly elevated, first and third with two rows, others with a single row, of coarse punctures (Fig. 625).
Attacks the roots of timothy and bluegrass; also found on corn and wheat.
New England to Florida and Texas.

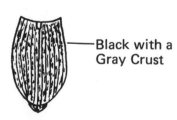

Fig. 625. Calendra parvula

Calendra melanocephala   Length: 7–11mm. Black, covered with a dull brownish crust. Pronotum longer than wide, median raised line ending at half the length of the pronotum and dilated posteriorly, coarsely and sparsely punctured, each side with a small, flattened elevation near apical angle; elytra narrowed to apices, striae fine with coarse punctures, intervals finely ·punctured.
On timothy and corn.
New England to Kansas and Georgia.

Calendra aequalis   The Clay Colored Billbug   Length: 11–17mm. Black, with a shiny coating varying in color, light bluish gray and pale yellowish to reddish brown; with three darkened elevated stripes on pronotum and sometimes dark stripes on the elytra.
On reeds and bulrushes, and also if the places where these grasses grow are plowed and planted with corn, the billbugs often attack the young corn plants.
New York to South Dakota.

Calendra zeae   The Timothy Billbug   Length: 6.5–9mm. Black or dark reddish brown, shining. Pronotum with three raised spaces, coarsely and densely punctured between elevations; each elytral interval with a row of fine punctures (Fig. 626).
On timothy, kentucky bluegrass, and corn.
New England to Florida and Kansas.

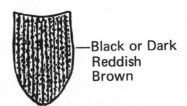

—Black or Dark Reddish Brown

Fig. 626.   Calendra zeae

Calendra pertinax   The Cattail Billbug   Length: 11–15mm. Black, shining, often with a reddish tinge; interspaces on pronotum and elytra covered with a whitish coating. Alternate elytral intervals elevated, irregular, and sometimes interrupted.
On cattail and calamus.
Throughout the United States.

Calendra naidis   The Maize Billbug   Length: 10–15mm. Blackish or dark reddish. Midline on pronotum, slightly elevated.
On corn; often a serious pest.
South Carolina to Alabama, Texas, and Kansas.

Sitophilus granaria   The Granary Weevil   Length: 3–4mm. Reddish brown to black, shining. Pronotum coarsely, sparsely punctured; elytra deeply striate, the striae punctured, the intervals smooth, except the sutural interval which has a row of elongate punctures. Beak two-thirds as long as pronotum, slender and cylindrical; antennal clubs oval (Fig. 627).

This species is wingless and is an indoor beetle found in houses, barns, and granaries where it injures wheat, corn, barley, and other grains.

Throughout the United States.

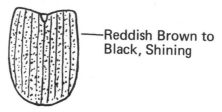

Fig. 627.   Sitophilus granaria

Maize Billbug; Calendra naidis

Maize Billbug; Calendra naidis; **larva, pupa, and adult**

Sitophilus oryzae   The Rice Weevil   Length: 2.1–2.8mm. Dull brown or reddish brown; elytra each with four reddish spots. Pronotum somewhat longer than wide, densely and coarsely punctured; elytra deeply striate, the striae coarsely and closely punctured, each puncture with a short yellowish seta. Beak slender, cylindrical, three-fourths as long as pronotum; antennal clubs oval (Fig. 628).
On rice, corn, wheat, barley, rye, and other grains; also found beneath bark and on leaves.
Throughout the United States.

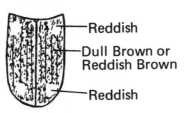

Reddish

Dull Brown or
Reddish Brown

Reddish

Fig. 628.   Sitophilus oryzae

Rice Weevil; Sitophilus oryzae

The Wide-Headed Ambrosia Beetles

Family Platypodidae

This is a small family represented in the United States by a single genus, *Platypus,* of which only five species seem to occur in our country. The beetles are slender and cylindrical, with a large head that is wider than the pronotum. They attack many kinds of conifers and deciduous trees in which they bore deeply, making "pinholes" that render the trees useless as lumber. The eggs are laid in the galleries, which the beetles excavate, and the larvae are fed on a fungus that is cultivated by the beetles and known as *ambrosia.*

Platypus wilsoni Length: 5.5mm. Brown, shining, densely covered with long yellowish hairs (Fig. 629).
Washington south to California.

Fig. 629. Platypus wilsoni

Platypus flavicornis Length: 5.5mm. Dark reddish brown; posterior ends of elytra prolonged at each outer third to form a blunt process in the female and which is much longer and sharper in the male. In various pines but also in other conifers and in several deciduous trees.
Southeastern States north to New Jersey.

Platypus compositus Length: 4.5–4.9mm. Light reddish brown. Pronotum finely, shallowly, and sparsely punctured, with a distinct, longitudinal groove on the posterior third, and with a small margined pit at each side, near the anterior end of the groove.
On a wide variety of trees, including hickory, birch, pecan, poplar, willow, oak, maple, basswood, elm, beech, wild cherry, sweet gum, and magnolia.
Southern States north to New York and southern Illinois.

The Engraver Beetles

Family Scolytidae

This is not a particularly large family but it is an important one, for the members are often quite destructive to trees. The beetles live, for the most part, between the bark and the wood where they carve numerous excavated galleries, each species having its own characteristic type of gallery, and the excavations often appear like an engraving on the wood, hence they are known as the *engraver beetles*. They are quite small and are so cylindrical and compact in form

and have such short legs that they look very much like miniature
bullets with both ends rounded. In these beetles the head is often
hidden by the pronotum; the beak is absent; the antennae are elbowed or bent at an angle; and the tarsi are each five segmented
(Fig. 630).

Both the adults and the larvae live beneath the bark of trees and,
though usually only dead or dying trees are attacked, some species
live in apparently healthy trees. They are especially destructive to
conifers.

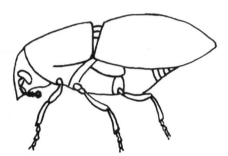

Fig. 630.   Engraver Beetle

Scolytus quadrispinosus   The Hickory Bark Borer   Length: 4–5mm.
Dark brown or black, shining. Pronotum longer than wide, sides
rounded, fringed with long hairs, finely punctured; each elytron
with ten to twelve striae, both the striae and intervals punctured;
head rather flattened; tibiae of front legs each with a long curved
hook on the outer apical angle, those of the middle and hind legs
sawlike (Fig. 631).
On hickory; the insect does considerable damage by boring into the
trunk and larger branches.
Eastern half of the United States.

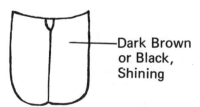

Dark Brown
or Black,
Shining

Fig. 631.   Scolytus quadrispinosus

Scolytus rugulosus   The Shot Hole Borer   Length: 2–2.5mm. Gray
black or reddish brown, slightly shining; elytra at apices, tibiae, and

tarsi reddish brown. Pronotum longer than wide, with many more or less oblong punctures; elytral striae finely, densely punctured, intervals densely punctured, the surface appearing rough; head in male flattened with long hairs, in female convex without hairs; tibiae of front legs each with a long, curved hook on outer apical angle, those of the middle and hind legs sawlike (Fig. 632).

On various fruit trees. The numerous small "worm holes," which give the outside of the bark the appearance of having been peppered with shot, hence the name of the beetle, are made by the adults when boring out.

Throughout the United States.

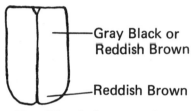

Fig. 632. Scolytus rugulosus

Scolytus multistriatus *The Smaller European Elm Bark Beetle* Length: 2.5–3.5mm. Brownish to black; elytra blackish red; antennae and legs light brown.

On recently cut, broken, or dying elm trees. This beetle, an introduced species, is probably the most important vector of the Dutch elm disease.

Polygraphus rufipennis *The Four-Eyed Spruce Bark Beetle* Length: 2–2.5mm. Reddish brown to black; elytra, legs, mouthparts, and antennae brownish red, sparsely covered with whitish pubescence. Pronotum wider than long, sides narrowed to apex, densely and minutely punctured; elytra parallel sided and rounded at apices, minutely punctured and with rows of larger punctures; antennal clubs elongate-oval, acute; eyes divided; coxae of front legs almost touching; third segment of each tarsus of front legs cylindrical (Fig. 633).

Beneath the green bark of living spruce, tamarack, and pine; also in stumps and injured or dying trees.

Throughout the United States.

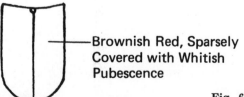

Fig. 633. Polygraphus rufipennis

Chramesus hicoriae   Length: 1–2mm. Black; antennae yellow; covered above with stiff, grayish hairs. Pronotum wider than long, narrowed to the apex, sides rounded, coarsely and sparsely punctured; elytra finely, rather densely punctured, basal margins more or less sawlike, intervals with rows of long erect bristles; antennae with unsegmented clubs; third segment of each tarsus of front legs widened and notched; body humpbacked.
On hickory.
Eastern half of the United States.

Phthorophloeus liminaris   *The Peach Bark Beetle*   Length: 1.5–2.2mm. Light brown to nearly black, slightly shining, sparsely covered with long, whitish pubescence. Pronotum somewhat square shaped, sides curved to apex, with a short median ridge, finely and densely punctured; elytra rounded to apices, with rows of deep, transverse punctures; antennal clubs each three segmented, the segments loosely joined and leaflike (Fig. 634).
On peach, plum, cherry, mulberry, hackberry, and mountain ash.
New England south to North Carolina and west to Michigan and Tennessee.

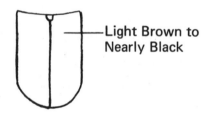

Fig. 634.   Phthorophloeus liminaris

Dendroctonus frontalis   *The Southern Pine Beetle*   Length: 2.5–4mm. Light reddish brown to blackish. Pronotum slightly wider than long, anterior margin somewhat notched, coarsely and sparsely punctured; elytra rounded to apices, striae punctured; head large, front of head with a prominent tubercle each side of a distinct median groove; antennae elbowed or bent at an angle, clubs short and obtuse, segments knob shaped; coxae of front legs nearly touching; third segment of each tarsus with two lobes; basal margins of elytra sawlike (Fig. 635).
On pine and spruce.
Eastern half of the United States.

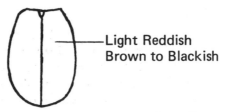

Fig. 635.   Dendroctonus frontalis

Dendroctonus simplex   The Eastern Larch Beetle   Length: 3.5–5mm.
Dark reddish brown to reddish, in part nearly black. Pronotum nar-
rowing to apex, with small and large punctures mixed; elytra each
with long hairs on basal half (Fig. 636).
On larch.
Maine south to West Virginia and west to Minnesota.

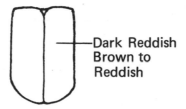

Fig. 636.   Dendroctonus simplex

Dendroctonus piceaperda   The Eastern Spruce Beetle   Length: 5–
5mm. Head, pronotum, and abdomen black; elytra reddish brown.
On red, white, and black spruce.
New England to Pennsylvania and west to Michigan.

Dendroctonus valens   The Red Turpentine Beetle   Length: 7–8mm.
Variable in color from light reddish to dark brown (Fig. 637).
On all species of pine.
Throughout the United States.

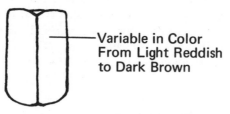

Fig. 637.   Dendroctonus valens

Hylurgopinus rufipes   Length: 2–2.5mm. Brownish black, thinly covered with short, stiff, yellowish hairs. Pronotum narrowed toward the apex, with a median indistinct ridge, densely and finely punctured; elytra with rows of somewhat square-shaped punctures; beak short; head coarsely punctured; antennal clubs each with four segments; coxae of front legs widely separated; third segment of each tarsus of front legs dilated with two lobes.
On elm, ash, and wild cherry.
New England south to Virginia and west to Iowa.

Hylurgops pinifex   Length: 4.5–5mm. Deep reddish brown to black, with a brown tinge; elytra with short pubescence; undersurface black. Pronotum wider than long, narrowed toward the apex, finely and densely punctured, with a fine median ridge; elytral striae with coarse, square-shaped punctures, intervals with rows of small granules, combined apices slightly wider than combined bases; beak ridged; antennal clubs four segmented, the first segment of each as long as the others combined; coxae of front legs nearly touching; tarsi of front legs with third segment of each very dilated and with two lobes (Fig. 638).
On pine, spruce, and larch.
Eastern half of the United States.

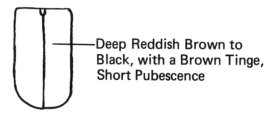

Deep Reddish Brown to Black, with a Brown Tinge, Short Pubescence

Fig. 638.   Hylurgops pinifex

Monarthrum mali   The Apple Wood Stainer   Length: 1.8–2mm. Brown or orange brown; pronotum at base and elytra lighter brown; antennae and legs brownish yellow; elytra covered with yellowish pubescence. Pronotum longer than wide, with tubercles and pubescence at the apex; elytra with rows of very fine punctures, apices obliquely cut off, one small tooth near apical suture on each side; head concealed from above by pronotum (Fig. 639).
On various trees, both deciduous and coniferous.
Eastern States.

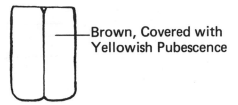

Fig. 639. Monarthrum mali

Monarthrum fasciatum Length: 2.5–3mm. Readily recognized by a pale yellow band across the middle of each elytron.
It infests most of the eastern hardwoods.
Throughout the eastern part of the United States but is much more common in the South.

Xyloterinus politus Length: 3–3.5mm. Yellow to deep brown, shining. Pronotum square shaped, apical margin rounded, fringed with hairs, finely punctured laterally, more coarsely anteriorly; elytra with rows of fine punctures, rounded at apices; head hidden from above by pronotum; antennal clubs oval, pubescent; eyes divided (Fig. 640).
On various hardwood trees.
Eastern States.

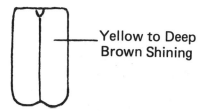

Fig. 640. Xyloterinus politus

Gnathotrichus materiarius The Pine Wood Stainer Length: 2.8–3.2mm. Brown, shining; elytra yellowish brown at bases; antennae and legs yellowish; undersurface sometimes black. Pronotum longer than wide, rounded at apex; elytra with indistinct rows of punctures, apices with scattered hairs; head hidden from above by pronotum; eyes notched; tibiae of front legs each sawlike on external margin (Fig. 641).
On pine and spruce.
Eastern half of the United States.

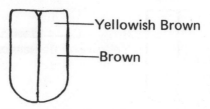

Fig. 641.   Gnathotrichus materiarius

Ips calligraphus   The Coarse Writing Bark Beetle   Length: 4.5–6.4mm. Blackish or dark yellow brown, shining, covered with yellowish or grayish pubescence; antennae yellow. Pronotum longer than wide, with a median longitudinal line, anterior part with tubercles and with transverse wrinkles, posterior part finely, sparsely punctured; elytral striae with transverse punctures, apices obliquely cut off and concave or hollowed out, the margin of each with six teeth; antennal clubs pubescent; eyes notched; tibiae of front legs each with several fine teeth (Fig. 642).
On pine; name derived because of peculiar engravings.
Eastern States.

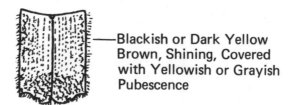

Fig. 642.   Ips calligraphus

Ips grandicollis   Length: 3.2–4–5mm. Bright orange brown to brownish black, slightly shining, thinly covered with pale yellowish or grayish hairs. Pronotum longer than wide, anterior part with tubercles and transverse wrinkles, posterior part finely punctured, median line narrow, smooth; elytral striae with somewhat square-shaped punctures, apices obliquely cut off and concave or hollowed out, the margin of each elytron toward apex with five teeth; antennal clubs pubescent; eyes notched; tibiae of front legs each with several fine teeth.
On pine and spruce.
Throughout the Southern States and north to Massachusetts.

Ips pini   Pine Bark Beetle   Length: 3.5–4.5mm. Brown, shining, sparsely covered with gray pubescence. Pronotum slightly longer than wide, rounded anteriorly, sparsely punctured at base, rough with raised points at the apex; elytral striae finely punctured; apices of elytra concave or hollowed out with four teeth on each side; antennal clubs pubescent; eyes notched; tibia of front legs each with several fine teeth (Fig. 643).

On pine and spruce.

Throughout the Northern States, from Massachusetts to Minnesota.

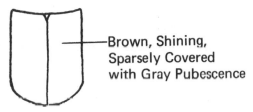

Brown, Shining, Sparsely Covered with Gray Pubescence

Fig. 643.   Ips pini

Orthotomicus caelatus   Length: 2.5–3mm. Brownish black to black; antennae and legs dark reddish yellow. Pronotum longer than wide, cylindrical, median line smooth, wrinkled and punctured at base; elytral striae with coarse, square-shaped punctures, intervals with rows of sparse, fine punctures, apices slightly hollowed, each side margin with about eight small teeth; antennal clubs pubescent; eyes notched; tibiae of front legs each with several fine teeth.

On pine, spruce, and fir.

Eastern States.

Xyleborus pubescens   Length: 2–2.5mm. Yellowish brown, shining; antennae and legs paler; upper surface covered with pale brownish pubescence. Pronotum longer than wide, basal half nearly smooth with fine, sparse punctures in the middle, anterior half and extreme sides coarsely wrinkled; elytra with rows of rather coarse punctures, intervals flat, slightly wrinkled and with scattered fine punctures; head completely hidden by pronotum; antennal clubs short and each broad with one or two recurved sutures (Fig. 644).

Eastern half of the United States.

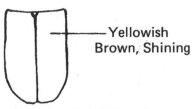

Yellowish Brown, Shining

Fig. 644.   Xyleborus pubescens

Xyleborus celsus   The Hickory Timber Beetle   Length: 2.7mm.
Brownish black, shining.
On various species of hickory.
From New York westward to Minnesota and Indiana and southward
to South Carolina and Mississippi.

Xyleborus xylographus   Length: 2.5mm. Reddish brown, shining, with
a covering of short hairs.
On various hardwoods.
From New York to Minnesota and southward to Florida.

Corthylus punctatissimus   The Sugar Maple Timber Beetle   Length:
3.7–4mm. Dark brown to black; antennae and legs reddish. Pronotum smooth and shining; elytra with prominent scattered punctures
(Fig. 645).
On sugar maple, sassafras, dogwood, ironwood, huckleberry, blueberry,
and rhododendron.
Eastern United States.

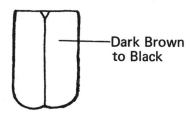

Fig. 645.   Corthylus punctatissimus

Glossary

ABBREVIATED Shortened, less than the usual length

ABDOMEN The third or posterior part of the insect body

ACUMINATE Pointed or tapering to a slender point

ACUTE Pointed, sharp, forming less than a right angle

ADULT The sexually mature stage of an insect

AERIAL Flying insects or those that live in the air

ANAL Refers to the last segment of the abdomen

ANAL APPENDAGE Any appendage attached to the posterior part of the abdomen

ANAL STYLE A pointed appendage on the terminal segment of the abdomen

ANGULATE Forming an angle

ANTENNA, ANTENNAE The segmented sensory organs attached to the head

ANTENNAL GROOVE A groove to receive and conceal each antenna

ANTENNAL TUBERCLE An elevation on the head to which each antenna is attached

ANTERIOR Toward the front

APEX, APICES The tip; the part farthest away from the body; the apex of the pronotum is the part nearest the head

APICAL Relating to, or at, the apex

APICES, APEX See APEX

APPENDAGE Any outlying part or organ attached to the body

APPENDICULATE With an appendage or appendages

APPRESSED   Closely applied to

AQUATIC   Living in water

ARTHROPOD   An invertebrate animal with segmented appendages

ATROPHIED   A part that stopped developing and perhaps decreased in size or disappeared altogether

BAND   A transverse marking wider than a line

BASAL   At or near the base

BASE   The part nearest the main body; base of pronotum is the part nearest the elytra

BASEMENT MEMBRANE   A delicate membrane composed of a single layer of flat cells, forming a substratum to the epithelial cells of many organs

BEAK   A prolongation of the head bearing the mouthparts

BIFURCATE   Divided into two branches; forked

BILOBED   With two lobes

BLOTCH   A large irregular marking

BLUNT   Opposed to sharp

BRASSY   Yellowish with the luster of metallic brass

BRISTLE   A stiff hair

BRONZED   Yellowish brown or reddish brown

BULB   The proximal end of the scape, that is, the first seyment of each antenna

CALLOSITY   A somewhat flattened elevation or hardened lump

CAPITATE   With a head, said of an antenna with a sudden, rounded knob at the apex

CERCI   A pair of lateral anal appendages

CHITIN   A complex organic substance occurring in the exoskeleton of arthropods

CHORDOTONAL ORGANS   Pertaining to or designating certain organs of insects found in various parts of the body and believed to be auditory

CILIA, CILIAE   A long hair, many usually forming a fringe

CLASS   A division of living organisms, higher than an ORDER but lower than a SUBKINGDOM

CLAVATE   Gradually thickened toward the apex

CLAVOLA   The part of each antenna except the first and second segments

CLAW   A hooklike structure arising from each last tarsal segment

CLEFT   Split, partially divided longitudinally

CLUB   Thickened or enlarged segments at the tip of an antenna

CLYPEUS A sclerite at the base of the labrum

COMPOUND EYE An eye made up of many parts or eye units, each having a more or less six-sided lens

COMPRESSED Pressed together

CONCAVE Hollowed out; curved like the inside of a circle or sphere

CONICAL Cone shaped

CONFLUENT Running together or overlapping

CONSTRICTED Narrowed

CONTIGUOUS Touching

CONVERGING Gradually narrowing or tapering

CONVEX Evenly and broadly rounded

CORNEA The outer surface of both the compound eye and of the individual facets

COXA, COXAE The first segment of the leg

COXAL CAVITY An opening in the underside of the thorax in which the leg is attached

CREST A ridge or ridgelike formation

CUTICULA A thin, noncellular outermost covering that protects the body and serves as a support for the internal organs

CYLINDRICAL Circular in cross section; like a cylinder

DEFLEXED Bent downward

DILATED Widened or expanded

DIMORPHISM Difference in size, structure, form, color, etc, between two types of the same species

DISK The central part of the pronotum or elytra apart from the margin

DISTAL The part or section of an appendage farthest from the body

DIURNAL Normally active by day

DIVERGENT Spread out; said of tarsal claws when they meet at a slight angle at the base

DORSAL Upper surface or relating to the upper surface

ELBOWED Said of an antenna that is sharply bent

ELEVATIONS Raised places

ELLIPTICAL Resembling oval but having the two rounded ends equal

ELONGATE Longer than wide

ELYTRA, ELYTRON The first wings or actually the hardened wing covers of beetles

ELYTRON, ELYTRA See ELYTRA

EMARGINATE Notched at the margin

ENTIRE Having the margin unbroken

EPITHELIAL   Pertaining to the sheet of cells covering either external or internal surfaces of the body

ERECT   Standing upright though not necessarily perpendicular

EXCAVATED   Hollowed out

EXOSKELETON   The hard outer wall of the beetles that serves as a support for the muscles

EXPANDED   Flattened or spread out

EXUVIA, EXUVIAE   The cast skin of an insect

FACE   The part of the head between the compound eyes and the mouth

FACET   The surface of one of the numerous small eyes that compose the compound eye

FAMILY   The next division following the ORDER, and which in turn is divided into GENERA

FEELER   Another name for antenna

FEMORA, FEMUR   See FEMUR

FEMUR, FEMORA   A segment of the leg, usually the largest or the first elongate one

FILAMENT   A slender threadlike process

FILIFORM   Threadlike, slender, of equal diameter

FLABELLATE   Folding like a fan, as in some antennae

FOOT   The tarsus of the leg

FREE   Free to move, not firmly united to another part

FRONT OR FRONTAL REGION   The part of the head between the base of each antenna and the compound eyes

FUNICLE   The part of each antenna between the club and ring joints or, when the ring joints are absent, between the club and pedicel

GALEA   The outer lobe of the maxilla

GENA   The part of the head below the eyes; the cheek

GENERA, GENUS   See GENUS

GENICULATE   Suddenly bent at an angle; elbowed

GENITAL CLASPERS   The appendages of the male connected with the reproductive organs

GENITALIA   External parts of the reproductive organs

GENUS, GENERA   The first word of a scientific name; the taxonomic subdivision of a FAMILY

GLOBOSE   Sphere shaped; spherical

GRANULATE   Appearing as if covered with small grains; with many small, flattened elevations on the surface

GRANULE   A small, grainlike elevation

GROOVES   Narrow furrows

GRUB   The larva of a beetle

GULA   A sclerite forming the throat

HABITAT   The place an insect inhabits

HEAD   The first of the three body regions of an insect that bears the eyes, antennae, and mouthparts

HIBERNATE   To pass the winter in a dormant condition

HORN   A pointed chitinous process on the head

HUMERAL   Near, or on, the shoulder or humerus

HUMERUS   The basal, external angle of each elytron

HYPODERMIS   The active living part of the body wall

IMPRESSED   Lying below the general surface; for instance, as if lines or dots were stamped into it

IMPRESSION   An indentation on the surface

INFLEXED   Bent or turned inward or downward

INSERTION   The place of attachment

INSTAR   The form of the larva between molts

INTEGUMENT   The outer covering or an outer enveloping cell layer

INTERRUPTED   The continuity broken but the tips of the broken segments in the same line with each other

INTERVAL   The area between two elytral striae

IRIDESCENT   Changing colors with different angles of light; reflecting colors of various hues

IRREGULAR   Unequal in distribution

KEEL   A ridge like the keel of a boat

LABIAL   On or belonging to the labrum

LABIAL PALPUS, LABIAL PALPI   The palpus of the labium; the appendage attached to the lower lip of an insect

LABIUM   The lower lip

LABRUM   The upper lip

LACINA   The inner lobe of each maxilla

LAMELLATE   Said of an antenna that has some of the distal segments expanded laterally to form leaflike or platelike structures

LARVA, LARVAE   The growing immature stage of beetles

LATERAL   Relating to the side

LIGULA   The central appendage of the labium

LOBE   Any prominent rounded process on a margin

LONGITUDINAL   In the direction of the long axis

LUMINESCENCE   The ability to produce light as in the fireflies

MANDIBLE   One of the upper jaws

MARGIN   The border or edge

MARGINED   With a distinct border

MAXILLA, MAXILLAE   One of the lower jaws

MAXILLARY PALPUS, MAXILLARY PALPI   Segmented antennalike sense organs borne on the maxillæ

MEMBRANOUS   Thin, semitransparent, like parchment

MENTUM   Part of the labium

MESO   A prefix meaning middle; refers to the middle segment of the thorax or its appendages

MESOSTERNUM   Middle segment of the thorax

MESOTHORAX   The second or middle segment of the thorax

META   A prefix meaning posterior; refers to the last segment of the thorax or its appendages

METASTERNUM   Last segment of the thorax

METALLIC   With a luster or color like metals

METAMORPHOSIS   The changes or stages in the life cycle of an insect

METATHORAX   The third or last segment of the thorax

MOLTING   The shedding of the larval skin to permit further growth

MONILIFORM   Beaded; made up of rounded segments like a string of beads

NAIADS   The young of aquatic insects with incomplete metamorphosis

NOCTURNAL   Normally active by night

NODE   A knob or swelling, a small knot or lump

NODULE   A small knot or lump

NOTCHED   Indented, usually on the margin

OBLIQUE   Any direction between the vertical and horizontal

OBLONG   A four-sided figure with one dimension longer than the other; longer than broad

OBSCURE   Not easily seen

OBTUSE   Not pointed, but blunt, with an angle greater than a right angle

OCCIPUT   The posterior-most part of the head, that is, the basal part of the head behind the vertex

OCELLI, OCELLUS   See OCELLUS

OCELLUS, OCELLI   Simple eyes (not common in beetles)

OMMATIDIA, OMMATIDIUM   See OMMATIDIUM

OMMATIDIUM, OMMATIDIA   One of the elongate, rodlike units of a compound eye of an insect

OPAQUE   Dull, in contrast to shining

ORBICULAR   Round and flat

ORDER   A subdivision of a CLASS

OVAL   Egg shaped

OVIPOSITOR   Tubular structure on last segment of female abdomen by means of which eggs are laid

PAD   Part between the claws

PALPI, PALPUS   See PALPUS

PALPIGER   The sclerite of the labium that bears the palpus

PALPUS, PALPI   A short, segmented appendage found both on the maxillae and labium

PARAGLOSSA   A paired structure of the labium

PARASITE   A species that lives in or on another animal and secures its food by consuming some part of its host

PECTINATE   With equal elongate process, like the teeth of a comb

PEDICEL   The second segment of each antenna

PITS   Small holes or rounded impressions

POSTERIOR   The rear or relatively nearer the hind end of the body

POSTERIOR ANGLES   The angles at the back of the pronotum

PRO   Prefix pertaining to the first division of the thorax or its appendages

PROCESS   Any marked prominence; an outgrowth or projection of the surface

PROMINENT   Rising above the surface or produced beyond the margin

PRONOTUM   Upper surface of the prothorax

PROSTERNUM   Area between the coxae of the front legs

PROTHORAX   The first segment of the thorax, bearing a pair of legs

PROTUBERANCE   An elevation above the surface

PUBESCENCE   A covering of short, soft hairs

PUNCTURE   A small depression, an impressed dot

PUNCTURED   Marked with small depressions or impressed dots

PUPA   The resting stage in which the beetle transforms from the larva to the adult

PUPATE   To become a pupa

PYGIDIUM   The last dorsal segment of the abdomen, often not covered by the elytra

RECTANGULAR   In the form of a right angle or rectangle

RECUMBENT   Lying down or reclining

REFLECTION   A throwing back or turning back of light or color

REFLEX   Reflected light or color

REFLEXED   Bent backward

RETRACTED   Being drawn back or in

RETRACTILE   Capable of being drawn back or in

RIDGES   Raised narrow strips

RING JOINTS   In certain insects the proximal segment or segments of the clavola

RUDIMENTARY   Undeveloped

SCALE   A broad, flattened hair

SCAPE   The first segment of an antenna

SCAVENGER   An animal that feeds on decaying matter

SCLERITE   Any piece of the body wall surrounded by sutures

SCULPTURE   Surface markings such as elevations and depressions

SCUTELLUM   The more or less triangular piece between the bases of the elytra

SEGMENT   A division marked by sutures or incisions

SERRATE   With notched edges, sawlike

SETA, SETAE   A bristle or long, stiff hair

SEXUAL COLOR DIMORPHISM   The two sexes of species differing in color, markings, or pattern

SHOULDER   The basal, external angle of each elytron; the humerus

SNOUT   A prolonged part of the head

SPARSE   Scattered

SPECIES   The second word in a scientific name

SPINE   A slender, sharp process

SPIRACLE   A breathing pore

SPUR   A short, stiff process, as at the end of each tibia

STADIUM   The period or interval between molts

STERNITE   A sclerite of the sternum

STERNUM   The middle part of the undersurface of the thorax, between the coxal cavities

STRIA, STRIAE   A depressed line extending lengthwise of the elytra, often with punctures

STRIATE   Marked with striae

STRIDULATE   To make a chirping or creaking sound

SUBCYLINDRICAL   Not quite cylindrical

SUBHUMERAL   Near the humerus

SUBMENTUM   Part of the labium

SUTURE   A line indicating the junction of two sections of the body wall; the line indicating the junction of the elytra

TARSAL LOBE   A membranous appendage on the underside of a tarsal segment

TARSI, TARSUS   See TARSUS

TARSUS, TARSI   The foot; the distal part of the leg and composed of from two to five segments

TERGUM   The dorsal portion of any body segment

TERMINAL   At the tip

TERRESTRIAL   Living on the land

THORAX   The middle or second region of an insect, bearing the wings and legs

TIBIA, TIBIAE   The part of the leg between the femur and the tarsus; usually long and slender

TOOTH   A short, pointed process from an appendage or margin

TRANSVERSE   Placed crosswise; when the longest dimension is across the body

TROCHANTER   A segment of the leg between the coxa and the femur

TUBERCLE   A small, knoblike prominence

VARIEGATED   Varied in color; of several colors in an indefinite pattern

VARIETY   A member of a species that differs markedly from the type species

VENTRAL   The undersurface or belonging to it

VERTEX   The tip part of the head, between the eyes, frontal region, and occiput

VESTIGIAL   A degenerate structure that was better developed or functional at one time

WING   An organ of flight

WING COVER   One of the first pair of wings in the beetles, which is horny and serves for protection rather than flight

WRINKLED   With cracks or creases

Bibliography

Borror, D. J., and White, R. E. *A Field Guide to the Insects*. Boston: Houghton Mifflin Company, 1970.

Comstock, J. H. *An Introduction to Entomology*. Ithaca, New York: Comstock Publishing Associates, 1940.

Dillon, E. S., and Dillon, L. S. *A Manual of Common Beetles of Eastern North America*. New York: Dover Publications, Inc., 1972.

Frost, S. W. *Insect Life and Insect Natural History*. New York: Dover Publications, 1959.

Jacques, H. E. *How To Know The Beetles*. Dubuque, Iowa: Wm. C. Brown Company, 1951.

Lutz, F. E. *Field Book of Insects*. New York: G. P. Putnam's Sons, 1948.

Swain, R. B. *The Insect Guide*. New York: Doubleday and Company, 1948.

Index